Reconfigurable Computing: Architecture, Logic and Applications

Reconfigurable Computing: Architecture, Logic and Applications

Edited by Naomi Bowman

CLANRYE
INTERNATIONAL
www.clanryeinternational.com

Clanrye International,
750 Third Avenue, 9th Floor,
New York, NY 10017, USA

ISBN: 978-1-63240-890-7

Cataloging-in-Publication Data

Reconfigurable computing : architecture, logic and applications / edited by Naomi Bowman.
    p. cm.
Includes bibliographical references and index.
ISBN 978-1-63240-890-7
1. Adaptive computing systems. 2. Computer architecture. 3. Computer logic. 4. Computer systems. I. Bowman, Naomi.
QA76.9.A3 R43 2019
621.395--dc23

For information on all Clanrye International publications
visit our website at www.clanryeinternational.com

Contents

Permissions

List of Contributors

Index

Preface

This book aims to highlight the current researches and provides a platform to further the scope of innovations in this area. This book is a product of the combined efforts of many researchers and scientists, after going through thorough studies and analysis from different parts of the world. The objective of this book is to provide the readers with the latest information of the field.

Reconfigurable computing is the computer architecture that combines the flexibility of software with high performing hardware by processing with high speed, flexible computing fabrics such as field-programming gate arrays (FPGAs). The central theories of reconfigurable computing are Tredennick's Classification and Hartenstein's Xputer. Modern reconfigurable computing systems include COPACOBANA, Intel, Xilinx, Mitrionics, etc. The classification of reconfigurable architectures is continuously being developed and redefined with the development of new architectures. The current classification is based on granularity, host coupling, rate of reconfiguration and routing interconnects. This book unravels the recent studies in the field of reconfigurable computing. Also included herein is a detailed explanation of the architecture, logic and applications of reconfigurable computing. This book, with its detailed analyses and data, will prove immensely beneficial to professionals and students involved in this area at various levels.

I would like to express my sincere thanks to the authors for their dedicated efforts in the completion of this book. I acknowledge the efforts of the publisher for providing constant support. Lastly, I would like to thank my family for their support in all academic endeavors.

Editor

Fuzzy Logic based Hardware Accelerator with Partially Reconfigurable Defuzzification Stage for Image Edge Detection

Aous H. Kurdi, Janos L. Grantner, and Ikhlas M. Abdel-Qader

Electrical and Computer Engineering Department, Western Michigan University, Kalamazoo, MI 49009, USA

Correspondence should be addressed to Aous H. Kurdi; aoushammad.kurdi@wmich.edu

Academic Editor: Yuko Hara-Azumi

In this paper, the design and the implementation of a pipelined hardware accelerator based on a fuzzy logic approach for an edge detection system are presented. The fuzzy system comprises a preprocessing stage, a fuzzifier with four fuzzy inputs, an inference system with seven rules, and a defuzzification stage delivering a single crisp output, which represents the intensity value of a pixel in the output image. The hardware accelerator consists of seven stages with one clock cycle latency per stage. The defuzzification stage was implemented using three different defuzzification methods. These methods are the mean of maxima, the smallest of maxima, and the largest of maxima. The defuzzification modules are interchangeable while the system runs using partial reconfiguration design methodology. System development was carried out using Vivado High-Level Synthesis, Vivado Design Suite, Vivado Simulator, and a set of Xilinx 7000 FPGA devices. Depending upon the speed grade of the device that is employed, the system can operate at a frequency range from 83 MHz to 125 MHz. Its peak performance is up to 58 high definition frames per second. A comparison of this system's performance and its software counterpart shows a significant speedup in the magnitude of hundred thousand times.

1. Introduction

Digital system design using Field Programmable Gate Arrays (FPGAs) focuses on performance, device utilization, and rapid development. Xilinx Vivado HLS offers a great development environment that enables the analysis of the system's performance and design optimization. It also facilitates modularized system design. The Vivado Design Suite provides the means for developing dynamic, partially reconfigurable designs in which different hardware modules can be swapped in and out to utilize available hardware resources on the fly. FPGAs, as a platform, represent one of the most qualified contenders for hardware implementation of digital signal processing systems [1]. In the Xilinx 7 Series devices, the programmable elements organized in blocks called Configurable Logic Block (CLB). Each CLB is comprised of two slices, and each slice is provided with a 6-input 1-output look-up table (LUT), distributed memory, shift register, high-speed logic for arithmetic functionality, a wide multiplexer, and a switching matrix to facilitate the access to routing elements on the chip [2]. The synthesizer tool assigns the chip's resources, mainly the CLBs, in accordance with the designer choice to implement sequential or combinational logic circuits.

Digital systems by nature rely on Boolean logic. Boolean logic has been, conventionally, the staple of knowledge representation for quite long. The main shortcoming in this regard is the incomplete applicability to situations of uncertainty and inaccuracy [3]. Thus, conventional approaches founded on Boolean logic do not provide suitable frameworks to represent human knowledge that is characterized by the uncertainty and fuzziness associated with the human cognitive function. Fuzzy logic, however, provides a mathematically feasible framework to represent degrees of truth and falsehood in contrast to the classic true or false values of Boolean logic. Fuzzy logic is referred to here in the wide-sense [4] that includes the concept of fuzzy sets [5] and approximate reasoning. For many applications, fuzzy logic has become an indispensable tool. Those applications include system control, intelligent systems, and image processing [6].

Most image processing algorithms contain edge detection as a vital part. Edge detection is, essentially, any method or algorithm that determines the set or sets of points within a digital image at which the gradient of intensity becomes a rapidly increasing or decreasing function of spatial coordinates [7, 8]. These points are grouped into curved line shapes called edges. Different methods have been developed to extract the edges in an image such as the Sobel operator, Laplacian, and Prewitt. These methods use specific parameters, such as a threshold, to complete the edge detection process [9].

Fuzzy logic based edge detection makes use of human knowledge to identify edges. A proposal for an improved edge detection algorithm using fuzzy logic was presented in [10]. The authors therein applied fuzzy logic techniques on a 3 × 3 pixels' mask. That mask is exploited in the process of examining each pixel's relation to its neighbor pixels. Each pixel is considered as a fuzzy input resulting in a multi-input-single-output (MISO) fuzzy system. Another approach used the pixels' gradient and standard deviation values as inputs to the fuzzy system [11]. In this paper, the suggested system works in such a way that it decides on which pixel is considered an edge, or not, by carrying out inference calculations utilizing a set of fuzzy IF-THEN rules. Using fuzzy logic to construct an edge detection algorithm would have the obvious potential. It could incorporate human knowledge and intuition into a model that can adapt to a substantial departure from the expected input images, such as the presence of noise in the input image, rather than using only a single real number to substantiate detection, that is, using a static threshold value. Fuzzy logic based systems work with a linguistic representation of knowledge in a way that describes uncertainty in the form of IF-THEN rules. Complex systems can be modeled using those rules that are intuitively recognizable to human beings [12]. To unlock the potential of fuzzy logic based systems in real life applications, practical platforms with low energy consumption and high computing power are crucially needed to implement them. Authors in [13], worked on utilizing FPGAs in implementing a fuzzy logic controller to track the maximum power point of the photovoltaic system. The authors used the Very High-Speed Hardware Description Language (VHDL) to design and implement a Mamdani-type [13] fuzzy controller.

The partial reconfiguration design approach aims to maximize device utilization efficiency by allowing different functional modules to use a specified set or sets of device resources called reconfigurable partition (PR) in interchangeable fashion while preserving the functionality of the rest of the system. In [14], a proposal for real-time tasks scheduling using partially reconfigurable FPGA design was discussed. The authors suggested dividing the FPGA fabric floor into homogenous blocks. Their experimental outcomes showed high resource utilization efficiency.

The rest of the paper is structured as follows: Section 2 introduces the proposed fuzzy edge detector system. The architecture of the hardware accelerator is described in Section 3. In Section 4, the dynamic partial reconfiguration design component of the edge detector system is discussed. The evaluation of the results is presented in Section 5. Conclusions are given Section 6.

2. The Proposed Fuzzy Edge Detector System

The proposed edge detector is a Mamdani-type [15] fuzzy system with four fuzzy inputs, one crisp output, and a knowledge base made of seven IF-THEN rules. It is important to note that in a Mamdani-type fuzzy system no implication functions [16] are used to create the fuzzy knowledge base representation. The first two inputs are the gradients on the x-axis and the y-axis out of a kernel of 3×3 pixels. GX and GY are the associated fuzzy sets, respectively. The third input is the output of a low-pass filter, and the corresponding fuzzy set is named LF, while the final input is the output of a high-pass filter, and the corresponding fuzzy input is referred to by HF.

2.1. Preprocessing. In preprocessing, a kernel of 3×3 pixels formed from the input image is used to compute the gradients in x-direction and y-directions, low-pass filter, and high-pass filter using (1), (2), (3), and (4), respectively. $I(x, y)$ stands for the kernel with the targeted pixel at the center.

$$GX = \begin{bmatrix} -1 & 0 & 1 \\ -2 & 0 & 2 \\ -1 & 0 & 1 \end{bmatrix} \cdot I(x, y), \quad (1)$$

$$GY = \begin{bmatrix} -1 & -2 & -1 \\ 0 & 0 & 0 \\ 1 & 2 & 1 \end{bmatrix} \cdot I(x, y), \quad (2)$$

$$LP = \begin{bmatrix} 1 & 1 & 1 \\ 1 & 1 & 1 \\ 1 & 1 & 1 \end{bmatrix} \cdot \frac{1}{9} \cdot I(x, y), \quad (3)$$

$$HP = \begin{bmatrix} -1 & -1 & -1 \\ -1 & 8 & -1 \\ -1 & -1 & -1 \end{bmatrix} \cdot \frac{1}{9} \cdot I(x, y). \quad (4)$$

2.2. Fuzzification. For fuzzification, crisp inputs are transformed into fuzzy inputs. Linguistic variables were created to represent the fuzzy qualities over a practical range of crisp values. For each linguistic variable three fuzzy sets were defined over the universal sets of discourse, namely, LOW, MED, and HIGH.

2.3. The Inference System. For each input variable, three membership functions (MF) were defined, LOW, MED, and HIGH. LOW and HIGH are trapezoid-shaped MFs while MED is a triangle-shaped one. The membership functions are distributed over the universal set of discourse ranging from 0 to 255 (the intensity range in a grayscale image) as illustrated in Figure 1.

The system features a Mamdani inference system [17]. The knowledge base is made up of seven fuzzy IF-THEN rules as shown in Table 1. All the rules are assigned the weight value of 1. Fuzzy intersection and union, in the implication process, are represented by MIN and MAX operators, respectively.

TABLE 1: The fuzzy rules.

Fuzzy inputs				Fuzzy output
GX	*GY*	HP	LP	*E*
LOW	LOW	x	x	LOW
MED	MED	x	x	MED
HIGH	HIGH	x	x	HIGH
LOW	x	LOW	x	MED
x	LOW	LOW	x	MED
LOW	x	x	LOW	LOW
x	LOW	x	LOW	LOW

2.4. Defuzzification. For the single output variable *E* (Edge), three membership functions were defined: LOW, MED, and HIGH. All those membership functions were chosen to be triangular as shown in Figure 2. They are distributed over the universal set of discourse ranging over values from 0 to 255 (the intensity range of a pixel in the edges output image). Three defuzzification methods were implemented to map the fuzzy output into a crisp value. These methods are the smallest of maxima (SOM), the mean of maxima (MOM), and the largest of maxima (LOM).

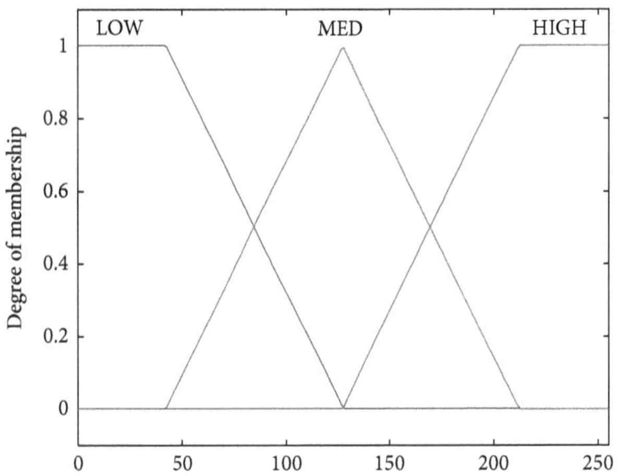

FIGURE 1: The membership functions of input *GX*, *GY*, HP, and LP.

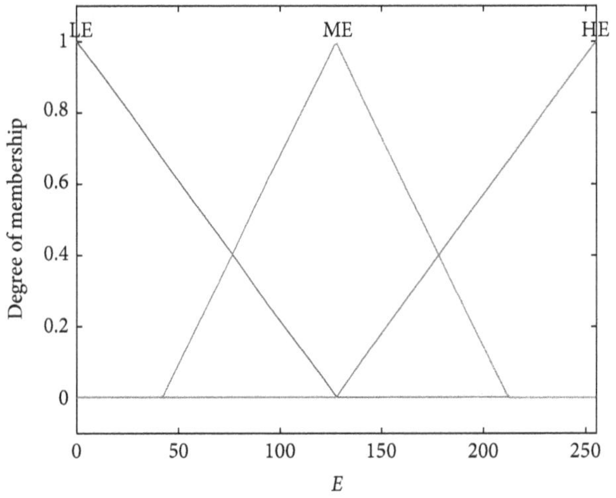

FIGURE 2: Membership functions for output *E*.

3. The Architecture of the Pipelined Hardware Accelerator

In this research, a pipelined hardware accelerator was designed and implemented on Xilinx 7000-series devices using Vivado HLS and Vivado Design Suite. The system consists of four main units: preprocessor, fuzzifier, inference system, and defuzzifier. They have implemented over seven pipeline stages. The latency of each stage is a single clock cycle. The preprocessor uses three stages; the inference system employs two stages while the other two blocks use one stage each. The defuzzifier unit was implemented using Vivado HLS while the rest were implemented as Register Transfer Level (RTL) design using VHDL in the Vivado Design Suite.

3.1. Preprocessing Unit. Figure 3 illustrates the preprocessor unit's functional block diagram. The hardware architecture of the preprocessor consists of a Block RAM (BRAM) Module that is configured as a Dual-Port RAM with asynchronous Read and Writes cycles. The memory organization is set up with a parallel data width of 72 bits by 512 locations. Each location is assigned the representation of the intensity of 9 pixels forming a 3×3 kernel window. The first stage of the pipeline reads one location from memory. Dedicated blocks of hardware were implemented for computing the gradients in the x- and the y-directions, the low-pass filter, and the high-pass filter, respectively. Each block employs two stages of the system's seven pipeline stages, working in parallel.

For *GX* and *GY*, two specialized subblocks were designed to execute the process of computing the positive and negative parts of the gradient masks as in (1) and (2). These subblocks work in parallel forming the second stage of the pipeline. The third stage performs the tasks as follows: addition of the outputs of the previous subblocks, followed by finding the magnitude of the sum and then scaling that down to the established maximum value (255 in this case) if the results surpassed that maximum.

For LF, three subblocks were designed to find the sum of each row as in (3). These subblocks work in parallel and occupy the second stage of the pipeline in the LP block. The third stage computes the sum of the results of the previous stage and divides it by 9 to find the average.

The last block is the HF that is also divided into two stages. The first one is composed of three subblocks. The first subblock performs multiplication of the first four elements of the HP mask as in (4) with their corresponding input pixels and calculates the sum. The second subblock does the same as the first one, but for the last four elements of the HF mask. The third subblock carries out the multiplication of the center element by 8. The second stage computes the sum of the previous stage and then divides it by 9.

3.2. Fuzzification Unit. The fourth stage of the hardware accelerator pipeline is the fuzzification unit. This unit performs the transformation of the crisp inputs into fuzzy

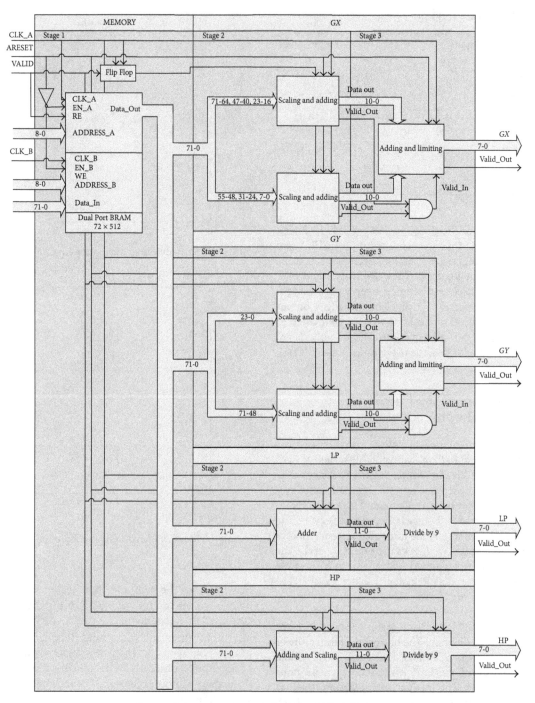

FIGURE 3: Preprocessing unit functional block diagram.

variables. The fuzzifier unit's functional block diagram is illustrated in Figure 4. The fuzzifier block consists of four identical subblocks working in parallel. These subblocks map the crisp inputs to linguistic labels in the corresponding fuzzy universal sets of discourse along with the degrees of consistency.

The inputs of the fuzzifier block are GX, GY, LP, and HP, which are the outputs of the preprocessor block, and control signals such as CLK, ARESET, and Valid_In. The outputs of the fuzzifier block are as follows: fuzzy variable GX

(GX_VF), degree of consistency of variable GX (GX_DoM), fuzzy variable GY (GY_FV), degree of consistency of variable GY (GY-DoM), fuzzy variable LP (LP_FV), degree of consistency of variable LP (LP_DoM), fuzzy variable HP (HP_VF), and degree of consistency of variable HP (HP_DoM), and Valid_Out.

3.3. Inference System Unit. The hardware design of the inference system utilizes two stages of the system's seven pipeline stages. The first stage implements the knowledge base, which

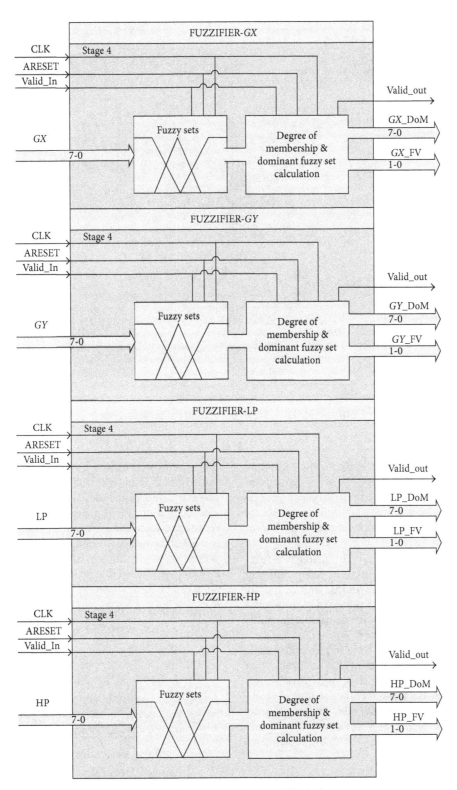

FIGURE 4: Fuzzification unit functional block diagram.

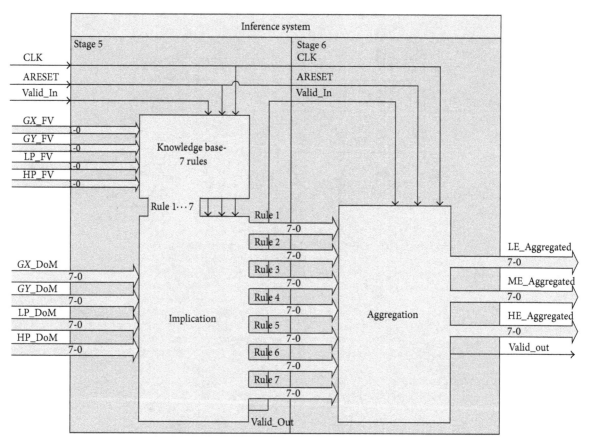

FIGURE 5: Inference system unit functional block diagram.

is composed of seven IF-THEN rules and computes the implication for each rule. The second stage completes aggregating the outcomes of the rules into three fuzzy variables LE, ME, and HE, respectively. The schematic Figure 5 represents the inference system unit functional block diagram.

3.4. Defuzzification Unit. In this unit, the aggregated fuzzy variables LE, ME, and HE are defuzzified using SOM, or MOM, or LOM defuzzification methods. The output of the defuzzification unit is an 8-bit representation of pixel intensity values in the output image. The defuzzification unit's block diagram is presented in Figure 6.

The defuzzification algorithms were implemented using Vivado HLS. The implementation of the defuzzification modules was written using C code along with a test bench. Vivado HLS synthesized the top-level function in the C code, named rModule_Defuzzification, into RTL design. Arbitrary precision integer of the length of 8 was used to implement the function interface. Pseudocode 1 shows the pseudocode for the implemented design.

4. Dynamic Partially Reconfigurable Design

At the time of writing this paper, the Vivado Design Suite supports only nonproject Tcl-based design flow for partial reconfiguration designs on FPGAs using bottom-up synthesis. The bottom-up approach uses multiple netlists from

different projects or design check points (DCP) to create the static design along with the reconfigurable partitions (RP). The static design includes all the logic that is not subject of reconfiguration. RP is a design element that is marked for reconfiguration. The portion of the design that will occupy the RP is known as reconfigurable module (RM) [18]. The process of generating a partially reconfigurable design from RTL to partial Bitstream generation using the Vivado Design Suite can be summarized as follows:

(1) Synthesize the static design and generate DCP.

(2) Synthesize the RM and generate DCP using bottom-up methodology.

(3) The DCP created before will be used to load the static design along with RM for each RP.

(4) Use the floor-planning tool to define each RP.

(5) Design rule checker (DRC) will be executed to verify the correctness of the floor-planning process.

(6) Optimize, place, and route the design and save DCP.

(7) Reiterate steps (3) to (6) for each single RM.

(8) Execute the PR_Verify command to validate the reconfigurable design.

(9) Generate partial Bitstream files for each single RM.

The partially reconfigurable design of the hardware accelerator implements the first six stages as a static portion while

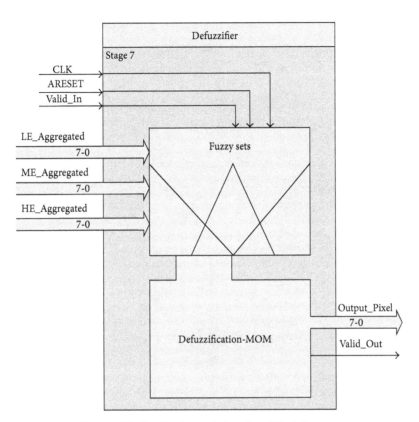

FIGURE 6: Defuzzification unit functional block diagram.

```
rModule_Defuzzification (uint8 LE, uint8 ME, unit8 HE, uint8 Output)
{
    If (LE > ME and LE> HE)
        Output= Calculate_Crisp (MF, LE)
    Else If (ME > LE and ME> HE)
        Output= Calculate_Crisp (MF, ME)
    Else If (HE > LE and HE> ME)
        Output= Calculate_Crisp (MF, HE)
}
Uint8 Calculate_Crisp (MembershipFunction MF, uint8 Value)
{
    If (MF is Triangle)
        Return Triangle_Crisp(Value)
    else
        Return Trapizoid_Crisp(Value)
}
```

PSEUDOCODE 1: Pseudocode for SOM defuzzification.

the defuzzification unit uses one RP and three RM modules as illustrated in Figure 7.

5. Evaluation of the Results

In this research, a hardware accelerator for fuzzy logic based edge detector with partially a reconfigurable defuzzification unit was designed, implemented, and tested. The hardware architecture was developed using Xilinx Vivado HLS and Vivado Design Suite. The performance of the hardware accelerator was investigated using a set of Xilinx Artix7 and Kintex7 devices. The fuzzy system's performance has been compared, in the presence of noise, to three traditional edge detection techniques.

5.1. The Performance of the Hardware Accelerator. The hardware accelerator design is based upon a pipeline architecture of seven stages. Each stage requires one clock cycle of execution time. The system was tested using three Xilinx Artix7 and three Xilinx Kintex7 devices with different speed

TABLE 2: Device utilization and maximum operating speed.

Device name	Maximum speed (MHz)	BRAM	DSP48E	FF	LUT
Artix7-Xc7a100t csg324-1	88.333	1	2	269	843
Artix7 Xc7a100t csg324-2	90.909	1	2	269	843
Artix7 Xc7a100t csg324-3	100.00	1	2	269	843
Kintex7 Xc7k160t fbg484-1	100.00	1	2	269	843
Kintex7 Xc7k160 tfbg484-2	111.111	1	2	269	843
Kintex7 Xc7k160 tfbg484-3	125.00	1	2	269	843

TABLE 3: Device utilization and maximum operating speed of (SOM) defuzzification module.

Design	Hardware		Timing			Utilization			
Design method	Device family	Device name	Targeted frequency (MHz)	Targeted time (ns)	Estimated time (ns)	Number of cycles required	BRAM	DSP48E	FF	LUT
Nonoptimized HLS	Artix-7	Xc7a100tcsg324-1	88.333	12	9.79	1–12	0	0	108	178
Optimized HLS	Artix-7	Xc7a100tcsg324-1	88.333	12	10.42	1	0	2	0	55
Optimized HLS	Artix-7	Xc7a100tcsg324-2	90.909	11	9.16	1	0	2	0	55
Optimized HLS	Artix-7	Xc7a100tcsg324-3	100.00	10	8.28	1	0	2	0	55
Optimized HLS	Kintex-7	Xc7k160tfbg484-1	100.00	10	8.21	1	0	2	0	55
Optimized HLS	Kintex-7	Xc7k160tfbg484-2	111.111	9	7.22	1	0	2	0	55
Optimized HLS	Kintex-7	Xc7k160tfbg484-3	125.00	8	6.56	1	0	2	0	55
RTL	Artix-7	Xc7a100tcsg324-1	88.333	12	11.07	1	0	0	9	65
RTL	Artix-7	Xc7a100tcsg324-2	90.909	11	9.87	1	0	0	9	65
RTL	Artix-7	Xc7a100tcsg324-3	100.00	10	8.91	1	0	0	9	65
RTL	Kintex-7	Xc7k160tfbg484-1	100.00	10	8.73	1	0	0	9	65
RTL	Kintex-7	Xc7k160tfbg484-2	111.111	9	7.51	1	0	0	9	65
RTL	Kintex-7	Xc7k160tfbg484-3	125.00	8	6.76	1	0	0	9	65

grades as indicated in Table 2. The tests showed that the system could work with a clock frequency rate of up to 125 MHz, hence, producing an output pixel in every eight ns.

Vivado HLS was used to implement the defuzzification unit. Two design approaches were investigated, the none-optimized design and the inline function optimization. The none-optimized design approach produces an RTL design that requires a latency of 1~12 cycles. The inline function optimization design utilizes DSP48E slices to perform the mathematical operation required to calculate crisp values. The execution time was optimized to just one clock cycle. The optimized approached showed better utilization and execution times compared to the hard-coded RTL design. The hardware utilization, timing, and design approach for the defuzzification unit using HLS and RTL on different devices are illustrated in Table 3. The timing simulations for the nonoptimized design and the inline function optimization for the SOM defuzzification module are shown in Figures 8 and 9, respectively.

Simulation results in Figure 10 show the system operating with an 11 ns clock cycle. The system needs 77 ns (7 cycles) to fill up the pipeline and after those another 176 ns (16 cycles) to produce 16 outputs as illustrated. To compare the performance of the hardware accelerator to its software

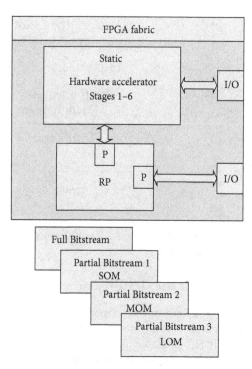

FIGURE 7: Partially reconfigurable system diagram.

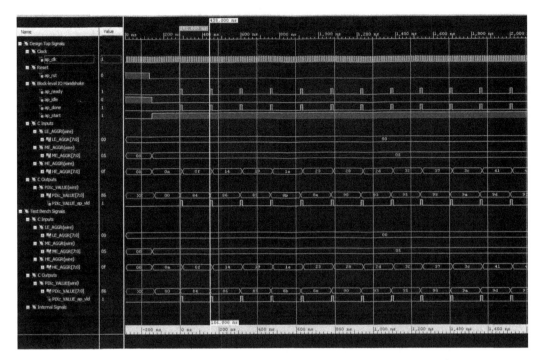

FIGURE 8: Simulation of the defuzzification unit using nonoptimized approach.

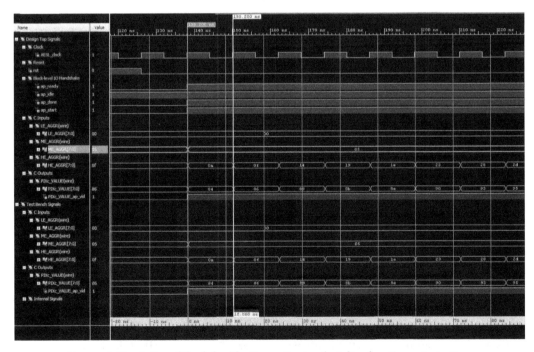

FIGURE 9: Simulation of the defuzzification unit using the inline function optimization.

counterpart, MATLAB was used to implement the system on a PC with Intel Core i7 processor and 8 GB of memory. The tests yield an execution time of 1.3178 milliseconds per pixel.

5.2. The Performance of the Proposed Fuzzy System. The proposed system was tested using two benchmark grayscale images, the cameraman and Lena. The performance results of the systems were also compared to other edge detection techniques such as Sobel's, Roberts's, and the Marr-Hildreth edge detection methods choosing Signal to Noise Ratio (SNR) as a quantitative measure. SNR, which is computed using (5), is the most widely used nondimensional parameter

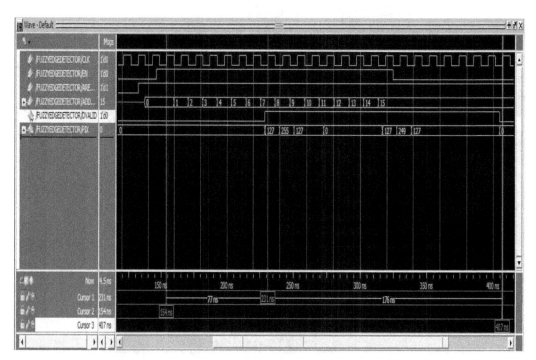

FIGURE 10: System simulation on Artix-7 Xc7a100tcsg324-2.

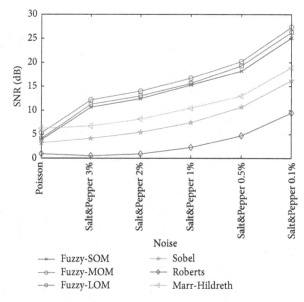

FIGURE 11: SNR in dB using different artificial noise (cameraman's image as source).

of the imaging system for measuring its sensitivity to noise [19].

$$\text{SNR} = 10 \log_{10} \frac{\sum_0^{n_x-1} \sum_0^{n_y-1} \left[r\left(x,y\right) \right]^2}{\sum_0^{n_x-1} \sum_0^{n_y-1} \left[r\left(x,y\right) - t\left(x,y\right) \right]^2}. \quad (5)$$

In (5), r and t stand for the respective grayscale intensities in the reference image and the image to be tested at pixel (x, y) in images of n_x by n_y size. The proposed system shows comparable or better immunity to noise compared to the other methods except the case with Poisson noise where

Marr-Hildreth algorithm showed a better performance. The noise test was performed using artificial noise added to the original image as shown Figures 11–14.

6. Conclusions

A seven-stage pipeline architecture for fuzzy logic edge detector with partially reconfigurable defuzzifier was proposed and implemented using Xilinx Vivado HLS and Xilinx Vivado Design Suite. Three Xilinx Artix7 and three Kintex7 devices were used to evaluate the system performance. The

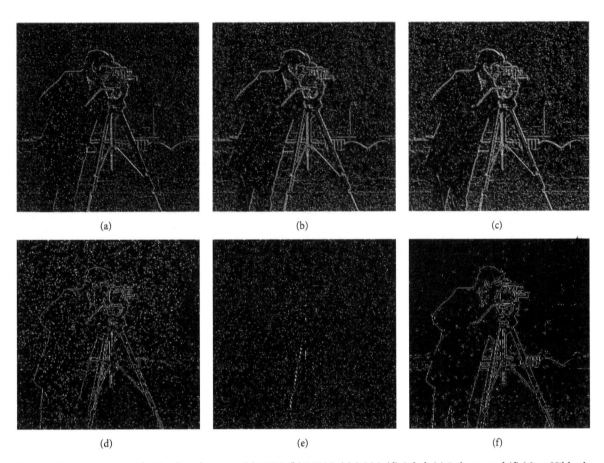

FIGURE 12: Cameraman with 3% salt and pepper: (a) SOM, (b) MOM, (c) LOM, (d) Sobel, (e) Roberts, and (f) Marr-Hildreth.

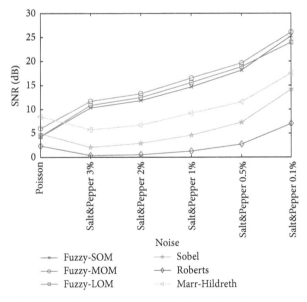

FIGURE 13: SNR in dB using different artificial noise (Lena's image as source).

performance of the hardware accelerator was compared to a functionally equivalent software counterpart and the results have shown a speedup of 109,618 times. The system's noise immunity was compared with other traditional methods using SNR as a quantitative performance measure. The system delivers better results in most of the comparisons. The defuzzification unit was implemented and optimized using Vivado HLS. The RTL code generated by HLS showed better performance and device utilization as compared to a hard-coded RTL that was generated by Vivado Design Suite using

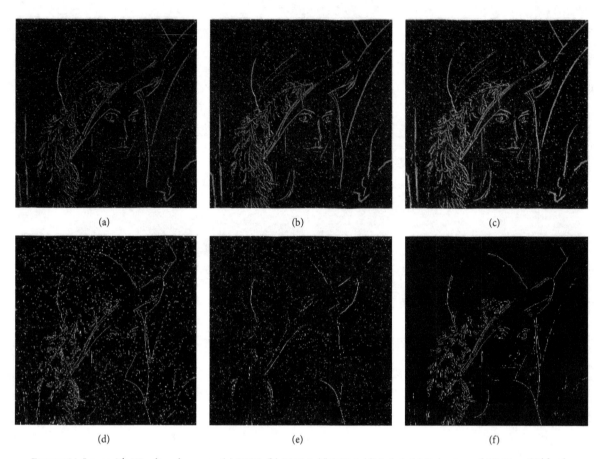

FIGURE 14: Lena with 1% salt and pepper: (a) SOM, (b) MOM, (c) LOM, (d) Sobel, (e) Roberts, and (f) Marr-Hildreth.

VHDL. Working with a system clock of 125 MHz, the system processed up to 58 HD frames per second. By attaching suitable input and output peripheral devices to the proposed hardware accelerator, it will make a powerful device for real-time applications.

Disclosure

Aous H. Kurdi was with Computer and Software Engineering Department, University of Technology, Baghdad, Iraq.

Competing Interests

The authors declare that there is no conflict of interests regarding the publication of this paper.

References

[1] C. Dick and F. Harris, "FPGA signal processing using Sigma-Delta modulation," *IEEE Signal Processing Magazine*, vol. 17, no. 1, pp. 20–35, 2000.

[2] Xilinx, "7 Series FPGAs Configurable Logic Block: User Guide. UG474 (v1.8)," September 2016.

[3] L. A. Zadeh, "Knowledge representation in fuzzy logic," *IEEE Transactions on Knowledge and Data Engineering*, vol. 1, no. 1, pp. 89–100, 1989.

[4] L. A. Zadeh, "What is Fuzzy Logic?" January 2013.

[5] L. A. Zadeh, "Fuzzy sets," *Information and Computation*, vol. 8, no. 3, pp. 338–353, 1965.

[6] K. Tanaka, *An Introduction to Fuzzy Logic for Practical Applications*, Springer, 1997.

[7] S. E. Umbaugh, *Digital Image Processing and Analysis: Human and Computer Vision Applications with CVIPtools*, CRC Press, 2016.

[8] J. Canny, "A computational approach to edge detection," *IEEE Transactions on Pattern Analysis and Machine Intelligence*, vol. 8, no. 6, pp. 679–698, 1986.

[9] Y. Becerikli and T. M. Karan, "A new fuzzy approach for edge detection," in *Proceedings of the 8th International Workshop on Artificial Neural Networks (IWANN '05): Computational Intelligence and Bioinspired Systems*, pp. 943–951, Springer, Vilanova i la Geltrú, Spain, June 2005.

[10] D. N. Oliveira, A. P. De Souza Braga, and O. Da Mota Almeida, "Fuzzy logic controller implementation on a FPGA using VHDL," in *Proceedings of the Annual North American Fuzzy Information Processing Society Conference (NAFIPS '10)*, 6, 1 pages, July 2010.

[11] A. D. Borkar and M. Atulkar, "Detection of edges using fuzzy inference system," *The International Journal of Innovative Research in Computer and Communication Engineering*, vol. 1, no. 1, 2013.

[12] F. A. Tab and O.-K. Shahryari, "Fuzzy edge detection based on pixel's gradient and standard deviation values," in *Proceedings of the International Multiconference on Computer Science and*

Information Technology (IMCSIT '09), pp. 7–10, IEEE, October 2009.

[13] L. Bouselham, M. Hajji, B. Hajji, A. E. Mehdi, and H. Hajji, "Hardware implementation of fuzzy logic MPPT controller on a FPGA platform," in *Proceedings of the 3rd International Renewable and Sustainable Energy Conference (IRSEC '15)*, pp. 1–6, IEEE, Marrakech, Morocco, December 2015.

[14] S. Saha, A. Sarkar, and A. Chakrabarti, "Scheduling dynamic hard real-time task sets on fully and partially reconfigurable platforms," *IEEE Embedded Systems Letters*, vol. 7, no. 1, pp. 23–26, 2015.

[15] E. H. Mamdani and S. Assilian, "Experiment in linguistic synthesis with a fuzzy logic controller," *International Journal of Man-Machine Studies*, vol. 7, no. 1, pp. 1–13, 1975.

[16] W. Bandler and L. J. Kohout, "Semantics of implication operators and fuzzy relational products," *International Journal of Man-Machine Studies*, vol. 12, no. 1, pp. 89–116, 1980.

[17] E. H. Mamdani, "Application of fuzzy logic to approximate reasoning using linguistic synthesis," *IEEE Transactions on Computers*, vol. C-26, no. 12, pp. 1182–1191, 1977.

[18] Xilinx, Vivado Design Suite User Guide Partial Reconfiguration UG909 (v2016.1), April 2016.

[19] R. C. Gonzalez and R. E. Woods, *Digital Image Processing*, Pearson, New York, NY, USA, 2008.

Software-Defined Radio FPGA Cores: Building towards a Domain-Specific Language

Lekhobola Tsoeunyane,[1] **Simon Winberg,**[1] **and Michael Inggs**[2]

[1]*Department of Electrical Engineering, University of Cape Town, Software Defined Radio Group, Rondebosch, Cape Town 7701, South Africa*
[2]*Department of Electrical Engineering, University of Cape Town, Radar Remote Sensing Group, Rondebosch, Cape Town 7701, South Africa*

Correspondence should be addressed to Lekhobola Tsoeunyane; lekhobola@gmail.com

Academic Editor: Michael Hübner

This paper reports on the design and implementation of an open-source library of parameterizable and reusable Hardware Description Language (HDL) Intellectual Property (IP) cores designed for the development of Software-Defined Radio (SDR) applications that are deployed on FPGA-based reconfigurable computing platforms. The library comprises a set of cores that were chosen, together with their parameters and interfacing schemas, based on recommendations from industry and academic SDR experts. The operation of the SDR cores is first validated and then benchmarked against two other cores libraries of a similar type to show that our cores do not take much more logic elements than existing cores and that they support a comparable maximum clock speed. Finally, we propose our design for a Domain-Specific Language (DSL) and supporting tool-flow, which we are in the process of building using our SDR library and the Delite DSL framework. We intend to take this DSL and supporting framework further to provide a rapid prototyping system for SDR application development to programmers not experienced in HDL coding. We conclude with a summary of the main characteristics of our SDR library and reflect on how our DSL tool-flow could assist other developers working in SDR field.

1. Introduction

Software-Defined Radio (SDR) approaches for rapid prototyping of radio systems using reconfigurable hardware platforms offer significant advantages over traditional analog and hardware-centered methods. In particular, time and cost savings can be achieved by reusing tested design artefacts. For example, a reconfigurable computer coupled to a commercial off-the-shelf (COTS) Radio Frequency (RF) daughterboard can reduce development time and lower costs in comparison to a custom-built PCB approach. A broad variety of SDR prototyping platforms is available, such as the USRP and Microsoft Sora [1], and rapid prototyping tools such as National Instruments LabView and GnuRadio [2]. The choice of SDR platform and components used to develop a complex SDR system is typically based on a variety of many interrelated selection decisions [3]. Important selection decisions

during development are influenced by the developers' familiarity with processor and platform architectures, coding languages, design approaches, support for legacy systems, and familiar design tools, among other factors. Development tool-chains and programming languages are highly influential in terms of developer productivity. Similarly, familiarity with the tools can impact the quality and reusability of the designs [3]. In this paper we consider a standard VHSIC Hardware Description Language (VHDL) approach to SDR prototyping, for which we develop a reusable library of Intellectual Property (IP) cores for use in Software-Defined Radio (SDR) application prototyping. We test the system using a legacy FPGA-based platform and recent add-on COTS daughterboard as a case study around which we build and test this library.

The aim of our investigation is to establish an effective selection of IP cores for baseline SDR applications, which can improve developer productivity using cores that can be further built upon to realize more specialized application needs. The Reconfigurable Hardware Interface for computatioN and radiO (RHINO) platform [4] is used as a case study for testing the library. In our effort to improve SDR productivity and reduce design complexity, we also propose a tool-flow that uses a Domain-Specific Language (DSL) as its entry-point to describe algorithms and automate the generation of HDL code. It exploits the parameters of SDR cores in order to integrate these existing library cores in the compilation flow hence enabling rapid prototyping of FPGA-based SDR at high-level of design abstraction.

The SDR IP core library comprises Digital Signal Processing (DSP) cores and input/output (I/O) interface cores. The library, which we are referring to as "SDR IP cores" library, is available for free under the General Public License (GPL) on https://github.com/lekhobola/Rhino-Processing-Blocks. It is designed around use by both the novice and experienced low-level HDL developers, providing novice users with experience of using IP cores that support open bus interfaces in order to exploit System-On-Chip (SoC) design without commercial, parameter, and bus compatibility limitations. The provided modules will be of particular benefit to the novice developers in providing ready-made examples of processing blocks, as well as parameterization settings for the interfacing cores and associated RF receiver side configuration settings. DSP cores can be used in any FPGA platforms whereas porting the I/O interface cores requires replacing Spartan-6 clock management and interconnecting libraries with new target-specific platform libraries.

The DSP cores are realized with fundamental DSP algorithms: Finite Impulse Response (FIR), Infinite Impulse Response (IIR), Fast Fourier Transform/Inverse Fast Fourier Transform (FFT/IFFT), and Digital Down Converter (DDC) algorithms. These DSP cores are accompanied by a description of how they can be integrated into a common Open Standard Interconnection Bus, namely, Wishbone. Furthermore, the I/O interface cores realize the interface control logic for Gigabit Ethernet (Gbe) and 4DSP FMC150 Analog-to-Digital Converter/Digital-to-Analog Converter (ADC/DAC) daughter board, both being part of RHINO. The Gbe interface core uses UDP protocol to enable high-speed data transfer between RHINO and external devices while FMC150 ADC/DAC provides an air interface for RHINO at high sampling rates. A Frequency Modulation (FM) receiver is then built from the IP cores to demonstrate the importance and reusability of the library of IP cores in the real world context of SDR.

The remainder of this paper is organized as follows. In Section 2, we provide a background to the SDR, FPGAs, and reconfigurable computing (RC). Next, the existing IP libraries are reviewed in Section 3. This is followed by the methodology used in developing and evaluating the library of SDR IP cores in Section 4. We continue with the design and implementation of a library of SDR IP cores in Section 5. In Section 6 we perform validation testing for SDR IP cores and results are compared to ideal Matlab simulation results. As a case study for SDR IP cores, we continue the testing by building an FM receiver in Section 7. This is followed by benchmarking all the SDR cores including an FM receiver in Section 8. Finally, we propose a tool-flow that enables high-level design using SDR IP cores in Section 9 while Section 10 covers conclusion.

2. Background

The ever increasing popularity and evolution of wireless communication technologies and standards are changing the manner in which wireless services and applications are used [6]. The demand and usage of these services by users are growing rapidly and are constantly pushing designs to their limits. Wireless devices are becoming more common and users are demanding the convergence of multiple services and technologies [7] in a single device. These lead to potential challenges in areas of equipment design, wireless service provision, security, and regulation [8].

2.1. SDR Systems. Configurable technologies are a solution to today's increasing user needs for wireless services and applications. These types of technologies are upgradable, reconfigurable, and adaptable to changes in technology standards and need [9]. One such technology that offers all these features is SDR. SDR is defined as radio in which hardware components or physical layer functions of a wireless communications system are all implemented in software [10].

SDR prototyping has opened doors to many possibilities in the field of radio communications. Owing to its rapid growth in recent years, it has gained popularity and has also found wide adoption in the analysis and implementation of many wireless communications systems. Traditional systems are now replaced by SDR systems because of their high reconfigurability and increased capabilities which suit modern wireless communications technology [9, 10].

SDR relies on a general purpose hardware that is easy to program and configure in software to enable a radio platform to adapt to multiple forms of operation such as multiband, multistandard, multimode, multiservice, and multicarrier [6, 10]. A typical SDR transceiver is depicted in Figure 1. The analog RF front-end converts RF signals to Intermediate Frequency (IF) signals in the receiver chain while the transmitter converts IF signals to RF signals. This is also where signal preconditioning and postconditioning using analog functions such as amplification and heterodyne mixing prior to ADC and after the DAC take place [6, 8]. The DSP performance largely depends on the digital computing hardware device used. Furthermore, improved and higher sampling ADCs and DACs are pushing the tasks traditionally performed in analog closer towards the antenna, hence allowing them to be processed digitally using processors or reconfigurable devices [11]. However, a drawback is that the ADCs and DACs are usually costly, and achieving high sampling rates (over millions of samples per second) remains a limitation in SDR [6]; this is a motivating factor for reusable SDR platforms for prototyping to share the cost of the same platform across multiple projects.

2.2. Overview of FPGAs and Reconfigurable Computing. The emergence of FPGA technology more than two decades ago

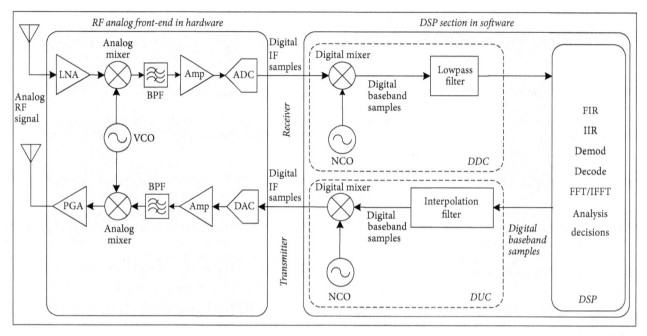

FIGURE 1: Radio transceiver architecture.

has revolutionized the field of SDR. FPGAs are made of highly reconfigurable and multiple logic blocks and cells together with switch matrix to route signals between them [12]. Their flexibility and speed have made them popular and are preferred to lay a general purpose hardware platform for SDR. The reconfigurable and parallel characteristics of FPGAs enable computationally intensive and complex tasks to be processed in real time with better performance and flexibility. These features have seen them gaining popularity over traditional general purpose processors (GPPs) and DSP processors [10]. For these reasons, they are used in RC as their structure can be reconfigured during start-up or runtime to perform advanced computations [13].

2.3. Design for Reuse. FPGAs have led to the concept of design for reuse which is a driving factor in enhancing the productivity and improving the system-level design in SDR applications. A library of parameterizable FPGA cores makes a design for reuse effective [14]. The timing, area, and power configurations are the key to SoC success as they allow mix-and-match of different IP cores so that the designer can apply the trade-offs that best suit the needs of the target application [15].

3. Review of Existing IP Libraries

The continuous design and implementation of a library of HDL cores, called IP cores in this paper, is increasingly driven by the desire to meet shortest possible time-to-market. This has led to greater demands of minimal development and debugging time [14, 16]. Many of the IP libraries have one or more of the characteristics listed below [14, 16–19]:

(i) Modularity

(ii) Parameterizability

(iii) Portability

(iv) Reusability

(v) Upgradability

(vi) Specific Technology Independency

(vii) Ability to consume fewer FPGA resources

Hardware designers are relying on predesigned IP cores from the IP libraries to increase productivity and reduce design time. However, many of the FPGA vendors and third-party IP libraries are static [18]. A static IP does not allow high performance to be achieved even when hardware resources or power budget is available nor does it achieve better performance to save both size and power consumption [18]. Integrating the third-party IPs can also be a challenge. It is often time-consuming and error-prone [19]. The IP libraries developed by private vendors are expensive and prohibitive to low-cost prototyping [20].

All the above shortcomings of private vendor IP libraries have led to new open-source hardware development models where reusable IPs are developed and made freely available to the public. Two examples of communities supporting open IP cores are OpenCores and GRLIB. OpenCores has the considerable number of IPs as well as Wishbone bus and its cores are accessible for free; however, OpenCores IPs are not parameterizable [20]. Likewise, GRLIB has many IP cores, interconnected by AMBA-2.0 AHB/APB bus on a SoC design. But a drawback of using GRLIB is that not all the IP cores are free [19].

4. Methodology

This objective of our investigation concerns making an effective selection of SDR cores needed to develop essential parts of an FPGA-based SDR application and from this to propose a DSL and initial selection of programming constructs that can facilitate the development of FPGA-based SDR applications without the programmer needing to have experience with HDL-based coding. The methodology we followed in this project comprises the following four aspects:

(1) Establish the design for an SDR IP core library that provides an essential collection of SDR building blocks that can serve as initial building blocks for FPGA-based SDR applications. Decide a suitable design and interfacing scheme for this set of SDR cores based on input from expert consultants.

(2) Testing the SDR cores independently on the physical FPGA-based SDR platform to confirm effective functionality of the cores.

(3) Developing a comprehensive SDR application from the SDR cores and testing this application on hardware to validate the operation of the cores working together.

(4) Benchmarking the SDR core library to ensure these cores are of an adequate standard in comparison to similar IP cores available in other libraries.

(5) Proposing a DSL-based tool-flow as an effective strategy for rapidly developing SDR applications for FPGA-based reconfigurable computing platforms using the SDR IP cores library.

The first step involved consultation with SDR experts. We interviewed and corresponded with these experts involved in FPGA-based design and implementation, both from industry and academia. Members of the engineering team at the Square Kilometre Array (SKA) were corresponded with in order to gain suggestions and feedback related to designs, processing requirements, and interfacing techniques; a total of three staff members contributed insights. We also met and corresponded with researchers involved with FPGA work at the University of Cape Town, including research scientists, postgraduate researchers, research officers, and academic staff; insights from four senior researcher staff and three postgraduate researchers were obtained at the university. The insights gained from this process were then used to prepare the design for the SDR core library and to decide the parameters that the cores should provide. The SDR cores were then coded using VHDL. Section 5 presents the subsequent design of the SDR IP cores library, starting by explaining the generic architecture that the cores fit into, then discussing the choice of SDR cores and how these were divided into DSP cores and I/O interface cores, and then explaining structure, parameters, and interface for each of the cores provided.

During the second step, testing of the individual cores was done to validate their operation; this was done using simulation and test vectors and by running the cores on a hardware platform. As part of this step, a reconfigurable hardware platform was chosen on which to test the cores. The chosen platform contained an FPGA that connected directly to a high-speed sampling card and to an Ethernet port for sending data. The results of this testing are shown in Section 6.

In the third step, we developed a representative SDR application that used the cores to confirm their operation and adequate performance when integrated as part of a complete SDR system. This application involved the development of an FM receiver for which digitally downconverted data was transferred over Ethernet to a host computer for demodulation and playback.

In the fourth step, our SDR cores were benchmarked against alternate cores available from other libraries. This benchmarking was done to confirm that the cores did not utilize an excessive number of logic elements compared to alternate solutions and that the operational clock rates of our cores were at adequate speed. Section 8 reports the benchmarking results.

In the final step, we propose a DSL to support rapid integration of the SDR cores for prototyping FPGA-based SDR applications without the programmer needing to have experience with the use of HDL coding. The proposed DSL and supporting tool-chain is presented in Section 9.

5. Design of SDR IP Cores

This section discusses the design of a library of SDR IP cores which is divided into DSP cores and I/O interface cores. For the design of DSP cores, we follow a modular coding approach using technology-independent logic elements which result in simple and reusable functional blocks. Likewise, for the design of I/O interface cores, the coding style is still modular but it comprises both technology-independent and technology-dependent functional blocks. Many commercial cores are closed source, licensed modules provided as monolithic hardware routing implementations optimized for and compatible with specific FPGA chips. A benefit of our cores is the availability of the underlying source code and therefore can be customized and be optimized further to meet the design requirements.

Although the SDR cores were tested on RHINO platform, the generic design of DSP cores using modular FPGA elements makes their portability possible without any changes or optimizations in the design, whereas porting of I/O interface cores to a wider range of platforms would still need an additional logic description or replacement of platform-specific elements in modules composed of such elements. Novice developers wanting to reuse these processing cores would consequently be advised to review the theoretical operation of the cores, possibly trying them in Octave or Matlab to gain a practical understanding of their behavior or limits, whereafter they would be familiar with the parameters concerned and be well prepared for moving to the FPGA, RHINO-based context of application of making these processing operations work in real time.

5.1. Design of DSP Cores. The design of the DSP cores presented in this paper is influenced by previous work performed for the design of hardware architectures to implement DSP algorithms. Wishbone bus slave interfaces were added to these designs to accommodate reusability, considering that the Wishbone standard is commonly used by developers making use of open-source or open-hardware IP. Some of

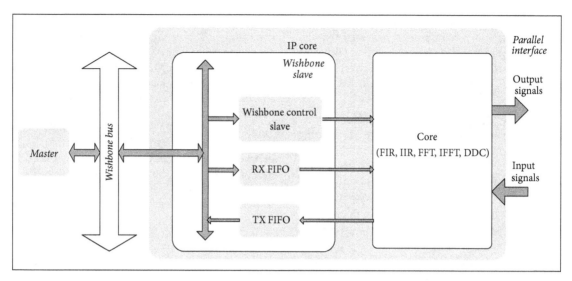

FIGURE 2: An overall architecture of a DSP IP core.

these DSP algorithms have been used by both commercial and open-source IP designers to implement their IP cores; however obtaining optimal results depends on the RTL coding style at a low level of design abstraction; thus the commercial solutions, in particular, are likely to have significant optimization performed for their proprietary implementations. Commercial IP cores are typically optimized for deployment on specific platforms whereas the open-source community hardly follows similar levels of consistency and standardization needed to implement such high-quality designs. In this work, we pay much attention to good RTL design conventions and practices typically obtained from consultation with experts and our own experience in FPGA design. The examples of technical recommendations that help in optimization of the cores during synthesis include (1) using modular coding style, (2) using a synchronous design approach, (3) avoiding latches, long combinatorial loops, and paths, (4) synchronizing resets at each clock domain, (5) using compatible platform-specific hardware resources such as memory, clock, and I/O management IP libraries, (6) isolating clock gating and switching, and (7) using clock PLLs and management blocks. All these design practices and many others not mentioned above make the optimization by low-level synthesis tools easier and effective. We also parameterize the cores to make it possible for future integration in the high-level synthesis tools.

The general structure of the design of the DSP cores is shown in Figure 2. These cores are implemented using fixed-point arithmetic [21] and are designed to operate with up to 130 MHz clock frequency. The configuration of core parameters such as data width, a number of filter coefficients, and FFT/IFFT length is performed through VHDL generics, hence providing a user with a wide range of options during the design process.

5.2. Selection of the DSP Cores. In this project, only restricted selection of IP cores was developed due to time constraint. These were chosen specially in consideration of common SDR

processing needs and was also based on a thorough literature review as well as establishing priorities on what was needed for RHINO platform. The following processing DSP IP cores were chosen for inclusion into the library: FIR filter, IIR filter, FFT/IFFT modules, and a parameterized and highly scalable DDC core. Furthermore, I/O interface cores, namely, FMC150 core and UDP/IP core, were developed for their importance in providing high-speed data communication with external devices.

5.3. Connecting the DSP Cores. As shown in Figure 2, the DSP cores can be interconnected with other cores using high-speed parallel interface at operating frequency of up to 130 MHz. The cores are also designed around a common SoC interface, namely, Wishbone, whose purpose is to further improve the reusability of these cores on a SoC design. The Wishbone slave control logic manages read-write operations of the slave registers while the first in first out (FIFO) memory stores incoming input data and outgoing processed data.

5.3.1. FIR IP Core. The FIR IP core is designed to enable modularity and scalability of SDR applications with the assurance of maximum attainable clock speed. With the support of five different FIR structures, the user has a wide range of choices to synthesize efficient FIR filter that meets the design needs under consideration. The top-level block diagram of the FIR IP core is depicted in Figure 3.

The proposed FIR core realizes a number of structures which include transposed parallel FIR structure, averaging FIR filter, and two optimized realizations, namely, even and odd symmetric parallel FIR filters [22, 23]. Parallel FIR architectures are designed around low-order, high-performance applications while optimized architectures are to be used in high-order, applications and where resources are limited.

The FIR core operation depends mainly on the structure chosen by the designer and the diagram that summarizes the operational flow based on the selected FIR structure is shown in Figure 4. Except for a moving average FIR filter, all

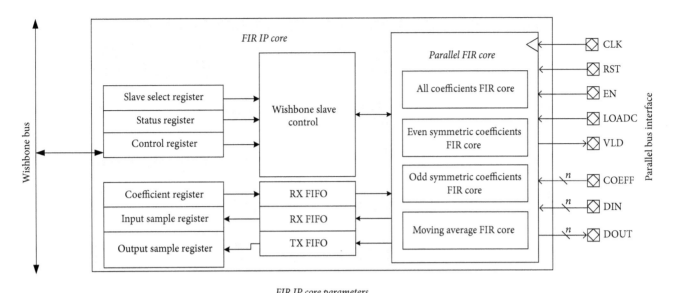

FIGURE 3: Architecture of FIR IP core.

Name	Description	Valid range
DIN_WIDTH	Width of data input	8
DOUT_WIDTH	Width of data output	8
COEFF_WIDTH	Width of a coefficient	8
NUM_OF_TAPS	Number of taps	2
COEFFS	Filter coefficients	Array size = taps size
LATENCY	FIR filter structure	0 = transpose 1 = odd symmetric 2 = even symmetric 3 = moving average

FIR IP core parameters

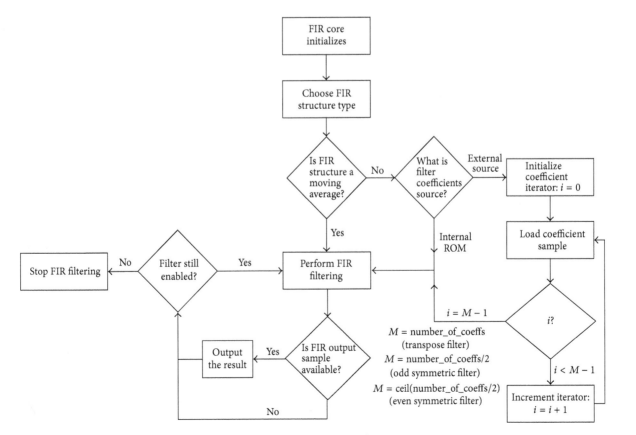

FIGURE 4: FIR core data flow diagram.

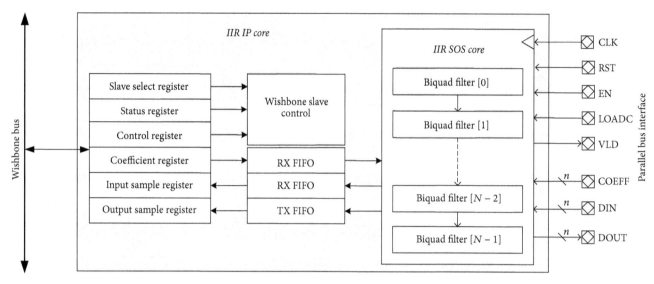

IIR IP core parameters		
Name	Description	Valid range
DIN_WIDTH	Width of data input	8
DOUT_WIDTH	Width of data output	8
COEFF_WIDTH	Width of a coefficient	8
STAGES	Number of biquad stages	1
a	Number of recursive coefficients	2
b	Number of recursive noncoefficients	3

FIGURE 5: An architecture of the IIR IP core.

other filter structures use coefficients stored in the distributed RAM or rather load coefficients from an external source. The user decides whether to use distributed RAM coefficients or to load them from an external memory. The FIR core does not begin filtering process until the coefficients loading is finished. If internal coefficients are used, filtering occurs immediately without waiting for loading to happen.

5.3.2. IIR IP Core. The core is built from a basic structure of a second-order IIR filter also known as biquad of Direct Form I [22]. IIR core allows cascading of the biquads to build higher order IIR filters without experiencing coefficient-sensitivity problems. This IIR structure with a cascade of biquads is called Second-Order Sections (SOS). The block diagram of IIR core designed is shown in Figure 5. The IIR core recursive and nonrecursive coefficients for each biquad are configured by the user.

5.3.3. FFT/IFFT IP Core. Radix-2^2 Single-Path Delay Feedback (R-2^2 SDF) algorithm [24] is exploited to implement a complex pipelined R-2^2 SDF architecture of the FFT on an FPGA. The high-level block diagram of the designed FFT IP core is shown in Figure 6. The implemented FFT core is further used to implement an IFFT core. The procedure is straightforward as the IFFT is computed by conjugating the twiddle factors of the corresponding forward FFT output [25]. Some benefits of using R-2^2 to design the FFT core are that its FFT architecture has simple pipeline control and reduced multipliers by a factor of $(N - 1)/2$ compared to

Radix-2 and Radix-4 which are used to design an FFT for Xilinx IP Cores Library [26]. The designed FFT/IFFT core length can be configured to 4, 8, 16, 32, 64, 128, 256, 512, 1024, 2048, and 4096 by the user. However, larger size FFTs can be implemented using a Matlab script accompanying a core.

An example of 32-point R-2^2 SDF FFT is illustrated in Figure 7. Data arrives at the input in a sequential order and output data leaves the core in a bit-reversed order. For an FFT with N points, a complete stage consists of two butterflies, namely, BFI and BFII, delay feedback shift register, and a twiddle factor complex multiplier. On the other hand, half a stage only has a single butterfly which is BFI.

5.3.4. DDC IP Core. The developed DDC core is highly configurable and can be tailored easily to meet many SDR multirate applications needs. Figure 8 illustrates the top-level block diagram of the DDC IP core. This can be used in SDR applications to perform the first processing after ADC. The DDC performs the tasks such as frequency downconversion, sample rate reduction, and high-speed filtering [27].

The DDC structure is realized as shown in Figure 9. The structure is composed of Numerically Controlled Oscillator (NCO), digital mixer; Cascaded Integrator Comb (CIC) and FIR filter were all designed to complete the structure of the DDC.

5.4. Design of I/O Interface Cores. This section presents a development of FMC150 ADC/DAC interface core and a UDP/IP core for Gbe which are designed to be operational on RHINO.

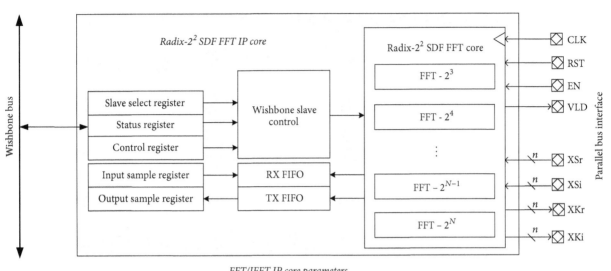

FFT/IFFT IP core parameters

Name	Description	Valid range
N	Number of FFT points	$= 2^N, N = 3$
DOUT_WIDTH	Width of data output	8–32
COEFF_WIDTH	Width of a coefficient	8–32
TF_WIDTH	Bit width of twiddle factors	8

FIGURE 6: An architecture of the FFT IP core.

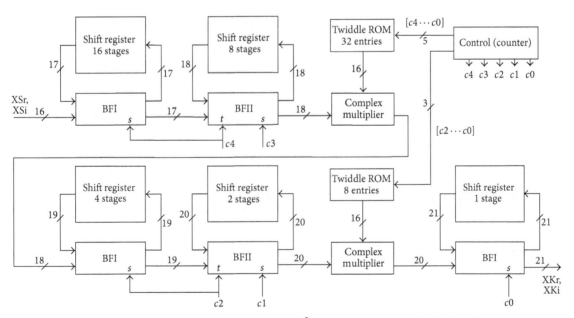

FIGURE 7: 32-point FFT structure using Radix-2^2 Single-Path Delay Feedback algorithm.

5.4.1. FMC150 Interface Core.

The FMC150 is designed with TI's ADS62P49/ADS4249 dual-channel 14-bit 250 MSPS ADC and TI's DAC3283 dual-channel 16-bit 800 MSPS DAC. The TI's CDCE72010 PLL is the clock distribution device that provides a clock to drive the DAC and ADC. The internal clock source can optionally be locked to onboard 100 MHz or external reference clock [28].

The FMC150 core presented in this section provides Low-Voltage Differential Signaling (LVDS) interface to a 4DSP FMC150 daughter card as depicted in Figure 10. A design example in Figure 10 is configured on ADC sampling rate of 61.44 MSPS and sends digital samples to DAC at 61.44 MSPS rate. The maximum sampling rates that FMC150 core were tested on using RHINO are 163.84 MSPS and 245.76 MSPS for ADC and DAC, respectively.

5.4.2. UDP/IP Core.

In order to make RHINO Gbe operational, an FPGA-based Gbe core is needed to configure,

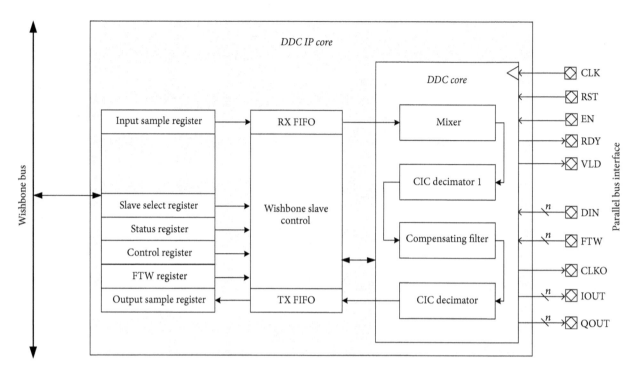

DDC IP core parameters

Name	Description	Valid range
N	Number of FFT points	8
DOUT_WIDTH	Width of data output	8
PHASE_WIDTH	NCO phase width	8
PHASE_DITHER_WIDTH	Phase dither width	PHASE_WIDTH
SELECT_CIC1	Activate CIC1 of a DDC	0 or 1
NUMBER_OF_STAGES1	Number of CIC1 Stages	>0
DIFFERENTIAL_DELAY1	Differential delay of CIC1	1 or 2
SAMPLE RATE_CHANGE1	Decimation factor of CIC1	>0
SELECT_CFIR	Use a compensating FIR filter of DDC	0 or 1
NUMBER_OF_TAPS	Number of coefficients	>0
FIR_LATENCY	Type of FIR filter structure	0, 1, 2, 3
COEFF_WIDTH	Coefficient bit width	8
COEFFS	Quantized integer filter coefficients	Array size = taps size
SELECT_CIC2	Activate CIC2 of a DDC	0 or 1
NUMBER_OF_STAGES2	Number of CIC2 stages	>0
DIFFERENTIAL_DELAY2	Differential delay of CIC2	1 or 2
SAMPLE RATE_CHANGE2	Decimation factor of CIC2	>0

FIGURE 8: An architecture of the DDC IP core.

monitor, and control the Ethernet interface. This section presents a design of a UDP/IP core based on the combination of Internet Protocol version-4 (IPv4) and User Datagram Protocol (UDP) in order to provide a high-speed and efficient solution for communication over a Gbe.

FPGA devices require Ethernet Media Access Controller (EMAC) to interface with the physical layer (PHY) chip on the board [29]. RHINO uses an integrated Marvell 88E111 PHY chip. The PHY is needed for the FPGA to connect with external devices. The user logic can be deployed to configure the EMAC physical interface [29] in a form of wrapper files. In our case, the wrapper files configure the OpenCores Trimode MAC [5] which is published under the GNU Lesser General Public License (LGPL). This is a very cost-effective

and nonrestrictive solution in comparison with proprietary Media Access Controllers (MACs) such as Xilinx's Trimode Ethernet Media Access Controller (TEMAC) [30] which is costly. Furthermore, the OpenCores Trimode MAC IP core supports data rates of 10, 100, and 1000 Mbps and is compliant with IEEE 802.3 specification [5]. Our UDP/IP core is only configured on 1000 Mbps speed.

The architecture of the UDP/IP core is illustrated in Figure 11. Address Resolution Protocol (ARP) is used to resolve the sender and receiver MAC addresses before packet data communication. An OpenCores Trimode MAC [5] is responsible for delivering data over a shared physical channel. The MAC consists of two user interfaces that simplify the connection to a PHY. It encodes/decodes packet data

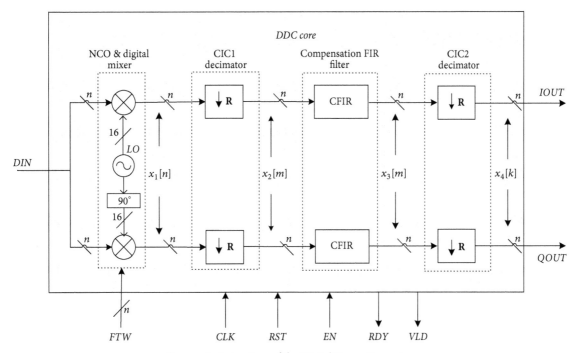

FIGURE 9: A structure of the Digital Down Converter.

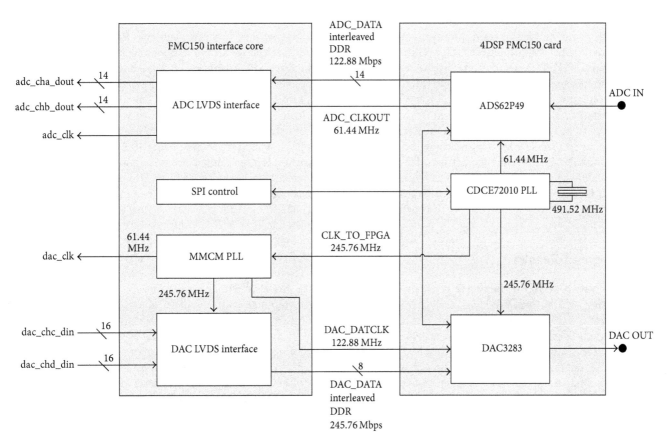

FIGURE 10: Structure of FMC150 core interfacing with the 4DSP FMC150 card.

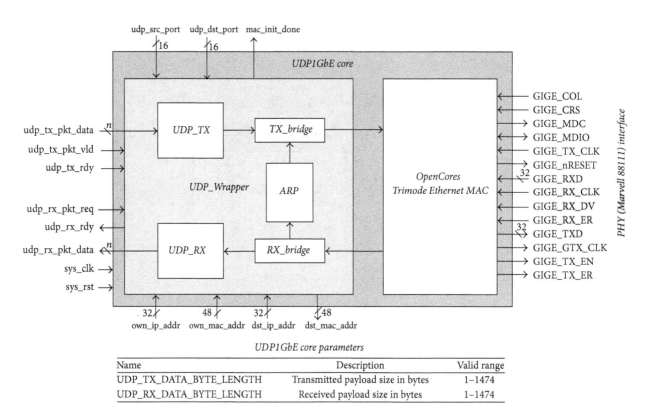

Name	Description	Valid range
UDP_TX_DATA_BYTE_LENGTH	Transmitted payload size in bytes	1–1474
UDP_RX_DATA_BYTE_LENGTH	Received payload size in bytes	1–1474

FIGURE 11: Structure of UDP/IP core for interfacing and control of a Gbe (uses OpenCores Trimode Ethernet MAC [5] to interface with a PHY).

to/from PHY during transmission and reception of data using Gigabit Media-Independent Interface (GMII) between a MAC and a PHY. The second interface is serial and it is called Management Data Input/Output (MDIO) bus. It transfers configuration data to a PHY and it is also used to read PHY status registers. The IPv4 is used by the designed UDP/IP core to deliver messages between the RHINO and a destination device. The IP addresses are configured statically and they must be in the same subnetwork for successful communication to happen. UDP is chosen as a transport layer protocol. It is used in this design for its simplicity and the fact that it supports high-speed and real-time data transfers [31, 32].

6. Testing and Results

In order to verify the functionality and correctness of these cores, testing which involved behavioral and functional simulation was performed. Each DSP core was successfully synthesized on Spartan-6 of RHINO and tested from input data generated using Matlab. After the core had processed the data, the results were stored in an output file as a vector of samples. Matlab scripts were used to plot graphs and perform further signal processing of the results for analysis. The general experimental setup for DSP cores is shown in Figure 13. The operating frequencies of 100 MHz were used when testing the FIR, IIR, and FFT cores. For a DDC core, 122.88 MHz of clock frequency was used.

6.1. Overview of RHINO Platform. Reconfigurable Hardware Interface for ComputatioN and RadiO (RHINO) is a standalone FPGA processing board and has commonalities with the better known Reconfigurable Open Architecture Computing Hardware (ROACH); however, it is a significantly cutdown and lower-cost alternative which has similarities in the interfacing and FPGA or processor interconnects of ROACH. RHINO was designed at the University Of Cape Town and is largely aimed around a lower-cost, totally open-source FPGA board which provides a good platform for the development of software-defined radio applications [4]. The RHINO platform was designed to be a combination of an education and training platform for learning about reconfigurable computing and as a research and prototyping platform for studies related to SDR [4, 33].

The two main processing elements of RHINO include ARM processor and Spartan-6 FPGA as shown in Figure 12. The computationally intensive functions are processed by the FPGA while the ARM processor provides configuration, control, and interface function with FPGA through Berkeley Operating System for Reprogrammable Hardware (BORPH) [4, 34]. BORPH is an extended Linux kernel that allows control of FPGA resources as if they were native computational resource [34]. This, as a result, allows users to program the FPGA with a given design or configuration and run it as software process within Linux.

Other building blocks of RHINO include FMC connectors which enable interface with ADC, DAC, and mixed

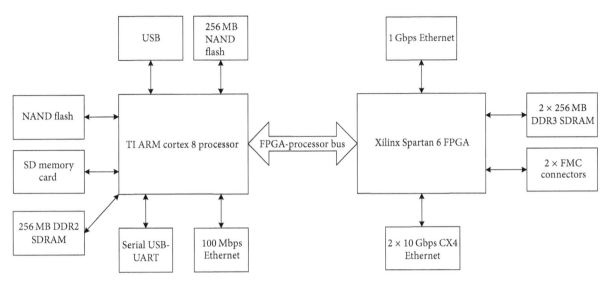

FIGURE 12: An architecture of RHINO platform building blocks.

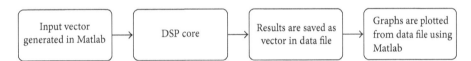

FIGURE 13: Process of configuring a DSP core.

signal daughter cards, supporting sample rates over 1GS/s [35]. The 1/10 Gbe connectors provide a high-speed network connection between the FPGA and remote devices using standard TCP or UDP transport layer protocols to convey packets of data.

6.2. Testing FIR Core. The FIR core was verified by designing length L = 95 FIR bandpass filter to specifications shown in Figure 14. The resulting Parks-McClellan optimal FIR coefficients of 16-bit width are illustrated in Figure 14(b) in a form of filter frequency response. The filter was tested on an input signal consisting of a sum of sinusoids at frequencies 440, 800, 2200, and 2500 Hz as shown in Figure 14(a) and only a 2200 Hz was isolated by a bandpass filter. The results shown in Figure 14(d) closely match with the results of the ideal filter in Matlab shown in Figure 14(c); however, the Signal-to-Noise Ratio (SNR) has slightly decreased due to quantization and round-off errors.

6.3. Testing IIR Core. Testing the IIR filter was similar to FIR testing in Section 6.2 except for filter response shown in Figure 15(b) which was designed with Chebyshev Type I filter to specifications shown in Figure 15. The results of the IIR core obtained are shown in Figure 15(d) which closely match the ideal Matlab results shown in Figure 15(c). In comparison to the FIR core results, the IIR core is highly selective and uses fewer coefficients leading to better results.

6.4. Testing FFT/IFFT Core. This testing involved generating an input vector (length = 1024) of a rectangular pulse as shown in Figure 16(a) and processing it with a 1024-point FFT/IFFT core. This was used at the input of the core operating in FFT mode. The output of the FFT core as shown in Figure 16(c) was later used as an input data to the IFFT core. The FFT core yielded the sinc waveform in Figure 16(c) which was the expected Fourier transform of a pulse waveform. This also matched with the Matlab generated FFT of the pulse wave shown in Figure 16(b). As expected, the IFFT core produced the original rectangular pulse waveform which is illustrated in Figure 16(d).

6.5. Testing DDC Core. Using Matlab and 122.88 MSPS sample rate, an FM signal vector was created by modulating 94.5 MHz sine wave with 15 kHz baseband signal. This vector was used as an input to a DDC core. Due to bandpass sampling used, the FM signal was centered at 28.38 MHz after sampling. Similarly, the carrier was also located at 28.38 MHz. In order to convert it to baseband, NCO signals are multiplied with input FM signal using the mixer. The product then becomes the desired signal component centered at DC and a spurious harmonic located at 56.76 MHz as shown in Figure 17(b). This undesired signal component was removed by a CIC filter which decimated the 122.88 MSPS ADC sample rate by a factor of 1 : 128 resulting in 960 kSPS sample rate as shown in Figure 17(c). The nonideal response of the CIC filter was corrected by introducing a compensation FIR filter in the final stage of the DDC and its output is shown in Figure 17(d).

After the digital downconversion, the FM demodulator was used to demodulate the FM signal. The magnitude

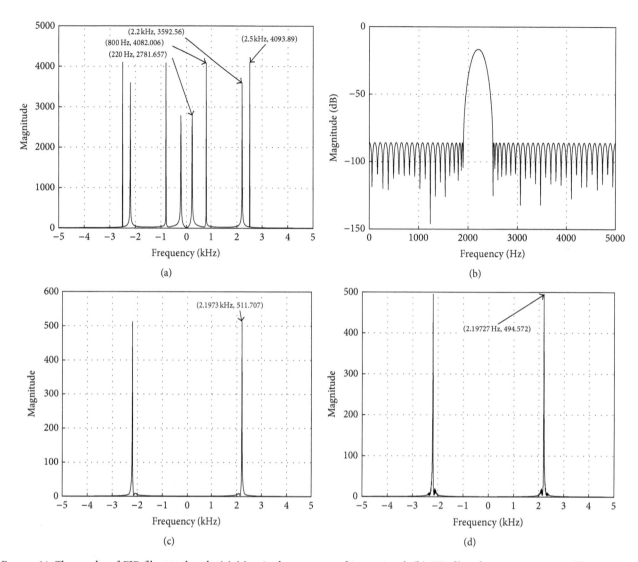

FIGURE 14: The results of FIR filter testbench. (a) Magnitude spectrum of input signal. (b) FIR filter frequency response (filter response parameters: *sampling frequency = 10 kHz, lower cutoff frequency = 2.190 kHz, higher cutoff frequency = 22.15 kHz, passband ripple = 3 dB, stopband attenuation = 80 dB,* and *number of coefficients = 95*). (c) Magnitude spectrum of Matlab FIR filter output. (d) Magnitude spectrum of FPGA FIR filter output.

spectrum and amplitude versus time graphs of the signal after demodulation are shown in Figures 18(a) and 18(b). This output has a transient response which is the effect of the FM demodulator. When the transient was removed, this resulted in steady-state response whose magnitude spectrum and time domain graphs are shown in Figures 18(c) and 18(d), and they represent the recovered 15 kHz baseband signal.

6.6. Testing FMC150 ADC Core and UDP/IP Core. The experimental setup is shown in Figure 19 and it involved stream-based processing that incorporated ADC and Gbe cores. The 20 MHz input tone to a 49.152 MSPS ADC was generated with a function generator as illustrated in Figure 20(a). The FMC150 interface core was used to capture the ADC samples and these samples were sent to a Desktop Personal Computer (PC) via a Gbe using UDP/IP core. At the PC end, the received samples were plotted as shown in Figure 20. The

Spurious Frequency Dynamic Range (SFDR) of the ADC signal was measured as 44 dBc, about 55% of the vendor specified ADC figure. The pronounced spurious harmonics are due to the high-level of distortion in the 10 dBm input signal from a function generator. A better function generator with a low distortion effect would improve results. The throughput speed recorded on a Gbe using Wireshark was 98.62 MB/s which is 89.65% of the theoretical figure of 110 MB/s (as specified by Huang et al. [36]).

6.7. Testing FMC150 DAC Core. The block diagram of the experimental setup is illustrated in Figure 21. The experiment used the NCO core designed in Section 5.3.4 to synthesize two different sine waveforms of frequencies 17.23 MHz and 28.38 MHz. The digital samples were sent to the DAC at 61.44 MSPS sampling rate. The DAC, in turn, converted

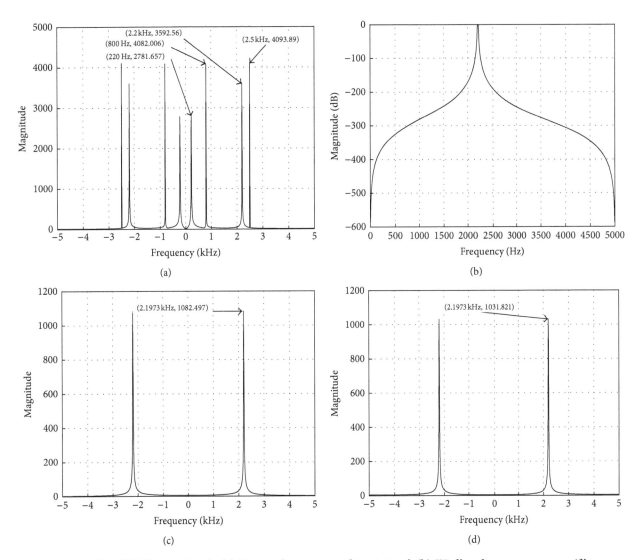

FIGURE 15: The results of IIR filter testbench. (a) Magnitude spectrum of input signal. (b) IIR filter frequency response (filter response parameters: *sampling frequency = 10 kHz, lower cutoff frequency = 2.190 kHz, higher cutoff frequency = 22.10 kHz, passband ripple = 0.1 dB, stopband attenuation = 200 dB, number of coefficients = 6*, and *number of sections = 6*). (c) Magnitude spectrum of Matlab IIR filter output. (d) Magnitude spectrum of FPGA IIR filter output.

digital data into analog signals which were measured on a spectrum analyzer and the results are shown in Figure 22.

7. Validation: Development of FM Receiver

This section reports on the development of a wideband digital FM receiver. This is used for validation of the proposed SDR IP cores library. Using the SDR IP cores which incorporate DSP cores and I/O interface cores, this prototype serves as a proof of concept that the cores can be used not only in this FM receiver design but also to prototype other real-time SDR applications. The complete design of FM receiver comprises an analog RF front-end circuitry and digital receiver which forms the largest part of the FM receiver processing.

7.1. Analog Front-End. The block diagram of the analog RF front-end design is shown in Figure 23 and is sensitive to

−65 dBm FM signal. The indoor FM antenna with a variable gain of 36 dB receives the FM signal in the frequency range of 88–108 MHz. The front-end also provides a bandpass filtering of FM band and a total gain of 75 dB to make the FM signal compatible with the input swing of the ADC. The overall gain is determined as

$$\text{Total Front-End Gain (dB)} = P_{\text{fm-signal}} + P_{\text{fmc150-ADC}}$$
$$= 10 + 65 = 75 \, \text{dB}, \tag{1}$$

where $P_{\text{fm-signal}}$ is FM signal power in dBm and $P_{\text{fmc150-ADC}}$ is ADC input signal power in dBm.

7.2. Digital Receiver. The digital receiver processing is implemented with a DDC core and the FM demodulator. The block diagram showing the processing blocks is shown in Figure 24. The 20 MHz bandwidth RF signal is digitized with a 14-bit

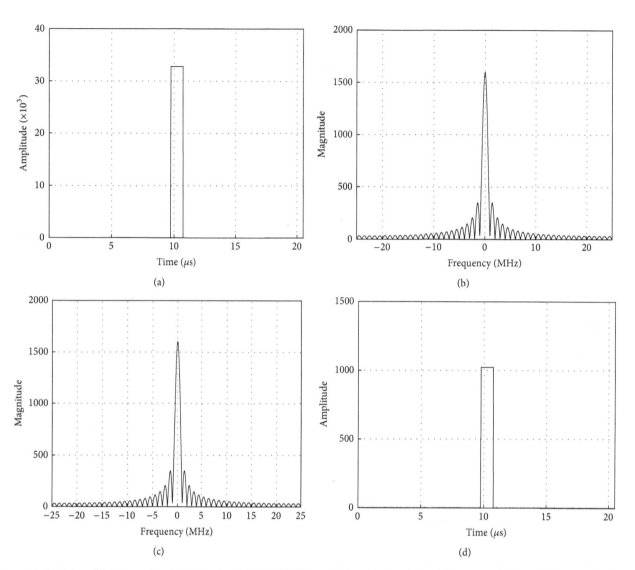

FIGURE 16: Matlab and FPGA results of a 1024-point FFT and IFFT core tested with rectangular pulse input waveform. (a) Rectangular pulse waveform, (b) 1024-point FFT core output using Matlab, (c) 1024-point FFT core output using FPGA, and (d) 1024-point IFFT core output using FPGA.

precision ADC. The ADC sampling rate f_s is determined by using a bandpass sampling criterion [37] in (2) where n falls in a range 1 to 5. We choose $n = 2$ and this results in a wide frequency range of 108 MHz–176 MHz valid for ADC bandpass sampling. We choose 122.88 MSPS as the ADC bandpass sampling speed. The chosen ADC sample rate results in the digitized FM signal downshifted from 88–108 MHz band to 14.88–34.88 MHz band.

$$\frac{2f_H}{n} \le f_s \le \frac{2f_L}{n-1}, \qquad (2)$$

where n is given by $1 \le n \le (f_H/(f_H - f_L))$, f_H is high frequency, and f_L is low frequency.

The 14-bit samples received from the ADC are extended to 16-bit signed words which are directed into the DDC core input. To generate a complex baseband I/Q signal, the sine and cosine waveforms are generated using the NCO core and

then multiplied with the FM signal using digital quadrature mixer. The frequency of the NCO output is equal to the frequency of a sampled FM signal and it ranges between 14.88 MHz and 34.88 MHz.

After mixing down the FM signal using the quadrature mixer, the image and mixer products are eliminated by the CIC filter which uses zero multipliers in its implementation. This CIC filter also decimates the 122.88 MSPS ADC rate to 960 kSPS by decimation ratio of 1:128. Despite its low cost and efficient and simple implementation, the CIC filter introduces undesirable droop in its filter response passband [38]. To correct this nonflat response in the passband of the CIC filter, the compensation FIR (C-FIR) filter is used.

The CIC and C-FIR filter specification parameters and their respective filter responses are shown in Figure 25. In this same figure, the total filter response is shown which results after decimation and compensation.

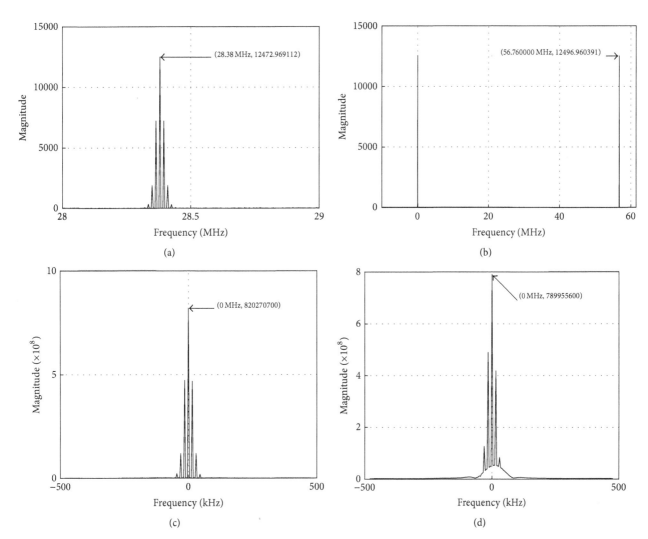

FIGURE 17: Results of DDC core and FM demodulator. (a) FM-modulated signal generated in Matlab, (b) magnitude spectrum of mixer, (c) magnitude spectrum of CIC-1, and (d) magnitude spectrum of a C-FIR filter.

7.3. Data Packetization. A data packet that is composed of 32-bit samples needs to be generated before the actual construction of a UDP packet. Each 32-bit is decomposed into 16-bit I/Q data samples. Generation of data packets is facilitated by a length-N double buffer that lies between a DDC core and UDP/IP core as shown in Figure 24. In this example, we choose $N = 33$. As illustrated in Figure 26, a double buffer accepts samples from a DDC core and writes them to *BUFFER 1* buffer. The UDP/IP core then reads samples from *BUFFER 2* as a unit to generate a data packet that is padded to a data field of a UDP packet. Furthermore, double buffering also solves a producer-consumer problem during concurrent read and write process by DDC core and UDP/IP core, respectively. Each data packet generated forms part of the UDP data field where each 32-bit sample in a packet is represented by 16-bit I/Q samples as shown in Figure 27.

7.4. Final Test: FM Receiver. The block diagram showing the experiment setup is shown in Figure 28. The test was performed by tuning to a local radio station at 94.5 MHz (K-FM). The final output of the FPGA processing was complex I/Q samples centered at DC as shown in Figure 29(a). These samples were then demodulated in Matlab using arctan/differentiation FM demodulator at the PC end. The output of the FM demodulator is a real-valued signal and is shown in Figure 29(b). The results clearly show the mono audio, pilot tone, stereo audio, and RBDS spectral components; however, stereo audio and RBDS are not distinguished due to a weak FM signal received by the ADC. The ADC tends not to be sensitive to signals with power way below 10 dBm. Increasing the analog RF front-end gain will improve results.

8. Benchmark Results

We benchmark our IP cores using Xilinx ISE v14.7, targeting the Spartan-6 xc6slx150t FPGA found on RHINO platform. We do the same with cores found in Xilinx DSP core library and OpenCores where they both represent commercial and open-source cores, respectively. The benchmark results

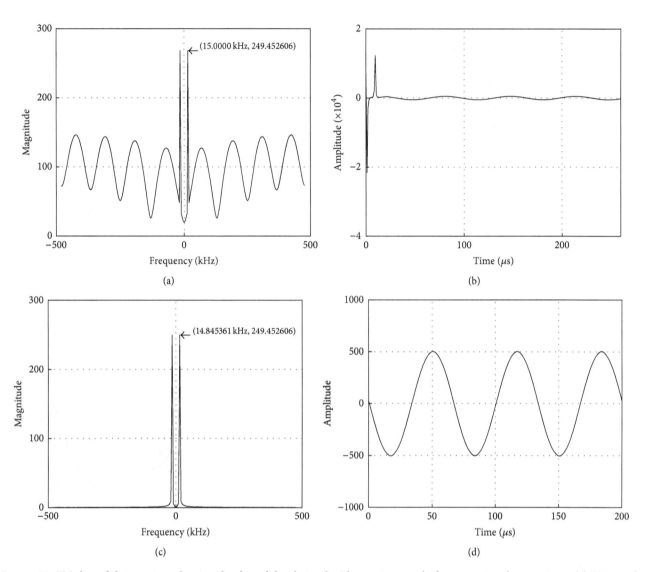

FIGURE 18: FM demodulator output showing the demodulated signal with transients and after removing the transients. (a) Magnitude spectrum of FM-demodulated signal, (b) FM-demodulated signal; (c) magnitude spectrum of FM-demodulated signal without transients, (d) FM-demodulated signal without transients.

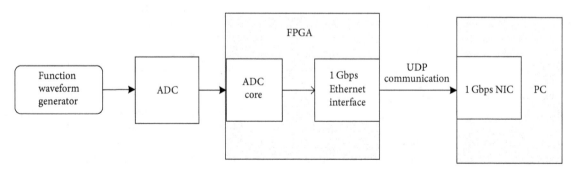

FIGURE 19: Experimental setup for a streaming core using FMC150 ADC core and Gbe core.

shown in Table 1 use metrics of FPGA resource utilization and the maximum clock speed that can safely be used to execute each core. The key parameter values for each of the SDR cores are as follows:

(1) The number of coefficients for the FIR core is 21 with data width set to 16 bits.

(2) The IIR core is benchmarked on 16 stages with 16-bit data.

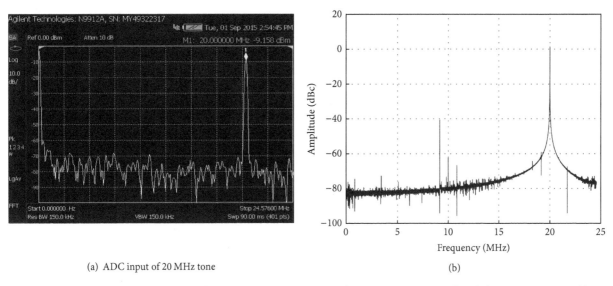

(a) ADC input of 20 MHz tone

(b)

FIGURE 20: 20 MHz tone ADC output streamed using UDP. (a) ADC input of 20 MHz tone generated with function generator, (b) FFT for 20 MHz ADC signal captured on a PC after streaming.

FIGURE 21: A block diagram showing experimental setup for DAC interface core.

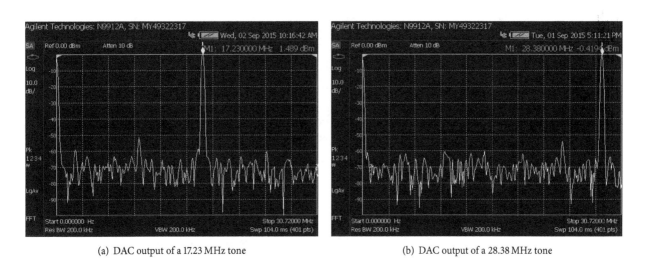

(a) DAC output of a 17.23 MHz tone

(b) DAC output of a 28.38 MHz tone

FIGURE 22: The spectra different sinusoids generated using NCO core and measured at the FMC150 DAC output.

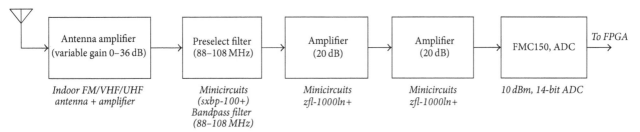

FIGURE 23: A block diagram of the analog RF front-end.

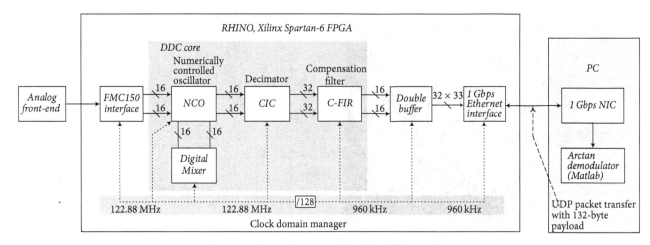

FIGURE 24: An architecture of the digital FM receiver.

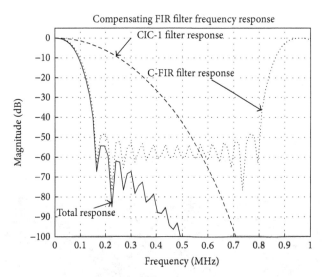

FIGURE 25: The total frequency response due to CIC and C-FIR frequency response. CIC parameters: *input sample = 122.88 MSPS, output sample rate = 960 kSPS, decimation factor (R) = 128, number of stages (N) = 10, differential delay (M) = 1.* C-FIR parameters: *input and output sample rate = 960 kSPS, number of coefficients = 21, cutoff frequency = 90 kHz, stopband attenuation = 10 dB.*

(3) The number of FFT core points is set to 1024 with data width set to 16 bits.

(4) The DDC core is configured to operate on 122.88 MSPS of an RF signal and output 1.28 MSPS of a baseband signal.

The Xilinx library does not have an IIR core while OpenCores does not have a DDC core needed to perform benchmarking.

The Xilinx DSP cores exhibit more performance and use the fewest FPGA resources overall. The static nature of the Xilinx cores allows easy access to generic parameters through a core generator wizard which makes it very complex to even modify the generated code. Our cores have performance that is slightly less than Xilinx cores but with comparable FPGA resource utilization. They also expose easy interface for configuration of generic parameters of the cores. The OpenCores cores have the lowest performance and the largest

resource occupation on the FPGA. Furthermore, they have other constraints such as limiting the number of FIR core coefficients to less than 22 and the FFT points are limited to 1024.

The results have shown that our SDR cores achieve significant performance and use less resources while exposing design parameters to the user in the VHDL code. Further benchmark tests for a Gbe core, FMC150 interface core, and the FM receiver application are performed and results shown in Table 1 show a satisfactory performance needed for SDR.

9. Proposed DSL and Tool-Flow for SDR

We briefly introduce a new SDR high-level synthesis, namely, SdrHls which enables the FPGA design of SDR applications using a Domain-Specific Language (DSL). Instead of translating a DSL into new FPGA functionality, SdrHls maps user design specifications in DSL onto parameterizable

TABLE 1: IP core benchmark results for Xilinx, OpenCores, and SDR cores.

Source	Cores	Slices (23038)	%	LUTs (92152)	%	Registers (184304)	%	RAM (21680)	%	DSP48A1s (180)	%	BUFGs (16)	%	Maximum Clock Frequency (MHz)
Xilinx library	FIR	30	1	50	1	96	1	13	1	1	1	1	1	303
	FFT	885	3	2294	2	3403	1	607	2	16	8	1	1	141
	DDC	680	2	1223	1	2179	1	472	2	7	3	1	1	134
OpenCores	FIR	1556	6	3872	4	691	1	0	0	21	11	1	1	80
	IIR	247	1	857	1	864	1	0	0	72	40	1	1	66
	FFT	1209	5	2768	3	3120	1	1024	4	16	8	1	1	84
SDR cores	FIR	43	1	132	1	304	1	0	0	30	16	1	1	130
	IIR	144	1	376	1	492	1	0	0	36	20	1	1	94
	FFT	930	4	2518	2	1267	1	642	2	16	8	1	1	118
	DDC	1404	6	4024	4	5179	2	0	0	2	1	1	1	129
	Gbe	1205	5	2701	1	2928	1	411	1	0	0	7	43	165
	FMC150	631	2	1335	1	1272	1	142	1	0	0	8	50	184
	FM Rec.	1404	6	4024	4	5179	2	0	0	2	1	1	6	154

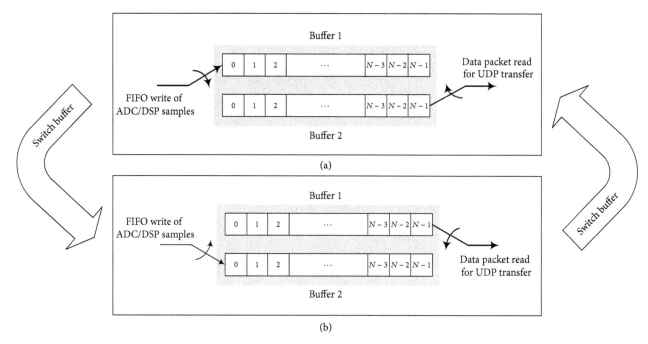

FIGURE 26: Double buffering used between the ADC or DSP output and Gbe input. (a) Writing DSP samples to BUFFER 1 and creating a data packet by concurrent reading of BUFFER 2 samples. (b) Writing DSP samples to BUFFER 2 and creating a data packet by concurrent reading of BUFFER 1 samples.

Data field of UDP packet	Sample 0	Sample 1	Sample 2	⋯	Sample 30	Sample 31	Sample 32
Word length in bits	32	32	32	⋯	32	32	32

Sample field of UDP data field	In-phase data	Quadrature data
Sample length in bits	16	16

FIGURE 27: UDP frame data field format. Data field is composed of 33 samples collected from a DDC core output.

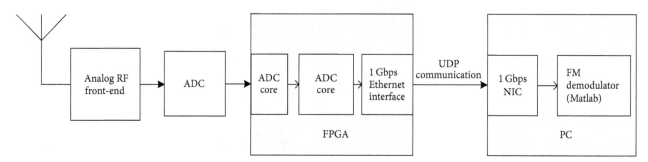

FIGURE 28: Experimental setup for a digital wideband FM receiver.

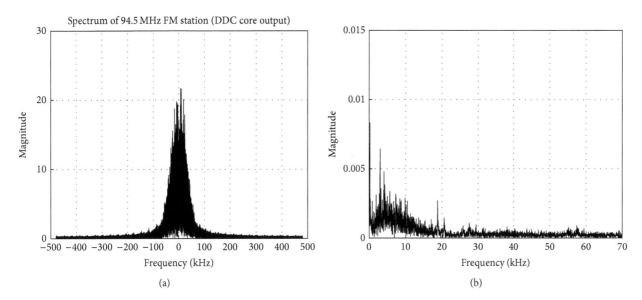

FIGURE 29: The results of FM receiver when tuning to 94.5 MHz radio station. (a) Spectrum of 94.5 MHz FM station baseband signal which is the output of a DDC core, (b) spectrum of FM-demodulated 94.5 MHz FM station in Matlab; the signal is real-valued after demodulation.

SDR IP cores and stitches the cores together to yield the desired FPGA design. It achieves this by adopting a model-based design approach employing a Synchronous Dataflow (SDF) [39] while also leveraging the high-level topological design patterns of a DSL that are based on a functional language called Scala. There are other dataflow-based HLS tools for fast prototyping of DSP applications such as Ptolemy [40], LabView [41], and Simulink [42]. These tools provide intuitive methodologies to specify, simulate, and/or execute DSP applications. However, they strive to provide generic solutions in all areas of DSP field thereby resulting in compromised efficiency of produced designs. SdrHls is a domain-specific tool optimized for producing efficient FPGA-based SDR designs and uses idioms and notations familiar to domain users of SDR.

An overview of our design flow for SdrHls is illustrated in Figure 30 and its description is backed by a typical SDR design example of the FM receiver discussed in Section 7.

9.1. A DSL and High-Level Compilation. We begin with an application specification that represents an SDR algorithm to be translated into an FPGA design in VHDL. This is specified using a DSL that employs a dataflow-based approach as shown Listing 1 and the corresponding SDF diagram is illustrated in Figure 31. The expressiveness and conciseness of the rich DSL syntax enable the intuitive description of a system, therefore, raising the low-level FPGA design abstraction to a higher level of design abstraction. This makes it easy for domain users with limited or no hardware design skills to generate hardware design and for skilled users to improve productivity.

Depending upon the system requirements, the user selects from the existing library of SDR cores the components needed to construct a complete system. The parameters for components can optionally be configured using a DSL and

the SdrHls will assign default values for the unset parameters during high-level synthesis. Furthermore, the parameters set in a DSL are later mapped to VHDL generics in the final hardware design. Such parameters can be defined as static values in a DSL or read from data files stored in a local memory. Most importantly, a DSL allows parameter values to be dynamically generated using a DSL itself and the compiler will assign static values for the parameters. A typical example is generating the filter coefficients for a FIR core.

The first six lines in Listing 1 include the SdrHls DSL compiler library and the Delite library and define an object for running the main SdrHls main application method. The fourth line generates a list of coefficients for a compensating filter of the CIC filter in Figure 24. The compensator constructor takes in parameters set with values as follows: sample rate change = 128, a number of stages = 10, and differential delay = 1. This is followed by the configuration of the parameters which correspond to VHDL generics of the IP cores. In this example, the ADC core takes no parameters as denoted by Nil, and the DDC core parameters set include data width and filter coefficients with other parameters not shown to make the code brief. The Gbe is set with 64 bytes of transmitted payload which is calculated using (3). The *Component* object is used to define the IP core and it takes in the VHDL component name of the IP core together with its generic parameters. The *Chain* object is a topological design pattern that creates a cascade of component objects connected to each other using FIFO channels. The square brackets after each of the components define the consumption and production rates of each component or actor in an SDF dataflow. The rate of zero denotes nonexisting input or output channel while the existence of a channel is denoted by the rate greater than zero. Lastly,

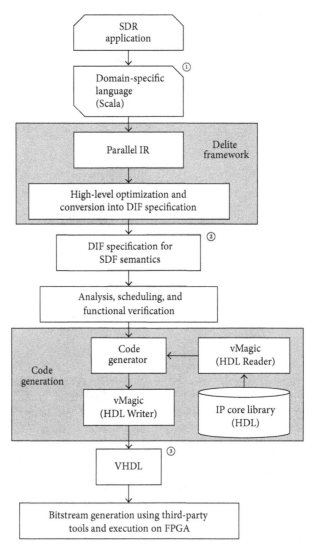

FIGURE 30: A high-level synthesis design flow for SDR.

FIGURE 31: An SDF diagram of the FM receiver.

the VHDL code of the system is generated by a *synthesize* method.

$$\text{UDP payload size} = \text{Gbe core consumption rate}$$
$$\times \text{baseband channels}$$
$$\times \text{data width} = 16 \times 2 \times 16 \quad (3)$$
$$= 512 \text{ bits} = 64 \text{ bytes}$$

The DSL application (Scala code) is input into a Delite framework compiler framework [43] which runs a *scalac* to convert the DSL into Java bytecode. The produced Java bytecode is then executed (staged) to create Intermediate Representation (IR) and perform optimizations. The Delite

IR comprises useful artefacts, namely, dependency graph and a sea of nodes representing DSL operations which are transformed into a dataflow model for the system. Delite is a highly extensible compiler framework and runtime environment developed by Stanford PPL. It provides developers with reusable components like parallel patterns, optimizations, and automatic code generators to facilitate construction of parallel embedded DSLs. The current support of resultant languages includes C++, CUDA, OpenCL, and Scala. Support for configuration of FPGAs and deployment of Delite-generated executables onto FPGA platforms for deployment onto Altera FPGA chips is being developed.

Recent breakthroughs in this work include defining a new FPGA intermediate representation language called Dataflow

```
// import SdrHls DSL compiler
import sdrg.dsl.sdrhls._
import sdrg.dsl.sdrhls.dsp.fir.Compensator
// include lms, delite libraries
object SdrHlsMainRunner extends SdrHlsApplicationRunner with SdrHlsMain
trait SdrHlsMain extends SdrHlsApplication {
    def main() {
        // generate a list of compensating filter coefficients
        val filter = Compensator(128, 10, 1)
        // set generic parameters for DDC
        valddcParams = ("DIN_WIDTH" -> 16, "DOUT_WIDTH" -> 16,
                "COEFFS" -> filter.coefficients,
                // other parameters
                   ...
                )
        // set generic parameters for Gigabit Ethernet
        valgbeParams = ("TX_BYTES", 64)
        // define FM receiver components
        valadc = Component("fmc150", Nil)
        valddc = Component("DDC", ddcParams)
        valgbe = Component("UDP1GbE", gbeParams)
        // the chain of system components
        val radio = Chain(adc[0:1], ddc[1:1], gbe[16:0])
        // generate VHDL code for the FM Receiver
        radio.synthesize("FmReceiver")
    }
}
```

LISTING 1: SdrHls source code for the FM Receiver[①].

Hardware Description Language (DHDL) and generating hardware code for Maxeler platform in MaxJ [44, 45]. However, DHDL only generates MaxJ for Maxeler platforms other than VHDL or Verilog which are used universally. DHDL is also targeted for applications in domains of machine learning, image processing, financial analytics, and internet search, all of which are not naturally related to SDR applications. In this work, we intend to improve productivity and performance of reconfigurable designs for SDR while also increasing portability using platform independent synthesizable VHDL.

9.2. System Modeling. The application model is specified using a Dataflow Interchange Format (DIF) Language [46] shown in Listing 2. A DIF specification formally captures the dataflow semantics of various dataflow models and performs analysis of topological information contained in a dataflow. We use SDF in our design for its straightforward static dataflow scheduling and analysability of throughput and buffer requirements. The DIF performs analysis, scheduling, and functional verification of the system modeled in SDF. When all these functions are complete, the application modeled in SDF is now ready for mapping onto a hardware.

9.3. Code Generation. This process involves generation of the VHDL code shown in Listing 3 which represents the design described using a DSL. The SDF dataflow-based design is converted into hardware description using SDR IP cores and FIFO buffers. The SDR IP cores become SDF actors and FIFO buffers act as SDF channels. We use VHDL Manipulation and Generation Interface (vMagic) [47] to read IP core library as well as writing the VHDL code of FPGA FM receiver system. The final step is the conversion of VHDL code into a bitstream using a third-party tool called Xilinx ISE. The bitstream is then loaded on the FPGA device for execution.

10. Conclusion

In this paper, we presented the design of a modular, reusable, and parameterizable library of SDR HDL cores. These cores provide both wishbone-compatible interfaces and direct parallel interfaces. DSP cores for processing and I/O cores for connecting to an ADC sampling daughterboard are provided together with an Ethernet data streaming core for sending data from the FPGA to a host computer. Functional validation testing was done for each core using a reconfigurable computing platform, namely, the RHINO platform (see Section 6.1), and the cores were tested working together in a representative SDR application, namely, an FM receiver shown in Section 7.4. In order to link the SDR processing cores to an input stream of sampled data, the FMC150-ADC core would need to be customized to be compatible with the sampling hardware. The test also demonstrated how the cores and their parameterizability allowed for rapid assembling of the SDR system. The SDR cores were benchmarked in

```
sdfFmReceiver{
    topology {
        nodes = adc, ddc, gbe;
        edges = channel1(adc, ddc),
            channel2(ddc, gbe);
    }
    parameter {
        gbeParams =[(tx_bytes => 64), ...];
        ddcParams =[(din_width => 16), ...];
    }
    production {
        channel1 = 1;
        channel2 = 1;
    }
    consumption {
        channel1 = 1;
        channel2 = 16;
    }
    delay {
        channel1 = 0;
        channel2 = 0;
    }
    actor adc{
        computation = "FMC150";
    }
    actor ddc{
        computation = "DDC";
        generics = ddcParams;
    }
    actor gbe{
        computation = "UDP1GbE";
        generics = gbeParams;
    }
}
```

LISTING 2: DIF source code for the FM Receiver[©].

Section 8, confirming that these cores provided adequate performance that was not greatly less than that exhibited by the closed source Xilinx IP cores. While the SDR cores had greater resource utilization than the Xilinx cores, the utilization of a particular type of resource (be it the number of slices, LUTs, registers, etc.) was generally below 200% of those used by the Xilinx cores. The SDR cores provided a better performance in terms of maximum supported clock rate and generally used fewer resources than similar OpenCores cores. The SDR cores thus provide a speed-area trade-off that makes them an open-source alternative to costly commercial IP cores. The SDR cores also provide greater code-based parameterizability than the other cores benchmarked.

In order to facilitate FPGA-based SDR application development for programmers not experienced in HDL coding, and as a possible approach to enhance productivity and reduce the complexity and amount of low-level coding needed for SDR application development using our SDR cores, we have proposed a DSL and accompanying tool-flow, which we are in the process of building. This tool-flow builds upon the Delite DSL framework and our SDR core library. It uses a range of parameters and the automatic code generation of Delite, to raise the level of design abstraction and as a potential means to speed up development time. The proposed DSL aims to capture system specifications easily and to automate the modeling of design characteristics such as system throughput and memory size while also optimizing the system for reduced area and the increased speed of the resulting FPGA design.

While our DSL is still at an early stage, we are hoping that the SDR cores we have provided will be of use to other researchers and developers working in the area of FPGA-based SDR application development and that we may gain feedback from any users of our resources and tools which we can use to further enhance our cores and our proposed DSL and supporting tools to assist in reuse of these cores.

```
-- FmReceiver library package
use work.SdrHlsPkg.all;
--FmReceiver top level entity
entity FmReceiver is
    port(
        ...
    );
end FmReceiver;
architecture rtl of FmReceiver is
    -- declare registers
    ...
begin
    -- instantiate adc component
    FMC150Inst: FMC150
    port map(...);
    -- instantiate adc to ddcfifo channel
    FMC150Inst_DDCInst_Channel1: sdf_channel
    generic map(
        DATA_BITS => 32, DEPTH => 2, PRD_RATE => 1, CNS_RATE => 1, INIT_DLY => 0)
    port map(...);
    -- instantiate ddc component
    DDInst: ddc
    generic map(
        DIN_WIDTH => 16, DOUT_WIDTH => 16,...)
    port map(...);
    -- instantiate ddc to Gbe fifo channel
    DDCInst_UDP1GbEIns_Channel2: sdf_channel
    generic map(
        DATA_BITS => 32, DEPTH => 18, PRD_RATE => 1, CNS_RATE => 16, INIT_DLY => 0)
    port map(...);
    -- instantiate Gigabit Ethernet
    UDP1GbEIns: UDP1GbE
    generic map(TX_BYTES => 64, RX_BYTES => 0)
    port map(...);
end rtl;
```

LISTING 3: VHDL source code for the FM Receiver[③].

Acknowledgments

The authors sincerely thank SKA for funding this project and members of the SDRG and RRSG groups at UCT for their support and advice.

References

[1] K. Tan, H. Liu, J. Zhang, Y. Zhang, J. Fang, and G. M. Voelker, "Sora: High-performance software radio using general-purpose multi-core processors," *Communications of the ACM*, vol. 54, no. 1, pp. 99–107, 2011.

[2] E. Blossom, "Gnu radio: tools for exploring the radio frequency spectrum," *Linux journal*, vol. 2004, no. 122, 4 pages, 2004.

[3] A. Haghighat, "A review on essentials and technical challenges of software defined radio," in *Proceedings of MILCOM 2002*, vol. 1, pp. 377–382, 2002.

[4] S. Winberg, A. Langman, and S. Scott, "The RHINO platform - charging towards innovation and skills development in Software Defined Radio," in *Proceedings of the Annual Conference of the South African Institute of Computer Scientists and Information Technologists (SAICSIT '11)*, pp. 334–337, October 2011.

[5] J. Gao, "10_100_1000 Mbps Tri-mode ethernet MAC specification," *OpenCores*, 2006.

[6] W. H. W. Tuttlebee, "Software-defined radio: Facets of a developing technology," *IEEE Personal Communications*, vol. 6, no. 2, pp. 38–44, 1999.

[7] J. Ghetie, "Fixed wireless and cellular mobile convergence: technologies, solutions, services," in *Proceedings of the 9th International Conference on Telecommunications (ConTel '07)*, 343 pages, 2007.

[8] C. E. Caicedo and P. D. Student, *Software defined radio and software radio technology: Concepts and application*, Department of Information Science and Telecommunications University of Pittsburgh, 2007.

[9] A. C. Tribble, "The software defined radio: fact and fiction," in *Proceedings of the IEEE Radio and Wireless Symposium (RWS '08)*, pp. 5–8, January 2008.

[10] T. J. Rouphael, *RF and digital signal processing for software-defined radio: a multi-standard multi-mode approach*, Newnes, 2009.

[11] O. Romain and B. Denby, "Prototype of a software-defined broadcast media indexing engine," in *Proceedings of the IEEE International Conference on Acoustics, Speech and Signal Processing (ICASSP '07)*, pp. II813–II816, April 2007.

[12] S. J. Olivieri, J. Aarestad, L. H. Pollard, A. M. Wyglinski, C. Kief, and R. S. Erwin, "Modular FPGA-based software defined radio for CubeSats," in *Proceedings of the IEEE International Conference on Communications (ICC '12)*, pp. 3229–3233, June 2012.

[13] A. Azarian and M. Ahmadi, "Reconfigurable computing architecture: survey and introduction," in *Proceedings of the 2nd IEEE International Conference on Computer Science and Information Technology (ICCSIT '09)*, pp. 269–274, August 2009.

[14] R. Woods, J. McAllister, G. Lightboy, and Y. Yi, *FPGA-based Implementation of Complex Signal Processing Systems*, John Wiley and Sons, 2008.

[15] R. Saleh, S. Wilton, S. Mirabbasi et al., "System-on-chip: Reuse and integration," *Proceedings of the IEEE*, vol. 94, no. 6, pp. 1050–1068, 2006.

[16] J. C. G. Pimentel and H. Le-Huy, "A vhdl library of ip cores for power drive and motion control applications," in *Proceedings of the Electrical and Computer Engineering, Canadian Conference*, vol. 1, pp. 184–188, 2000.

[17] A. Parsons, D. Backer, C. Chang et al., "A new approach to radio astronomy signal processing: Packet switched, fpga-based, upgradeable, modular hardware and reusable, platform-independent signal processing libraries," in *Proceedings of the 30th General Assembly of the International Union of Radio Science*, pp. 4–7, 2006.

[18] F. Fang, J. Hoe, M. Pueschel, S. Misra, C.-M. U. P. P. D. ELECTRICAL, and C. ENGINEERING., *Generation of Custom DSP Transform IP Cores: Case Study Walsh-Hadamard Transform*, Defense Technical Information Center, 2002.

[19] J. Gaisler, "A dual-use open-source vhdl ip library," in *Proceedings of the MAPLD International Conference*, pp. 8–10, 2004.

[20] A. López-Parrado and J.-C. Valderrama-Cuervo, "OpenRISC-based system-on-chip for digital signal processing," in *Proceedings of the 19th Symposium on Image, Signal Processing and Artificial Vision (STSIVA '14)*, pp. 1–5, September 2014.

[21] W. T. Padgett and D. V. Anderson, "Fixed-point signal processing," *Synthesis Lectures on Signal Processing*, vol. 9, pp. 1–129, 2009.

[22] U. Meyer-Baese and U. Meyer-Baese, *Digital signal processing with field programmable gate arrays*, vol. 65, Springer, 2007.

[23] mikroelectronika, "Chapter 2: Fir filters - digital filter design," http://www.mikroe.com/chapters/view/72/chapter-2-fir-filters/.

[24] S. He and M. Torkelson, "A new approach to pipeline fft processor," in *Proceedings of the 10th International on Parallel Processing Symposium (IPPS '96)*, pp. 766–770, April 1996.

[25] A. Saeed, M. Elbably, G. Abdelfadeel, and M. I. Eladawy, "Efficient fpga implementation of fft/ifft processor," in *Proceedings of the International Journal of Circuits*, vol. 3, pp. 103–110, 2009.

[26] I. LogiCORE, *fast fourier transform*, vol. 8, INTECH, 2012.

[27] S.-M. Tseng, J.-C. Yu, and Z.-H. Lin, "Software digital-down-converter design and optimization for dvb-t systems," *ResearchGate*, pp. 57–61, 2012.

[28] 4DSP, "FMC150 User Manual," 2013.

[29] N. Alachiotis, S. A. Berger, and A. Stamatakis, "Efficient PC-FPGA communication over Gigabit Ethernet," in *Proceedings of the 10th IEEE International Conference on Computer and Information Technology, CIT-2010, 7th IEEE International Conference on Embedded Software and Systems, ICESS-2010 and 10th IEEE International Confernce Scalable Computing and Communications (ScalCom '10)*, pp. 1727–1734, July 2010.

[30] I. LogiCORE, *Tri-mode ethernet mac v4. 5 user guide*, XILINX Inc, 2011.

[31] M. R. Mahmoodi, S. M. Sayedi, and B. Mahmoodi, "Reconfigurable hardware implementation of gigabit UDP/IP stack based on spartan-6 FPGA," in *Proceedings of the 6th International Conference on Information Technology and Electrical Engineering (ICITEE '14)*, October 2014.

[32] N. Alachiotis, S. A. Berger, and A. Stamatakis, "A versatile udp/ip based pc-fpga communication platform," in *Proceedings of the International Conference on Reconfigurable Computing and FPGAs (ReConFig '12)*, pp. 1–6, December 2012.

[33] M. Inggs, G. Inggs, A. Langman, and S. Scott, "Growing horns: applying the Rhino software defined radio system to radar," in *Proceedings of the 2011 IEEE Radar Conference: In the Eye of the Storm (RadarCon '11)*, pp. 951–955, May 2011.

[34] H. K.-H. So, A. Tkachenko, and R. Brodersen, "A unified hardware/software runtime environment for FPGA-based reconfigurable computers using BORPH," in *Proceedings of the 4th International Conference on Hardware Software Codesign and System Synthesis (CODES+ISSS '06)*, pp. 259–264, October 2006.

[35] S. Scott, *Rhino: Reconfigurable hardware interface for computation and radio [M.S. thesis]*, University Of Cape Town, 2011.

[36] B. K. Huang, R. G. L. Vann, S. Freethy et al., "FPGA-based embedded Linux technology in fusion: The MAST microwave imaging system," *Fusion Engineering and Design*, vol. 87, no. 12, pp. 2106–2111, 2012.

[37] R. G. Vaughan, N. L. Scott, and D. R. White, "The theory of bandpass sampling," *IEEE Transactions on Signal Processing*, vol. 39, no. 9, pp. 1973–1984, 1991.

[38] Altera, "Understanding CIC Compensation Filters," apn455, 2007.

[39] D. G. Messerschmitt, "Static Scheduling of Synchronous Data Flow Programs for Digital Signal Processing Edward Ashford Lee," *IEEE Transactions on Computers*, vol. C-36, no. 1, pp. 24–35, 1987.

[40] J. Eker, J. W. Janneck, E. A. Lee et al., "Taming heterogeneity—the ptolemy approach," *Proceedings of the IEEE*, vol. 91, no. 1, pp. 127–143, 2003.

[41] H. A. Andrade and S. Kovner, "Software synthesis from dataflow models for g and labview," in *Proceedings of the IEEE Asilomar Conference on Signals, Systems, and Computers*, pp. 1705–1709, 1998.

[42] T. E. Dwan and T. E. Bechert, "Introducing simulink into a systems engineering curriculum," in *Proceedings of the 23rd Annual Conference on Frontiers in Education: Engineering Education: Renewing America's Technology*, pp. 627–631, November 1993.

[43] K. J. Brown, A. K. Sujeeth, H. J. Lee et al., "A heterogeneous parallel framework for domain-specific languages," in *Proceedings of the 20th International Conference on Parallel Architectures and Compilation Techniques (PACT '11)*, pp. 89–100, October 2011.

[44] D. Koeplinger, R. Prabhakar, Y. Zhang, C. Delimitrou, C. Kozyrakis, and K. Olukotun, "Automatic generation of efficient accelerators for reconfigurable hardware," in *Proceedings of the 43rd International Symposium on Computer Architecture (ISCA '16)*, pp. 115–127, June 2016.

[45] R. Prabhakar, D. Koeplinger, K. J. Brown et al., "Generating configurable hardware from parallel patterns," in *Proceedings of the 21st International Conference on Architectural Support for Programming Languages and Operating Systems (ASPLOS '16)*, pp. 651–665, ACM, New York, NY, USA, April 2016.

[46] C. Hsu, F. Keceli, M. Ko, S. Shahparnia, and S. S. Bhattacharyya, "DIF: an interchange format for dataflow-based design tools," in *Computer Systems: Architectures, Modeling, and Simulation*, vol. 3133 of *Lecture Notes in Computer Science*, pp. 423–432, Springer, Berlin, Germany, 2004.

[47] C. Pohl, C. Paiz, and M. Porrmann, "vmagic-automatic code generation for vhdl," *International Journal of Reconfigurable Computing*, vol. 2009, pp. 1–9, 2009.

3

How to Efficiently Reconfigure Tunable Lookup Tables for Dynamic Circuit Specialization

Amit Kulkarni and Dirk Stroobandt

ELIS Department, Computer Systems Lab, Ghent University, Sint-Pietersnieuwstraat 41, 9000 Ghent, Belgium

Correspondence should be addressed to Amit Kulkarni; amit.kulkarni@ugent.be

Academic Editor: Fernando Pardo

Dynamic Circuit Specialization is used to optimize the implementation of a parameterized application on an FPGA. Instead of implementing the parameters as regular inputs, in the DCS approach these inputs are implemented as constants. When the parameter values change, the design is reoptimized for the new constant values by reconfiguring the FPGA. This allows faster and more resource-efficient implementation but investigations have shown that reconfiguration time is the major limitation for DCS implementation on Xilinx FPGAs. The limitation arises from the use of inefficient reconfiguration methods in conventional DCS implementation. To address this issue, we propose different approaches to reduce the reconfiguration time drastically and improve the reconfiguration speed. In this context, this paper presents the use of custom reconfiguration controllers and custom reconfiguration software drivers, along with placement constraints to shorten the reconfiguration time. Our results show an improvement in the reconfiguration speed by at least a factor 14 by using Xilinx reconfiguration controller along with placement constraints. However, the improvement can go up to a factor 40 with the combination of a custom reconfiguration controller, custom software drivers, and placement constraints. We also observe depreciation in the system's performance by at least 6% due to placement constraints.

1. Introduction

An ability to modify some parts of the logic blocks of an FPGA while the rest remains active is called partial run-time reconfiguration and has been commercially available for quite a while through the Xilinx partial reconfiguration (PR) flow [1]. Members of our research group developed a technique called Dynamic Circuit Specialization (DCS) which is a partial reconfiguration technique tailored to parameterized applications [2]. A parameterized application contains a set of inputs for which some of the input values change much less frequently than the other inputs. The infrequently changing inputs are called parameters. DCS uses the run-time reconfiguration technique to specialize the parameterized design depending on the values of the infrequently changing inputs (parameters). Hence for every change in the parameter value, a new specialized bitstream is generated and the FPGA is reconfigured with the specialized bitstreams. Because the

actual reconfiguration bitstream is computed at run-time instead of at compile-time, DCS allows wider applicability of PR for implementation with a lot of different possible implementation variants.

Our experiments for conventional DCS implementation on a self-reconfigurable platform [3] have shown the Hardware Internal Configuration Access Port (HWICAP) to be a main bottleneck for the reconfiguration speed, since its throughput is not high enough to match with the speed of the embedded processor used during the reconfiguration process. However, experiments described in [4] have shown that the bottleneck depends on the experiment setup and the different components that participate during the reconfiguration process.

In the conventional implementation of a DCS system, the Xilinx HWICAP is used as a reconfiguration controller. The HWICAP driver function "XhwIcap_setClb_bits" is used to reconfigure the truth table entries of a single Lookup

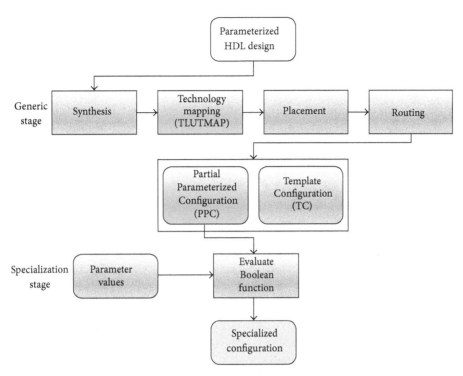

FIGURE 1: Dynamic Circuit Specialization tool flow (TLUT tool flow).

Table (LUT). With existing Xilinx FPGA column based architectures, we propose to reconfigure multiple LUTs at the same time [5]. We do this by using design placement constraints to cluster the bits that have to be changed in the same reconfiguration columns and customizing the HWICAP's "XhwIcap_setClb_bits" function. This gives us a significant improvement in reconfiguration speed. However, this improvement comes at the cost of a slight reduction in the performance of the design. In this paper we show the trade-off between the design performance and the reconfiguration speed achieved by employing placement constraints and a custom HWICAP driver.

We proposed two custom reconfiguration controllers: MiCAP [6] and MiCAP-Pro that are specifically designed to provide efficient reconfiguration for the DCS system. The controllers have higher throughput than the standard HWICAP. We used the custom reconfiguration drivers along with the placement constraints on the Zynq-SoC FPGAs for implementing 8-bit FIR filters using DCS.

Our main contribution in this paper is that we extend the principle of reconfiguring multiple LUTs to the software drivers of the custom reconfiguration controllers: MiCAP and MiCAP-Pro, thus resulting in a drastic improvement in DCS reconfiguration speed. We also propose a concept to store the frames in a memory (that acts as a reconfiguration cache) after reconfiguration so that we bypass the read frames' activity for every future reconfiguration of the same LUTs. The extended principle also contains considering an existing approach to use placement constraints to cluster possible truth table entries of the LUTs in a minimal number of CLB columns.

In Section 2, we briefly introduce DCS and its implementation on the Xilinx FPGAs. In Section 3, we describe a brief overview of the column based Xilinx FPGA architecture of the Zynq-SoC. The reconfiguration controllers used for implementing DCS are presented in Section 4, followed by the description of custom reconfiguration software drivers in Section 5. A brief overview of placement constraints and how to improve reconfiguration speed using placement constraints is presented in Section 6. In Section 7, we explain our experimental setup and the parameterized design implemented using DCS. In Section 8 we discuss the results of our experiments and interpret our results and finally we conclude in Section 9.

2. Dynamic Circuit Specialization

Dynamic Circuit Specialization (DCS) enables us to implement a parameterized application with less FPGA resources (mainly Lookup Tables) compared to the classic static FPGA implementation. An average reduction of 42% in FPGA resources is observed for an 8-bit, 16-tap adaptive Finite Impulse Response (FIR) filter application. This also helps in shortening the critical path of the design and thus it improves the filter's performance [2].

The tool flow that implements DCS consists of two stages: a *generic stage* and a *specialization stage*. In the generic stage, a parameterized application (or design) described in a Hardware Description Language (HDL) is processed to yield a Partial Parameterized Configuration (PPC) and a Template Configuration (TC) as depicted in Figure 1. The PPC contains bitstreams expressed as Boolean functions of input parameters of a parameterized design. The TC contains static bits (ones and zeros) and is used for the non-reconfigurable parts of the problem. Members of our research group have found an automatic method to map a parameterized design onto virtual Lookup Tables (LUTs) called Tunable Lookup Tables (TLUTs) [2]. TLUTs are the intermediate representation of physical LUTs with truth table entries (a part of the bitstreams) that are expressed as Boolean functions of the parameters instead of regular bitstreams. (A TLUT is a virtual version of a physical LUT whose features are identical to the physical LUT of an FPGA, except that the truth table entries are dependent on the parameters.) Therefore, during the reconfiguration, only the truth table entries of the TLUTs are replaced with the specialized bits that are generated during the specialization stage.

In the specialization stage, the Boolean functions are evaluated for specific values of the parameters thus generating specialized bitstreams. For every infrequent change in parameter values, the Boolean functions are evaluated by a specialized configuration generator (SCG). The SCG can be implemented on an embedded processor such as the Power-PC or the ARM Cortex-A9 present within the FPGA core.

The SCG reconfigures the FPGA via a configuration interface called the Internal Configuration Access Port (ICAP) by swapping the specialized bitstreams into the FPGA configuration memory. The configuration controller such as HWICAP (in conventional DCS implementation, the HWICAP is used as a reconfiguration controller) encapsulates the ICAP primitive (port) of the FPGA and forms a controller that orchestrates the swapping of specialized bitstreams via the interface port ICAP. The bitstreams are accessed in the form of frames and a frame is defined as the smallest addressable element of FPGA configuration data. Each frame contains reconfiguration bits of tens of LUTs and has its unique frame address that can be used to point to the frame during the reconfiguration. The software to implement DCS is available as an open source project on GitHub [7].

2.1. DCS on the Xilinx FPGAs. The conventional implementation of DCS on the Xilinx FPGAs, such as the Zynq-SoC, is shown in Figure 2. The SCG is realized on an embedded processor (ARM Cortex-A9 dual core processor or a MicroBlaze soft core processor).

The PPC Boolean functions are stored in the memory such as DRAM memory of the Zynq-SoC.

The ICAP is used as a configuration interface. The HWICAP reconfiguration controller is responsible for orchestrating the replacement of the stale frames with specialized frames present in the configuration memory of the FPGA.

2.2. The HWICAP Driver "XhwIcap_setClb_bits" Function. The HWICAP supports a software driver function called "XhwIcap_setClb_bits" to perform the reconfiguration. This function accepts two crucial function arguments:

(1) Location coordinates of a TLUT: this information is used to generate the frame address that is used to point to the frame that contains truth table entries of the TLUT.

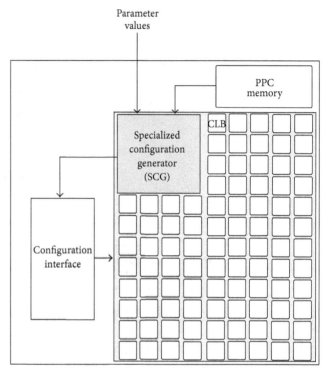

FIGURE 2: Dynamic Circuit Specialization on Xilinx FPGAs.

(2) Truth table entries: these are the specialized bits generated after the specialization stage of the DCS tool flow. The TLUT truth table entries need to be overwritten with these specialized bits.

The reconfiguration takes place in 3 steps:

(1) Read frames: using the frame address, a set of four consecutive frames containing the truth table entries of a TLUT are read from the configuration memory.

(2) Modify frames: the current truth table entries of a TLUT are replaced by the specialized bits. The modified frames contain specialized bitstreams.

(3) Write-back frames: using the same frame address, the modified four frames are written back to the configuration memory, thus accomplishing the *micro-reconfiguration*.

Micro-reconfiguration is a fine grain form of reconfiguration used for DCS [8].

Therefore, a reconfiguration controller in this case should be capable of reading, modifying, and writing the frames from the configuration memory and a processor should take care of executing the cycle of read, modify, and write-back frames.

The micro-reconfiguration incurs 4 major costs. These costs are major drawbacks of DCS:

(1) *PPC Memory Size.* Memory space required to store all the Boolean functions of the parameterized application.

(2) *Evaluation Time.* Time taken by the SCG to evaluate the Boolean function for a specific set of parameter values.

(3) *Reconfiguration Time.* Time taken to update all the TLUTs of a parameterized design with the specialized bits; in other words, time taken to accomplish the micro-reconfiguration.

(4) *Power Consumption.* The idle and dynamic power consumed by the reconfiguration infrastructure during the micro-reconfiguration.

The reconfiguration time is a major overhead of the DCS approach [8]. Using the HWICAP, the time taken to reconfigure one TLUT is 230 μs. Custom reconfiguration controllers such as the MiCAP and the MiCAP-Pro offer much higher reconfiguration speeds compared to the HWICAP at the extra cost of FPGA resources.

3. Column Based Xilinx FPGA Architecture

In order to exploit reconfiguration in modern FPGA architectures, we have to adjust to the specific reconfiguration infrastructure in current column based FPGA architectures from Xilinx for our experiments. Since the custom reconfigurations controllers are designed to be specific to the Zynq-SoC architecture, we conduct our experiments on the Zynq-SoC FPGA only. However, the idea of improving the reconfiguration speed using custom drivers along with placement constraints can be applied to any column based Xilinx FPGA.

The Xilinx FPGA on the Zynq-SoC contains an array of Configurable Logic Blocks (CLBs) which encapsulate LUTs, flip-flops, and multiplexers. Each CLB contains 8 LUTs and is capable of realizing combinational and sequential logic. The array of CLBs is divided into a number of clock regions. Each clock region contains CLB columns with a fixed number of CLBs and the height of the CLB column remains the same in all the clock regions. There are multiple CLB columns adjacent to each other thus forming CLB rows as shown in Figure 3. There are other columns such as DSP and BRAM columns that exist in between CLB columns.

3.1. Frame Structure. A frame of an FPGA is the smallest addressable element of an FPGA configuration. It can be viewed as a vertical stack of a fixed number of bits spanning a complete height of a row [9]. A fixed data size of 2 words (1 word = 32 bits) is assigned to each CLB within the entire frame. This means a set of LUT entries present in one CLB can be configured within those 2 words. However, the complete configuration data of an entire CLB containing multiple LUTs spans over four frames and each frame has its own unique frame address [9]. It should be noted that there exists one extra word called "HCLK config word" for each column within one frame as shown in Figure 4.

A single frame can contain truth table entries of multiple LUTs which are located in a single CLB column. In the Zynq-7000 family, there are 50 CLBs in one column, so a total of $50 \times 2 + 1 = 101$ words exist in one frame. The frame size plays an important role during the reconfiguration

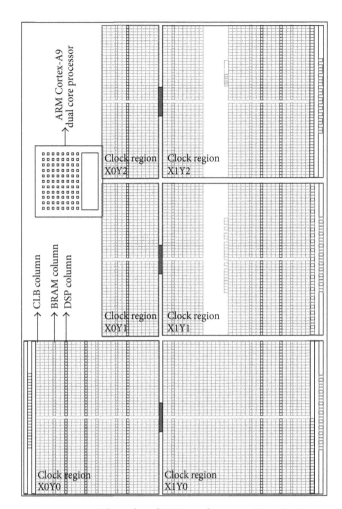

FIGURE 3: Column based FPGA architecture: Zynq-SoC.

process. Since a frame is the smallest addressable element, for every reconfiguration process, at least one frame has to be accessed via the HWICAP. Thus the time taken to reconfigure a LUT is affected by the frame size. For a fixed HWICAP throughput, an increase in frame size results in an increase in reconfiguration time and thus reduces the reconfiguration speed.

4. Reconfiguration Controllers

The configuration data of an FPGA can be internally accessed frame by frame by an embedded processor such as the ARM Cortex-A9 (dual core) present in the Zynq-SoC. The processor can access the frames via an internal configuration interface called ICAP. The ICAP is a hardware macro or a primitive that needs a hardware driver (controller) to write or read the configuration data from the configuration memory. The maximum data throughput the ICAP supports is 400 MBps [10].

The processor has to send a series of commands to the ICAP in order to access the bitstreams from the configuration memory. There are different sets of commands to read and write the frames into the configuration memory. The

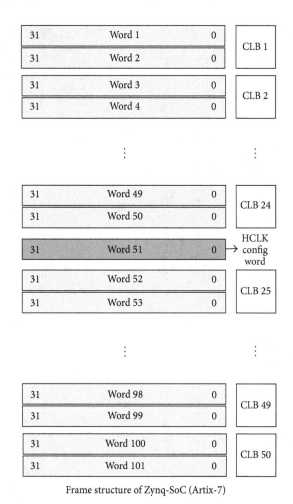

Frame structure of Zynq-SoC (Artix-7)

FIGURE 4: Frame structure of a column based Xilinx Zynq-SoC.

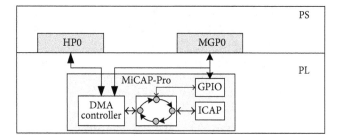

FIGURE 5: MiCAP-Pro architecture on the Zynq-SoC.

commands and the bitstreams. We have shown that MiCAP improves the reconfiguration speed by 17% and consumes 50% less resources than the HWICAP. However, the MiCAP suffers from a major bottleneck while transferring the data between PL and PS regions of the Zynq-SoC.

The MiCAP software driver function "*MiCAP_setClbbits*" uses the same principle (read-modify-write-back frames) of the "XhwIcap_setClb_bits" function. The function reconfigures only a single TLUT for every function call.

4.3. MiCAP-Pro. The pro. version of the MiCAP overcomes the data transfer bottleneck between the Processor System (PS) region and the Programmable Logic (PL) region of the Zynq-SoC. The data transfer between the ICAP and the processor occurs via High Performance (HP) ports of the SoC. It uses a DMA controller for a high speed data transaction. The reconfiguration speed is improved by a factor ≈ 3. However, the improvement of reconfiguration speed comes at the cost of the FPGA resource that is ≈ 3 times higher than the HWICAP. The block diagram of the MiCAP-Pro is shown in Figure 5.

The MiCAP-Pro uses the same driver "*MiCAP_setClbbits*" that includes minor changes to use DMA related functions to transfer the data via HP ports of the Zynq-SoC.

The MiCAP-Pro is a more advanced controller than other reconfiguration controllers such as the ZyCAP [10] and the FaRM [11]. The ZyCAP does not support configuration read-back and the FaRM supports configuration read-back but the controller can be implemented only on the PLB bus. The MiCAP-Pro is capable of reading and writing the configuration frames compatible with the AXI bus.

5. Custom Reconfiguration Drivers

In this section, we propose two different principles to modify the reconfiguration drivers of the corresponding reconfiguration controllers. These modifications optimize the read activity during the *micro-reconfiguration*.

5.1. Type 1: Mutliread, Multimodify, and Multiwrite. The conventional drivers follow the read-modify-write-back principle to reconfigure every TLUT separately. In order to exploit the advantage of the existing frame structure that is imposed by the column based Xilinx FPGA architecture, we propose to modify truth table entries of multiple TLUTs within a single read activity. If multiple TLUTs of a parameterized design are

reconfiguration controller receives these commands from the processor, channelizes them to the ICAP, and orchestrates the bitstream transactions between the processor and the configuration memory.

4.1. Hardware ICAP (HWICAP). The HWICAP is an IP provided by Xilinx. The controller is mainly intended for the partial reconfiguration and therefore contains a complex state machine with a tiny FIFO buffer. The buffer is used to temporarily store the frames before they are sent to or received from the configuration memory. The HWICAP can support a maximum clock frequency of 100 MHz. The maximum data throughput of the HWICAP is 19 MBps [10]. The "XhwIcap_setClb_bits" is a HWICAP software driver that is responsible for reconfiguring a LUT given its location coordinates and the truth table entries. Therefore, this driver is used for the implementation of DCS.

4.2. MiCAP. The Micro-Reconfigurable Configuration Access Port (MiCAP) is a custom reconfiguration controller used to micro-reconfigure the frames of a parameterized design [6]. The controller has a simple state machine and an individual input and output buffer. The depth of the buffers is sufficient to hold all the required data including ICAP

placed in a single column then each of these TLUTs has a certain set of truth table entries that are located in the same frame. However, all 64 entries of a single TLUT are spread over 4 different frames. We have modified the reconfiguration process (into driver type 1) that takes place in 3 steps:

(1) Read multiple frames: with the help of the frame address, four frames containing all the truth table entries of a column of TLUTs and LUTs are read from the configuration memory. If there are multiple TLUTs placed in a single column, the truth table values of multiple TLUTs are read with a single read activity.

(2) Modify frames: before modification, the function locates the truth table bits of all the TLUTs that are present in the frame. The current truth table entries of these TLUTs are replaced with the specialized truth table bits, which are generated by the SCG. Thus multiple TLUTs are specialized in a single attempt.

(3) Write-back frames: with the help of the same frame address, the modified or specialized truth table values are updated in all the TLUTs of the column by swapping in multiple frames into the configuration memory of the FPGA. This updates all the truth table entries of multiple TLUTs that are placed in a single column.

Hence for a single read frames activity, multiple TLUTs can be reconfigured and this proves to be efficient since reading and writing back the frames for each TLUT can be avoided in contrast to the case of the conventional driver.

If the number of TLUTs in a parameterized design is higher than what fits in a single CLB column then multiple CLB columns containing multiple TLUTs can be used in order to achieve the gain in reconfiguration speed.

The TLUTs can be forcibly placed in a single column by using design placement constraints. However, the main concern with using the placement constraints is the design performance. Strict placement constraints would lead to hindrance of the design performance. There will be a trade-off between the reconfiguration speed and the design performance which is investigated in Section 7.

5.2. Type 2: Read Once, Multimodify, and Multiwrite. The type 1 reconfiguration driver can be further optimized at the cost of DRAM memory. The memory is used as a cache to store the frames that are read during a reconfiguration. We have optimized the read frame activity for future reconfiguration of the same TLUTs.

(1) Read Frames Once. With the help of the frame address, four frames containing all the truth table entries of a column of TLUTs and LUTs are read from the configuration memory. If there are multiple TLUTs placed in a single column, the truth table values of multiple TLUTs are read with a single read activity. Once the frames are read, each frame is stored in DRAM memory of the Zynq-SoC. If the processor has to reconfigure the same TLUTs at a later time, it can directly access the frames from the DRAM memory instead of

TABLE 1: Dimensions for the placement constraints.

	16-tap FIR	32-tap FIR	64-tap FIR
Number of TLUTs to be clustered	384	768	1536
Zynq-SoC	50×5	50×11	50×14

Note: the above dimensions are in the form of length × width of the CLB columns. Each column contains 200 LUTs.

requesting the same frames from the configuration memory via the ICAP. Since the data access from the DRAM memory is faster than the configuration memory, the read frame activity can be bypassed for the future reconfigurations of the same TLUTs.

The rest of the reconfiguration steps: multimodify and multi-write-back frames remain unchanged. However, the bitstream's cache is updated for every write-back activity in order to keep the cached bitstream consistent with the actual configuration of the FPGA.

6. Placement Constraints

The main aim of using placement constraints in our setting is to force multiple TLUTs to cluster all their truth table entries in a minimal number of frames. The placement constraints are used to restrict where the design's logic is placed. It forces the placer to use a certain area of the FPGA. We have described the correlation between the CLB columns and the frame structure in Section 3. Our approach is to force more TLUTs to be placed in a single CLB column so that their truth table entries can be reconfigured with a minimal access of configuration frames.

We have used the "AREA_GROUP" constraint [12]. This constraint allows us to specify that certain parts of the design can only be placed in a predetermined rectangular region of the FPGA's CLBs. To determine the exact size of this rectangular region the maximum length of the CLB column and minimum width of the CLB rows have to be considered. The maximum length of the CLB column is equal to its height (50 for the Zynq-SoC) in a given clock region and it ensures that more TLUTs can fit the specified area, while the minimum CLB rows ensure that we use the minimal number of CLB columns possible.

We first used the constraint to place the TLUTs in an exact minimum number of CLB columns determined by the number of LUTs present in it. For example, in the Zynq-SoC each column has 200 LUTs. Therefore to place the 64-tap FIR filter (1536 TLUTs), it is sufficient to use 8 columns. However with 8 columns, the router was not able to route the design. Hence we increased the width of the rectangular area by increasing the number of columns until the router was able to route the whole design. The width of the rectangular area in terms of CLB columns for different configurations of the FIR filter is tabulated in Table 1.

For a 64-tap FIR filter, the average number of TLUTs clustered in a single CLB column of the Zynq-SoC is 110 which is 52% of the total LUTs available in a single CLB column and there are a maximum of 156 TLUTs clustered in a single

TABLE 2: TLUTs cluster rate of a 64-tap FIR filter in a single CLB column.

	Zynq-SoC	
	Average	Maximum
Clustered TLUTs	52%	75%
Unclustered TLUTs	48%	25%

TABLE 3: FIR filter configurations.

Taps	Multipliers	TLUTs
16	32	384
32	64	768
64	128	1536

column which is 75%. The remaining LUTs are not a part of the reconfiguration process and hence they are used for the nonreconfigurable parts of the problem. Table 2 shows the percentage of TLUTs clustered.

7. Experimental Setup

In order to evaluate the performance of the reconfiguration controllers after using custom reconfiguration drivers, we first set up a DCS system on a self-reconfigurable platform. In this section, we describe the experimental setup of the parameterized design implemented using DCS with different reconfiguration controllers. We implemented the controllers and used modified drivers (type 1 and type 2) on a self-reconfigurable DCS platform and measured the reconfiguration speed.

7.1. Parameterized FIR Filter. We implement an 8-bit FIR filter with three different tap configurations as a parameterized design. Each filter tap contains two 4-bit multipliers and each multiplier is mapped onto 12 TLUTs [3]. We use the FIR filters with different configurations as listed in Table 3.

Figure 6 shows the structure of the filter. All coefficients form the parameterized inputs and for every change in the coefficient value, a specialized bitstream is generated and the filter taps containing multiplications are reconfigured accordingly.

7.2. Self-Reconfigurable Platform. We have used a self-reconfigurable platform [3] for implementing a parameterized FIR filter using DCS. Three different reconfiguration controllers (HWICAP, MiCAP, and MiCAP-Pro, each clocked at 100 MHz) were used for individual experiments. The platform is depicted in Figure 7.

We used a Zynq-SoC (XC7Z020-CLG484-1, ZedBoard) FPGA and Xilinx XPS v14.7 for the project system builder. The PPC Boolean functions are stored in the DRAM memory of the Processor System (PS) and all the actions of the micro-reconfiguration are controlled by the ARM Cortex-A9 processor (clocked at 667 MHz). Therefore, the user can use a simple program to run software on the processor to control and measure the reconfiguration activity. The whole system

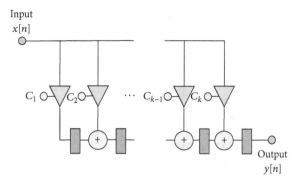

FIGURE 6: k-tap, 8-bit FIR filter.

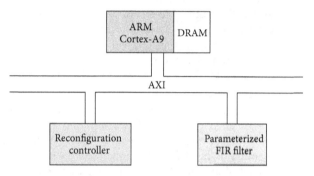

FIGURE 7: A self-reconfigurable platform for DCS implementation.

is connected using the AXI bus (clocked at 100 MHz) for the data transfer.

7.3. Reconfiguration Speed Measurement. We measured the reconfiguration speed of a single TLUT of a parameterized design using soft-timers. We also evaluated the total time to reconfigure all the TLUTs of the parameterized design (total reconfiguration time). First the experiments were conducted without placement constraints. The experiments were performed using both types of reconfiguration software drivers (type 1 and type 2) on individual reconfiguration controllers separately. Further, the experiments were conducted by constraining the TLUTs to cluster their truth table entries in the same frames by using placement constraints.

Using placement constraints results in a reduction of the design's performance. Therefore, we have measured the maximum clock frequency the design can support for the experiments using placement constraints and without placement constraints.

8. Results and Discussion

In this section, we present the results of our experiments. Table 4 shows the reconfiguration time distribution of a TLUT using three different reconfiguration controllers. Clearly, MiCAP-Pro is the fastest reconfiguration controller between all three controllers. In order to evaluate the effect of using custom reconfiguration drivers on the three controllers, we consider the total reconfiguration time (time taken to reconfigure all the TLUTs of the DCS system).

TABLE 4: Reconfiguration time distribution of a single TLUT.

Reconfiguration controller	Micro-reconfiguration task	Time (μs)	TLUT reconfiguration time (μs)
HWICAP	Read frames	111.5	234
	Boolean evaluate and modify	18	
	Write-back frame	100.5	
MiCAP	Read frames	97	210
	Boolean evaluate and modify	18	
	Write-back frames	95	
MiCAP-Pro	Read frames	23	64.1
	Boolean evaluate and modify	18	
	Write-back frames	23.1	

TABLE 5: CLB columns TLUTs placed without placement constraints.

	16-tap FIR	32-tap FIR	64-tap FIR
Number of TLUTs to be clustered	384	768	1536
CLB columns	25	42	50

There were 3 different experiments conducted on each of the reconfiguration controllers:

(1) Experiments with type 1 reconfiguration drivers and without placement constraints.

(2) Experiments with type 1 reconfiguration drivers and with placement constraints.

(3) Experiments with type 2 reconfiguration drivers and with placement constraints.

8.1. Experiments with Type 1 Reconfiguration Drivers and without Placement Constraints. In this experiment, we have not used placement constraints and hence the TLUTs were automatically placed by the placer without constraints from the user. The placer tool had full freedom to choose its own place for the TLUTs in different CLB columns.

Table 5 shows the number of columns in which the TLUTs were placed by the placer without any placement constraints. Further investigations have shown that there were multiple TLUTs placed for a given CLB column and therefore, we can still use the principle of modifying multiple TLUTs for a single read activity.

The TLUTs of the parameterized FIR filter design were reconfigured with 3 different reconfiguration controllers. We used custom reconfiguration drivers of type 1. The corresponding time required to reconfigure all the TLUTs of the parameterized design and the Improvement Factor (IF) is tabulated in Table 6.

Clearly, there was a drastic reduction in the reconfiguration time compared to the standard reconfiguration drivers. The reconfiguration speed was improved drastically at least by a factor of 12 for the HWICAP and the MiCAP. Similarly, the improvement in reconfiguration tunation speed by a factor of ≈ 8 was observed for the MiCAP-Pro. This improvement was achieved since we overcome the reading of the same frames that contain configuration of multiple TLUTs.

The data transfers between PS and PL regions of the Zynq-SoC are the major bottleneck for the HWICAP and the MiCAP. Therefore, bypassing the frame read activities in the driver contributes a lot to the reconfiguration speed and is the major reason for the improvement in the reconfiguration speed.

Since we did not use any placement constraints, the overall performance of the DCS system remains unchanged.

8.2. Experiments with Type 1 Reconfiguration Drivers and with Placement Constraints. In this experiment, we force the placer tool to place the maximum possible number of TLUTs in an exact minimum number of CLB columns by using "AREA_GROUP" placement constraints. Table 1 shows the minimum CLB columns in which the TLUTs were placed.

The parameterized design was reconfigured using type 1 drivers using three different controllers. The total reconfiguration time is tabulated in Table 7.

Clearly, the reconfiguration speed was even further improved by at least a factor ≈ 20 for the HWICAP and MiCAP. The reconfiguration speed was improved at least by a factor ≈ 8 for the MiCAP-Pro. The improvement is due to the placement of TLUTs in a reduced number of CLB columns compared to the previous experiment.

With the help of the placement constraints, the truth table entries of multiple TLUTs were clustered in a single CLB column. Therefore, this method gives an advantage of modifying more TLUTs for a single frame read activity. The type 1 driver exploits the advantage and reconfigures multiple TLUTs thereby reducing the reconfiguration time.

The improvement in the reconfiguration speed comes at the cost of a reduction in the design performance. Introducing the placement constraints causes the design to have a longer critical path than the conventional implementation. This causes a decrease in the maximum clock frequency the design can support as observed in Table 8. Clearly, an increase in the number of TLUTs decreases the design performance. The overall average deterioration in design performance is about 6 MHz (or a deterioration of $\approx 6\%$).

8.3. Experiments with Type 2 Reconfiguration Drivers and with Placement Constraints. In this experiment, we used a custom

TABLE 6: Total reconfiguration time without placement constraints.

FIR filter taps	TLUTs	Reconfiguration controller	Total reconfiguration time (ms)	IF
16	384	HWICAP	88.3/7.4	12
		MiCAP	80.6/6.9	12
		MiCAP-Pro	24.6/3.3	8
32	768	HWICAP	176.6/13.1	13
		MiCAP	161.2/12.2	13
		MiCAP-Pro	49.2/6.2	8
64	1536	HWICAP	353.2/18.4	19
		MiCAP	322.4/17.4	19
		MiCAP-Pro	98.4/12.1	8

Note 1: the above timing values are in the form of normal reconf. drivers/custom type 1 reconf. drivers.
Note 2: IF stands for Improvement Factor.

TABLE 7: Total reconfiguration time with placement constraints.

FIR filter taps	TLUTs	Reconfiguration controller	Total reconfiguration time (ms)	IF
16	384	HWICAP	88.3/4.4	20
		MiCAP	80.6/4.3	19
		MiCAP-Pro	24.6/3.1	8
32	768	HWICAP	176.6/9	20
		MiCAP	161.2/8.7	19
		MiCAP-Pro	49.2/6	8
64	1536	HWICAP	353.2/16.4	22
		MiCAP	322.4/16.1	20
		MiCAP-Pro	98.4/9.6	10

Note 1: the above timing values are in the form of normal reconf. drivers/custom type 1 reconf. drivers.
Note 2: IF stands for Improvement Factor.

TABLE 8: Maximum clock the design can support on the Zynq-SoC.

	16-tap FIR	32-tap FIR	64-tap FIR
Number of TLUTs to be clustered	384	768	1536
Clock frequency in MHz	108.6/102.8	108.6/102.2	108.6/101.2

Note: the above values are in the form without placement constraints/with placement constraints.

reconfiguration driver of type 2. Introducing the placement constraints reduces the number of CLB columns in which the TLUTs are placed. When using a custom driver of type 2, the frames that contain TLUT truth table entries are stored in the DRAM of the Zynq-SoC after they are read during the reconfiguration of the TLUTs for the first time. The DRAM acts as a cache so that we can reuse the truth table entries for reconfiguring the same TLUTs in future requests. Therefore, we bypass the frame read activity and hence the reconfiguration time is reduced.

Table 9 shows the reconfiguration time of the DCS system after using the type 2 reconfiguration driver. Clearly, we observe an improvement in reconfiguration speed by 12% compared to the type 1 driver. However, this small improvement comes at the cost of memory that is used to store the frames for reconfiguring the TLUTs. The DRAM

should store at least 404 words (1 word = 32 bits) of the frame data to reconfigure multiple TLUTs present in a single CLB column.

We limit the use of the type 2 driver to the experiments with placement constraints only. This is because the number of frames that contain truth table entries of TLUTs is small compared to the number of frames without placement constraints and therefore it is worth storing minimum possible frames rather than storing the frames that contain TLUTs which are widespread across the multiple clock regions of the FPGA.

For a 64-tap parameterized FIR filter, in order to store all the frames (that contain truth table entries of 1536 TLUTs) in the DRAM memory, we need a memory space of 5656 words ($14 \times 404 = 5656$) or $\approx$23 KB in the DRAM memory.

The comparison of the reconfiguration time of the parametrized FIR filter with 64 taps implemented using DCS using different reconfiguration controllers is depicted in Figure 8. The naming conventions used in Figures 8–11 are described in Table 10.

Clearly, the TLUTs of the parameterized design are reconfigured efficiently with less overhead of reconfiguration time using custom reconfiguration controllers when used along with custom type 1 and type 2 reconfiguration drivers.

8.4. Functional Density. The effect of variations in the reconfiguration speed and the effect of introducing the placement

TABLE 9: Reconfiguration time using type 2 drivers.

FIR filter taps	TLUTs	Reconfiguration controller	Total reconfiguration time (ms)
16	384	HWICAP	4.4/3.8
		MiCAP	4.3/3.8
		MiCAP-Pro	3.1/2.8
32	768	HWICAP	9/7.7
		MiCAP	8.7/7.7
		MiCAP-Pro	6/5.4
64	1536	HWICAP	16.4/14.7
		MiCAP	16.1/14.7
		MiCAP-Pro	9.6/9

Note: the above values are in the form of custom type 1 drivers/type 2 drivers.

TABLE 10: Naming convention for reconfiguration controllers.

Reconfiguration controllers	Definition
(Reconf_Controller)1	DCS system with (Reconf_Controller) and standard reconfiguration driver (read, single modify, and write).
(Reconf_Controller)2	DCS system with (Reconf_Controller), with custom type 1 reconfiguration driver and without placement constraints.
(Reconf_Controller)3	DCS system with (Reconf_Controller), with custom type 1 reconfiguration driver, and with placement constraints.
(Reconf_Controller)4	DCS system with (Reconf_Controller), with custom type 2 reconfiguration driver, and with placement constraints.

Note: (Reconf_Controller) can be HWICAP, MiCAP, and MiCAP-Pro in the above naming convention.

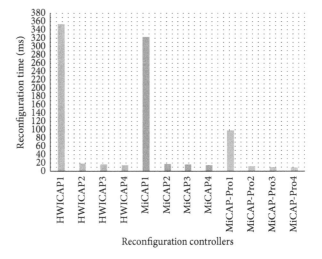

FIGURE 8: Reconfiguration time comparison between standard reconfiguration driver and custom reconfiguration drivers.

constraints to improve the reconfiguration speed in DCS can be best explained using the functional density curve [13]. The functional density is defined as the number of computations (N) that can be performed per unit area (A) and unit time (T) as shown in

$$F_d = \frac{N}{A \times T}. \tag{1}$$

In our experiments, the computations are all the operations in the FIR filter. The value of "A" depends on the resources of the FPGA used by the FIR filter (mainly TLUTs). The value of "T" is the reconfiguration time, the execution time, and the time to specialize. A higher functional density signifies a more efficient usage of implementation area.

The functional density curve was plotted against the rate of change of the input parameters for the parameterized design implementation. We have plotted the functional density curve for each reconfiguration controller and observed the variation in functional density of the DCS system after using standard, custom type 1 without placement constraints and type 1 and custom type 2 drivers with placement constraints.

The functional density curves for the HWICAP, the MiCAP, and the MiCAP-Pro are depicted in Figures 9, 10, and 11, respectively. The naming conventions for the reconfiguration controllers are listed in Table 10. The x-axis represents the average time (in clock cycles) between two parameter value changes. We observe a similar behavior of functional density curves in the DCS systems implemented using three different reconfiguration controllers.

The functional density for the DCS with custom type 1 driver (without placement constraints) rises well before the functional density of the DCS that uses the standard reconfiguration driver, introducing the placement constraints for type 1 and type 2 custom drivers improves the reconfiguration speed furthermore, and hence the corresponding functional density curves rise earlier compared to the functional density curve with standard reconfiguration drivers. This shows that improving the reconfiguration speed allows the parameters to change faster with the same gain in area compared to

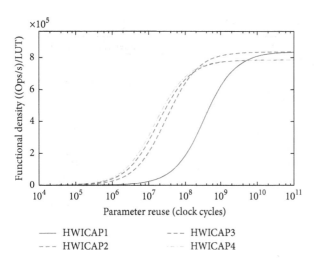

FIGURE 9: Functional density curves for HWICAP with different reconfiguration drivers.

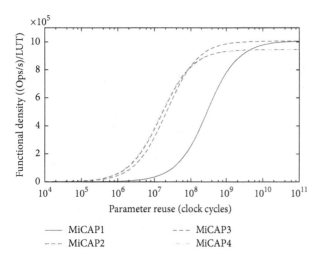

FIGURE 10: Functional density curves for MiCAP with different reconfiguration drivers.

DCS whose reconfiguration speed is slow. However, since the design performance is slightly reduced due to placement constraints, the magnitude of the functional density curves is relatively lower compared to the DCS without placement constraints forming the main trade-off.

The HWICAP and the MiCAP have similar functional density curves (except the MiCAP has a higher magnitude of functional density) since they have approximately equal throughput [6]. Using the custom reconfiguration drivers improves the reconfiguration speed drastically.

However, the functional density curves for the MiCAP-Pro only show a small improvement in reconfiguration speed after using type 1 and type 2 reconfiguration drivers. Since the data throughput of the MiCAP-Pro is very high, the effect of using custom reconfiguration drivers to improve the reconfiguration speed is relatively lower. The impact of using placement constraints can be also seen in the functional density curves of the MiCAP-Pro.

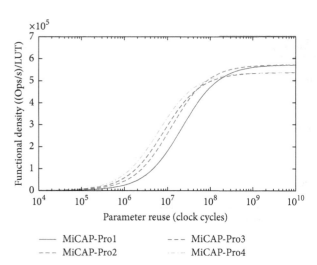

FIGURE 11: Functional density curves for MiCAP-Pro with different reconfiguration drivers.

Commercial applications such as Ternary Content Addressable Memories (TCAMs) used for packet classification in network routers [14] can benefit from DCS. An entry (content) of the memory is an infrequently changing input value and, therefore, can be used as a parameter input. However, in the network routing if the content of the TCAM has to be updated then the reconfiguration speed plays an important role. If the reconfiguration speed is too slow then it affects the network router's performance. The parameterized TCAMs can benefit from our proposed methods and overcome the barrier of the reconfiguration time without affecting the router's performance.

9. Conclusion

In order to efficiently reconfigure the TLUTs of a DCS system with less reconfiguration time overhead, we have proposed two different custom reconfiguration software drivers: type 1 and type 2. The reconfiguration time can be further suppressed using design placement constraints. We constrained the TLUTs of the FIR filter within the minimal number of columns possible. The custom reconfiguration drivers of type 1 were optimized to read and write the frames only once to reconfigure multiple TLUT entries. Further, in custom type 2 drivers, the frames that are read (during micro-reconfiguration) are stored in DRAM memory. These stored frames are used by the processor to modify the TLUTs in the future reconfiguration of the same TLUTs, thus saving the time to read the same frames for the future reconfiguration requests.

The concept of optimization (type 1 and type 2) was applied to the reconfiguration drivers of the custom reconfiguration controllers MiCAP and MiCAP-Pro. Improvements in the reconfiguration speed were observed. We have shown that there is a drastic improvement in the reconfiguration speed but this comes at the cost of a slight reduction in performance of the design (due to placement constraints). The functional density curves were used to analyze the impact of using high speed reconfiguration controllers in the DCS system.

The custom reconfiguration controllers MiCAP and MiCAP-Pro can be accessed at [15] and [16], respectively. The custom reconfiguration drivers type 1 and type 2 can be accessed at [17] and [18], respectively.

Competing Interests

The authors declare that they have no competing interests.

Acknowledgments

This work was supported by the European Commission in the context of the H2020-FETHPC EXTRA project (no. 671653). The authors would like to thank Dr. Karel Heyse, Dr. Tom Davidson, Dr. Vipin Kizheppatt, and Dr. Robin Bonamy for their timely advice and valuable suggestions.

References

[1] P. Lysaght, B. Blodget, J. Mason, J. Young, and B. Bridgford, "Invited paper: enhanced architectures, design methodologies and CAD tools for dynamic reconfiguration of Xilinx FPGAS," in *Proceedings of the International Conference on Field Programmable Logic and Applications (FPL '06)*, pp. 1–6, Madrid, Spain, August 2006.

[2] K. Bruneel, W. Heirman, and D. Stroobandt, "Dynamic data folding with parameterizable FPGA configurations," *ACM Transactions on Design Automation of Electronic Systems*, vol. 16, no. 4, pp. 1–29, 2011.

[3] K. Bruneel, F. Abouelella, and D. Stroobandt, "Automatically mapping applications to a self-reconfiguring platform," in *Proceedings of the Design, Automation and Test in Europe Conference and Exhibition (DATE '09)*, pp. 964–969, Leuven, Belgium, April 2009.

[4] K. Papadimitriou, A. Dollas, and S. Hauck, "Performance of Partial Reconfiguration in FPGA systems: a survey and a cost model," *ACM Transactions on Reconfigurable Technology and Systems*, vol. 4, pp. 1–24, 2011.

[5] A. Kulkarni, T. Davidson, K. Heyse, and D. Stroobandt, "Improving reconfiguration speed for dynamic circuit specialization using placement constraints," in *Proceedings of the International Conference on ReConFigurable Computing and FPGAs (ReConFig '14)*, pp. 1–6, Cancun, Mexico, December 2014.

[6] A. Kulkarni, V. Kizheppatt, and D. Stroobandt, "MiCAP: a custom reconfiguration controller for dynamic circuit specialization," in *Proceedings of the International Conference on ReConFigurable Computing and FPGAs (ReConFig '15)*, pp. 1–6, IEEE, Cancun, Mexico, December 2015.

[7] *TLUT Tool Flow Based Dynamic Circuit Specialization*, 2013, https://github.com/UGent-HES/tlut_flow.

[8] A. Kulkarni, K. Heyse, T. Davidson, and D. Stroobandt, "Performance evaluation of dynamic circuit specialization on Xilinx FPGAs," in *Proceedings of the FPGA World Conference*, Stockholm, Sweden, September 2014.

[9] *7 Series FPGAs Configuration: User Guide*, UG470 (v1.10), Xilinx Inc, 2015.

[10] K. Vipin and S. A. Fahmy, "ZyCAP: efficient partial reconfiguration management on the xilinx zynq," *IEEE Embedded Systems Letters*, vol. 6, no. 3, pp. 41–44, 2014.

[11] F. Duhem, F. Muller, and P. Lorenzini, "Reconfiguration time overhead on field programmable gate arrays: reduction and cost model," *IET Computers and Digital Techniques*, vol. 6, no. 2, pp. 105–113, 2012.

[12] Xilinx, *Constriants Guide (cgd 10.1)*, Xilinx, San Jose, Calif, USA, 2015.

[13] A. DeHon, *Reconfigurable Architectures for General-Purpose Computing*, Massachusetts Institute of Technology Artificial Intelligence Laboratory, 1996.

[14] K. Pagiamtzis and A. Sheikholeslami, "Content-Addressable Memory (CAM) circuits and architectures: a tutorial and survey," *IEEE Journal of Solid-State Circuits*, vol. 41, no. 3, pp. 712–727, 2006.

[15] MiCAP: A custom Reconfiguration Controller for Dynamic Circuit Specialization, 2015, https://github.com/UGent-HES/MiCAP.

[16] *MiCAP-Pro: A High Speed Custom Reconfiguration Controller for Dynamic Circuit Specialization*, 2015, https://github.com/UGent-HES/MiCAP-Pro.

[17] Custom Reconfiguration Drivers for DCS (Type 1), 2015, https://github.com/UGent-HES/Custom-Reconfiguration-Drivers-for-DCS-Type-1.

[18] Custom Reconfiguration Drivers for DCS (Type 2), 2015, https://github.com/UGent-HES/Custom-Reconfiguration-Drivers-for-DCS-Type-2.

4

A High-Level Synthesis Scheduling and Binding Heuristic for FPGA Fault Tolerance

David Wilson,[1] Aniruddha Shastri,[2] and Greg Stitt[1]

[1]*Department of Electrical and Computer Engineering, University of Florida, Gainesville, FL 32611, USA*
[2]*National Instruments Corp., 11500 N Mopac Expwy, Austin, TX 78759, USA*

Correspondence should be addressed to David Wilson; d.wilson@ufl.edu

Academic Editor: Michael Hübner

Computing systems with field-programmable gate arrays (FPGAs) often achieve fault tolerance in high-energy radiation environments via triple-modular redundancy (TMR) and configuration scrubbing. Although effective, TMR suffers from a 3x area overhead, which can be prohibitive for many embedded usage scenarios. Furthermore, this overhead is often worsened because TMR often has to be applied to existing register-transfer-level (RTL) code that designers created without considering the triplicated resource requirements. Although a designer could redesign the RTL code to reduce resources, modifying RTL schedules and resource allocations is a time-consuming and error-prone process. In this paper, we present a more transparent high-level synthesis approach that uses scheduling and binding to provide attractive tradeoffs between area, performance, and redundancy, while focusing on FPGA implementation considerations, such as resource realization costs, to produce more efficient architectures. Compared to TMR applied to existing RTL, our approach shows resource savings up to 80% with average resource savings of 34% and an average clock degradation of 6%. Compared to the previous approach, our approach shows resource savings up to 74% with average resource savings of 19% and an average heuristic execution time improvement of 96x.

1. Introduction

Recently, computing systems in space and other extreme environments with high-energy radiation (e.g., high-energy physics, high altitudes) have been turning to field-programmable gate arrays (FPGAs) to meet performance and power constraints not met by other computing technologies [1]. One challenge for FPGAs in these environments is susceptibility to radiation-induced single-event upsets (SEUs), which can alter the functionality of a design by changing bits in memories and flip-flops. Although radiation-hardened FPGAs exist, some of those devices are still susceptible to SEUs and commonly have prohibitive costs compared to commercial-off-the-shelf (COTS) devices [2].

To mitigate these issues, designers often use triple-modular redundancy (TMR) on COTS FPGAs. TMR is a well-known form of hardware redundancy that replicates a design into three independent modules with a voter at the outputs to detect and correct errors. Research has shown that TMR with frequent configuration scrubbing (i.e., reconfiguring faulty resources) provides an effective level of fault tolerance for many FPGA-based space applications [3].

One key disadvantage of TMR is the 3x resource overhead, which often requires large FPGAs that may exceed cost or power constraints for embedded systems. Although resource sharing is a common strategy for reducing this overhead, designers often apply TMR to register-transfer-level (RTL) code, where the productivity challenge of exploring resource sharing and scheduling options is often impractical. Furthermore, RTL code is not available for the common case of using encrypted or presynthesized IP cores, making such exploration impossible.

In this paper, we automate this exploration during high-level synthesis (HLS) by integrating resource sharing and TMR into a scheduling and binding heuristic called the *Force-Directed Fault-Tolerance-Aware* (FD-FTA) *heuristic* that provides attractive tradeoffs between performance, area, and redundancy. More specifically, the heuristic explores the impact of varying hardware redundancy with the capability to correct an error, which we measure as an *error-correction percentage*. Our heuristic is motivated by the observation that, for many situations, error correction is not as critical as error detection. By allowing a designer to specify an error-correction percentage constraint that is appropriate for their application, our heuristic can explore numerous options between performance and area that would be impractical to do manually.

Although other FPGA work has also approached fault tolerance through high-level synthesis, that earlier work mainly focused on different fault models or reliability goals. For example, Golshan et al. [4] introduced an HLS approach for minimizing the impact of SEUs on the configuration stream, which is complementary to our approach. Shastri et al. [5] presented a conceptually similar HLS approach, but that work focused on minimizing the number of coarse-grained resources without considering their FPGA implementation costs, while also suffering from long execution times and the need for manual parameter tuning. This paper presents an extension of [5] that addresses previous limitations with an automated approach, showing resource savings of up to 74% compared to the earlier approach, while also reducing heuristic execution time by 96x on average.

Similarly, high-level synthesis for ASICs has introduced conceptually similar techniques [6], but whereas ASIC approaches must deal with transient errors, FPGAs must pay special attention to SEU in configuration memory that will remain until scrubbing or reconfiguration (referred to as *semipermanent errors* for simplicity). Due to these semipermanent errors, FPGA approaches require significantly different HLS strategies.

Compared to the common strategy of applying TMR to existing RTL code, our heuristic has average resource savings of 34% and displays significant improvements as the latency constraint and the benchmark size increases. For a latency constraint of 2x the minimum-possible latency, our heuristic shows average resource savings of 47%, which achieves a maximum of 80% resource savings in the largest benchmark.

The paper is organized as follows. Section 2 describes related work on studies pertaining to areas such as FPGA reliability and fault-tolerant HLS. Section 3 defines the problem and the assumptions of our fault model. Section 4 describes the approach and implementation of the FD-FTA heuristic. Section 5 explains the experiments used to evaluate the FD-FTA heuristic, and Section 6 presents conclusions from the study.

2. Related Work

With growing interest in FPGAs operating in extreme environments, especially within space systems, a number of studies have been done on assessing FPGA reliability in these environments. Some of these studies rely on analyzing FPGA reliability through models. For example, Ostler et al. [7] investigated the viability of SRAM-based FPGAs in Earth-orbit environments by presenting a reliability model for estimating mean time to failure (MTTF) of SRAM FPGA designs in specific orbits and orbital conditions. Similarly,

Héron et al. [8] introduced an FPGA reliability model and presented a case study for its application on a XC2V3000 under a number of soft IP cores and benchmarks. In addition to reliability models, a number of studies have been done on emulating and simulating faults in FPGAs (e.g., [9, 10]). Rather than relying on costly testing in a radiation beam, such approaches facilitate cost-effective testing of fault-tolerant designs. Although many studies analyze SRAM-based technologies, other studies have also considered antifuse FPGAs and flash FPGAs. For example, McCollum compares the reliability of antifuse FPGAs to ASICs [11]. Wirthlin highlights the effects of radiation in all three types of FPGAs and explores the challenges of deploying FPGAs in extreme environments, such as in space systems and in high-energy physics experiments [2]. In this paper, we complement these earlier studies by presenting an HLS heuristic that transparently adds redundancy to improve the reliability of SRAM-based FPGA designs. As described in Section 3, the fault model for our heuristic makes several assumptions based on the findings of these earlier works.

In our approach, we leverage the use of TMR to apply fault tolerance to FPGA designs. TMR is a well-studied fault tolerance strategy in FPGAs that has been studied in different use cases and under additional modifications. Morgan et al. [12], for example, compared TMR with several alternative fault-tolerant designs in FPGAs and showed that TMR was the most cost-effective technique for increasing reliability in a LUT-based architecture. Other works have introduced modifications that are complementary to our TMR design and may be incorporated into our heuristic. For example, Bolchini et al. [13] present a reliability scheme that uses TMR for fault masking and partial reconfiguration for reconfiguring erroneous segments of the design. Our work focuses on automatically applying the TMR architecture from high-level synthesis and could incorporate partial reconfiguration regions for enhanced reliability at the cost of producing device-specific architectures.

Work by Johnson and Wirthlin [14] approaches the issue of voter placement for FPGA designs using TMR and compares three algorithms for automated voter insertion based on strongly connected component (SCC) decomposition. Compared to the naive approach of placing voters after every flip-flop, these algorithms are designed to insert fewer voters through feedback analysis. Since FPGA TMR designs consist of both applying redundancy and voter insertion, our paper focuses specifically on the problem of automated TMR and can be potentially used alongside these voter insertion algorithms.

Although scheduling and binding in high-level synthesis is a well-studied problem [15–17], many of those studies do not consider fault tolerance or error-correction percentage. More recent works have treated reliability as a primary concern in the high-level synthesis process but focus on different reliability goals in ASIC designs. For example, Tosun et al. [18] introduce a reliability-centric HLS approach that focuses on maximizing reliability under performance and area constraints using components with different reliability characterizations. Our work, in contrast, focuses on minimizing area under performance and reliability constraints

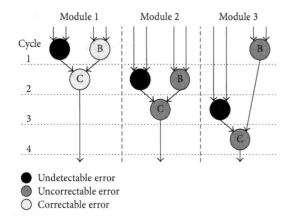

FIGURE 1: An example binding onto three color-coded resources. For this binding, a single fault can result in an undetectable, uncorrectable (but detectable), or correctable error, depending on the resource.

using components with the same reliability characterizations. Antola et al. [6] present an HLS heuristic that applies reliability by selectively replicating parts of the datapath for self-checking as an error-detection measure. Our heuristic differs by applying reliability through TMR with resource sharing. Our heuristic additionally varies the reliability through an error-correction percentage constraint that enables selective resource sharing between TMR modules.

Other work has notably used HLS to apply reliability through other means than replication. For example, Chen et al. [19] introduce an HLS approach that uses both TMR and gate-level hardening technique called gate sizing on different resources to minimize both soft error rate and area overhead. In another example, Hammouda et al. [20] propose a design flow that automatically generates on-chip monitors to enable runtime checking of control flow and I/O timing behavior errors in HLS hardware accelerators. Our heuristic focuses specifically on scheduling and binding and may be complementary to several of these approaches. Although our heuristic could also be potentially applied to ASIC design with modification, we have tailored scheduling and binding to the FPGA architecture, which notably has different HLS challenges compared to ASICs [21], and have compared its effectiveness with other FPGA-specific approaches. Our heuristic is especially applicable to FPGAs given the rise of FPGAs in space missions which commonly implement fault-tolerant logic through TMR and configuration scrubbing [3].

Compared to ASICs, far fewer reliability-centric high-level synthesis studies have targeted FPGAs. Golshan et al. [4] introduced a TMR-based HLS process for datapath synthesis, placement, and routing that targets SRAM-based FPGAs. Although conceptually similar to our work, that study focused on mitigating the impact of SEUs in the configuration bitstreams by enforcing self-containment of SEUs within a TMR module and by minimizing potential SEU-induced bridging faults that connect two separate nets in a routing resource. By contrast, our work focuses on minimizing the resources needed for TMR and can intentionally neglect self-containment of SEUs within a TMR

module for additional resource savings. Dos Santos et al. [22] investigated another TMR-based HLS design flow on SRAM-based FPGAs and compares the reliability of these designs with their respective unhardened equivalents. Compared to our work, our heuristic focuses on making tradeoffs between redundancy and area, which can include full TMR. Shastri et al. [5] introduced a TMR-based HLS heuristic that focused on solely minimizing coarse-grained resources under latency and redundancy constraints. By contrast, our work considers each resource's implementation costs and uses improved scheduling and binding algorithms for better scalability in larger benchmarks and increased latency constraints. At a 2x normalized latency constraint, our heuristic provides average resource savings of 34% compared to TMR applied to existing RTL and achieves resource savings of 74% relative to [5] approach on the largest benchmark.

3. Problem Definition

Although there are different optimization goals that could be explored while varying the amount of error correction, in this paper we focus on the problem of *minimum-resource, latency- and error-constrained scheduling and binding*, which for brevity we simply refer to as *the problem*. To explain the problem, we introduce the following terms:

  (i) Fault: a resource with an SEU-induced error

 (ii) Module: one instance of the dataflow graph (DFG), analogous to a module in TMR

(iii) Error: any fault where one or more of the three modules output an incorrect value

(iv) Undetectable error: any fault where all three modules output the same incorrect value

 (v) Detectable error: any fault where one or more modules output different values

(vi) Uncorrectable error: any fault where two or more modules output incorrect values

(vii) Correctable error: any fault where two or more modules output a correct value

(viii) Error-correction % (EC%): the percentage of total possible errors that are correctable by a given solution.

Figure 1 illustrates several example error types, where all operations with the same color are bound to a single resource. If the black resource experiences a fault, this binding results in an undetectable error because all three modules will produce the same incorrect value. If there is a fault in the medium-gray resource, this binding causes an uncorrectable error because two modules (2 and 3) will produce incorrect values. A fault in the light-gray resource results in a correctable error because modules 2 and 3 both produce correct outputs. Note that both gray resources result in detectable errors because at least one module outputs a different value than the other modules. We consider the error correction to be 100% if all errors can be classified in this way as correctable errors, although failures that occur in other parts of the system may still cause incorrect outputs.

The input to the problem is a dataflow graph (DFG) D, a latency constraint L expressed in number of cycles, and an error constraint E specified as the minimum acceptable EC%. The output is a solution X, which is a combination of a schedule S and binding B for a redundant version of D. Given these inputs and outputs, we define the problem as follows:

$$
\begin{aligned}
\text{Minimize} \quad & \text{NumResources}(X) \\
\text{Subject to} \quad & \text{Latency}(X.S) \leq L, \\
& \text{ErrorCorrection}(X.B) \geq E, \\
& \text{ErrorDetection}(X.B) = 100\%.
\end{aligned}
\tag{1}
$$

In other words, the goal of the problem is to find a schedule and binding that minimizes the number of required resources, where the schedule does not exceed the latency constraint L, the binding does not exceed the error constraint E, and all errors are detectable. We provide an informal proof that this problem is NP-hard as follows. If we remove both error constraints from the problem definition, the problem is equivalent to minimum-latency and resource-constrained scheduling followed by binding, which are both NP-hard problems [15]. The correctable and detectable error constraints only make the problem harder by expanding the solution space with replicated versions of the input.

Note that a more complete definition of this problem would include other FPGA resources (e.g., DSP units, block RAM), as opposed to solely using LUTs. However, because there is no effective relative cost metric for different FPGA resources, comparison between solutions with different types of FPGA resources is difficult. For example, it is not clear whether or not a solution with 100 DSPs and 10,000 LUTs is preferable to a solution with 10 DSPs and 100,000 LUTs. An alternative to this approach would be minimizing one resource while using constraints on the other resources. This approach however may exclude solutions that minimize multiple selected resources. For ease of explanation and comparison, the presented heuristic implements coarse-grained resources using only LUTs and focuses on minimizing the design's overall LUT count.

We assume that scrubbing occurs frequently enough so there cannot be more than one faulty resource at a time, which is often true due to the low frequency of SEUs in many contexts. For example, in the Cibola Flight Experiment [23], the experiment's Virtex FPGAs experienced an average SEU rate of 3.51 SEUs/day compared to their scrubbing cycle of 180 ms. With this assumption, based on our definitions, the total number of possible faults (and errors) is equal to the total number of resources used by the solution. Due to the likely use of SRAM-based FPGAs, we assume that all faults persist until scrubbing removes the fault. This contrasts with earlier work that focuses on *transient* faults [24–26]. We assume the presence of an implicit voter at the output of the modules, potentially using strategies from [14].

One potential challenge with error correction is the possibility of two modules producing incorrect errors that have the same value, which we refer to as *aliased errors*. Although we could extend the problem definition to require no instances of aliased errors, this extension is not a requirement for many usage cases (e.g., [26]). In addition, by treating aliased errors as uncorrectable errors, good solutions will naturally tend to favor bindings that have few aliased errors. To further minimize aliased errors, our presented heuristic favors solutions with the highest EC% when there are multiple solutions that meet the error constraint with equivalent resources.

4. Force-Directed Fault-Tolerance-Aware (FD-FTA) Heuristic

To solve the problem of minimum-resource, latency- and error-constrained scheduling and binding, we introduce the Force-Directed Fault-Tolerance-Aware (FD-FTA) heuristic, which performs scheduling and binding during high-level synthesis while simultaneously applying TMR and resource sharing to reduce overhead. By using an error-correction constraint combined with a latency constraint, the heuristic explores various tradeoffs between area, performance, and redundancy. As described in Algorithm 1, the heuristic first triplicates the DFG, schedules the triplicated DFG under a given latency constraint, and then binds the scheduled operations under a given EC% constraint.

The heuristic is divided into two key parts: scheduling and binding. We discuss the scheduling algorithm in Section 4.1 and the binding algorithm in Section 4.2.

4.1. Scheduling. In high-level synthesis, scheduling is the process of assigning each operation into a specific cycle or control state. The resulting schedule for the entire application is then implemented using a finite-state machine. In this section, we discuss the limitations of previous fault-tolerance-aware schedulers (Section 4.1.1) and then present a heuristic that adapts Force-Directed Scheduling (FDS) [27] to address those limitations (Section 4.1.2).

4.1.1. Previous Fault-Tolerance Aware Scheduling. The previous work on fault-tolerance-aware scheduling from [5] used the *Random Nonzero-Slack List Scheduling*. As a variant form of minimum-resource, latency constraint (MR-LC) list scheduling, this scheduling algorithm is a greedy algorithm that makes scheduling decisions on a cycle-by-cycle basis based on a resource bound and operation slack (i.e., the difference between the latest possible cycle start time and the cycle under consideration). To minimize resource usage, the algorithm iterates over each cycle and schedules operations ordered from lowest to highest slack up to the resource bound. If there are still zero-slack operations in a particular cycle once the resource bound is reached, those operations are scheduled and the resource bound is updated to match this increased resource usage. This process continues until all of the operations are scheduled. Unlike MR-LC list scheduling, the Random Nonzero-Slack List Scheduling schedules nonzero-slack operators with a 50% probability up to the resource bound. With this randomness, the scheduling algorithm is intended to produce different schedules for each TMR module which would increase the likelihood of intermodule operations bindings following scheduling. To escape local optima, this previous work used the scheduling

Input: Dataflow graph D, latency constraint L, error correction constraint E
Output: Solution X that minimizes resources
begin
    Step 1. Triplicate D into D_{FT};
    Step 2. Schedule the operators of D_{FT} with constraint L to obtain S;
    Step 3. Bind the operators of S with constraint E to obtain B;
    Step 4. Return solution X from S and B;
end

ALGORITHM 1: Force-Directed Fault-Tolerance-Aware (FD-FTA) heuristic.

Input: Dataflow graph representation of the design
Output: Operator assignments to cycles
while *there are unscheduled operations* **do**
    Step 1. Evaluate time frames;
    Step 2. Update distribution graphs;
    Step 3. Calculate self-forces for every feasible cycle;
    Step 4. Calculate total force from self-force, predecessor force, and successor force;
    Step 5. Schedule operation with lowest force;
end

ALGORITHM 2: Force-Directed Scheduling.

algorithm in a multipass approach that would collect the best result from a series or phase of scheduling and binding runs. The heuristic would then continue to run these phases until the best result of a phase showed no significant improvement compared to the previous phase's result.

There are several key disadvantages of using the previous heuristic with this scheduling algorithm that we address in this paper. One primary disadvantage is the heuristic's lengthy execution time from its multipass approach, which relies on randomness in the schedule to find an improved solution. Using a user-defined percentage, the heuristic continues to another phase with double the amount of scheduling and binding runs if the current phase's result is not significantly better than the previous phases. The execution time can therefore be largely influenced by the randomness and the data dependencies between operations. In addition to long execution times, the heuristic requires fine-tuning of starting parameters to avoid premature exiting, which worsens productivity and can be error prone. The heuristic also has the disadvantage of exploring a restricted solution space by favoring the scheduling of operations in earlier cycles. This scheduling tendency results from the use of a fixed 50% scheduling probability for nonzero-slack operations in each cycle. By contrast, our proposed heuristic performs the scheduling and binding process *once*, using a more complex force-directed scheduler, which generally reduces the execution time and improves quality without the need for manually tuning heuristic parameters.

In terms of complexity, both heuristics consist of scheduling followed by binding. As such, the proposed heuristic consists of $\mathcal{O}(cn^2)$ complexity for the force-directed scheduler [27] described in the next subsection and $\mathcal{O}(n^2)$ for the binder described in Section 4.2 [28]. The overall complexity

is therefore $\mathcal{O}(cn^2)$ where c is the latency constraint and n is the number of operations. In contrast, the previous heuristic consists of $\mathcal{O}(n)$ complexity for its variant list-scheduler and $\mathcal{O}(n^2)$ for its clique partitioning binder. Since the previous heuristic will generally limit the number of phases or total number of scheduling and binding runs in its multipass approach, the overall complexity is $\mathcal{O}(pn^2)$, where p is a user-defined limit on total iterations and n is the number of operations. The proposed heuristic therefore has a lower complexity than the previous heuristic when $c < p$ which is commonly true as the user will generally set p such that $p \gg c$ to avoid premature exiting.

Additionally, the previous heuristic suffers from the same disadvantages as general MR-LC list scheduling. Notably, it is a local scheduler that makes decisions on a cycle-by-cycle basis using operation slack as a priority function. Such an approach has a tendency towards locally optimal operation assignments that often leads to suboptimal solutions when providing a latency constraint that is significantly larger than the minimum-possible latency. Similarly, the heuristic's use of slack may present suboptimal results in scenarios where operation mobility may underestimate resource utilization. By contrast, Force-Directed Scheduling is a global stepwise-refinement algorithm that selects operation assignments from any cycle based on its impact on operation concurrency.

4.1.2. Force-Directed Scheduling. Force-Directed Scheduling is a latency-constrained scheduling algorithm that focuses on reducing the number of functional units by balancing the concurrency of the operations assigned to the units. Algorithm 2 presents an overview of the algorithm. A more detailed description can be found in [27].

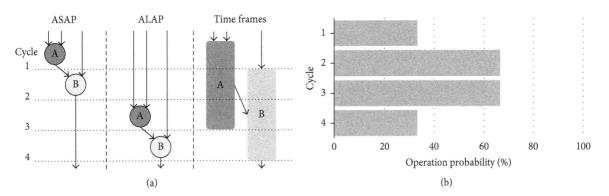

FIGURE 2: Illustrations of different structures used in Force-Directed Scheduling. The diagram in (a) shows the ASAP and ALAP schedule of a DFG and the respective time frames of the operations. The chart in (b) shows the distribution graph assuming both operations use the same resource type.

As demonstrated in Algorithm 2, Force-Directed Scheduling balances operation concurrency by using time frames, distribution graphs, and force values. *Time frames* refer to the possible cycles to which an operation may be assigned, such that the resulting schedule does not violate the latency constraint. Intuitively, the assignment of an operation to a specific cycle may impact the time frames of other operations if there are data dependencies. *Distribution graphs* refer to the probability that a given operation type is assigned to a specific cycle for each cycle within the latency constraint. For each cycle, the algorithm assigns probabilities to the distribution graphs by finding all operations of the same type that can be scheduled at a given cycle and then sums their individual probabilities.

To better illustrate these structures, Figure 2 shows the time frames and distribution graphs of a DFG that consists of two operations and is subject to a latency constraint of 4 cycles. In Figure 2(a), the DFG is shown scheduled with an as-soon-as-possible (ASAP) schedule and an as-late-as-possible (ALAP) schedule. The ASAP schedule focuses on scheduling an operation at the earliest possible cycle given data dependencies. Notice how operation B cannot be scheduled on cycle 1 because it is dependent on operation A. Similarly, the ALAP schedule focuses on scheduling an operation at the latest possible cycle. Force-Directed Scheduling uses these two schedules to form the time frame of each operation, which represents the cycle bounds of an operation assignment.

Figure 2(b) shows the distribution graphs of the DFG before any operation has been scheduled. Assuming operations 1 and 2 are of the same type (or can share a resource), each operation has a uniform 33% chance of being scheduled in any cycle of its 3-cycle time frame. The distribution graph therefore shows a 33% probability of that operation type being scheduled in cycles 1 and 4 and a 66% probability for the cycles where the time frames of the operations overlap.

Force-Directed Scheduling abstracts each distribution graph as a series of springs (for each cycle) connected to each operation of the DFG. Therefore, any spring displacement exerts a "force" on each operation. In this abstraction, the spring's strength is the distribution graph's value in a particular cycle and the displacement is a change in probability in

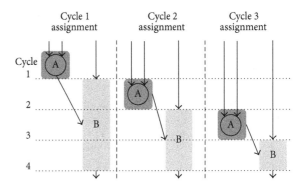

FIGURE 3: Illustrations of the DFG's time frames after a tentative assignment of operation A.

a cycle due to a tentative assignment. A tentative operation assignment will therefore cause displacements in the cycle it is assigned to, whose probability is now 100%, and in the cycles it can no longer be assigned to, whose probabilities are now 0%. Using this abstraction, each operation assignment has an associated total *force* value that reflects the assignment's impact on the time frames and distribution graphs of the operation and its preceding and succeeding operations. While there are unscheduled operations, the algorithm schedules the operation assignment with the lowest force value reflecting the lowest impact on operation concurrency.

Figure 3 depicts several examples of how an operation assignment may impact the time frames of other operations using the DFG from Figure 2. In each of these examples, operation A is scheduled in a specific cycle, which limits the operation's time frame to that cycle. For the first diagram, operation A is scheduled in cycle 1 and has no impact on operation B's time frame. In contrast, scheduling operation A in cycle 2 or 3 reduces operation B's time frame, since operation A must be scheduled in a cycle before operation B.

Figure 4 depicts the corresponding distribution graph after such cycle assignments. Notice that an operation assignment in a particular cycle changes the probability of that operation type being scheduled to 100%. In (a), operation A contributes a 100% probability in cycle 1, while operation B

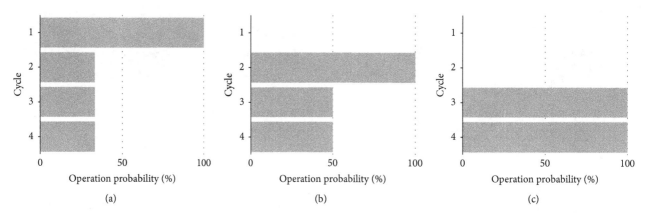

FIGURE 4: Distribution graphs for a cycle 1 assignment (a), for a cycle 2 assignment (b), and for a cycle 3 assignment (c) of operation A.

contributes a uniform 33% probability over its time frame from cycle 2 to cycle 4. In (b), operation A still contributes a 100% probability in its scheduled cycle, while operation B contributes a uniform 50% probability over its reduced time frame. Noticeably, in (c), operation A's assignment in cycle 3 will effectively force operation B's later assignment to cycle 4 due to data dependencies. It should be noted that a distribution graph may have probabilities over 100% which can represent multiple operation assignments of that type in the same cycle. The main goal of Force-Directed Scheduling is to balance operation concurrency such that the distribution graph for each operation type will have a relatively uniform probability over each cycle after all operations are scheduled. Using the equations for *force*, the assignment of operation A to cycle 1 would have the lowest force value of the three possible assignments since it balances the operation probability across the most cycles.

In [27], the authors describe an adjustment for optimization in scenarios with resources with different realization costs. This adjustment involves scaling the force values by a cost factor reflecting the relative realization costs. In our proposed heuristic, we scale the force values by the LUT requirements of the resource.

4.2. Binding. In high-level synthesis, binding refers to the process of assigning operations and memory access to hardware resources. When following scheduling, the binding process yields a mapping of operations to hardware resources at specific cycles.

4.2.1. Singleton-Share Binding. Our proposed heuristic, referred to as *Singleton-Share Binding*, involves a two-stage process that first performs binding in each TMR module separately and then merges nonconflicting bindings between TMR modules. By binding operations from different TMR modules to the same resource, the heuristic has therefore made tradeoffs between the circuit's capability to correct an error and the total area needed by the circuit. Using the aforementioned EC% constraint, a designer can limit the total amount of intermodule binding that can occur.

Algorithm 3 displays the pseudocode of Singleton-Share Binding.

In the first stage, Singleton-Share Binding considers each TMR module separately and binds the module's operations to resources using the Left Edge Algorithm (LEA) as originally described in [29]. Although originally introduced as a method for packing wire segments, this algorithm has found popularity in resource binding that focuses on binding as many operations to a resource as possible before binding on another resource.

In the second stage, the binding algorithm consolidates singleton bindings (i.e., resources with only one mapped operation) and attempts to merge each singleton binding with a nonconflicting binding from another module. By merging these bindings, a single resource will contain operation bindings from different TMR modules which will reduce the circuit's error-correcting capability at the benefit of a lower area cost. This binding process will therefore reduce the total number of resources used in the design at the cost of reducing the design's EC%. As mentioned before, the heuristic maintains 100% error detection by limiting the resource sharing to only two modules. This process allows the design to detect errors, albeit uncorrectable, in the event of a fault in a shared resource. Algorithm 3 shows the pseudocode for the second stage which first merges bindings between singleton and nonsingleton bindings and then merges bindings between singleton binding pairs. Bindings may only be merged if the resulting binding does not involve multiple operations scheduled on the same cycle or operations of all three modules.

The key requirement of the second stage is ensuring that the EC% does not fall under the error constraint E. Since the number of uncorrectable errors equals the number of resources that have been shared across two modules, this constraint satisfaction is illustrated as shown in

$$\frac{\text{resources}_{\text{used}} - \text{resources}_{\text{Shared}}}{\text{resources}_{\text{used}}} \times 100\% \geq E \qquad (2)$$

which can be reduced to

$$\text{resources}_{\text{Shared}} \leq \text{resources}_{\text{used}} \times \left(1 - \frac{E}{100}\right). \qquad (3)$$

These equations however do not reveal a limit on the number of shares that can be done by the second stage binder. Since sharing a resource also reduces the number of

```
Input: Operator assignments to control-steps, S
Output: Operator bindings to resources, B_stg2
begin
    /* Stage 1 Binding                                              */
    B_stg1 ← ∅;
    foreach module m do
        B_stg1 ← B_stg1 ∪ LeftEdgeAlgorithm(S_m)
    end
    /* Stage 2 Binding                                              */
    shares ← 0;
    limit ← GetLimit(B_stg1);
    singleton, non-singleton ← SeparateRes(B_stg1);
    /* Stage 2: Merge singletons with non-singletons               */
    foreach resource s of singleton do
        foreach resource n of non-singleton do
            if shares = limit then break;
            ;
            if IsMergeable(s, n) then
                add operator of s to n and remove s from singleton;
                shares ← shares + 1;
            end
        end
    end
    /* Stage 2: Merge singletons with other singletons             */
    foreach pair of singleton (s, n) do
        if shares = limit then break;
        ;
        if IsMergeable(s, n) then
            add operator of s to n and remove s and n from singleton;
            add n to non-singleton;
            shares ← shares + 1;
        end
    end
    B_stg2 ← singleton ∪ non-singleton;
    return B_stg2
end
```

ALGORITHM 3: Singleton-Share Binding.

resources, the relationship between the number of shares i and the initial number of bindings is related in

$$i \leq \left(\text{usage}_{\text{stg1}} - i\right) \times \left(1 - \frac{E}{100}\right). \quad (4)$$

Since the number of shares must be an integer, we define the integer $limit$ as the maximum number of shares done by the second stage binder while meeting the error constraint. We simplify (4) in terms of $limit$ in

$$\text{limit} \leq \left\lfloor \text{usage}_{\text{stg1}} \times \frac{100 - E}{200 - E} \right\rfloor. \quad (5)$$

Figure 5 depicts an example of the binding process. In these subfigures, each nonsingleton resource is represented by a node with a solid color, whereas each singleton resource is represented by a node with a pattern. The format A_n on each node refers to an operation A from the original DFG performed on module n. Figure 5(a) therefore displays three modules each with distinct singleton and nonsingleton resources and represents a possible scheduling and binding after the first stage of binding.

Using a 50% EC constraint and (5), the second stage of binding may share up to two resources to meet the EC% constraint. As the first step, the binding process attempts to merge singleton bindings with nonsingleton bindings. In Figure 5(a), the only candidates for sharing is singleton bindings of either node B_1 or node A_3, with the nonsingleton binding containing nodes A_2, C_2, and D_2 (the light-gray resource). The singleton binding containing B_2 is ineligible since all nonsingleton bindings already have a conflicting operation scheduled during cycle 2. Similarly, no other nonsingleton binding can be merged with a singleton as each contains a conflicting operation during cycles 1 and 2. Merging singleton binding of node B_1 with the candidate nonsingleton binding, the binding process produces Figure 5(b). Notice that node B_1 is now part of the nonsingleton binding of A_2, C_2, and D_2, as represented by the same color.

Since there are no more candidate pairs, the binding process then attempts to merge singleton binding pairs. In

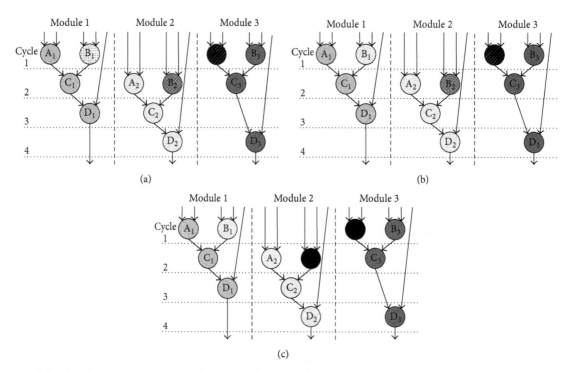

FIGURE 5: Sample binding for a latency constraint of 4 cycles and error constraint of 50%. The binding in (a) depicts the first stage of binding, whereas the bindings in (b) and (c) represent bindings following different steps in the second stage. The binding in (b) depicts the merging of a singleton with a nonsingleton, and the binding in (c) depicts the merging of a pair of singletons.

Figure 5(b), there is only one candidate pair between the singleton of B_2 and of A_3. Merging these bindings, the binding process produces a nonsingleton binding containing these two nodes, as seen in Figure 5(c) with the solid black color. At this point, the binding process completes as the number of shared resources has met the limit. Instead of using the initial size resources, the final design now produces a scheduling and binding on four resources with a 50% EC. If the limit had not been reached, the binding process may continue until there are no more candidate pairs.

For register-binding, our heuristic provides a register unit for each functional unit to avoid relatively expensive multiplexers on the FPGA's LUT-based architecture while also providing register sharing for compatible variables originating from the same functional unit. Due to the FPGA's register-rich fabric, register sharing can be more expensive than register duplication and is rarely justified [30].

5. Experiments

In this section, we evaluate the effectiveness of the FD-FTA heuristic in a variety of benchmarks. Section 5.1 describes the experimental setup. Section 5.2 shows a comparison in resource savings with TMR applied to existing RTL. Section 5.3 shows a comparison in resource savings with a previous approach. Section 5.4 shows a comparison in execution time with the previous approach. Section 5.5 illustrates a comparison of clock frequencies using the different approaches.

5.1. Experimental Setup. To evaluate our heuristic, we implemented Algorithm 1 in C++, while also using Vivado 2015.2 to provide LUT counts for each resource and the clock frequency of the final solution. Our target architecture was a Xilinx Virtex-7 xc7vx485tffg1761-2, which uses Xilinx 7 Series Configurable Logic Blocks with 6-input LUTs.

5.1.1. Benchmarks. Table 1 summarizes the benchmarks and shows the numbers of nodes and edges and the operation types. To represent signal-processing applications, we used DFGs for 5×5 convolution, 8-point radix-2 butterfly FFT, 16-point radix-2 butterfly FFT, and 4-point radix-4 dragonfly FFT. Of these, the radix-4 FFT efficiently expands the complex arithmetic involved to equivalent real operations as in [31]. For the radix-2 FFTs, we use resources capable of directly performing complex operations. To represent fluid-dynamics and similar applications, we used two DFGs that solve 5-dimensional linear equations ($Ax = B$) using the Jacobi iterative method and the successive overrelaxation (SOR) iterative method [32]. We also used two DFGs that solve Laplace's equation ($\nabla^2 f = 0$) using the Jacobi and SOR methods. We also supplement these real benchmarks with synthetic benchmarks (small0–small7, medium0–medium4) that we created using DFGs generated through random directed acyclic graphs.

5.1.2. Baselines. Two baselines were used to evaluate our proposed heuristic: a common approach where designers apply TMR to existing RTL (collectively referred to as *TMR-RTL*

TABLE 1: Benchmark summary.

Benchmark	Description	Number of nodes	Number of edges	Operation types
conv5x5	5x5 convolution kernel.	49	190	Add, Mult
conv9x9	9x9 convolution kernel.	161	932	Add, Mult
fft8	8-point radix-2 DIT FFT based on butterfly architecture.	32	116	Add, Sub, Mult
fft16	16-point radix-2 DIT FFT based on butterfly architecture.	88	648	Add, Sub, Mult
fftrad4	4-point radix-4 FFT based on dragonfly architecture. Efficiently decomposing complex operations into real operations.	40	232	Add, Sub, Mult
linsor	Single iteration kernel to solve a system of linear equations ($Ax = B$) in 5 variables, using successive-overrelaxation (SOR) method.	64	2657	Add, Sub, Mult, Div
linjacobi	Single iteration kernel to solve a system of linear equations in 5 variables, using Jacobi method.	60	230	Add, Sub, Mult, Div
lapsor	Single iteration kernel to solve Laplace's equation ($\nabla^2 f = 0$), using successive-overrelaxation (SOR) method.	7	16	Add, Sub, Mult
lapjacobi	Single iteration kernel to solve Laplace's equation using Jacobi method.	5	9	Add, Sub, Mult
small0–7	8 randomly generated DFGs with <20 operations.	4–19	2–36	Add, Mult
medium0–4	5 randomly generated DFGs with <130 operations.	88–127	346–642	Add, Sub, Mult, Div

for simplicity) and the approach from [5] (referred to as the *previous* approach). We use the TMR-RTL approach baseline to motivate the benefits of our heuristic over common use cases and the previous approach baseline to demonstrate improvements over the state of the art.

We model the TMR-RTL approach based on two observations: (1) designers often deal with existing RTL code and (2) designers may not be willing or capable of performing an extensive exploration of fault-tolerance tradeoffs. Because most existing RTL is implemented without considering the effects of TMR, the code is generally not written to minimize area. To approximate this use case, we use an ASAP schedule and LEA bindings. Although a designer could certainly use an approach that reduces area, we have observed that ASAP schedules are common in RTL cores, likely due to ease of implementation.

5.2. Comparison with TMR Applied to Existing RTL. In this section, we evaluate the effectiveness of our FD-FTA heuristic compared to TMR-RTL under different EC% and latency constraints. Unlike a simple triplicated RTL circuit, an HLS RTL circuit may use more extensive resource sharing during high-level synthesis to automatically target different latency and redundancy constraints. Applying triplication to an existing circuit, in contrast, limits the designer to the circuit's existing architecture and leaves little opportunities to target different constraints, especially when using encrypted or presynthesized IP cores. Table 2 presents the resources savings where the rows correspond to different benchmarks and the columns correspond to different EC% and latency constraints. We vary the latency constraint from the DFG's minimum-possible latency (as determined by an ASAP schedule) up to 2x the minimum latency, in increments of 0.2x. The EC% constraint is explored for 100% and 70%. On average, the FD-FTA heuristic shows savings compared

to the TMR-RTL for each pair of normalized latency and EC% constraints. Although relatively small at the lowest latency constraint, these average savings become significant at higher latency constraints reaching 45% and 49% savings at 2.0x normalized latency constraint for both 100% and 70% EC constraints, respectively. For individual benchmarks, the FD-FTA heuristic shows significant savings at each set of constraints except for benchmarks with low operation counts and for certain benchmarks at low normalized latency constraints.

From Table 2, we observe results consistent with expectations. For a normalized latency constraint of 1.0x and a EC constraint of 100%, the FD-FTA heuristic yielded no savings for about half of the benchmarks and up to 65% savings for the remainder. The lack of savings for certain benchmarks is expected given that some benchmarks have no flexibility to schedule operations on different cycles when constrained by the minimum-possible latency. In such cases, designers should use the lowest complexity scheduling algorithm as all algorithms will produce similar schedules. For the other benchmarks, up to 65% savings correspond to benchmarks with little to some flexibility, whereas the 65% savings in the *linsor* benchmark correspond to DFGs with large operation flexibility. In these cases, we start to see a trend of growing resource savings as operation flexibility increases. Additionally, the FD-FTA heuristic displayed a minimal degradation between −2% and −1%, on some benchmarks. Further investigation of each approach's output reveals that nonoptimal bindings by the FD-FTA heuristic resulted in multiplexers with more inputs than their counterparts in the TMR-RTL approach.

For a normalized latency constraint of 2.0x and a EC constraint of 100%, the FD-FTA heuristic yielded savings up to 75% with savings above 50% for about half of the benchmark set. We expect such high savings due to the large

TABLE 2: Resource savings (LUT%) of FD-FTA heuristic compared to TMR-RTL for 100% and 70% EC.

Benchmark	Normalized latency and EC% constraints											
	1.0x		1.2x		1.4x		1.6x		1.8x		2.0x	
	100%	70%	100%	70%	100%	70%	100%	70%	100%	70%	100%	70%
lapjacobi	0%	0%	0%	0%	5%	30%	2%	5%	2%	2%	5%	4%
lapsor	0%	0%	−1%	−1%	−1%	−1%	−1%	2%	−2%	0%	−2%	0%
conv5x5	18%	18%	52%	52%	58%	65%	64%	67%	62%	71%	68%	71%
fft8	0%	0%	12%	13%	13%	29%	19%	25%	24%	32%	38%	37%
fftRadix4	0%	0%	−1%	15%	21%	29%	21%	39%	28%	43%	32%	43%
fft16	0%	0%	16%	28%	9%	18%	11%	25%	−10%	5%	18%	27%
linjacobi	27%	28%	50%	52%	47%	59%	61%	67%	63%	68%	62%	70%
linsor	65%	69%	68%	68%	70%	72%	70%	72%	71%	72%	70%	74%
conv9x9	19%	19%	50%	50%	66%	70%	69%	74%	76%	78%	75%	80%
Average	14%	15%	27%	31%	32%	41%	35%	42%	35%	41%	40%	45%
small0	1%	1%	1%	1%	10%	13%	10%	13%	2%	11%	48%	57%
small1	0%	1%	0%	1%	0%	1%	3%	30%	3%	30%	2%	4%
small2	0%	0%	0%	0%	20%	22%	20%	22%	19%	30%	39%	40%
small3	30%	30%	30%	30%	57%	57%	53%	57%	45%	58%	58%	57%
small4	30%	49%	30%	49%	38%	38%	49%	57%	40%	49%	57%	57%
small5	27%	44%	35%	54%	37%	45%	28%	30%	38%	39%	45%	46%
small6	5%	5%	5%	5%	11%	20%	29%	38%	29%	28%	31%	49%
small7	0%	0%	0%	0%	31%	35%	39%	47%	50%	57%	54%	58%
medium0	3%	3%	37%	42%	50%	52%	50%	55%	57%	61%	52%	60%
medium1	3%	3%	32%	44%	49%	54%	51%	55%	58%	62%	60%	64%
medium2	0%	0%	38%	42%	51%	54%	58%	63%	60%	63%	62%	67%
medium3	6%	6%	33%	39%	45%	50%	49%	55%	52%	57%	52%	59%
medium4	0%	0%	33%	37%	43%	51%	49%	51%	52%	57%	57%	60%
Average	8%	11%	21%	27%	34%	38%	37%	44%	39%	46%	48%	52%
Total average	11%	13%	24%	28%	33%	39%	37%	43%	37%	44%	45%	49%

operation flexibility granted by the latency constraint which enables the FD-FTA heuristic's global scheduling approach to balance the operation concurrency over 2x as many cycles as the minimum-possible latency. The TMR-RTL approach, in contrast, will maintain a static scheduling approach despite the larger latency constraint. Like any basic triplication approaches, the TMR-RTL approach is unable to target new constraints without manual intervention and may suffer from a higher area cost due to fewer opportunities for resource sharing. Despite these savings, there are a few benchmarks where the FD-FTA heuristic experienced little to no savings. These benchmarks (e.g., *labjacobi*, *lapsor*, and *small1*) are however very small in operation count and represent cases where the FD-FTA heuristic's attempt to balance operation concurrency will yield output similar to the TMR-RTL approach. Overall, these results have supported our expectation that the FD-FTA heuristic performs better with increasing latency constraints due to larger scheduling flexibility.

Comparing the results from nonsynthetic benchmarks and synthetic benchmarks, Table 2 shows that the trends found in each individual benchmark set are similar to the trends found when both sets are considered together. For nonsynthetic benchmarks, the FD-FTA heuristic yielded no savings for about half of the benchmarks and up to 65%

savings for the remainder at a latency constraint of 1.0x and EC constraint of 100%. As the latency constraint increased, the FD-FTA heuristic generally showed increased savings with exception to *lapsor* and *fftRadix4* which displayed minimal degradation between −2% and −1% under certain latency constraints. At a latency constraint of 2.0x, the FD-FTA heuristic yielded savings up to 75%. Similarly, in the synthetic benchmarks, the FD-FTA heuristic also yielded no savings for about half of the benchmarks and up to 30% savings for the remainder at a latency constraint of 1.0x and EC constraint of 100%. As the latency constraint increased, the FD-FTA heuristic also generally showed increased savings but at a slower rate than the nonsynthetic benchmarks. At a latency constraint of 2.0x, the FD-FTA heuristic showed savings up to 62%. With similar trends, both benchmark sets also showed averages within 5% of their respective total averages.

To better illustrate these trends, Figure 6 shows the LUT savings of certain benchmarks that exemplify the different behaviors observed. In this graph, four benchmarks are displayed with EC constraints of 70% and 100%. Each benchmark entry is shown with six bars representing the LUT savings compared to the TMR-RTL approach for the six normalized latency constraints.

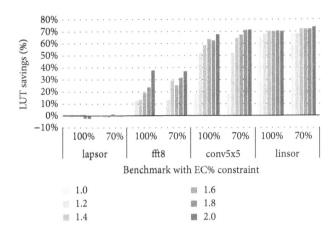

FIGURE 6: Resource savings of FD-FTA heuristic under different normalized latency constraints for selected benchmarks and EC% constraints when compared to TMR-RTL.

As one may expect, the impact of a latency constraint for HLS has a quite varied impact depending on the DFG structure. For the *lapsor* and other small benchmarks, increasing the latency constraint generally had a minimal impact in resource savings since the FD-FTA heuristic is likely to produce a similar schedule as TMR applied to existing RTL at small DFG operation counts. Similarly, the *linsor* benchmark also experienced small increases in savings as the latency constraint increased, despite the large initial savings. This behavior is caused by the benchmark's innate structure that enables much operation scheduling flexibility, even for the minimum-possible latency constraint. Due to the large flexibility, the FD-FTA heuristic's scheduling algorithm can balance the operation concurrency easier and experiences diminished benefits from additional flexibility granted by an increased latency constraint. In contrast, the *fft8* and *conv5x5* benchmarks show significant increases in savings when the latency constraint is increased. We attribute this behavior to minimal scheduling flexibility at the minimum-possible latency constraint which is alleviated with larger latency constraints.

When comparing the savings of 70% EC with 100% EC, Table 2 shows that the experiments under the 70% EC constraint had additional savings up to 27% compared to experiments under the 100% EC constraint with the same latency constraint. Similar to previous observations, the decreased EC% largely had no impact in experiments with a normalized latency constraint of 1x which is primarily due to the lack of operation flexibility. For this baseline latency constraint, the singletons of each module are likely scheduled on the same cycle and are therefore not eligible for singleton-sharing as seen in a majority of the benchmarks. Otherwise, the 70% EC iterations generally showed additional savings compared to their counterpart 100% EC iterations as the latency constraint is increased. Notably, these additional savings remain relatively similar once savings occur. Such savings are expected as EC% reflects the number of resources that may be shared across modules which places an upper bound on the additional savings due to EC.

Despite the overall positive impact by decreasing the EC%, there are a few cases where decreasing the EC% also decreased the LUT savings. For those cases, the savings due to sharing were offset by the cost of increasing the number of inputs on the interconnection multiplexers for the remaining resources. This trend is however only largely noticeable in the smaller DFGs, where the cost of input multiplexers may be comparable to the cost of resources. Similarly, there are also cases were decreasing the EC% showed a sudden increase in resource savings for a single latency constraint, but not for others, as seen in the *lapjacobi* benchmark. In these scenarios, the specific latency constraint of increased resource savings may present the only scenario where the Singleton-Share Binding is capable of sharing singletons. In contrast, the heuristic may present incompatible singleton bindings due to inflexible schedules at lower latency constraints or suboptimal schedules at higher latency constraints due to the force-directed global scheduling approach. Overall, determining the impact of the EC% constraint is counterintuitive as the constraint's impact relies primarily on the heuristic's distribution of singletons among cycles within each module. This distribution cannot be easily determined from the benchmark or constraints as the scheduling and binding process may vary the singleton distribution at the slightest change of constraints or in DFG structure. This impact is further affected by the shared resource type and by whether the sharing has increased the size of the resource's input multiplexer.

5.3. Comparison with Previous Approach. In this section, we evaluate the effectiveness of our FD-FTA heuristic compared to the approach of previous work described in [5] under different EC% and latency constraints. Table 3 presents the resource savings of the FD-FTA heuristic compared to the previous approach and uses the same presentation style as Table 2. On average, the FD-FTA heuristic shows savings compared to the previous work for each pair of normalized latency and EC% constraints. Although minimal at the lowest latency constraint, these savings become significant at higher latency constraints reaching 21% and 23% average savings at 2.0x normalized latency constraint for 100% and 70% EC, respectively. For individual benchmarks, the FD-FTA heuristic commonly shows significant savings at each set of constraints except for benchmarks with low operation counts and for most benchmarks at low normalized latency constraints.

Like the previous experiment, Table 3 expresses some similar results for benchmarks under the minimum-possible latency constraint. For the normalized latency constraint of 1.0x and 100% EC constraint, the FD-FTA heuristic generally has a small degradation ranging from −1% down to −5% in *fft8*. Similar to the results in Table 2, the FD-FTA heuristic has a tendency to make nonoptimal bindings that result in larger input multiplexers than the previous approach. Although present in all iterations of the experiment, such behavior is usually amortized by better utilization on fewer resources, especially on larger latency constraints. For the few cases where the FD-FTA heuristic experienced savings under these constraints, these iterations involved benchmarks with some flexibility to schedule operations on different cycles. In the case of the largest savings in the *small5* benchmark,

TABLE 3: Resource savings (LUTS) of FD-FTA heuristic compared to previous work for 100% and 70% EC.

| Benchmark | Normalized latency and EC% constraints | | | | | | | | | | | |
| | 1.0x | | 1.2x | | 1.4x | | 1.6x | | 1.8x | | 2.0x | |
	100%	70%	100%	70%	100%	70%	100%	70%	100%	70%	100%	70%
lapjacobi	0%	0%	0%	0%	2%	28%	−2%	−2%	−5%	−6%	−2%	−42%
lapsor	19%	19%	−1%	−1%	1%	−5%	1%	−2%	0%	−38%	0%	−33%
conv5x5	0%	0%	40%	41%	49%	56%	54%	59%	53%	64%	59%	63%
fft8	−5%	−5%	10%	9%	12%	27%	17%	22%	22%	29%	36%	35%
fftRadix4	0%	−2%	−6%	11%	12%	22%	9%	30%	12%	31%	13%	27%
fft16	−3%	−1%	15%	28%	9%	18%	11%	25%	−9%	6%	18%	27%
linjacobi	−1%	0%	29%	32%	24%	41%	43%	52%	44%	53%	42%	54%
linsor	0%	7%	−7%	−12%	−8%	−1%	−18%	−33%	−20%	−33%	−46%	−25%
conv9x9	−1%	0%	38%	38%	57%	63%	61%	67%	69%	72%	67%	74%
Average	1%	2%	13%	16%	18%	28%	20%	24%	18%	20%	21%	20%
small0	1%	1%	1%	1%	0%	4%	0%	4%	−21%	−10%	26%	40%
small1	0%	1%	0%	1%	0%	1%	2%	2%	2%	2%	0%	−35%
small2	0%	0%	0%	0%	11%	13%	11%	13%	−1%	12%	13%	15%
small3	0%	0%	0%	0%	34%	30%	25%	24%	1%	19%	20%	−4%
small4	10%	35%	10%	35%	11%	11%	15%	−5%	−18%	−25%	−4%	−4%
small5	27%	45%	28%	48%	22%	31%	−2%	−1%	3%	0%	−1%	−25%
small6	2%	2%	2%	2%	−1%	10%	11%	22%	1%	−1%	−11%	−19%
small7	0%	0%	0%	0%	28%	32%	34%	42%	43%	52%	46%	51%
medium0	0%	0%	33%	39%	44%	46%	44%	48%	49%	53%	40%	50%
medium1	0%	−2%	27%	40%	42%	48%	43%	47%	49%	53%	48%	53%
medium2	0%	0%	37%	41%	50%	53%	55%	60%	56%	60%	58%	63%
medium3	0%	0%	27%	33%	38%	43%	41%	48%	42%	49%	39%	49%
medium4	0%	0%	31%	35%	39%	48%	43%	47%	46%	52%	48%	52%
Average	3%	6%	15%	21%	24%	28%	25%	27%	19%	24%	25%	22%
Total average	2%	4%	14%	19%	22%	28%	23%	26%	19%	23%	23%	21%

the solution produced by the FD-FTA heuristic used far less multipliers than the previous approach's solution. This better utilization of the costly multipliers ultimately contributed to a smaller design.

Table 3 expresses some clear trends in the results of this experiment. These trends are general increases in resource savings as both the latency constraint and the number of operations in the benchmark increase. The experiment displays these trends in a majority of benchmarks and constraint sets with a few exceptions. These trends however are expected as the FD-FTA heuristic was designed to address disadvantages of the previous approach's scheduling algorithm. As mentioned in Section 4.1, the previous approach's scheduling algorithm had a number of scalability issues. The first trend of savings increasing with increased latency constraint can be attributed to the MR-LC scheduling algorithm that the previous approach is based on. Since MR-LC tries to minimize resources in a local cycle basis, this algorithm keeps a maximum operation count that limits the number of operations that may be scheduled in a cycle. These counts are only increased if the number of zero-slack operations in a cycle exceeds its current resource count. This behavior

noticeably causes problems for latency constraints larger than the minimum-possible latency constraint since all operations are guaranteed to have nonzero slacks in the first few cycles. In this case, the algorithm will only schedule at most one operation per cycle until it experiences numerous zero-slack operations at later cycles. This lack of initial operation concurrency will likely cause large operation concurrency at later cycles. The design will therefore be forced to instantiate additional resources to meet this large concurrency. The result is a large number of resources that are underutilized in early cycles. By contrast, the FD-FTA heuristic's scheduling algorithm aims to balance the operation concurrency among all cycles such that all resources maintain a high utilization and therefore uses fewer overall resources.

Comparing the results from nonsynthetic benchmarks and synthetic benchmarks, Table 3 shows that the trends found in each individual benchmark set are similar to the trends found when both sets are considered together. For nonsynthetic benchmarks, the FD-FTA heuristic yielded no savings for most benchmarks and up to 19% savings for the remainder at a latency constraint of 1.0x and EC constraint of 100%. As the latency constraint increased, the FD-FTA

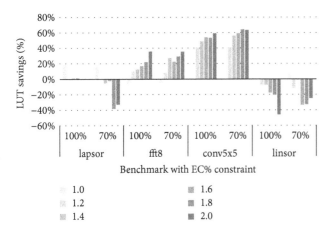

FIGURE 7: Resource savings of FD-FTA heuristic under different normalized latency constraints for selected benchmarks and EC% constraints when compared to the previous approach.

heuristic generally showed increased savings with exception to *lapjacobi* and *linsor* which decreased in savings. At a latency constraint of 2.0x, the FD-FTA heuristic yielded savings up to 67%. Similarly, in the synthetic benchmarks, the FD-FTA heuristic also yielded no savings for most benchmarks and up to 27% savings for the remainder at a latency constraint of 1.0x and EC constraint of 100%. As the latency constraint increased, the FD-FTA heuristic also generally showed increased savings but at a slower rate than the nonsynthetic benchmarks. At a latency constraint of 2.0x, the FD-FTA heuristic showed savings up to 58%. With similar trends, both benchmark sets also showed averages within 3% of their respective total averages.

To better illustrate these trends, Figure 7 shows the resource savings of certain benchmarks that exemplify the different behaviors observed. In this graph, four benchmarks are displayed with EC constraints of 70% and 100%. Each benchmark entry is shown with six bars representing the LUT savings compared to the previous approach for different normalized latency constraints.

Similar to Figure 6, the impact of a latency constraint for HLS has a quite varied impact depending on the DFG structure and on the effectiveness of the previous approach. For the *lapsor* and other small benchmarks, increasing the latency constraint generally had a small impact in resource savings since the FD-FTA heuristic is likely to produce a similar schedule to the previous approach. This behavior is mainly caused by the small operation count which limits the number of possible schedules. For a 70% EC constraint and 2.0x normalized latency constraint, the FD-FTA heuristic even displays a notable loss in savings. It should be cautioned that, at such small DFGs, any "significant" gain or loss of savings may be only the difference of one additional adder.

For the fft8 and conv5x5 benchmarks, we observe a significant increase in savings as the latency constraint increases. This trend represents the general case where the previous approach has difficulties finding an optimal schedule with larger operation counts. There are exceptions to this trend as seen in the linsor benchmark where the previous approach performs better than the FD-FTA heuristic under

most latency constraints. In fact, the FD-FTA heuristic does progressively worse as the latency constraint increases.

The second trend of increased savings with increased operation count can be attributed to the previous approach's iterative approach and its randomness in the scheduling algorithm. Since that approach largely relies on finding an optimal schedule randomly over many iterations, that approach is much more likely to find an optimal schedule in small DFGs rather than in larger DFGs given good starting parameters. As a result, as the size of the DFG increases, the previous approach finds less optimal solutions and encounters its exit condition much earlier. Although a design could modify the starting parameters to find a better solution at different sizes, such an approach requires much fine-tuning and is not a scalable solution. In contrast, the FD-FTA heuristic uses a global scheduling approach that balances operation concurrency over all possible cycles which allows the heuristic to scale with the size of the DFG at the expense of additional complexity.

5.4. Heuristic Execution Time Comparison. This section compares the average heuristic execution times of the FD-FTA heuristic with the previous approach. In this context, execution time refers to the duration of the scheduling and binding process and does not include the placement and routing of the design on a FPGA. We provide this comparison to demonstrate the scalability of these heuristics, which may limit the practical use cases of a heuristic. For FPGAs, long execution times may be an acceptable tradeoff due to placement and routing generally dominating compiling times. Relatively short execution times may make a heuristic amenable to fast recompilation in areas such as FPGA overlays [33].

Figure 8 presents the results of this experiment comparing the execution time of the two approaches with a 100% EC constraint and a 2x the normalized latency constraint. The figure is arranged such that the horizontal axis represents benchmarks arranged by operation count from smallest to largest and that the vertical axis represents execution time in milliseconds on a logarithmic scale. It should be noted that each tick of the horizontal axis does not represent the same increase in operation count between benchmarks. Similarly, benchmarks of the same operation count may vary in execution for both heuristics based on the overall DFG structure.

Generally, the results of this experiment match our expectations on execution time. The figure shows that, for each benchmark, the previous approach's execution time is orders of magnitude longer than the FD-FTA heuristic with an average speedup of 96x, a median speedup of 40x, and a max speedup of 570x in the *fft*16 benchmark. Our switch to the proposed FD-FTA heuristic was intended to address the previous approach's long execution time.

Based on the experiments on resource savings, these results suggest that both heuristics and the TMR-RTL approach have Pareto-optimal solutions within the design space for execution times, resource requirements, and latency constraints. Although the TMR-RTL approach does not require any scheduling and binding, results from Table 3 indicate a much smaller design may be achievable with the other

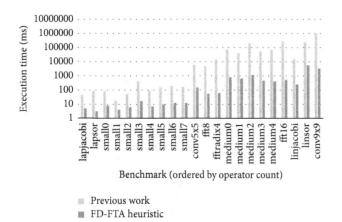

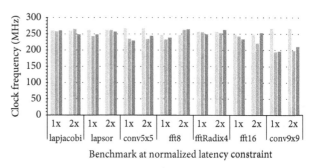

FIGURE 8: Execution times of the three approaches in the benchmark set under a 2x normalized latency constraint and a 100% EC constraint.

FIGURE 9: Clock frequency of the three approaches in a subset of nonsynthetic benchmarks under 1x and 2x normalized latency constraints and a 100% EC constraint.

approaches, especially at a larger latency constraint. Similarly, the approach of previous work may take vastly longer than other approaches but may achieve significantly smaller designs for latency constraints at the minimum-possible latency at a negligible difference in execution time for small DFGs. Notably, the FD-FTA heuristic achieves significantly more savings than the previous work at increased latency constraints and on larger DFGs.

5.5. Clock Results. This section compares the clock frequencies of designs generated by the proposed heuristic, the TMR-RTL approach, and the previous approach. Since increased resource sharing can increase the size of input multiplexers and potentially the critical path, we include this experiment to explore the impact of each approach on a design's clock frequency. Since synthesis tools perform placement and routing with a pseudorandom process, we determine an approach's clock frequency over multiple compilation runs through a script that does a binary search over the possible clock-constraint space and determines the theoretical max clock frequency based on a target frequency and slack values. Due to the lengthiness of this process, we provide this comparison only on a subset of nonsynthetic benchmarks and on a reduced set of constraints. For constraints, we test each selected benchmark at 1x and 2x normalized latency constraint with 100% EC constraint. Since the TMR-RTL approach does not rely on the latency constraint, we repeat the value in both latency constraints for comparison purposes.

To obtain these results, we convert the solution's netlist provided the C++ code into RTL code through scripts. We then use Vivado 2015.2 for compilation and for determining clock frequencies after placement and routing. For resources, we use IP cores from Xilinx for each respective resource and configure them to be implemented in LUTs and with single-cycle latencies.

Figure 9 shows the results of this experiment. In this figure, each approach has a bar for each benchmark and normalized latency constraint pairing. On the horizontal axis, the results are clustered by benchmark and then by

normalized latency constraint relative to the minimum-possible latency. On the vertical axis, the clock frequency is reported in MHz.

For each benchmark and latency constraint pairing, Figure 9 presents similar results for each approach. Compared to the TMR-RTL approach, the previous approach and the FD-FTA heuristic had an average clock degradation of 7.08% and 6.03%, respectively. This clock overhead is unexpectedly small since sharing increases the steering logic and the FD-FTA heuristic and previous approach incorporate much more sharing than the TMR-RTL approach. Upon further analysis of the timing reports, each approach had different critical paths. For the TMR-RTL approach, the critical path was generally a path from an input register to the output register of a multiplier. For the other approaches, the critical path was usually a path from the output register of one resource to the output register of a multiplier. These results suggest that the larger routing problem associated with using more resources in the TMR-RTL approach had a similar impact on a design's clock frequency as the steering logic for the other approaches. The one exception to this trend was the *Conv9x9* benchmark where the TMR-RTL approach had much higher clock frequencies than the other two approaches. In terms of increasing the latency constraint, both the FD-FTA heuristic and the previous approach generally showed minor increases in clock frequency.

6. Conclusions

This paper introduced the Force-Directed Fault-Tolerance-Aware (FD-FTA) heuristic to solve the minimum-resource, latency- and error-constrained scheduling and binding problem. Compared to TMR applied to existing RTL (TMR-RTL) and to a previous approach, this heuristic provides attractive tradeoffs by efficiently performing redundant operations on shared resources. The FD-FTA heuristic improves upon previous work with improved scheduling and binding algorithms for better scalability on larger benchmarks and with increased latency constraints. Compared to TMR-RTL implementations, the FD-FTA heuristic had average savings of 34%

and displayed average savings of 47% at a 2x normalized latency constraint. Although skewed by small benchmarks which have little opportunities for sharing, the FD-FTA heuristic had savings up to 80% under a 2x normalized latency constraint, with most savings occurring in the larger benchmarks. Compared to the previous approach, the FD-FTA heuristic had average savings of 19% and displayed average savings of 22% at a 2x normalized latency constraint. The FD-FTA's comparisons with the previous approach are also skewed by small benchmarks and showed up to 74% resource savings under a 2x normalized latency constraint with most savings occurring in the larger benchmarks. Additionally, the FD-FTA showed a 96x average heuristic execution time improvement compared to the previous approach and produced FPGA designs with a 6% average clock degradation compared to the TMR-RTL implementations. Future work includes support for pipelined circuits and for alternative strategies for FPGA fault-tolerance.

Acknowledgments

This work is supported in part by the I/UCRC Program of the National Science Foundation, under Grant nos. EEC-0642422, IIP-1161022, and CNS-1149285.

References

[1] N. Wulf, A. D. George, and A. Gordon-Ross, "Memory-aware optimization of FPGA-based space systems," in *Proceedings of the IEEE Aerospace Conference (AERO '15)*, pp. 1–13, IEEE, March 2015.

[2] M. Wirthlin, "High-reliability FPGA-based systems: space, high-energy physics, and beyond," *Proceedings of the IEEE*, vol. 103, no. 3, pp. 379–389, 2015.

[3] M. J. Wirthlin, "FPGAs operating in a radiation environment: Lessons learned from FPGAs in space," *Journal of Instrumentation*, vol. 8, no. 2, Article ID C02020, 2013.

[4] S. Golshan, H. Kooti, and E. Bozorgzadeh, "SEU-aware high-level data path synthesis and layout generation on SRAM-based FPGAs," *IEEE Transactions on Computer-Aided Design of Integrated Circuits and Systems*, vol. 30, no. 6, pp. 829–840, 2011.

[5] A. Shastri, G. Stitt, and E. Riccio, "A scheduling and binding heuristic for high-level synthesis of fault-tolerant FPGA applications," in *Proceedings of the 26th IEEE International Conference on Application-Specific Systems, Architectures and Processors (ASAP '15)*, pp. 202–209, July 2015.

[6] A. Antola, V. Piuri, and M. Sami, "High-level synthesis of data paths with concurrent error detection," in *Proceedings of the IEEE International Symposium on Defect and Fault Tolerance in VLSI Systems*, pp. 292–300, Austin, Tex, USA, November 1998.

[7] P. S. Ostler, M. P. Caffrey, D. S. Gibelyou et al., "SRAM FPGA reliability analysis for harsh radiation environments," *IEEE Transactions on Nuclear Science*, vol. 56, no. 6, pp. 3519–3526, 2009.

[8] O. Héron, T. Arnaout, and H.-J. Wunderlich, "On the reliability evaluation of SRAM-based FPGA designs," in *Proceedings of the International Conference on Field Programmable Logic and Applications (FPL '05)*, pp. 403–408, August 2005.

[9] O. Boncalo, A. Amaricai, C. Spagnol, and E. Popovici, "Cost effective FPGA probabilistic fault emulation," in *Proceedings of the 32nd NORCHIP Conference (NORCHIP '14)*, pp. 1–4, October 2014.

[10] A. Janning, J. Heyszl, F. Stumpf, and G. Sigl, "A cost-effective FPGA-based fault simulation environment," in *Proceedings of the 8th International Workshop on Fault Diagnosis and Tolerance in Cryptography (FDTC '11)*, pp. 21–31, September 2011.

[11] J. McCollum, "ASIC versus antifuse FPGA reliability," in *Proceedings of the IEEE Aerospace Conference*, pp. 1–11, March 2009.

[12] K. S. Morgan, D. L. McMurtrey, B. H. Pratt, and M. J. Wirthlin, "A comparison of TMR with alternative fault-tolerant design techniques for FPGAs," *IEEE Transactions on Nuclear Science*, vol. 54, no. 6, pp. 2065–2072, 2007.

[13] C. Bolchini, A. Miele, and M. D. Santambrogio, "TMR and partial dynamic reconfiguration to mitigate SEU faults in FPGAs," in *Proceedings of the 22nd IEEE International Symposium on Defect and Fault-Tolerance in VLSI Systems, DFT 2007*, pp. 87–95, September 2007.

[14] J. M. Johnson and M. J. Wirthlin, "Voter insertion algorithms for FPGA designs using triple modular redundancy," in *Proceedings of the 18th Annual ACM SIGDA International Symposium on Field-Programmable Gate Arrays (FPGA '10)*, pp. 249–258, ACM, Monterey, Calif, USA, February 2010.

[15] P. G. Paulin and J. P. Knight, "Scheduling and binding algorithms for high-level synthesis," in *Proceedings of the 26th ACM/IEEE conference*, pp. 1–6, June 1989.

[16] C.-T. Hwang, J.-H. Lee, and Y.-C. Hsu, "A formal approach to the scheduling problem in high level synthesis," *IEEE Transactions on Computer-Aided Design of Integrated Circuits and Systems*, vol. 10, no. 4, pp. 464–475, 1991.

[17] P. Coussy, D. D. Gajski, M. Meredith, and A. Takach, "An introduction to high-level synthesis," *IEEE Design and Test of Computers*, vol. 26, no. 4, pp. 8–17, 2009.

[18] S. Tosun, N. Mansouri, E. Arvas, M. Kandemir, and Y. Xie, "Reliability-centric high-level synthesis," in *Proceedings of the Design, Automation and Test in Europe (DATE '05)*, vol. 2, pp. 1258–1263, March 2005.

[19] X. Chen, W. Yang, M. Zhao, and J. Wang, "HLS-based sensitivity-inductive soft error mitigation for satellite communication systems," in *Proceedings of the 22nd IEEE International Symposium on On-Line Testing and Robust System Design (IOLTS '16)*, pp. 143–148, July 2016.

[20] M. B. Hammouda, P. Coussy, and L. Lagadec, "A unified design flow to automatically generate on-chip monitors during high-level synthesis of hardware accelerators," *IEEE Transactions on Computer-Aided Design of Integrated Circuits and Systems*, vol. 36, no. 3, pp. 384–397, 2017.

[21] S. Hadjis, A. Canis, J. H. Anderson et al., "Impact of FPGA architecture on resource sharing in high-level synthesis," in *Proceedings of the ACM/SIGDA International Symposium on Field Programmable Gate Arrays (FPGA '12)*, pp. 111–114, ACM, Monterey, Calif, USA, February 2012.

[22] A. F. Dos Santos, L. A. Tambara, F. Benevenuti, J. Tonfat, and F. L. Kastensmidt, "Applying TMR in hardware accelerators generated by high-level synthesis design flow for mitigating multiple bit upsets in SRAM-based FPGAs," in *Applied Reconfigurable Computing*, pp. 202–213, Springer, 2017.

[23] H. Quinn, D. Roussel-Dupre, M. Caffrey et al., "The cibola flight experiment," *ACM Transactions on Reconfigurable Technology and Systems*, vol. 8, no. 1, article no. 3, 2015.

[24] A. Orailoglu and R. Karri, "Automatic synthesis of self-recovering VLSI systems," *IEEE Transactions on Computers*, vol. 45, no. 2, pp. 131–142, 1996.

[25] K. Kyriakoulakos and D. Pnevmatikatos, "A novel SRAM-based FPGA architecture for efficient TMR fault tolerance support," in *Proceedings of the International Conference on Field Programmable Logic and Applications*, pp. 193–198, August 2009.

[26] T. Inoue, H. Henmi, Y. Yoshikawa, and H. Ichihara, "High-level synthesis for multi-cycle transient fault tolerant datapaths," in *Proceedings of the IEEE 17th International On-Line Testing Symposium (IOLTS '11)*, pp. 13–18, July 2011.

[27] P. G. Paulin and J. P. Knight, "Force-directed scheduling for the behavioral synthesis of ASIC's," *IEEE Transactions on Computer-Aided Design of Integrated Circuits and Systems*, vol. 8, no. 6, pp. 661–679, 1989.

[28] F. J. Kurdahi and A. C. Parker, "Real: a program for register allocation," in *Proceedings of the 24th ACM/IEEE Design Automation Conference*, pp. 210–215, June 1987.

[29] A. Hashimoto and J. Stevens, "Wire routing by optimizing channel assignment within large apertures," in *Proceedings of the 8th Design Automation Workshop (DAC '71)*, pp. 155–169, ACM, Atlantic City, NJ, USA, June 1971.

[30] A. Canis, J. Choi, M. Aldham et al., "LegUp: high-level synthesis for FPGA-based processor/accelerator systems," in *Proceedings of the 19th ACM/SIGDA International Symposium on Field Programmable Gate Arrays (FPGA '11)*, pp. 33–36, ACM, Monterey, Calif, USA, March 2011.

[31] J. A. Vite-Frias, R. D. J. Romero-Troncoso, and A. Ordaz-Moreno, "VHDL core for 1024-point radix-4 FFT computation," in *Proceedings of the proceedings of the IEEE International Conference on Reconfigurable Computing and FPGAs (RECONFIG '05)*, pp. 4–24, Puebla, Mexico, September 2005.

[32] J. Hu, *Solution of partial differential equations using reconfigurable computing [PhD. thesis]*, The University of Birmingham, 2010.

[33] J. Coole and G. Stitt, "Fast, flexible high-level synthesis from OpenCL using reconfiguration contexts," *IEEE Micro*, vol. 34, no. 1, pp. 42–53, 2014.

5

An FPGA-Based Quantum Computing Emulation Framework based on Serial-Parallel Architecture

Y. H. Lee, M. Khalil-Hani, and M. N. Marsono

VeCAD Research Laboratory, Faculty of Electrical Engineering, Universiti Teknologi Malaysia (UTM), 81310 Skudai, Johor Bahru, Malaysia

Correspondence should be addressed to M. Khalil-Hani; khalil@fke.utm.my

Academic Editor: João Cardoso

Hardware emulation of quantum systems can mimic more efficiently the parallel behaviour of quantum computations, thus allowing higher processing speed-up than software simulations. In this paper, an efficient hardware emulation method that employs a serial-parallel hardware architecture targeted for field programmable gate array (FPGA) is proposed. Quantum Fourier transform and Grover's search are chosen as case studies in this work since they are the core of many useful quantum algorithms. Experimental work shows that, with the proposed emulation architecture, a linear reduction in resource utilization is attained against the pipeline implementations proposed in prior works. The proposed work contributes to the formulation of a proof-of-concept baseline FPGA emulation framework with optimization on datapath designs that can be extended to emulate practical large-scale quantum circuits.

1. Introduction

Quantum computing is based on the properties of quantum mechanics, namely, superposition and entanglement. Superposition allows a quantum state to be in more than one basis state simultaneously, whereas entanglement is the strong correlation between multiqubit (quantum bit) basis states in a quantum system. Superposition and entanglement facilitate massive parallelism which enables exponential speed-ups to be achieved in the well-known integer factoring and discrete logarithms algorithms [1] and quadratic speed-ups in solving classically intractable brute-force searching and optimization problems [2, 3].

Similar to classical computing, quantum algorithms are developed long before any large-scale practical quantum computer is physically available. In 1994, Shor proposed the integer factoring and discrete logarithms algorithms [1] that brought the world's attention to the enormous potential of quantum computing. An example of this is the Rivest-Shamir-Adleman (RSA) security scheme [4] which is widely applied in current public key cryptosystem. It is based on the assumption that integer factoring of large number is intractable in classical computing. Shor's proposal, which,

in contrast, factors integer in polynomial time, would make such security scheme no longer secure. In [5], Grover proposed a quantum search algorithm that is capable of identifying a specific element in an unordered m elements database in $(\Pi/4)\sqrt{m}$ attempts. This algorithm achieves a quadratic speed-up over the corresponding classical method that requires $m/2$ queries on average, to retrieve the desired data. Although the solution is only polynomially faster than the classical approach, Grover's quantum algorithm is an important one as it can be generalized to be applied in many intractable computer science problems. Recently, quantum equivalents for random walks [6], genetic algorithms [3], and NAND tree evaluation [7] have been developed.

Shor in [8] categorized quantum algorithms known to provide substantial speed-up over the classical approach into three types: (a) algorithms that achieve notable speed-up by applying quantum Fourier transform (QFT) in periodicity finding; examples of this type of algorithm include integer factoring and discrete logarithms algorithms [1], Simon's periodicity algorithm [9], Hallgren's algorithms for Pell's equation [10], and the quantum algorithms for solving hidden subgroup problems [11, 12]; (b) Grover's search algorithm and its extensions [2, 13] which in general offer square root speed improvements over their classical counterparts; and (c) algorithms for simulating or solving problems in quantum mechanics [14].

Physical realization of a quantum computer is proving to be extremely challenging [15]. With research into viable large-scale quantum computers still ongoing, various technologies, namely, ion trap [16], nuclear magnetic resonance [17], and superconductor [18], were attempted. Nevertheless, only small-scale quantum computation implementations have been achieved [19, 20]. Instead of focusing on the realization of quantum gates, a different approach known as quantum annealing which solves optimization problems by finding the minimum point is used in the 128-qubit D-Wave One, 512-qubit D-Wave Two, and 1000-qubit D-Wave 2X systems [21, 22]. However, based on the research report presented in [23], the expected quantum speed-ups were not found in the D-Wave systems.

In parallel to efforts to develop physical quantum computers, there is also much effort in the theoretical research of quantum algorithms. Until large-scale practical quantum computers become prevalent, quantum algorithms are currently developed using the classical computing platform. However, due to their inherent sequential behaviour, classical computers that are based on Von Neumann architecture cannot simulate the inherent parallelism in quantum systems efficiently. On the other hand, the technology of field programmable gate array (FPGA) offers the potential of massive parallelism through hardware emulation. Consequently, significant improvement in speed performance over the equivalent software simulation can be achieved. However, FPGA is still a form of classical digital computing, and resource utilization on such a classical computing platform grows exponentially as the number of qubits increases. The problem is further compounded with the fact that accurate modelling of quantum circuit in FPGA technology is nonintuitive and therefore difficult, providing the research motivation for this paper.

This paper presents an efficient FPGA emulation framework for quantum computing. In the proposed emulation model, quantum computations are mapped to a serial-parallel architecture that facilitates scalability by managing the exponential growth of resource requirement against number of qubits. Quantum Fourier transform and Grover's search are chosen as case studies in this work since they are the core of many useful quantum algorithms, and in addition, they have been used as benchmarking models in prior works on FPGA emulation. Experimental results on the efficiencies of different FPGA emulation architectures and fixed point formats are presented, which will sufficiently demonstrate the feasibility of proposed framework.

The rest of this paper is organized as follows: Section 2 discusses prior works on FPGA-based quantum computing emulation, emphasizing issues of hardware architecture and modelling of quantum system on FPGA platform. In Section 3, the theoretical background on quantum computing and related quantum algorithms is provided. Section 4 presents the design of the proposed FPGA emulation models for QFT and Grover's search algorithms. Experimental results

and analysis are given in Section 5. Finally, concluding remarks are made in Section 6.

2. Related Work

Modelling of a quantum system on classical computing platform is a challenging task. Hence, it is even more difficult to map quantum algorithms for emulation on classical computing environment based on FPGA, which is highly resource-constrained. Many attempts have been made in the last decade in FPGA emulation of quantum algorithms, and these works include [24–27]. However, details of the critical design processes such as mapping of the quantum algorithms into the FPGA emulation models and the verification of the implementations are not revealed in these prior works.

For software-based simulation using classical computer, various types of quantum simulators have been proposed. An open source C library, *libquantum*, for simulation of quantum computing is presented in [28] where pure quantum computer simulation as well as general quantum simulation is supported by the tool. In 2007, a variant of binary decision diagram named quantum information decision diagram (QuIDD) for compact state vector storage was introduced in [29] for efficient quantum circuit simulation. García and Markov [30] proposed a compact data structure based on stabilizer formalism called stabilizer frames.

Most of the previous FPGA emulation works are based on the quantum circuit model, which is essentially an interconnection of quantum gates. A different approach was taken by Goto and Fujishima [24] where a general purpose quantum processor was developed instead of applying the quantum circuit model. However, Fujishima's quantum processor assumed that the amplitudes of a quantum state can be either all zeros or with evenly distributed probability. In its emulation of Shor's integer factoring algorithm, details of the implementation are inadequate for its results to be verified as claimed. For instance, it is stated in [24] that a 64-bit factorization was demonstrated using their emulator with only 40 Kbits of classical memory instead of 320 qubits as required with Shor's algorithm in a quantum computer. This statement was not supported by design and implementation details on how factorization of such a large integer can be done with only 40 Kbits memory, where typically it would require at least 2^{320} bytes to represent a quantum state of such a scale on the classical platform.

In [25], FPGA emulation of 3-qubit QFT and Grover's search are proposed. In this work, which is based on the quantum circuit model, qubit expansion is performed prior to the application of multiqubit quantum gate transformations. This leads to an inaccurate modelling of a quantum algorithm, since, according to [31], the input quantum state to QFT circuit should first be placed in superposition of basis states, where signal samples are encoded as sequence of amplitudes. In the work by [26], hardware emulation of QFT restricts its input quantum state to the computational basis state, implying that superposition is not included in the modelling. Rivera-Miranda et al. in [26] claims 16-qubit QFT emulation is achieved. However, the emulator can only process up to 32 input signal samples in one evaluation, which is equivalent to a 5-qubit QFT emulation if effects of superposition and entanglement are included.

From the above discussion it should be noted then that the critical quantum properties of superposition and entanglement were not considered in these previous works, resulting in inaccurate modelling of quantum algorithms. Without the superposition and entanglement effects, the power of quantum parallelism cannot fully be exploited. Previous works reported in [25–27] applied pipeline architecture in their FPGA emulation implementations so as to obtain high throughput and low critical path delay. However, a pipeline design imposes high resource utilization (due to the requirement of additional pipeline registers and associated logic), thus limiting FPGA emulation to be deployed in more practical quantum computing applications that typically require high qubit sizes. In these pipeline implementations proposed in prior works, resource growth was exponential to the increase in qubit sizes.

In this paper, the issues outline above is addressed. The efficiencies of different hardware architectural designs for FPGA emulation purposes are evaluated based on the chosen case studies of QFT and Grover's search. We propose an accurate modelling of quantum system for FPGA emulation, targeting efficient resource utilization while maintaining significant speed-up over the equivalent simulation approach. Since our proposed FPGA emulation framework applies the state vector approach, simulation models based on the *libquantum* library are selected in this work for benchmarking purposes.

3. Theoretical Background

In general, quantum algorithms obey the basic process flow structure. The computation process begins with a system set in a specific quantum state, which is then converted into superposition of multiple basis states. Unitary transformations are performed on the quantum state according to the required operations of the algorithm. Finally, measurement is carried out, resulting in the qubits collapsing into classical bits.

3.1. Quantum Bit (Qubit). In classical computing, the smallest unit of information is the *bit*. A bit can be in either state 0 or state 1, and the state of a *bit* can be represented in matrix form as

$$\begin{aligned} \text{state } 0 &= \begin{array}{c} 0 \\ 1 \end{array} \begin{bmatrix} 1 \\ 0 \end{bmatrix}, \\ \text{state } 1 &= \begin{array}{c} 0 \\ 1 \end{array} \begin{bmatrix} 0 \\ 1 \end{bmatrix}. \end{aligned} \tag{1}$$

On the other hand, in quantum computing, the smallest unit of information is the *quantum bit* or a *qubit*. To distinguish the classical bit with the quantum qubit, Dirac *ket* notation is used. Using the *ket* notation, the quantum computational basis state is represented by $|0\rangle$ and $|1\rangle$. A qubit can be in state $|0\rangle$, or in state $|1\rangle$, or in superposition of both basis states. The state of a qubit can be represented as

$$|\psi\rangle = \alpha |0\rangle + \beta |1\rangle \equiv \begin{array}{c} 0 \\ 1 \end{array} \begin{bmatrix} \alpha \\ \beta \end{bmatrix}, \tag{2}$$

where both α and β are complex numbers and $|\alpha|^2 + |\beta|^2 = 1$. $|\alpha|^2$ is the probability where the qubit is in state $|0\rangle$ and $|\beta|^2$ is the probability where the qubit is in state $|1\rangle$ upon measurement. An n-qubit quantum state vector contains 2^n complex numbers which represents the measurement probability of each basis state. However, on measurement, the superposition is destroyed and the qubits return to the classical state of bits depending on the probability derived from the complex-valued state vector.

3.2. Tensor/Kronecker Product. Tensor product or Kronecker product is the basic operation that is applied in the formation of a larger quantum system as well as multiqubit quantum transformations. A quantum state vector that can be written as the tensor of two vectors is separable, whereas a state vector that cannot be expressed as the tensor of two vectors is entangled [15]. The tensor operation on any arbitrary two 1-qubit transformations is shown below:

$$\begin{bmatrix} a_0 & a_1 \\ a_2 & a_3 \end{bmatrix} \otimes \begin{bmatrix} b_0 & b_1 \\ b_2 & b_3 \end{bmatrix} = \begin{bmatrix} a_0 b_0 & a_0 b_1 & a_1 b_0 & a_1 b_1 \\ a_0 b_2 & a_0 b_3 & a_1 b_2 & a_1 b_3 \\ a_2 b_0 & a_2 b_1 & a_3 b_0 & a_3 b_1 \\ a_2 b_2 & a_2 b_3 & a_3 b_2 & a_3 b_3 \end{bmatrix}. \tag{3}$$

3.3. Quantum Circuit Model. A quantum algorithm is a description of a sequence of quantum operations (or transformations) applied upon qubits to generate new quantum states. The model most widely used in describing the evolution of a quantum system is the quantum circuit model, first proposed in [32]. A quantum circuit is the interconnection of quantum gates with quantum wires, and gate operations are represented by unitary matrices.

All unitary matrices are invertible and the products of unitary matrices as well as the inverse of unitary matrix are unitary. An N-by-N matrix U is unitary if $UU^\dagger = U^\dagger U = I_N$, where $U^\dagger$ is the adjoint (conjugate transpose) of U. Since all quantum transformations are reversible, quantum gate operations can always be undone. Fundamental quantum gates include the Hadamard gate, phase-shift gate, and swap gate, and these gates are described as follows.

Hadamard gate H is one of the most useful single qubit quantum gates. It operates by placing the computational basis state into superposition of basis states with equal probability. The Hadamard transform can be represented by the following unitary matrix:

$$H = \frac{1}{\sqrt{2}} \begin{bmatrix} 1 & 1 \\ 1 & -1 \end{bmatrix}. \tag{4}$$

The following example illustrates the application of Hadamard gates in mapping a 2-qubit basis state $|00\rangle$ to a superposition of basis states with equal probability:

$$|00\rangle \xrightarrow{H \otimes H} \frac{1}{2} (|00\rangle + |01\rangle + |10\rangle + |11\rangle),$$

$$\left(\frac{1}{\sqrt{2}} \begin{bmatrix} 1 & 1 \\ 1 & -1 \end{bmatrix} \otimes \frac{1}{\sqrt{2}} \begin{bmatrix} 1 & 1 \\ 1 & -1 \end{bmatrix} \right) \begin{bmatrix} 1 \\ 0 \\ 0 \\ 0 \end{bmatrix} = \frac{1}{2} \begin{bmatrix} 1 \\ 1 \\ 1 \\ 1 \end{bmatrix}. \quad (5)$$

Controlled phase-shift gate $^{C}R_k$ operates on 2 qubits, one of which is the control qubit and the other is the target qubit. If the control qubit is true, a phase-shift operation is performed on the target qubit; otherwise, there is no operation. The operation is represented by the following matrix:

$$^{C}R_k = \begin{bmatrix} 1 & 0 & 0 & 0 \\ 0 & 1 & 0 & 0 \\ 0 & 0 & 1 & 0 \\ 0 & 0 & 0 & e^{2\pi i/2^k} \end{bmatrix}. \quad (6)$$

Quantum SWAP gate is used for swapping two qubits. It switches the amplitudes of a quantum state vector. The operation of a 2-qubit SWAP gate is represented by matrix in

$$\text{SWAP} = \begin{bmatrix} 1 & 0 & 0 & 0 \\ 0 & 0 & 1 & 0 \\ 0 & 1 & 0 & 0 \\ 0 & 0 & 0 & 1 \end{bmatrix}. \quad (7)$$

3.4. Quantum Fourier Transform (QFT). The Fourier transform is deployed in wide range of engineering and physics applications such as signal processing, image processing, and quantum mechanics. It is a reversible transformation that converts signals from time/spatial domain to frequency domain and vice versa. The Fourier transform is defined in (8) for continuous signals and in (9) for discrete signals:

$$X(f) = \int_{-\infty}^{\infty} x(t) e^{-i2\pi f t} dt, \quad (8)$$

$$X_k = \sum_{n=0}^{N-1} x_n e^{-i2\pi(kn/N)}. \quad (9)$$

The quantum Fourier transform (QFT) is a transformation on qubits and is the quantum equivalent of the discrete Fourier transform. It should be noted that a quantum computer performs QFT with exponentially less number of operations than the classical Fourier transform. However, QFT does not reduce the execution time of the algorithm when classical data is used. This is due to the characteristic of the quantum computer that does not allow parallel read-out of all quantum state amplitudes. In addition, there is no

known method that can effectively instantiate the desired input state amplitudes to be Fourier-transformed [33].

In order to harness the power of quantum computing on Fourier transform, QFT has to be deployed within other practical applications. QFT is pivotal in quantum computing since it is part of many quantum algorithms. These algorithms include integer factorization and discrete logarithms algorithms [1], Simon's periodicity algorithm [9], and Hallgren's algorithms [10]. They offer significant speed-up over their classical counterparts. QFT has also found applications in many real-world problems such as image watermarking [34] and template matching [35].

To compute Fourier transform in quantum domain, discrete signal samples are encoded as the amplitude sequences of a quantum state vector which is in superposition of basis states [31]. An n-qubit QFT operation which transforms an arbitrary superposition of computational basis states is expressed in

$$|\psi\rangle = \frac{1}{\sqrt{2^n}} \sum_{j=0}^{2^n-1} f(j\Delta t) |j\rangle$$

$$\xrightarrow{\text{QFT}} \frac{1}{\sqrt{2^n}} \sum_{k=0}^{2^n-1} \sum_{j=0}^{2^n-1} f(j\Delta t) e^{2\pi i(jk/2^n)} |k\rangle. \quad (10)$$

As the requirement for a valid quantum state, $|\psi\rangle$ must be normalized such that it fulfils (11). If the original signal inputs do not comply with this requirement, the amplitudes of the signal samples have to be divided by the normalization factor, $\sqrt{\sum_{l=0}^{2^n-1} |f(l\Delta t)|^2}$. In most cases, the input states formed by the normalized signal samples are entangled:

$$\sum_{j=0}^{2^n-1} |f(j\Delta t)|^2 = 1. \quad (11)$$

From (10), it can be observed that the term $j/2^n$ in QFT equation is a rational number in the range of $0 \le j/2^n < 1$. As qubit representation is typically used in computations, the j in base-10 integer is redefined in base-2 notation as individual bit such that the binary fraction form as expressed in (12) can be conveniently adopted:

$$\begin{aligned} (j)_{10} &\equiv (j_1 j_2 \cdots j_n)_2 \\ &= \left(2^{n-1} j_1 + 2^{n-2} j_2 + \cdots + 2^0 j_n \right)_{10} \\ &= 2^n \left(2^{-1} j_1 + 2^{-2} j_2 + \cdots + 2^{-n} j_n \right)_{10} \\ &= 2^n \left(0 \cdot j_1 j_2 \cdots j_n \right)_2. \end{aligned} \quad (12)$$

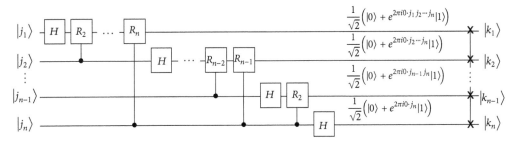

FIGURE 1: Quantum circuit model for n-qubit QFT.

With some algebraic manipulations, the QFT equation can be derived from (13) to form (14) [33]:

$$\text{QFT}_{2^n}|j\rangle = \frac{1}{\sqrt{2^n}} \sum_{k=0}^{2^n-1} e^{2\pi i(jk/2^n)}|k\rangle \tag{13}$$

$$= \frac{1}{\sqrt{2^n}}\left(|0\rangle + e^{2\pi i 0 \cdot j_n}|1\rangle\right)$$

$$\cdot\left(|0\rangle + e^{2\pi i 0 \cdot j_{n-1} j_n}|1\rangle\right)\cdots\left(|0\rangle + e^{2\pi i 0 \cdot j_1 j_2 \cdots j_n}|1\rangle\right). \tag{14}$$

Since the term $e^{2\pi i 0 \cdot j_1}$ produces either -1 if $j_1 = 1$ or $+1$ otherwise, Hadamard computation on the first qubit results in $(1/\sqrt{2})(|0\rangle + e^{2\pi i 0 \cdot j_1}|1\rangle)$. Computations of the consecutive bits in the binary fraction are obtained using controlled phase-shift gates according to (14). QFT circuit consists of three types of elementary gates which are Hadamard gate, H, controlled phase-shift gate, ${}^C R_k$, and SWAP gate. The circuit model of an n-qubit QFT is depicted in Figure 1.

The size of a QFT circuit grows exponentially as the number of input qubits increases. An n-qubit QFT involves $\sum_{k=1}^{n} k+1$ unitary transformations and could process up to 2^n input samples in one evaluation (provided the input samples are encoded as the amplitude sequences of a superposition of computational basis states).

3.5. Grover's Search Algorithm.

In computer science area, a typical search problem is to identify the desired element from an unordered array. For many computing applications, it is critical that the search technique is efficient. In terms of a function, the search problem $f : \{0,1\}^n \rightarrow \{0,1\}$ is given with assurance that there exists one binary string x_0 where $f(x) = 1$ if $x = x_0$; else, $f(x) = 0$.

In classical computing, $m/2$ queries on average are required to search for a particular element in an unordered array with m elements. In quantum computing, Grover's search algorithm can complete the job in $(\Pi/4)\sqrt{m}$ queries (for the rest of the text and figures in Section 3.5, the required Grover iterations are abbreviated as $\sqrt{2^n}$ times). Although the speed-up achieved is only quadratic, Grover's algorithm and its extensions are extremely useful in enhancing current methods in solving database searching and optimization problems, which include 3-satisfiability [36], global optimization [37], minimum point searching [38], and pattern matching [39]. The core operations of Grover's algorithm are phase inversion and inversion about mean. Phase inversion

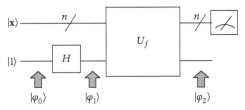

FIGURE 2: Quantum circuit for phase inversion [15].

inverts the phase of the state-of-interest, and its quantum circuit model is given in Figure 2.

In Figure 2, the top n-qubit, $|\mathbf{x}\rangle$, is the target qubit, and the bottom qubit is called the ancilla qubit. The function of U_f is to pick out the desired binary string. To apply phase inversion on target qubits, Hadamard gate operation is performed on the ancilla qubit, which is initialized as $|1\rangle$. This is to complement the effect of U_f which takes $|\mathbf{x}, y\rangle$ to $|\mathbf{x}, f(\mathbf{x}) \oplus y\rangle$.

In terms of matrices, the phase inversion operation can be expressed as $U_f(I_n \oplus H)|\mathbf{x}, 1\rangle$, and the corresponding quantum states are described as follows:

$$|\varphi_0\rangle = |\mathbf{x}, 1\rangle,$$

$$|\varphi_1\rangle = |\mathbf{x}\rangle\left[\frac{|0\rangle - |1\rangle}{\sqrt{2}}\right] = \left[\frac{|\mathbf{x}, 0\rangle - |\mathbf{x}, 1\rangle}{\sqrt{2}}\right],$$

$$|\varphi_2\rangle = |\mathbf{x}\rangle\left[\frac{|f(\mathbf{x}) \oplus 0\rangle - |f(\mathbf{x}) \oplus 1\rangle}{\sqrt{2}}\right]$$

$$= |\mathbf{x}\rangle\left[\frac{|f(\mathbf{x})\rangle - |\overline{f(\mathbf{x})}\rangle}{\sqrt{2}}\right] \tag{15}$$

$$= (-1)^{f(\mathbf{x})}|\mathbf{x}\rangle\left[\frac{|0\rangle - |1\rangle}{\sqrt{2}}\right]$$

$$= \begin{cases} -1\,|\mathbf{x}\rangle\left[\dfrac{|0\rangle - |1\rangle}{\sqrt{2}}\right], & \text{if } \mathbf{x} = \mathbf{x}_0, \\ +1\,|\mathbf{x}\rangle\left[\dfrac{|0\rangle - |1\rangle}{\sqrt{2}}\right], & \text{if } \mathbf{x} \neq \mathbf{x}_0. \end{cases}$$

Inversion about mean boosts the phase separation between the element-of-interest and other elements in the unordered arrays (after phase inversion operation is applied to invert the phase of the target element). The mean of

(1) Start with $|0\rangle$ as the target input qubits
(2) Apply n-qubit Hadamard gate on target qubits, $H^{\otimes n}$
(3) **for** $\sqrt{2^n}$ times **do**
(4)   Apply phase inversion operation, $U_f(I \otimes H)$
(5)   Apply inversion about mean operation on the target qubits, $-I + 2A$
(6) **end for**
(7) Measure the target qubits

ALGORITHM 1: Grover's search algorithm.

all elements is computed and inversions are made about the mean. The overall mean remains unchanged after the inversion process. This is because the distance between one element and the mean is the same before and after inversion. The only change is if the original sequence is above the mean, during the inversion it is flipped about the mean to the same distance below the mean and vice versa. In general, the inversion about mean operation can be expressed as

$$v' = -v + 2a, \qquad (16)$$

where a is the mean, v is the value of an element in the array, and v' is the new value of that element after inversion.

In terms of matrices, the mean of a 2^n elements vector V is obtained by the product of matrices A and V where all the elements in the 2^n-by-2^n matrix A are set to $1/2^n$. Hence, inversion about mean in matrix form becomes

$$V' = -V + 2AV = (-I + 2A)V. \qquad (17)$$

In order to achieve high confidence of getting the desired element, the amplitude amplification process (amplitude amplification in Grover's search algorithm involves phase inversion and inversion about mean operations) has to be repeated for $\sqrt{2^n}$ times. This is because the probability of success changes sinusoidally by the number of amplitude amplification iterations (as illustrated in Figure 3) and the highest probability of success first happened after the required iterations. Pseudocode for a generic Grover's search algorithm is given in Algorithm 1.

There are two approaches to model Grover's search quantum algorithm. The first approach, which is based on quantum circuit model, is discussed next. The second method is modelling using arithmetic functions, and this is presented in Section 4.2 since this approach is applied in this paper.

As shown in Figure 4, Grover's search circuit given in [15] is constructed with assumption that black box modules U_f and $-I + 2A$ are available. Descriptions of the U_f and $-I + 2A$ modules have been given earlier.

On the other hand, the circuit model for n-qubit Grover's algorithm presented in [33] is shown in Figure 5(a). In this figure, H is the Hadamard gate, and G is the Grover iteration circuit, which is illustrated in Figure 5(b).

The function of Grover iteration circuit is equivalent to the phase inversion and inversion about mean. In order to achieve high probability of successful search, G is concatenated for $\sqrt{2^n}$ times. In Figure 5(b), the role of oracle module is to recognize the solution to a particular search

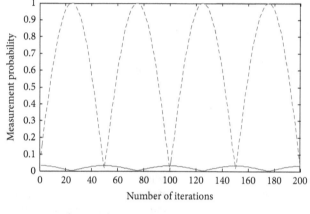

FIGURE 3: Probability of success by the number of amplitude amplification iterations amongst 2^{10} probabilities. For 10-qubit search, first highest probability of success happens at 25th iteration.

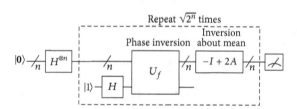

FIGURE 4: Modelling of Grover's search based on quantum circuit model [15].

problem in the phase inversion operation. By monitoring the oracle qubit, a solution to the search problem can be detected through the changes of the oracle qubit. The design of oracle module varies with different search applications, and an example of the oracle circuit for a simple 3-bit search task is shown in Figure 6. In Figure 6, the X symbol represents Pauli-X matrix. The open circle notation indicates conditioning on the qubit being set to zero, whereas the closed circle indicates conditioning on the qubit being set to one.

Deriving from the circuits in Figure 5, the corresponding 3-qubit Grover's search circuit is provided in Figure 7. This circuit model is made up of Hadamard, oracle, quantum NOT, and multiqubit controlled-NOT gates.

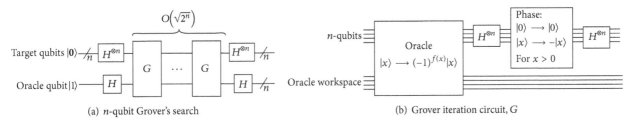

(a) n-qubit Grover's search   (b) Grover iteration circuit, G

FIGURE 5: Quantum circuit model for Grover's search algorithm [33].

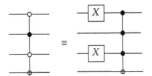

FIGURE 6: Oracle circuit for recognizing binary string "010".

4. Proposed FPGA-Based Hardware Emulation

This section presents our approach in modelling quantum Fourier transform and Grover's search algorithms for FPGA emulation. The proposed techniques can be generalized to FPGA emulation of more complex quantum algorithms that apply QFT or Grover's algorithm. This paper extends our earlier work presented in [40, 41]. In these previous works, the hardware architecture proposed was restricted to the serial design with resource sharing facilitated at the register level. In this paper, we enable resource sharing at the operator (or computational) level that allows for more efficient emulation of the quantum algorithms. Furthermore, additional case study on Grover's search algorithm is included for generalization of the proposed framework. The choice of hardware architecture varies based on the need of different applications. Based on the selected case studies, the efficiencies of different hardware architectures for quantum computing emulation purposes are discussed and analysed in this work. The goal is to achieve scalability and also efficient resource utilization for emulating practical larger qubit size quantum systems.

4.1. Modelling QFT for FPGA Emulation. The derivation of quantum circuit model for n-qubit QFT was discussed earlier is Section 3.4. Here, we present the modelling of QFT for FPGA emulation based on a 3-qubit example. According to (14), the mathematical expression for 3-qubit QFT is derived as shown in

$$\text{QFT}_{2^3} |j\rangle = \frac{1}{\sqrt{2^3}} \left(|0\rangle + e^{2\pi i 0 \cdot j_3} |1\rangle \right)$$

$$\cdot \left(|0\rangle + e^{2\pi i 0 \cdot j_2 j_3} |1\rangle \right) \quad (18)$$

$$\cdot \left(|0\rangle + e^{2\pi i 0 \cdot j_1 j_2 j_3} |1\rangle \right).$$

Deriving from the general n-qubit QFT circuit provided in Figure 1, the corresponding quantum circuit for 3-qubit QFT is obtained as shown in Figure 8.

The circuit consists of Hadamard gates, H, controlled phase-shift gates, $^CR_2$ and $^CR_3$, and also the SWAP gate. Referring to the functional block diagram given in Figure 9, this quantum circuit model corresponds to a sequence of unitary transformations, Ui, i = 1 to 7, defined by

$$U1 = H \otimes I \otimes I, \quad (19)$$

$$U2 = {}^CR_2 \otimes I, \quad (20)$$

$$U3 = (I \otimes \text{SWAP}) \cdot \left({}^CR_3 \otimes I \right) \cdot (I \otimes \text{SWAP}), \quad (21)$$

$$U4 = I \otimes H \otimes I, \quad (22)$$

$$U5 = I \otimes {}^CR_2, \quad (23)$$

$$U6 = I \otimes I \otimes H, \quad (24)$$

$$U7 = \text{SWAP}_{2^3}. \quad (25)$$

Note that, in Figure 9, the modelling of n-qubit quantum system with superposition and entanglement properties resulted in a circuit with 2^n signals. Since the input samples to QFT circuit are encoded as sequence of amplitudes in an entangled superposition of basis states (discussed in Section 3.4), modelling based on individual qubit with separate quantum gate operations is unable to reflect the effects of applying a quantum gate on entangled qubits correctly.

In order to model the effect of superposition and entanglement, derivation of each unitary transformation is made through the tensor product of individual quantum gate and identity matrix to form unitary matrix of equal dimension with the quantum state vector. Detailed derivations of the quantum unitary matrices for the 3-qubit QFT have been presented in our previous paper [41].

Since these quantum unitary matrices are mostly sparse matrices, we extract minimal number of useful arithmetic operations (due to nonzero elements in the matrices), resulting in an optimal realization of the model that can be mapped to an efficient FPGA emulation architecture. Incidentally, a software program has been developed to automate this mapping, hence easily scaling up the circuit model to larger qubit sizes. From these arithmetic functions, the corresponding data-flow graph for the 3-qubit QFT is derived as shown in Figure 10.

In Figure 10, each IN and OUT signal is a fixed point complex number register for an element of the quantum state vector. The operation of module F corresponds to out_r = −in_i and out_i = in_r, where F is the multiplication

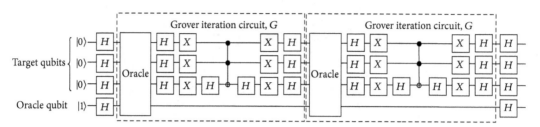

FIGURE 7: Modelling of 3-qubit Grover's search based on quantum gates.

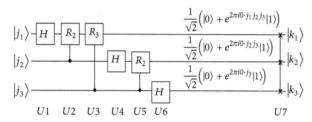

FIGURE 8: Quantum circuit for 3-qubit QFT.

FIGURE 9: The 3-qubit QFT in terms of a sequence of unitary transformations.

of the input complex number with imaginary number i. This is applied in unitary transformations $U2$ and $U5$. The operation of module CMULT in Figure 10 is described in (26). The function of CMULT is the multiplication of the input complex number with a constant complex number which is derived based on the controlled phase-shift gate. As expressed previously in (21), it is used in unitary transformation $U3$:

$$out\_r = (in\_r \times constant\_r) - (in\_i \times constant\_i),$$
$$out\_i = (in\_i \times constant\_r) + (in\_r \times constant\_i). \tag{26}$$

4.2. Modelling Grover's Search for FPGA Emulation. As mentioned earlier, the second approach of modelling Grover's quantum search is modelling using arithmetic functions (based on mathematical model). In this work, we have chosen this approach of modelling Grover's algorithm for FPGA emulation. In contrast to the quantum circuit model approach that involves complex large dimensional matrix operations (i.e., matrix multiplication and tensor product), the chosen method can utilize the computational resources available on FPGA such as comparators, adders/subtracters, and multiplexers for efficient emulation of Grover's search algorithm.

This technique is based on phase inversion and inversion about mean as described in Section 3.5. As shown in Figure 11, mathematically, Grover's search for a database with 2^n elements mainly involves the processes of inverting the phase of target element, function F, and performing

inversion about mean on all elements, function $-I + 2A$, for $\sqrt{2^n}$ times. Initialization of the quantum state vector with equal probability, function INIT, is carried out once in the beginning of the process.

For the case study of a 3-bit search problem, we derive the data-flow graphs and obtain the result of the required arithmetic functions as shown in Figure 12. For experimental purposes, the oracle module is developed by comparing all elements in database with targeted element using comparators, COMP modules. The arithmetic functions of the inversion about mean are derived through straightforward computations that involve summation, bit shift, and subtraction.

4.3. Architecture of Proposed FPGA Emulation Model. It is clear that if implemented on classical computing platforms, the resource utilization for a quantum system would grow exponentially. Hence, the choice of suitable architecture is critical for FPGA-based quantum computing emulation. Here, we discuss the efficiencies of different architectural choices in datapath: concurrent, pipeline, serial, and serial-parallel. The block diagram of various architectures is constructed based on the example of 3-qubit QFT.

4.3.1. Concurrent Processing. In concurrent processing of an algorithm, all computations are completed within a clock cycle. In the case of 3-qubit QFT, computation blocks between the input and output registers, through the functional blocks, $U1$ to $U7$ are performed in one clock cycle (refer to Figure 13(a)). However, such an architecture consumes enormous resources, such that the number of registers required to emulate an n-qubit QFT is 2^{n+1}. In addition, the critical path delay is very high which results in unrealistic low operating frequency.

4.3.2. Pipeline Architecture. Most of the prior works on FPGA-based quantum circuit emulation [25–27] are developed based on pipeline architecture. The pipeline architecture has the advantages of high throughput and much shorter critical path delay. Figure 13(b) shows the proposed pipeline architecture of the 3-qubit QFT. However, the main issue of this approach is that resource utilization grows drastically by the number of qubits, due to the circuit augmentation of pipeline registers. $2^n(\sum_{k=1}^{n} k+2)$ pipeline registers are required to emulate n-qubit QFT. Consequently, hardware emulation scalability is highly constrained by the available resources in FPGA.

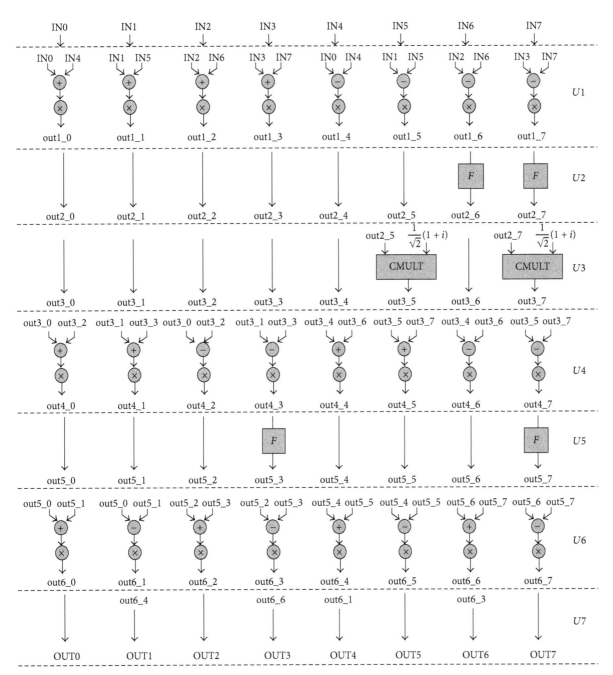

FIGURE 10: Data-flow graph for 3-qubit QFT. The multipliers shown in this diagram represent the multiplication of input complex number with constant $1/\sqrt{2}$.

4.3.3. Serial Processing.

Although serial design requires multiple iterations to perform a complex computation, it opens up the opportunity for resource sharing. Serial processing is suitable for applications where resource utilization is a critical design constraint. Figure 13(c) depicts the serial form of the 3-qubit QFT circuit that consists of a control unit and a datapath unit. As resources can be reused between transformations, a serial-based n-qubit QFT consumes 2^n registers, a register utilization that is much lower than in concurrent or pipeline architectures. However, pure serial approach forfeits the purpose of conducting FPGA emulation whose aim is to exploit the parallelism inherent in a quantum system, as it would still suffer from slow sequential behaviour as exhibited in simulation on classical computer.

4.3.4. Proposed Serial-Parallel Architecture.

In this paper, we propose a hybrid serial-parallel architecture for FPGA emulation of quantum algorithms. The proposed approach takes advantage of both serial and parallel design techniques.

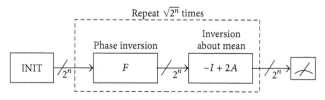

FIGURE 11: Mathematical modelling of Grover's search algorithm.

Applying the concepts of quantum parallelism and quantum dynamics modelled by sequential transformations on a quantum state vector, it is found that the proposed serial-parallel architecture is suitable for efficient and accurate quantum computing emulation on FPGA platform.

Figure 14 shows the functional block diagram of the proposed serial-parallel FPGA emulation architecture of the 3-qubit QFT. The serial-parallel design of the datapath unit involves a number of quantum computation units that can perform parallel computations for each stage of unitary transformation whereby the same computational resources can be reused for the following stage of transformations.

For data storage and synchronization purposes, 2^n registers are shared between unitary transformations. As compared to the pipeline design, our proposed serial-parallel approach achieves linear reduction on the usage of registers to emulate the same quantum system. The arithmetic logic unit (ALU) in the datapath unit contains multiple custom processing elements and the allocation of resources in ALU varies based on the target application. The number of processing elements is basically determined based on the desired 2^n parallelism in the n-qubit quantum system.

As illustrated in Figures 10 and 12, the data-flow graph of QFT and Grover's search algorithm exhibit similar repetitive pattern between unitary transformations. This implies that the proposed serial-parallel approach can be generalized for the two case studies to achieve balance in both resource utilization and speed performance. For the case of Grover's search, the ALU would be the Grover iteration module shown in Figure 12, whereas the control unit is designed to keep track on the number of Grover iterations required by the target search problem.

5. Experimental Results

The proposed emulation designs are modelled in SystemVerilog HDL, synthesized using Altera Quartus II software, and implemented into target emulation platform which is based on Altera Stratix IV EP4SGX530KF43C4 FPGA. In Section 5.1, we discuss the verification of the hardware emulation designs for the QFT and Grover's search case studies. In addition, the automated process for scaling up the design to larger qubit size is described. In Section 5.2, investigation is conducted to study the effects of the number of mantissa bits used in our fixed point representation format on resource utilization and precision error. In the section that follows, we analyse, for different emulation architectures, how the increase in qubit size impacts on resource growth and maximum operating frequency allowed in the designs.

Finally, the runtime speeds in simulation and emulation for quantum algorithms with different qubit sizes are compared.

5.1. Design Verification. To show that the quantum algorithms have been modelled accurately, design verification of the proposed emulation hardware is performed. Golden references based on the software simulation models (in C) are developed and their outputs are compared with the emulation hardware under test (which are described in SystemVerilog HDL).

In our QFT case study, FFTW3 [42], a widely applied fast Fourier transform library in C, is used to perform Fourier transform computations on the signal samples that are used in this work. The outputs of the classical Fourier transform then serve as the golden reference model in verification of the proposed emulation model. Furthermore, since the discrete Fourier transform (DFT) is a linear transformation that can be defined in unitary matrix form, the functional correctness of our QFT hardware emulation model can be conveniently verified against the DFT matrix. The expression of an n-qubit DFT matrix is shown in

$$\text{DFT} = \frac{1}{\sqrt{2^n}} \begin{bmatrix} 1 & 1 & 1 & \dots & 1 \\ 1 & \omega^1 & \omega^2 & \dots & \omega^{2^n-1} \\ 1 & \omega^2 & \omega^4 & \dots & \omega^{2(2^n-1)} \\ \vdots & \vdots & \vdots & \vdots & \vdots \\ 1 & \omega^{2^n-1} & \omega^{2(2^n-1)} & \dots & \omega^{(2^n-1)(2^n-1)} \end{bmatrix}, \quad (27)$$

where ω is the 2^nth root of unity; that is, $\omega = e^{2\pi i/2^n}$. The choice of $e^{2\pi i/2^n}$ or $e^{-2\pi i/2^n}$ is purely a matter of convention as both the term $e^{2\pi i/2^n}$ and the term $e^{-2\pi i/2^n}$ to the power of 2^n are equal to 1.

On the other hand, the design of Grover's search FPGA emulation model is verified against the mathematical model provided in literature. The simulation model of Grover's search algorithm also serves as the golden reference model for verification purposes.

For the development of FPGA emulation models for practical quantum computing applications, it is important that the emulation hardware can be scaled up to larger qubit size architectures. In this work, the designs are scaled up with the aid of software program developed in-house. HDL codes of the two case studies are autogenerated by the software program based on the proposed modelling techniques (as discussed in Section 4). The generated HDL code produces efficient hardware emulation model based on the proposed serial-parallel architecture.

5.2. Fixed Point Representation. As defined in (2), a quantum state vector is represented by complex floating point numbers. To ensure effective resource utilization in our FPGA emulation hardware, floating point numbers are replaced by fixed point representations. In this work, a fixed point format with 1 sign bit, 1 integer bit, and N mantissa bits (as shown in Figure 15) is used. Since the amplitudes of a quantum state, that is, the probabilities of collapsing into computational basis

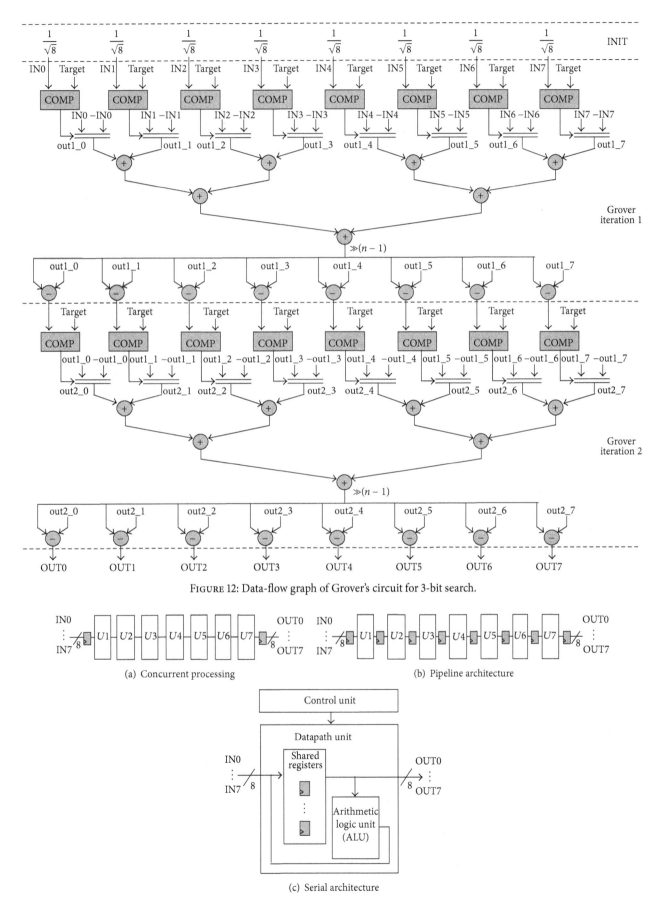

FIGURE 12: Data-flow graph of Grover's circuit for 3-bit search.

(a) Concurrent processing

(b) Pipeline architecture

(c) Serial architecture

FIGURE 13: Three-qubit QFT implemented using different hardware architectures.

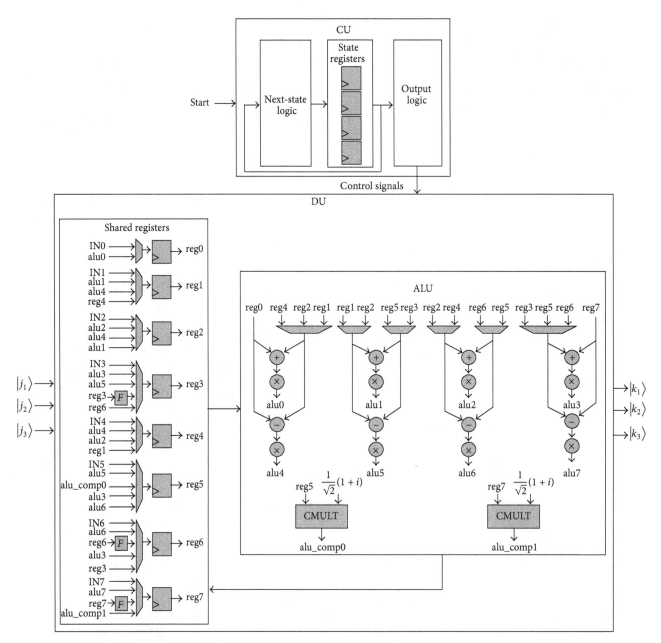

FIGURE 14: Proposed serial-parallel architecture for 3-qubit QFT. The multipliers shown in this diagram represent the multiplication of input complex number with constant $1/\sqrt{2}$.

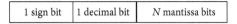

1 sign bit	1 decimal bit	N mantissa bits

FIGURE 15: Fixed point representation format.

states after measurement, are constrained in the range of 0 to 1, only one bit is required to represent the integer part.

Due to the limitations of the classical digital computing platform, representation of qubit amplitudes with infinite precision is infeasible. In the context of quantum computer modelling, particularly for quantum systems with large qubit sizes, minimising precision loss is critical to preserve the consistency of the quantum state during the modelling process [43]. Here, we investigate how precision error is affected by the number of mantissa bits used in our fixed point representation format. The corresponding experimental results are given in Figure 16.

Precision error shown in Figure 16 is computed based on the following equations:

$$\text{error\_}r = \sum_{m=0}^{2^n-1} \frac{\left|\text{emulate\_}r_m - \text{simulate\_}r_m\right|}{\left|\text{simulate\_}r_m\right|},$$

$$\text{error\_}i = \sum_{m=0}^{2^n-1} \frac{\left|\text{emulate\_}i_m - \text{simulate\_}i_m\right|}{\left|\text{simulate\_}i_m\right|}, \quad (28)$$

$$\text{precision\_error} = \frac{1}{2^{n+1}}\left(\text{error\_}r + \text{error\_}i\right),$$

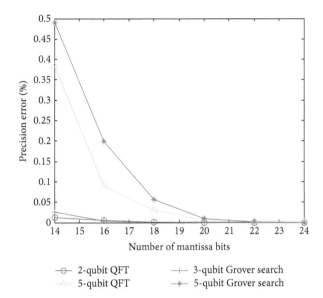

FIGURE 16: Precision error against different fixed point formats used.

where simulate_r and simulate_i are the floating point real and imaginary amplitudes of the reference output state generated from simulation, whereas emulate_r and emulate_i are the amplitudes extracted from the output state of proposed FPGA emulator (converted from original fixed point format to floating point for verification purposes).

Figure 16 shows that 16-bit fixed point format (14 mantissa bits) incurs significant precision error for 5-qubit emulations in both case studies. However, the error produced by 2-qubit emulations is insignificant. This behaviour is because the amplification of the fixed point truncation errors grows with the size of quantum system. For FPGA emulation purposes, precision error due to fixed point representation can be reduced by increasing the number of mantissa bits with trade-off on resource utilization. By expanding the number of mantissa bits up to 24-bit (which results in 26, total number of bits), negligible precision error for 5-qubit emulations is attained. It is important to note that the proposed FPGA emulator is parameterizable in terms of the number of mantissa bits for fixed point representation. This is crucial to ensure different fixed point formats can be applied to emulate quantum circuit of various sizes based on the demanded precision error tolerance and resource constraint.

The size of our fixed point number format also affects resource utilization. The corresponding experimental results for QFT case study are shown in Figure 17. Since the resources available on FPGA device are mostly in blocks or multiples of 8 bits, the choice of 26-bit fixed point format is not suitable. Hence, we apply 22-mantissa-bit size (i.e., total number of bits is 24) in our fixed point representation formats. Note that, for Grover's search emulations, the experiment on resource utilization of DSP blocks is not relevant because FPGA emulation model developed here (as depicted in Figure 12) does not involve multiplication.

5.3. *Efficiency of Proposed FPGA Emulation Architecture.* In this subsection, we investigate how the increase in qubit size

impacts resource growth and maximum allowable operating frequency in different emulation architectures (i.e., concurrent, pipeline, and serial-parallel). In the case of QFT emulation model, we have two versions of serial-parallel architectures. Type 1 serial-parallel uses DSP blocks to perform multiplications, whereas type 2 replaces the multiplications (required in Hadamard gate operations, $U1$, $U4$, and $U6$, in the 3-qubit QFT case) with shift-add operations. Although conventional hardware design methods encourage the usage of shift-add operation instead of multiplication to reduce resource utilization, the case is now different with FPGA devices containing efficient built-in DSP blocks. Figures 18 and 19 show the results of the experiments conducted on QFT and Grover's search algorithms, respectively.

Based on the experimental results shown in Figure 18, when comparing to type 1, type 2 method consumes less DSP blocks but more logic elements due to the construction of adders needed in shift-add operations. As the number of qubits increases, resource utilization of logic elements for type 1 emulation grows rapidly when available DSP blocks are used up and it ends up with similar resource utilization as the type 2 approach. Hence, we can conclude that, for large-scale FPGA emulations, both methods would lead to similar resource utilization. Thus, the first approach is preferred due to the ease of design process where DSP blocks are utilized by default when implementing the design with the FPGA design automation tool.

In contrast to the concurrent and pipeline designs, the experimental results for QFT and Grover's search show that the proposed serial-parallel architecture achieves balance on both resource utilization and operating frequency. The proposed architecture has significantly reduced resource growth in the application of logic elements, dedicated logic registers, and DSP block, yet maintaining reasonable operating frequency. With the concurrent and pipeline architectures, 5-qubit QFT emulation completely used up the resources available in the Altera Stratix IV FPGA device used in this work. However, the same device can support up to 7-qubit QFT emulation with the proposed serial-parallel architecture. It is important to note that the processing power of 7-qubit QFT is far higher than the 5-qubit implementation as an n-qubit QFT can process up to 2^n samples in one evaluation.

For scalability, software simulation would depend on resources available on the computer servers. The scalability of the FPGA emulation framework would depend on the resources available on target FPGA devices. As there have been rapid advances in FPGA technology in recent years, by designing an efficient architecture that is implemented in a high-density FPGA device (such as the Altera Stratix 10 that contains up to 5.5 million logic elements), one can actually emulate large qubit size quantum circuit on a single FPGA chip. Furthermore, new approach to FPGA emulation may be made through the exploration of efficient data structures and modelling methods. Thus, the proposed work contributes to the formulation of a proof-of-concept baseline FPGA emulation framework with optimization on datapath designs that can be extended to emulate practical large-scale quantum circuits.

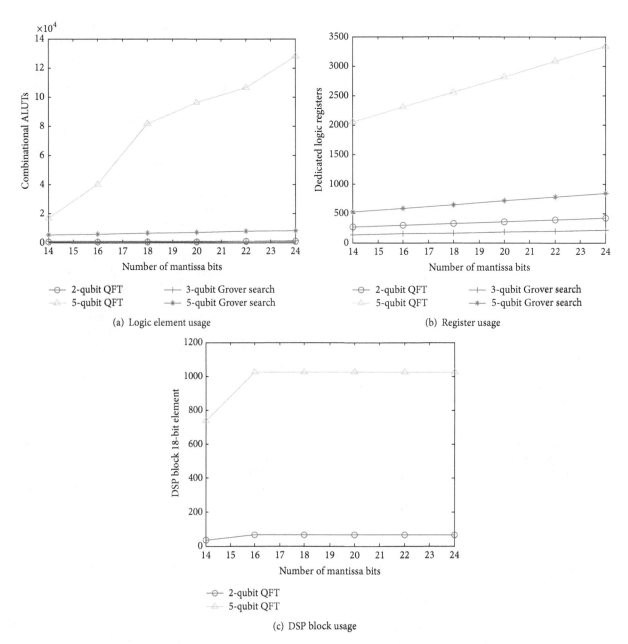

(a) Logic element usage

(b) Register usage

(c) DSP block usage

FIGURE 17: Resource utilization for different fixed point formats used.

5.4. Benchmarking between Simulation and Emulation. Here, our emulation models are benchmarked against the equivalent software simulations. The simulation models used are based on an open source quantum library, *libquantum* [28]. Software simulation is performed on an Intel Core i7-4790 eight-core processor with 3.6 GHz clock rate running on a Linux-based Ubuntu 14.04 kernel, whereas hardware emulation is based on the Altera Stratix IV EP4SGX530KF43C4 FPGA. Table 1 shows the runtime comparison between simulation and our emulation.

Figure 20 illustrates the runtime speed-up (simulation/emulation) of Grover's search case study. It is important to note that the proposed hardware emulation is implemented based on 24-bit fixed point format (which is determined

TABLE 1: Comparison of runtime between simulation and emulation.

	QFT runtime (s)		Grover's search runtime (s)	
	Simulation	Emulation	Simulation	Emulation
2-qubit	15.5×10^{-6}	35.8×10^{-9}	29.6×10^{-6}	4.6×10^{-9}
3-qubit	46.6×10^{-6}	80.5×10^{-9}	74.0×10^{-6}	12.0×10^{-9}
4-qubit	51.0×10^{-6}	134.4×10^{-9}	220.7×10^{-6}	21.4×10^{-9}
5-qubit	56.5×10^{-6}	219.3×10^{-9}	398.8×10^{-6}	36.7×10^{-9}
6-qubit	—	—	1069.6×10^{-6}	62.7×10^{-9}
7-qubit	—	—	2771.4×10^{-6}	96.8×10^{-9}

based on the experimental work presented in Section 5.2) whereas 32-bit single precision float is used in the software

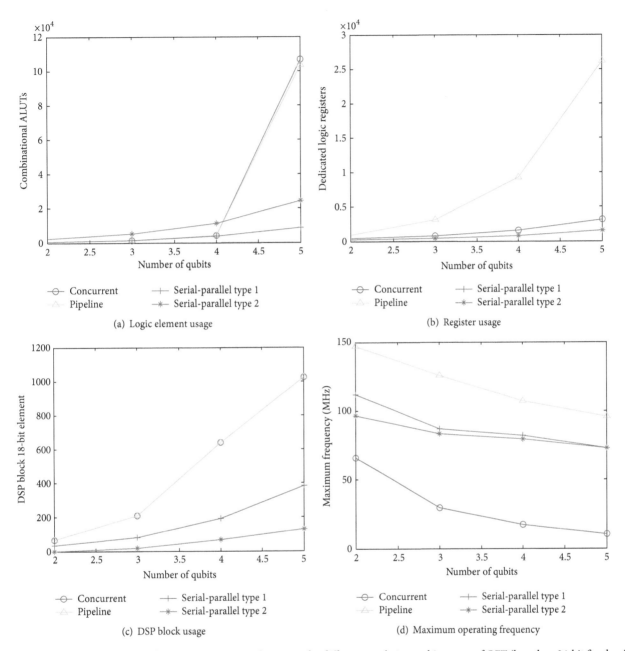

FIGURE 18: Resource utilization and maximum operating frequency for different emulation architectures of QFT (based on 24-bit fixed point format).

simulation to describe the quantum state. For a larger qubit size quantum circuit, the number of mantissa bits for fixed point representation has to be increased accordingly to ensure similar precision as in software simulation can be achieved with trade-offs on resource utilization and execution speed [44].

From Figure 20, it can be observed that the proposed hardware emulation provides significant speed-up over software simulation using *libquantum*. It is important to note that the achieved speed-up increases drastically as the number of qubits increases. This result further supports the notion that hardware emulation has significant potential in the modelling of a large-scale quantum system on the classical computing platform based on FPGA.

As the number of required I/O pins for emulating QFT and Grover's search algorithms with parallel read-outs is too much to fit in the existing FPGA devices, board-level verification is infeasible. Although the usage of multiplexers reduces the number of output pins, resource consumption rises significantly with the increase in the number of qubits, and this affects the analysis of the overall experiment. Thus, the estimated runtime of the proposed FPGA emulation architecture is obtained based on the hardware clock cycle and the operating frequency that is acquired from the FPGA development tool. This is not a critical issue in future practical deployment as the selected case studies are meant to work as core modules within other quantum applications that might not require parallel read-out.

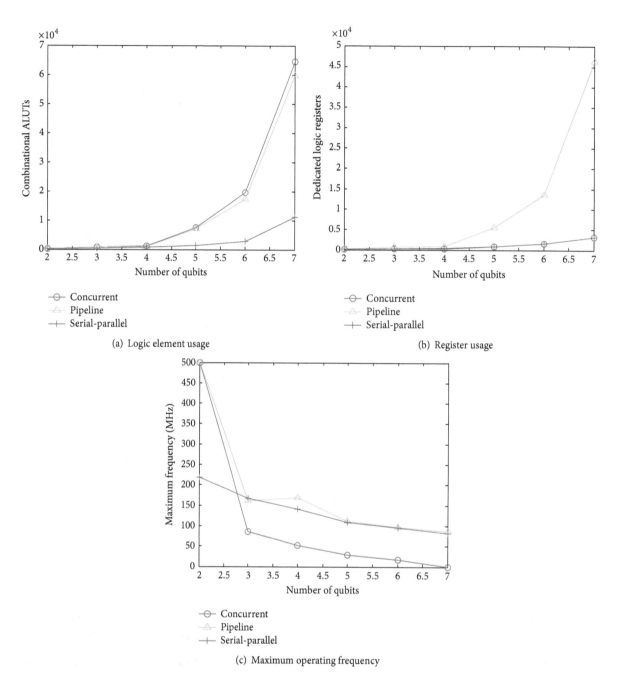

(a) Logic element usage

(b) Register usage

(c) Maximum operating frequency

FIGURE 19: Resource utilization and maximum operating frequency for different emulation architectures of Grover's search (based on 24-bit fixed point format).

6. Conclusion and Future Work

Efficient resource utilization is critical for FPGA-based implementations especially for emulating quantum computing applications as they typically exhibit exponential resource requirement with increasing number of qubits. In this paper, we proposed a baseline FPGA emulation framework with focus on the datapath design optimization based on the conventional state vector model as well as an effective methodology that facilitates accurate modelling of quantum algorithms for FPGA emulation. A serial-parallel architecture

with efficient resource utilization for FPGA-based emulation of quantum computing is presented. The proposed emulation architecture achieves linear reduction in resource utilization compared to pipeline implementations as found in previous works. This work has also demonstrated the advantage of FPGA emulation over software simulation where hardware emulation of 7-qubit Grover's search is about 3×10^4 times faster than the software simulation performed on Intel Core i7-4790 eight-core processor running at 3.6 GHz clock rate.

However, experimental results obtained in this work show that it is difficult to realize a scalable and flexible

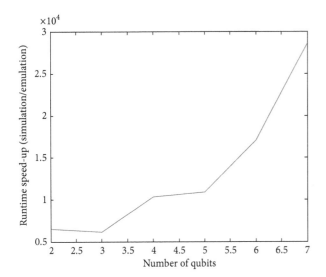

FIGURE 20: Runtime speed-up against number of qubits in Grover's search emulation.

emulation platform for large qubit size real-world quantum system using the approach that applies existing state vector quantum models. This concurs with [45] that states that the practical limit on the size of the quantum system that can be modelled on classical computing platform can hardly be overcome due to exponentially large memory requirements for storing the entire state vector. Hence, this suggests that a model with a more effective data structure to represent quantum systems is required. Recently, the work on stabilizer frames [30] has shown promise in providing a more suitable data structure for quantum models targeted for FPGA emulation. This is the subject of future work in our research in applying FPGA emulation in modelling of large-scale quantum systems. In addition, the error-correction structure available with stabilizer frames will be considered for application in practical quantum computations. With a more efficient modelling technique, FPGA can represent a more efficient emulation strategy of quantum systems.

Competing Interests

The authors declare that they have no competing interests.

Acknowledgments

This work is supported by the Ministry of Higher Education (MOHE) and Universiti Teknologi Malaysia (UTM) under Fundamental Research Grant Scheme (FRGS) Vote number 4F422.

References

[1] P. W. Shor, "Algorithms for quantum computation: discrete logarithms and factoring," in *Proceedings of the 35th IEEE Annual Symposium on Foundations of Computer Science (SFCS '94)*, pp. 124–134, Santa Fe, NM, USA, November 1994.

[2] L. K. Grover, "Quantum mechanics helps in searching for a needle in a haystack," *Physical Review Letters*, vol. 79, no. 2, pp. 325–328, 1997.

[3] A. Malossini and T. Calarco, "Quantum genetic optimization," *IEEE Transactions on Evolutionary Computation*, vol. 12, no. 2, pp. 231–241, 2008.

[4] R. L. Rivest, A. Shamir, and L. Adleman, "A method for obtaining digital signatures and public-key cryptosystems," *Communications of the ACM*, vol. 21, no. 2, pp. 120–126, 1978.

[5] L. K. Grover, "A fast quantum mechanical algorithm for database search," in *Proceedings of the 28th Annual ACM Symposium on Theory of Computing*, pp. 212–219, ACM, 1996.

[6] N. Shenvi, J. Kempe, and K. B. Whaley, "Quantum random-walk search algorithm," *Physical Review A: Atomic, Molecular, and Optical Physics*, vol. 67, no. 5, Article ID 052307, 2003.

[7] E. Farhi, J. Goldstone, and S. Gutmann, "A quantum algorithm for the Hamiltonian NAND tree," *Theory of Computing*, vol. 4, pp. 169–190, 2008.

[8] P. W. Shor, "Why haven't more quantum algorithms been found?" *Journal of the ACM*, vol. 50, no. 1, pp. 87–90, 2003.

[9] D. R. Simon, "On the power of quantum computation," *SIAM Journal on Computing*, vol. 26, no. 5, pp. 1474–1483, 1997.

[10] S. Hallgren, "Polynomial-time quantum algorithms for Pell's equation and the principal ideal problem," *Journal of the ACM*, vol. 54, article 4, 2007.

[11] M. Mosca and A. Ekert, "The hidden subgroup problem and eigenvalue estimation on a quantum computer," in *Quantum Computing and Quantum Communications*, pp. 174–188, Springer, Berlin, Germany, 1999.

[12] D. Bacon, A. M. Childs, and W. Van Dam, "From optimal measurement to efficient quantum algorithms for the hidden subgroup problem over semidirect product groups," in *Proceedings of the 46th Annual IEEE Symposium on Foundations of Computer Science (FOCS '05)*, pp. 469–478, IEEE, October 2005.

[13] L. K. Grover and A. M. Sengupta, "From coupled pendulums to quantum search," in *Mathematics of Quantum Computation*, pp. 119–134, Chapman and Hall/CRC, 2002.

[14] R. P. Feynman, "Simulating physics with computers," *International Journal of Theoretical Physics*, vol. 21, no. 6-7, pp. 467–488, 1982.

[15] N. S. Yanofsky and M. A. Mannucci, *Quantum Computing for Computer Scientists*, vol. 20, Cambridge University Press, Cambridge, UK, 2008.

[16] C. Monroe, D. M. Meekhof, B. E. King, W. M. Itano, and D. J. Wineland, "Demonstration of a fundamental quantum logic gate," *Physical Review Letters*, vol. 75, no. 25, pp. 4714–4717, 1995.

[17] N. A. Gershenfeld and I. L. Chuang, "Bulk spin-resonance quantum computation," *Science*, vol. 275, no. 5298, pp. 350–356, 1997.

[18] J. E. Mooij, T. P. Orlando, L. Levitov, L. Tian, C. H. Van der Wal, and S. Lloyd, "Josephson persistent-current qubit," *Science*, vol. 285, no. 5430, pp. 1036–1039, 1999.

[19] I. L. Chuang, N. Gershenfeld, and M. Kubinec, "Experimental implementation of fast quantum searching," *Physical Review Letters*, vol. 80, no. 15, article 3408, 1998.

[20] R. Barends, J. Kelly, A. Megrant et al., "Superconducting quantum circuits at the surface code threshold for fault tolerance," *Nature*, vol. 508, no. 7497, pp. 500–503, 2014.

[21] M. H. Amin, N. G. Dickson, and P. Smith, "Adiabatic quantum optimization with qudits," *Quantum Information Processing*, vol. 12, no. 4, pp. 1819–1829, 2013.

[22] A. D. King, E. Hoskinson, T. Lanting, E. Andriyash, and M. H. Amin, "Degeneracy, degree, and heavy tails in quantumannealing," http://arxiv.org/abs/1512.07325.

[23] T. F. Rønnow, Z. Wang, J. Job et al., "Defining and detecting quantum speedup," *Science*, vol. 345, no. 6195, pp. 420–424, 2014.

[24] Y. Goto and M. Fujishima, "Efficient quantum computing emulation system with unitary macro-operations," *Japanese Journal of Applied Physics*, vol. 46, no. 4, pp. 2278–2282, 2007.

[25] A. U. Khalid, Z. Zilic, and K. Radecka, "FPGA emulation of quantum circuits," in *Proceedings of the IEEE International Conference on Computer Design: VLSI in Computers and Processors (ICCD '04)*, pp. 310–315, IEEE, October 2004.

[26] J. F. Rivera-Miranda, Á. J. Caicedo-Beltrán, J. D. Valencia-Payán, J. M. Espinosa-Duran, and J. Velasco-Medina, "Hardware emulation of quantum Fourier transform," in *Proceedings of the IEEE 2nd Latin American Symposium on Circuits and Systems (LASCAS '11)*, pp. 1–4, IEEE, Bogata, Colombia, February 2011.

[27] M. Aminian, M. Saeedi, M. S. Zamani, and M. Sedighi, "FPGA-based circuit model emulation of quantum algorithms," in *Proceedings of the IEEE Computer Society Annual Symposium on VLSI (ISVLSI '08)*, pp. 399–404, IEEE, Montpellier, France, April 2008.

[28] H. Weimer, M. Müller, I. Lesanovsky, P. Zoller, and H. P. Büchler, "A Rydberg quantum simulator," *Nature Physics*, vol. 6, no. 5, pp. 382–388, 2010.

[29] G. F. Viamontes, *Efficient quantum circuit simulation [Ph.D. thesis]*, The University of Michigan, Ann Arbor, Mich, USA, 2007.

[30] H. J. García and I. L. Markov, "Simulation of quantum circuits via stabilizer frames," *IEEE Transactions on Computers*, vol. 64, no. 8, pp. 2323–2336, 2015.

[31] C. P. Williams and S. H. Clearwater, *Explorations in Quantum Computing*, Springer, Berlin, Germany, 1998.

[32] A. Barenco, D. Deutsch, A. Ekert, and R. Jozsa, "Conditional quantum dynamics and logic gates," *Physical Review Letters*, vol. 74, no. 20, pp. 4083–4086, 1995.

[33] M. A. Nielsen and I. L. Chuang, *Quantum Computation and Quantum Information*, Cambridge University Press, 2000.

[34] W.-W. Zhang, F. Gao, B. Liu, Q.-Y. Wen, and H. Chen, "A watermark strategy for quantum images based on quantum Fourier transform," *Quantum Information Processing*, vol. 12, no. 2, pp. 793–803, 2013.

[35] D. Curtis and D. A. Meyer, "Towards quantum template matching," in *Proceedings of the SPIE 48th Annual Meeting in Quantum Communications and Quantum Imaging*, pp. 134–141, International Society for Optics and Photonics, August 2003.

[36] R. Schützhold and G. Schaller, "Adiabatic quantum algorithms as quantum phase transitions: first versus second order," *Physical Review A*, vol. 74, no. 6, Article ID 060304, 2006.

[37] W. P. Baritompa, D. W. Bulger, and G. R. Wood, "Grover's quantum algorithm applied to global optimization," *SIAM Journal on Optimization*, vol. 15, no. 4, pp. 1170–1184, 2005.

[38] C. Durr and P. Hoyer, "A quantum algorithm for finding the minimum," http://arxiv.org/abs/quant-ph/9607014.

[39] A. Montanaro, "Quantum pattern matching fast on average," *Algorithmica*, 2015.

[40] Y. H. Lee, M. Khalil-Hani, and M. N. Marsono, "FPGA-based quantum circuit emulation: a case study on Quantum Fourier transform," in *Proceedings of the 14th International Symposium on Integrated Circuits (ISIC '14)*, pp. 512–515, IEEE, Singapore, December 2014.

[41] M. Khalil-Hani, Y. H. Lee, and M. N. Marsono, "An accurate FPGA-based hardware emulation on quantum fourier transform," in *Proceedings of the Australasian Symposium on Parallel and Distributed Computing (AusPDC '15)*, vol. 1, Sydney, Australia, 2015, a1b3.

[42] M. Frigo and S. G. Johnson, "The design and implementation of FFTW3," *Proceedings of the IEEE*, vol. 93, no. 2, pp. 216–231, 2005.

[43] D. Wecker and K. M. Svore, "LIQUi|>: a software design architecture and domain-specific language for quantum computing," http://arxiv.org/abs/1402.4467.

[44] S. Kilts, *Advanced FPGA Design: Architecture, Implementation, and Optimization*, John Wiley & Sons, New York, NY, USA, 2007.

[45] M. Smelyanskiy, N. P. D. Sawaya, and A. Aspuru-Guzik, "qHiPSTER: the quantum high performance software testing environment," http://arxiv.org/abs/1601.07195.

6

FPGA based High Speed SPA Resistant Elliptic Curve Scalar Multiplier Architecture

Khalid Javeed[1,2] and Xiaojun Wang[2,3]

[1]*Electrical Engineering Department, COMSATS Institute of Information Technology, Abbottabad, Pakistan*
[2]*School of Electronic Engineering, Dublin City University, Dublin, Ireland*
[3]*School of Computer & Software, Nanjing University of Information Science and Technology, Nanjing, Jiangsu, China*

Correspondence should be addressed to Khalid Javeed; khalidjaveed@ciit.net.pk

Academic Editor: Michael Hübner

The higher computational complexity of an elliptic curve scalar point multiplication operation limits its implementation on general purpose processors. Dedicated hardware architectures are essential to reduce the computational time, which results in a substantial increase in the performance of associated cryptographic protocols. This paper presents a unified architecture to compute modular addition, subtraction, and multiplication operations over a finite field of large prime characteristic GF(p). Subsequently, dual instances of the unified architecture are utilized in the design of high speed elliptic curve scalar multiplier architecture. The proposed architecture is synthesized and implemented on several different Xilinx FPGA platforms for different field sizes. The proposed design computes a 192-bit elliptic curve scalar multiplication in 2.3 ms on Virtex-4 FPGA platform. It is 34% faster and requires 40% fewer clock cycles for elliptic curve scalar multiplication and consumes considerable fewer FPGA slices as compared to the other existing designs. The proposed design is also resistant to the timing and simple power analysis (SPA) attacks; therefore it is a good choice in the construction of fast and secure elliptic curve based cryptographic protocols.

1. Introduction

Elliptic curve based cryptography (ECC) proposed independently by Miller [1] and Koblitz [2] has established itself as a proper alternative to the traditional systems such as Ron Rivest, Adi Shamir, and Leonard Adleman (RSA) [3]. The National Institute of Standards and Technology (NIST) recommended 256 bits of key lengths for ECC to achieve the same level of security as 3072 bits of RSA.

Due to the fact that ECC offers similar security with considerable smaller key sizes than RSA, it has been standardized by IEEE and NIST [4]. Thus, as the result of smaller key sizes, its implementation led to substantial reduction in power consumption and storage requirements and offers potentially higher data rates. These inherent properties rank it as a strong candidate for providing security in resource-constrained devices. Unfortunately, due to the underlying complex mathematical structure, its implementation on general-purpose

processors (GPP) struggles to meet the speed requirements of many real-time applications.

Thus, several new implementation platforms have been explored during the last years. Field programmable gate array (FPGA) has been established as a proper platform for implementation of security algorithms such as ECC and RSA. Its shorter design cycle time, lower design cost, and its reconfigurability make it more attractive than other platforms, such as Application Specific Integrated Circuits (ASICs).

Elliptic curve scalar point multiplication is the central and most time consuming operation in all ECC based schemes. Its efficient implementation on various platforms is very critical. It is achieved by manipulating points on a properly chosen elliptic curve over a finite field. Mathematically, it is expressed as $Q = sP$, where P is a base point, s is an integer value, and Q is the resultant point of multiplication of s and P. For example, it can be achieved by adding P to itself $(s - 1)$ times. The strength of any ECC schemes is based on the computational hardness of finding s given P and Q known as Elliptic Curve Discrete Logarithm Problem (ECDLP).

There are several elliptic curve representations satisfying different performance and security requirements. A flexible design capable of supporting different values for elliptic curve parameters and a prime p is more demanding. The ECDLP is not the only way of finding scalar s; it can also be revealed by monitoring the timing [5] and power consumption of cryptographic devices known as side channel attacks (SCAs) [6]. The simplest SCAs are based on the timing and simple power consumption analysis (SPA). Detailed surveys on known SCAs, countermeasures, and secure ECC implementations are reported previously in [7, 8].

Elliptic curve scalar point multiplication involves many basic modular arithmetic operations such as addition, subtraction, multiplication, inversion, and division. Hence, optimization of these operations can significantly improve the performance of ECC schemes.

Elliptic curve cryptosystems can be designed on a finite field either with prime characteristics $GF(p)$ or with binary characteristics $GF(2^m)$. The $GF(2^m)$ arithmetic is easier to implement in hardware than $GF(p)$ because of carry-free arithmetic. However, field parameters in $GF(2^m)$ are mostly fixed and are not very flexible. Some efficient ECC implementations over $GF(2^m)$ are presented in [9–14]. A very good survey of high speed hardware implementations of ECC has been reported in [15].

Several hardware based elliptic curve processors over $GF(p)$ have also been proposed in the literature [5, 16–26]. The design reported in [21] proposed two architectures to speed up the EC point multiplication operation. Both these architectures are based on incorporating parallel dedicated hardware units to compute arithmetic operations such as addition, subtraction, multiplication, and division over $GF(p)$. The $GF(p)$ multiplication unit [21] is based on a bit-serial interleaved multiplication while, for a division over $GF(p)$, a dedicated hardware unit based on a binary version of the extended Euclidean algorithm is used. Ghosh et al. proposed a speed and area optimized architecture for EC point multiplication by exploiting a concept of shared hardware arithmetic over $GF(p)$ [20]. The saving in area is achieved by sharing hardware resources among different $GF(p)$ arithmetic operations, while multiple copies of the arithmetic units are used to speed up EC point multiplication.

1.1. Contribution. Modern FPGAs have dedicated built-in arithmetic components (dedicated multipliers, block RAMs, etc.) to perform different signal processing tasks efficiently. However, in this work these components are not used due to the limitations of the adopted technique to perform a modular multiplication, that is, Interleaved Multiplication (IM) algorithm [27], which interleaved the reduction step by reducing each partial product. To the best of authors knowledge, no work has been reported targeting a digit-wise implementation of the IM technique. However, available small-sized dedicated multipliers inside an FPGA can be very effective in case of the Montgomery multiplication [28] and the NIST recommended primes [29]. A modular

multiplication using these methods can be performed by integers multiplication followed by a modular reduction.

This paper presents a novel architecture to speed up the EC point multiplication in affine coordinates. The proposed design is based on a unified $GF(p)$ adder, subtractor, and multiplier (Add/Sub/Mul) unit. The unified Add/Sub/Mul unit is an extension of our previous $GF(p)$ multiplier design reported in [30]. The proposed unified unit in this work performs modular addition and subtraction in a single clock cycle, while modular multiplication is performed in $\lceil K/3 \rceil + 2$ clock cycles, where $K = \log_2 p$. The careful FPGA implementation of the proposed EC point multiplication architecture outperforms the other existing designs. The main advantages of the proposed design are as follows.

(i) It reduces the number of required clock cycles and computation time of EC point multiplication to almost 40% and 35%, respectively, with considerably smaller FPGA area consumption. The reduction in clock cycles and computation time is mainly due to the proposed $GF(p)$ multiplier [30].

(ii) Furthermore, the adopted algorithm for EC point multiplication with careful implementation of $GF(p)$ arithmetic primitives is capable of resisting the timing and SPA attacks [5].

(iii) It is flexible; all parameters (curve parameter a, EC point P, scalar value s, and the prime value p) can be easily changed without FPGA reconfiguration.

This paper is organized as follows. Section 2 briefly explains EC group operations such as EC point addition and EC point doubling. In addition, this section also describes the Montgomery ladder structure for the EC point multiplication algorithm. The unified Add/Sub/Mul unit over $GF(p)$ is presented in Section 3. Section 4 proposes a novel architecture for EC point multiplication based on the $GF(p)$ unified Add/Sub/Mul unit. Implementation results and performance evaluation are presented in Section 5, and finally the paper is concluded in Section 6.

2. Elliptic Curve Group Operations

In this paper, we consider an elliptic curve $\mathbb{E}$, defined over a prime field $GF(p)$, where p is a large prime characteristic number. Field elements are represented as integers in the range $[0, p - 1]$. An elliptic curve $\mathbb{E}$ over $GF(p)$ in short Weierstrass form is represented as

$$\mathbb{E} : y^2 = x^3 + ax + b, \tag{1}$$

where, a, b, x, and $y \in GF(p)$ and $4a^3 + 27b^2 \neq 0$ (modulo p). The set of all points (x, y) that satisfies (1), plus the point at infinity, makes an abelian group. EC point addition and EC point doubling operations over such groups are used to construct many elliptic curve cryptosystems. The EC point addition and EC point doubling operations in affine coordinates can be represented as follows: let $P_1 = (x_1, y_1)$ and $P_2 = (x_2, y_2)$ be two points on the elliptic curve. The group

---

Input: An integer s and a point P on elliptic curve
Output: sP
(1) $S_1 \leftarrow P$
(2) $S_2 \leftarrow 2P$
(3) **for** $i = K - 2$ ***downto*** 0 **do** // K is the bit length of s //
(4)   **if** $s_i = 1$ **then**
(5) $S_1 \leftarrow S_1 + S_2$ ‖ EC Point addition
(6) $S_2 \leftarrow 2S_2$ ‖ EC Point doubling
(7)   **else**
(8) $S_2 \leftarrow S_1 + S_2$
(9) $S_1 \leftarrow 2S_1$
(10) **return** S_1

ALGORITHM 1: Montgomery ladder for EC point multiplication [20].

operation is the point addition, $P_3(x_3, y_3) = P_1(x_1, y_1) + P_2(x_2, y_2)$, which is defined by the group law and is given as

$$x_3 = \lambda^2 - x_1 - x_2$$
$$y_3 = \lambda(x_1 - x_3) - y_1, \tag{2}$$

where

$$\lambda = \begin{cases} \dfrac{y_2 - y_1}{x_2 - x_1} & \text{if } P_1 \neq P_2 \\[2ex] \dfrac{3x_1^2 + a}{2y_1} & \text{if } P_1 = P_2. \end{cases} \tag{3}$$

If $P_1 = P_2$, then a special case of adding a point to itself is called EC point doubling operation. In affine coordinates the EC point addition requires one division, two multiplications, and six addition or subtraction operations, whereas the EC point doubling can be performed by using one division, three multiplications, and seven addition or subtraction operations. Therefore, optimization of these operations impacts significantly on the overall performance of the EC point multiplication operation.

2.1. Elliptic Curve Scalar Multiplication. EC cryptosystems are mostly based on the EC point multiplication operation. This operation can be performed as a sequence of EC point addition and EC point doubling operations given in Algorithm 1, which is known as the Montgomery ladder for EC point multiplication. Algorithm 1 works on the binary representation of s and it is assumed that the most significant bit is equal to 1. The EC point addition and EC point doubling operations are not dependant on the bit pattern of s, so these operations can be performed in parallel. As these can be executed concurrently, therefore Algorithm 1 gives an extra feature of protection against the timing and simple power analysis (SPA) attacks.

3. Unified Add/Sub/Mul Unit

In this section we present a unified modular adder, subtractor, and multiplier (unified Add/Sub/Mul) unit. This unit is capable of performing modular addition, subtraction, and multiplication operations and supports any prime p; therefore it

is able to provide hardware support for ECC over a variety of elliptic curves. Normally, to achieve a better performance of EC point multiplication on dedicated hardware, multiple copies of GF(p) adder, subtractor, multiplier, and divider units are integrated. These multiple copies can help to execute several operations in parallel at the expense of area and cost, which can also result in more power consumption. Our objective is to accelerate the computation of EC point multiplication operation with minimum number of dedicated arithmetic units. Modular multiplication is a critical component in the architecture of EC point multiplication operation. In this regard, several modular multipliers have been proposed. The design reported in [19] is based on an iterative addition and reduction algorithm. In every iteration addition and reduction modulo p of partial products are performed. It computes a K-bit modular multiplication in $K + 1$ clock cycles. Two novel architectures based on radix-4 and radix-8 Booth encoding techniques are reported in [30, 31].

In [30] the radix-4 Booth encoded version computes a modular multiplication operation in $K/2 + 1$ clock cycles, whereas the radix-8 Booth encoded multiplier takes $\lceil K/3 \rceil + 2$ clock cycles. The radix-8 Booth encoded multiplier given in Algorithm 2 is based on an iterative addition and reduction modulo p of partial products technique proposed by Blakley reported in [27]. The two main components in the design are as follows:

(i) Three-bit left shift modulo p unit (Step (3)).

(ii) Addition and subtraction modulo p unit (Steps (7), (9), (11), and (13)).

There is also a logic circuit for Booth encoding in addition to these two core components. The presented unified Add/Sub/Mul unit is based on the same design. The radix-8 Booth encoded modular multiplier design has a modular adder/subtractor unit. Hence this paper modified the radix-8 Booth encoded modular multiplier design in such a way that it becomes capable of performing modular addition and subtraction operations in addition to its main task, that is, a modular multiplication operation. Due to the proposed modification dedicated hardware units for modular addition and subtraction operations are not needed.

The top-level block of unified Add/Sub/Mul unit is shown in Figure 1. The whole logic components of the radix-8 Booth encoded modular multiplier are mainly divided into shared and unshared logic parts. The shared logic components can be shared to perform modular addition, subtraction, and multiplication operations, whereas the unshared logic components are only dedicated to a modular multiplication operation. A control unit is responsible for decoding instructions on the basis of two bits of operational code (opcode) and generates appropriate signals for the shared and unshared logic parts.

The shared logic is comprised of a modular adder/subtractor unit while the unshared logic consists of three-bit left shift modulo p unit and Booth encoding logic. The adder/subtractor and three-bit left shift modulo p units are shown in Figure 2. The three-bit left shift modulo p unit is comprised of three identical D1 units cascaded in series. Each

---

Input: $p, a, b : 0 \le a, b < p$
Output: $z = a \times b \bmod p$
(1) $z = 0$, $R_1 = 2a \bmod p$, $R_2 = 3a \bmod p$, $R_3 = 4a \bmod p$.
(2)   **for** $i = K$ *downto* 0; $i = i - 3$ **do** // K is the bit length of p //
(3) $z := 8z \bmod p$
(4)   **if** $(b_{(i,i-1,i-2,i-3)}) = (\{0000\} \mid \{1111\})$ **then**
(5) $z := z$
(6)   **else if** $(b_{(i,i-1,i-2,i-3)}) = (\{0001\} \mid \{0010\}\{1101\} \mid \{1110\})$ **then**
(7) $z := z \pm a$
(8)   **else if** $(b_{(i,i-1,i-2,i-3)}) = (\{0011\} \mid \{0100\}\{1011\} \mid \{1100\})$ **then**
(9) $z := z \pm R_1$
(10)   **else if** $(b_{(i,i-1,i-2,i-3)}) = (\{0101\} \mid \{0110\}\{1001\} \mid \{1010\})$ **then**
(11) $z := z \pm R_2$
(12)   **else**
(13) $z := z \pm R_3$
(14) **return** z

ALGORITHM 2: Radix-8 BE IM algorithm [30].

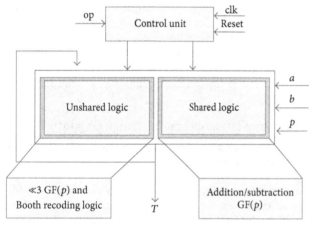

FIGURE 1: Unified Add/Sub/Mul unit.

TABLE 1: Operation codes for unified Add/Sub/Mul unit.

Logic operation	Opcode	Shared logic	Unshared logic
GF(p) addition	00	$(a+b) \bmod p$	—
GF(p) subtraction	01	$(a-b) \bmod p$	—
GF(p) multiplication	10	$(d1 \pm d2) \bmod p$	$8d \bmod p$

decodes the opcode and activates the shared logic block; that is, the adder/subtractor unit and sets $c_{in} = 0$. The adder/subtractor unit consists of two K-bit adders and logic for input output multiplexing shown in Figure 2. The first K-bit adder performs addition of operands $(a + b)$ and the result is fed into the second K-bit adder where a modulus p is subtracted from it. Similarly, a GF(p) subtraction is performed by the same unit by setting opcode = 01; the first K-bit adder performs subtraction $(a - b)$ followed by the addition of a modulus p. The result of modular addition and subtraction becomes available at port T after a single clock cycle. In the case of GF(p) multiplication indicated by opcode = 10, the control unit generates appropriate signals for the shared and unshared logic components. Partial products addition or subtraction $(d1 \pm d2 \bmod p)$ is computed by the shared logic components depending on cin signal generated by the Booth recoding logic, while three-bit left shift modulo p $(8d \bmod p)$ operation is computed by the unshared logic components. The detailed execution procedure and control signals for both shared and unshared logic components are given in [30]. The unified Add/Sub/Mul architecture takes $\lceil K/3 \rceil + 2$ clock cycles to produce a GF(p) multiplication result at port T. The main advantages of the proposed unified Add/Sub/Mul units are a single unit that can handle GF(p) addition, subtraction, and multiplication instructions. It eliminates a need for dedicated hardware units for GF(p) addition and subtraction operations, which consumes two K-bit adders in addition to I/O multiplexers. The proposed unit is not only optimized for hardware resources and required

D1 unit performs a single bit left shift modulo p operation and it consists of one K-bit adder and a multiplexer. Hence, in total, the unshared logic consists of three K-bit adders, three multiplexers, and an additional logic for Booth recoding. The adder/subtractor unit consists of two K-bit adders and five multiplexers.

In the proposed unified Add/Sub/Mul unit, these hardware logic resources are shared with other resources, so two K-bit adders and five multiplexers are saved. This unit is not capable of performing modular addition, subtraction, and multiplication operations in parallel. However, EC point representation in affine coordinates has a very limited scope of parallelism. Therefore, the proposed unified Add/Sub/Mul unit can increase the performance of EC point multiplication in affine coordinates with a lower area overhead. The proposed unified Add/Sub/Mul unit performs modular addition, subtraction, and multiplication operations as given in Table 1 in the following manner.

A GF(p) addition is performed by the shared logic unit, if the two-bit input opcode = 00. The control unit

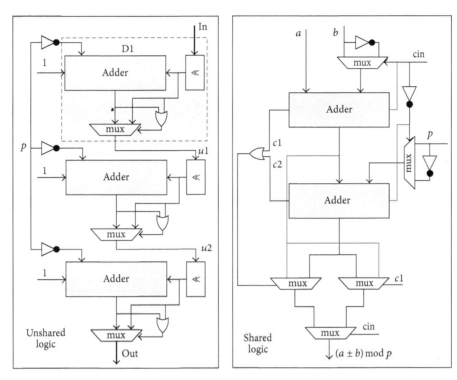

FIGURE 2: Shared and unshared logic components.

number of clock cycles for $GF(p)$ multiplication operation, but it is also programmable and supports any value for a modulus p.

4. Elliptic Curve Scalar Multiplier Architecture

ECC based schemes heavily rely on the EC scalar multiplication operation; therefore, its efficient implementation can greatly improve the performance of associated ECC based protocols.

The EC scalar multiplication is the computation of sP operation, where s is an integer and P is a base point of a chosen elliptic curve. Several algorithms have been proposed to compute the EC scalar multiplication operation [29]. Standard double-and-add, nonadjacent form (NAF), and a Montgomery ladder for EC point multiplication are mostly used. EC point addition and EC point doubling operation can be executed in parallel using a Montgomery ladder method given in Algorithm 1. As these EC point operations are not dependant on the respective scalar bit s_i, hence, power consumptions of these operations are symmetric and it is not possible for an attacker to extract any information regarding a secret value s. Therefore, this technique provides a protection against simple power analysis attacks. This section presents an efficient architecture for EC scalar multiplication in affine coordinates based on the proposed unified Add/Sub/Mul unit in Section 3. The proposed EC scalar multiplier architecture executes a scalar multiplication as a sequence of EC point addition and EC point doubling operations. These EC point operations can be achieved as a sequence of $GF(p)$ arithmetic operations as given in Table 2.

The EC point addition operation requires six $GF(p)$ subtraction, two $GF(p)$ multiplication, and one $GF(p)$ division operations. On the other hand, three $GF(p)$ addition, four $GF(p)$ subtraction, two $GF(p)$ multiplication, and single $GF(p)$ division operations are required to perform EC point doubling operation. As depicted in Table 2, the EC point operations in affine coordinates also require $GF(p)$ division operation in addition to $GF(p)$ addition, subtraction, and multiplication operations. A $GF(p)$ division and inversion can be performed either by Fermat little theorem or by Extended Euclidean algorithm (EEA). The binary version of EEA given in [29] is the mostly adopted algorithm for $GF(p)$ division. The EEA implementation in this work is based on the guidelines presented in [34]. It takes $2K$ clock cycles to perform a K-bit $GF(p)$ division or inversion operation.

It is evident from Table 2 that, in the computation of EC point operations, a scope of parallelism among $GF(p)$ arithmetic operations is very limited. Therefore, a semiparallel architecture for EC scalar multiplication is shown in Figure 3.

It consists of two $GF(p)$ unified Add/Sub/Mul units, two $GF(p)$ divider units, two register files (each comprised of 3 K-bit registers), I/O multiplexers, and a main controller. The $GF(p)$ unified Add/Sub/Mul unit executes a $GF(p)$ addition, subtraction, or multiplication operations at a time, while $GF(p)$ division unit executes $GF(p)$ division (a/b modulo p) operation in $2K$ clock cycles. Therefore, the proposed design can execute two $GF(p)$ addition, subtraction, or multiplication operations in parallel to two $GF(p)$ division operations. We grouped these $GF(p)$ arithmetic units into SAU1 and SAU2 units. Each SAU1 and SAU2 consists of one $GF(p)$ unified Add/Sub/Mul unit, one $GF(p)$ divider

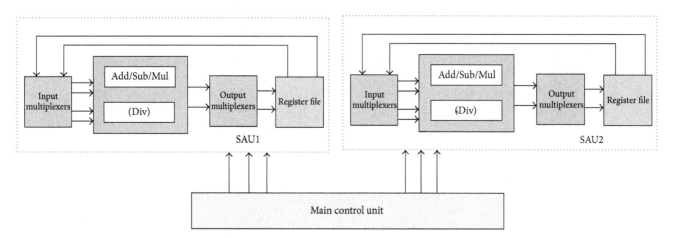

FIGURE 3: Proposed EC scalar multiplier architecture.

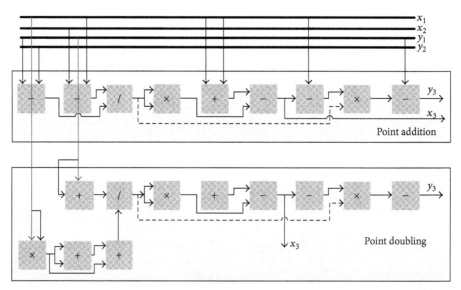

FIGURE 4: Scheduling of point operations.

unit, and one register file. The EC point addition operation and EC point doubling operation in Algorithm 1 can be performed in parallel. Therefore, the proposed architecture performs these EC point operations in parallel; however, on the unified Add/Sub/Mul unit, GF(p) addition, subtraction, and multiplication operations can only be performed in a serial fashion. The SAU1 unit is dedicated to perform the EC point addition operation, while the EC point doubling operation is executed by SAU2 unit. The register files store intermediate results during execution of EC point addition and EC point doubling operations based on control signals generated and managed by the main controller.

4.1. Scheduling Strategy. A scheduling policy to compute EC point addition and EC point doubling operations on the proposed SAU1 and SAU2 units is shown in Figure 4, where GF(p) addition, subtraction, multiplication, and division operations are denoted as +, −, ×, and /, respectively. Coordinates of two input points P_1, P_2 are denoted by x_1, x_2, y_1, y_2, while resultant point coordinates are shown as

x_3, y_3. The results of + and − operations are available after one clock cycle, whereas × and / operations are completed in $\lceil K/3 \rceil + 2$ and $2K$ clock cycles, respectively. The register transfer logic of EC point addition and EC point doubling operations on SAU1 and SAU2 units can be analyzed using Figure 4 and Table 2. Initially registers R_{x_1}, R_{y_1}, R_{x_2}, and R_{y_2} are loaded with coordinates of EC input points P and $2P$, while register R_a is initialized with the EC parameter a. The computation of EC point addition on the proposed SAU1 unit is completed in $(11 + 8\lceil K/3 \rceil)$ clock cycles, whereas SAU2 unit takes $(15 + 3K)$ number of clock cycles to execute EC point doubling operation. Therefore, a single iteration of Algorithm 1 is completed in $(15 + 3K)$ clock cycles and registers R_{x_1}, R_{y_1}, R_{x_2}, and R_{y_2} are updated with new values of EC point addition and EC point doubling. Let K_n be the total number of required clock cycles to compute the EC point multiplication operation; then on the proposed architecture it can be estimated as

$$K_n = \left(\log_2 (s-1) \right) (15 + 3K). \tag{4}$$

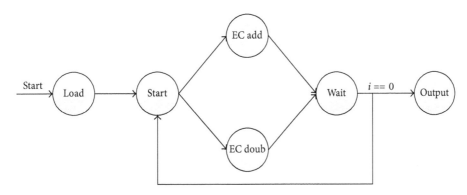

FIGURE 5: State diagram for main controller.

TABLE 2: Sequences of GF(p) operations for EC point operations.

GF(p) operation	EC point addition	#cc	GF(p) operation	EC point doubling	#cc
Subtraction	$f_1 = y_2 - y_1$	1	Multiplication	$f_1 = x_1 \times x_1$	1
Subtraction	$f_2 = x_2 - x_1$	2	Addition	$f_2 = f_1 + f_1$	$\lceil K/3 \rceil + 3$
Division	$f_1 = f_1 / f_2$	3	Addition	$f_1 = f_1 + f_2$	$\lceil K/3 \rceil + 4$
Multiplication	$f_2 = f_1 \times f_1$	$2K + 4$	Addition	$f_1 = f_1 + a$	$\lceil K/3 \rceil + 5$
Subtraction	$f_3 = x_1 - x_2$	$7\lceil K/3 \rceil + 6$	Addition	$f_2 = y_1 + y_1$	$\lceil K/3 \rceil + 6$
Subtraction	$f_3 = f_2 - f_3$	$7\lceil K/3 \rceil + 7$	Division	$f_1 = f_1 / f_2$	$\lceil K/3 \rceil + 7$
Subtraction	$f_2 = x_1 - f_3$	$7\lceil K/3 \rceil + 8$	Multiplication	$f_2 = f_1 \times f_1$	$7\lceil K/3 \rceil + 8$
Multiplication	$f_1 = f_1 \times f_2$	$7\lceil K/3 \rceil + 9$	Addition	$f_3 = x_1 + x_1$	$8\lceil K/3 \rceil + 10$
Subtraction	$f_2 = f_1 - y_1$	$8\lceil K/3 \rceil + 11$	Subtraction	$f_3 = f_2 - f_3$	$8\lceil K/3 \rceil + 11$
			Subtraction	$f_2 = x_1 - f_3$	$8\lceil K/3 \rceil + 12$
			Multiplication	$f_1 = f_1 \times f_2$	$8\lceil K/3 \rceil + 13$
			Subtraction	$f_1 = f_1 - y_1$	$3K + 15$

4.2. Main Controller Logic. The main controller is shown in Figure 5; it is based on a finite state machine (FSM) logic comprised of six states. The control unit is responsible for generating appropriate control signals required to execute EC point addition and EC point doubling on the proposed SAU1 and SAU2 units according to the scheduling strategy shown in Figure 4. It waits for the respective done signals, checks the ith bit of scalar s, and either decides to update the register files with new values or outputs the result and stops execution.

5. Implementation Results and Discussion

The elliptic curve scalar multiplier architecture presented in the previous section has been implemented in Verilog HDL. For simulation, synthesis, mapping, and routing purposes Xilinx ISE 9.1 design suite has been used.

Table 3, shows the performance of the proposed architecture for 160, 192, 224, and 256 bits field sizes on several different FPGA platforms. It takes 3.2 ms, 2.3 ms, and 1.4 ms while running at a maximum frequency of 35 MHz, 48 MHz, and 81 MHz for 192-bit implementation on Virtex-II pro, Virtex-4, and Virtex-6 FPGA platforms, respectively. As, ISE 9.1 design suit does not have a support for Virtex-6 FPGA, so implementation on Virtex-6 FPGA has been done using Xilinx ISE 14.7.

For 192-bit field size our implementation on Virtex-4 computes a single EC scalar multiplication in 2.3 ms in 113,472 clock cycles running at a maximum frequency of 48 MHz. The 192-bit implementation consumes 8,500 slices of Virtex-4 FPGA and has a throughput of 83.5 Kbps. The same design on Virtex-II pro takes 3.2 ms at a maximum frequency of 35 MHz and it uses 7,930 slices. Performance comparison among the proposed architecture and other FPGA implementations is analyzed on the basis of clock cycles, computation time, frequency, occupied FPGA slices, and throughput (TP).

Table 4 shows the required number of clock cycles to compute the EC scalar multiplication operation. The proposed design computes EC point addition and EC point doubling operations in $(11 + (8\lceil K/3 \rceil))$ and $(15 + 3K)$ clock cycles, respectively. As in the proposed design EC point operations are executed concurrently; therefore a single iteration of Algorithm 1 is completed in $(15+3K)$ clock cycles. The designs reported in [21] take $(13+5K)$ clock cycles, which is almost 40% more than the proposed design. Similarly, [18, 24–26] require 48%, 179%, 85%, and 62% more clock cycles to perform the EC scalar multiplication, respectively.

Table 5 demonstrates performance analysis of the several existing FPGA based implementations of EC scalar multiplier. The design reported in [21] is based on parallel dedicated hardware units for GF(p) addition, subtraction,

TABLE 3: Performance evaluation on different FPGA platforms.

Field size	Virtex-II pro		Virtex-4		Virtex-6	
	Freq (MHz)	Time (ms)	Freq (MHz)	Time (ms)	Freq (MHz)	Time (ms)
160	40	1.9	53	1.4	86	0.9
192	35	3.2	48	2.3	81	1.4
224	31	4.9	43	3.5	76	2
256	27	7.4	40	5	70	2.8

TABLE 4: Clock cycles requirements for different designs.

Design	Field size	Point addition	Point doubling	EC point multiplication
This work	160	437	495	79,200
	192	523	591	113,472
[21]	160		814	130,240
	192		974	187,008
[25]	160	868	668	153,000
[18]	160	809	972	283,000
[24]	167	2120	2540	545,040
[26]	192	—	—	300,000
[22]	192	—	—	120,000

TABLE 5: Performance comparison with exiting FPGA implementations.

Design	Field size	Platform	Area (slices)	Freq (MHz)	Time (ms)	TP (Kbps)
This work	160	Virtex-4	7,088	53	1.4	114
	192		8,590	48	2.3	83.5
	224		10,800	43	3.5	64
	256		13,158	40	5	51
This work	160	Virtex-II pro	6,492	40	1.9	84
	192		7,930	35	3.2	60
	224		9,308	31	4.9	45
	256		11,104	27	7.4	34
[21]	160	Virtex-4	12,415	60	2.2	72
	192		14,858	53	3.5	55
	224		17,331	47	5.4	41
	256		20,123	43	7.7	33
[18]	160	Virtex-II	3,433	40	7.1	22
	192		4,135	35	11.6	16.5
	224		4,808	33	16.8	13.3
[16]	192	Virtex-II pro	20,793	49	7.24	26
[32]	192	Virtex-II pro	3,173	93	9.90	19.3
[33]	256	Virtex-II pro	15,775	39	5.99	42.7
[20]	192	Virtex-II pro	8,972	43	4.47	42
	224		10,386	40	6.50	34
	256		11,953	36	9.38	27.2

multiplication, and division. It computes a 192-bit EC scalar multiplication in 3.5 ms at a maximum frequency of 53 MHz on the Virtex-4 platform. On the same platform the proposed design is 34% faster and requires 39% fewer clock cycles with 40% lower FPGA slice consumption as compared to [21]. The proposed design completes a 160-bit EC point multiplication in 79,200 clock cycles at a maximum frequency of 40 MHz.

It consumes 6,492 Virtex-II pro FPGA slices. Embedded multicore design reported in [32] computes 192-bit EC scalar multiplication in 9.9 ms running at a maximum frequency of 93 MHz and consumed 3,173 Virtex-II pro FPGA slices. It also uses 6 block BRAMs (BRAM) and sixteen 18 × 18-bit embedded multipliers. Compared to our design, it is 210% slower, but it consumes 149% fewer FPGA slices if we ignore the slices for BRAM and dedicated embedded multipliers. The design presented in [33] consumes 15,775 slices and takes 5.99 ms to compute one EC scalar multiplication. On the same platform it is 25% faster but it consumes 28% more FPGA slices. The design proposed by Daly et al. in [18] is 262% slower but it consumes 47% lower slices. The design reported in [20] is 40% slower and consumes 13% more FPGA slices as compared to the proposed design.

Performance comparison on the basis of throughput rate is depicted in the last column of Table 5. The proposed design has 0.5 times, 2.64 times, 1.30 times, 2.1 times, and 0.42 times higher throughput rate as compared to the designs [21], [18], [16], [32], and [20], respectively. The design [33] has 1.25 times higher throughput rate as compared to our design; however, it consumes 1.42 times more FPGA slices. Therefore, our design is better in terms of the computation time, slice area, and throughput rate as compared to all the designs listed in Table 5. As the proposed design executed EC point addition and EC point doubling operations concurrently in a fixed amount of time $(15 + 3K)$, therefore, it provides a protection against the timing and simple power analysis attacks, which is an important feature in modern day security applications. Due to the lower computation time and high throughput rate it is suitable for network applications like *SSL* and *IPsec*. It is also suitable in the low power resource-constrained environments because of the smaller area and reduced clock cycles.

6. Conclusion

This paper first introduces a unified arithmetic architecture for GF(p) addition, subtraction, and multiplication operations. Then, a high speed elliptic curve scalar multiplier is developed on the basis of the unified arithmetic architecture. The proposed design has been synthesized using Xilinx ISE 9.1 and 14.2 Design Suites targeting various Xilinx FPGA devices. Performance is shown for 160-, 192-, 224-, and 256-bit elliptic curve scalar multiplication operation. Compared with other contemporary designs, it gives 34% and 40% better performance in terms of computation time and number of required clock cycles, respectively. It is programmable for any value of prime p and is also resilient to timing and simple power analysis attacks. Therefore, it is a good choice in ECC based cryptosystems.

Competing Interests

The authors declare that there are no competing interests regarding the publication of this paper.

Acknowledgments

This work is supported by the Telecommunication Graduate Initiative (TGI) scheme funded by the Higher Education Authority (HEA), Ireland.

References

[1] V. S. Miller, "Use of elliptic curves in cryptography," in *Advances in Cryptology—CRYPTO '85 Proceedings*, pp. 417–426, Springer, 1986.

[2] N. Koblitz, "Elliptic curve cryptosystems," *Mathematics of Computation*, vol. 48, no. 177, pp. 203–209, 1987.

[3] R. L. Rivest, A. Shamir, and L. Adleman, "A method for obtaining digital signatures and public-key cryptosystems," *Communications of the Association for Computing Machinery*, vol. 21, no. 2, pp. 120–126, 1978.

[4] IEEE standard specifications for Public, "Key cryptography," IEEE Standards 1363-2000, 2000.

[5] P. C. Kocher, "Timing attacks on implementations of Diffie-Hellman, RSA, DSS, and other systems," in *Advances in Cryptology—CRYPTO '96*, Lecture Notes in Computer Science, pp. 104–113, Springer, Berlin, Germany, 1996.

[6] F.-X. Standaert, "Introduction to side-channel attacks," in *Secure Integrated Circuits and Systems*, I. M. R. Verbauwhede, Ed., Integrated Circuits and Systems, pp. 27–42, Springer, Berlin, Germany, 2010.

[7] J. Fan, X. Guo, E. De Mulder, P. Schaumont, B. Preneel, and I. Verbauwhede, "State-of-the-art of secure ECC implementations: a survey on known side-channel attacks and countermeasures," in *Proceedings of the IEEE International Symposium on Hardware-Oriented Security and Trust (HOST '10)*, pp. 76–87, Anaheim, Calif, USA, June 2010.

[8] J. Fan and I. Verbauwhede, "An updated survey on secure ECC implementations: attacks, countermeasures and cost," in *Cryptography and Security: From Theory to Applications*, pp. 265–282, Springer, 2012.

[9] H. Eberle, N. Gura, C. Sheueling, and V. Gupta, "A cryptographic processor for arbitrary elliptic curves over GF(2m)," *International Journal of Embedded Systems*, vol. 3, no. 4, pp. 241–255, 2008.

[10] J. Lutz and A. Hasan, "High performance FPGA based elliptic curve cryptographic co-processor," in *Proceedings of the International Conference on Information Technology: Coding and Computing (ITCC '04)*, vol. 2, pp. 486–492, Las Vegas, NV, USA, April 2004.

[11] N. Mentens, S. B. Ors, and B. Preneel, "An FPGA implementation of an elliptic curve processor over GF(2^m)," in *Proceedings of the 14th ACM Great Lakes Symposium on VLSI (GLSVLSI '04)*, pp. 454–457, ACM, Boston, Mass, USA, April 2004.

[12] S. Okada, N. Torii, K. Itoh, and M. Takenaka, "Implementation of elliptic curve cryptographic coprocessor over GF(2^m) on an FPGA," in *Cryptographic Hardware and Embedded Systems—CHES 2000*, Ç. K. Koç and C. Paar, Eds., vol. 1965 of *Lecture Notes in Computer Science*, pp. 25–40, Springer, Berlin, Germany, 2000.

[13] G. Orlando and C. Paar, "A high performance reconfigurable elliptic curve processor for GF (2m)," in *Cryptographic Hardware and Embedded Systems—CHES 2000: Second International Workshop Worcester, MA, USA, August 17-18, 2000 Proceedings*, vol. 1965 of *Lecture Notes in Computer Science*, pp. 41–56, Springer, Berlin, Germany, 2000.

[14] N. A. Saqib, F. Rodríguez-Henriquez, and A. Díaz-Pérez, "A parallel architecture for fast computation of elliptic curve scalar multiplication over GF (2 m)," in *Proceedings of the 18th International Parallel and Distributed Processing Symposium (IPDPS '04)*, pp. 1967–1974, April 2004.

[15] G. Meurice de Dormale and J.-J. Quisquater, "High-speed hardware implementations of elliptic curve cryptography: a survey," *Journal of Systems Architecture*, vol. 53, no. 2-3, pp. 72–84, 2007.

[16] K. Ananyi, H. Alrimeih, and D. Rakhmatov, "Flexible hardware processor for elliptic curve cryptography over NIST prime

fields," *IEEE Transactions on Very Large Scale Integration (VLSI) Systems*, vol. 17, no. 8, pp. 1099–1112, 2009.

[17] G. Chen, G. Bai, and H. Chen, "A high-performance elliptic curve cryptographic processor for general curves over GF(p) based on a systolic arithmetic unit," *IEEE Transactions on Circuits and Systems II: Express Briefs*, vol. 54, no. 5, pp. 412–416, 2007.

[18] A. Daly, W. Marnane, T. Kerins, and E. Popovici, "An FPGA implementation of a GF(*p*) ALU for encryption processors," *Microprocessors and Microsystems*, vol. 28, no. 5-6, pp. 253–260, 2004.

[19] S. Ghosh, M. Alam, I. S. Gupta, and D. R. Chowdhury, "A robust GF(p) parallel arithmetic unit for public key cryptography," in *Proceedings of the 10th Euromicro Conference on Digital System Design Architectures, Methods and Tools (DSD '07)*, pp. 109–115, Lübeck, Germany, August 2007.

[20] S. Ghosh, D. Mukhopadhyay, and D. Roychowdhury, "Petrel: power and timing attack resistant elliptic curve scalar multiplier based on programmable GF(*p*) arithmetic unit," *IEEE Transactions on Circuits and Systems. I. Regular Papers*, vol. 58, no. 8, pp. 1798–1812, 2011.

[21] S. Ghosh, M. Alam, D. R. Chowdhury, and I. S. Gupta, "Parallel crypto-devices for GF(p) elliptic curve multiplication resistant against side channel attacks," *Computers and Electrical Engineering*, vol. 35, no. 2, pp. 329–338, 2009.

[22] G. Orlando and C. Paar, "A scalable GF(*p*) elliptic curve processor architecture for programmable hardware," in *Cryptographic Hardware and Embedded Systems—CHES 2001*, pp. 348–363, Springer, Berlin, Germany, 2001.

[23] S. B. Örs, L. Batina, B. Preneel, and J. Vandewalle, "Hardware implementation of an elliptic curve processor over GF(p)," in *Proceedings of the IEEE International Conference on Application-Specific Systems, Architectures, and Processors (ASAP '03)*, pp. 433–443, IEEE, June 2003.

[24] E. Öztürk, B. Sunar, and E. Savaş, "Low-power elliptic curve cryptography using scaled modular arithmetic," in *Cryptographic Hardware and Embedded Systems—CHES 2004: 6th International Workshop Cambridge, MA, USA, August 11–13, 2004. Proceedings*, vol. 3156 of *Lecture Notes in Computer Science*, pp. 92–106, Springer, Berlin, Germany, 2004.

[25] A. Satoh and K. Takano, "A scalable dual-field elliptic curve cryptographic processor," *IEEE Transactions on Computers*, vol. 52, no. 4, pp. 449–460, 2003.

[26] W. Shuhua and Z. Yuefei, "A timing-and-area tradeoff GF(p) elliptic curve processor architecture for FPGA," in *Proceedings of the International Conference on Communications, Circuits and Systems*, vol. 2, pp. 1308–1312, May 2005.

[27] G. R. Blakley, "A computer algorithm for calculating the product AB modulo M," *IEEE Transactions on Computers*, vol. 32, no. 5, pp. 497–500, 1983.

[28] K. Javeed and X. Wang, "Efficient montgomery multiplier for pairing and elliptic curve based cryptography," in *Proceedings of the 9th International Symposium on Communication Systems, Networks and Digital Signal Processing (CSNDSP '14)*, pp. 255–260, Manchester, UK, July 2014.

[29] D. Hankerson, A. Menezes, and S. Vanstone, *Guide to Elliptic Curve Cryptography*, Springer, New York, NY, USA, 2004.

[30] K. Javeed and X. Wang, "Radix-4 and radix-8 booth encoded interleaved modular multipliers over general Fp," in *Proceedings of the 24th International Conference on Field Programmable Logic and Applications (FPL '14)*, pp. 1–6, September 2014.

[31] K. Javeed, X. Wang, and M. Scott, "Serial and parallel interleaved modular multipliers on FPGA platform," in *Proceedings of the 25th International Conference on Field Programmable Logic and Applications (FPL '15)*, pp. 1–4, London, UK, September 2015.

[32] J. Fan, K. Sakiyama, and I. Verbauwhede, "Elliptic curve cryptography on embedded multicore systems," *Design Automation for Embedded Systems*, vol. 12, no. 3, pp. 231–242, 2008.

[33] C. J. McIvor, M. McLoone, and J. V. McCanny, "Hardware elliptic curve cryptographic processor over GF(p)," *IEEE Transactions on Circuits and Systems I*, vol. 53, no. 9, pp. 1946–1957, 2006.

[34] A. Daly, W. Marnane, T. Kerins, and E. Popovici, "Fast modular division for application in ECC on reconfigurable logic," in *Field Programmable Logic and Application*, pp. 786–795, Springer, Berlin, Germany, 2003.

7

OpenCL-Based FPGA Accelerator for 3D FDTD with Periodic and Absorbing Boundary Conditions

Hasitha Muthumala Waidyasooriya,[1] **Tsukasa Endo,**[1]
Masanori Hariyama,[1] **and Yasuo Ohtera**[2]

[1]*Graduate School of Information Sciences, Tohoku University, Aoba 6-3-09, Aramaki-Aza-Aoba, Sendai, Miyagi 980-8579, Japan*
[2]*Graduate School of Information Sciences, Tohoku University, Aoba 6-3-05, Aramaki-Aza-Aoba, Sendai, Miyagi 980-8579, Japan*

Correspondence should be addressed to Hasitha Muthumala Waidyasooriya; hasitha@ecei.tohoku.ac.jp

Academic Editor: João Cardoso

Finite difference time domain (FDTD) method is a very poplar way of numerically solving partial differential equations. FDTD has a low operational intensity so that the performances in CPUs and GPUs are often restricted by the memory bandwidth. Recently, deeply pipelined FPGA accelerators have shown a lot of success by exploiting streaming data flows in FDTD computation. In spite of this success, many FPGA accelerators are not suitable for real-world applications that contain complex boundary conditions. Boundary conditions break the regularity of the data flow, so that the performances are significantly reduced. This paper proposes an FPGA accelerator that computes commonly used absorbing and periodic boundary conditions in many 3D FDTD applications. Accelerator is designed using a "C-like" programming language called OpenCL (open computing language). As a result, the proposed accelerator can be customized easily by changing the software code. According to the experimental results, we achieved over 3.3 times and 1.5 times higher processing speed compared to the CPUs and GPUs, respectively. Moreover, the proposed accelerator is more than 14 times faster compared to the recently proposed FPGA accelerators that are capable of handling complex boundary conditions.

1. Introduction

Finite difference time domain (FDTD) method is a very important and widely used one in many areas such as electromagnetic field analysis [1], optoelectronics [2], and antennas [3]. FDTD computation is an iterative method where a grid is updated in each iteration according to a fixed computation pattern. It is one of the most researched subjects and there are many proposals for new algorithms and accelerators. FPGA accelerators [4–10] are getting popular recently since they use deeply pipelined architectures by exploiting streaming data flows in FDTD computation. Streaming data flow computing is ideal for applications with low operational intensity [11] such as FDTD. The operational intensity refers to the amount of operations per data movement. In spite of the success, many FPGA accelerators are purely academic and cannot be used efficiently for real-world applications. The main reason

for this is the lack of support for boundary conditions or the inefficiency of computing them.

Commonly available boundary conditions in FDTD computation are Dirichlet, periodic, and absorbing boundary conditions. Dirichlet or the fixed boundary condition is the simplest one where a constant (usually zero) is used for the data on the boundaries. Fixed boundaries are used when the outside of a grid is a perfect electric or a magnetic conductor. In this case, the fields on the boundaries equal zero. Most of the existing works use fixed boundary conditions to gain high speedups by preserving the regularity of the data flow. Absorbing boundary condition (ABC) is often used to simulate infinite domains by applying absorbing layers close to the boundary. Implementing ABC computation could break the regularity of the data flow due to the data dependency near the boundaries. Periodic boundary condition (PBC) is used to simulate infinite periodic structures by computing a small portion called a "unit." PBCs are applied at the boundaries so that the same unit cell is replicated. Implementing PBC computation without breaking the regularity of the data flow is even more difficult, due to the data dependency among different boundaries. However, many real-world FDTD applications [12–14] use both absorbing and periodic boundaries, and their efficient implementation is very important.

In this paper, we propose an FPGA accelerator for 3D FDTD computation that efficiently supports absorbing and periodic boundary conditions. This paper is an extension of our previous work [15] which introduces the basic FPGA accelerator architecture. In this paper, we improve the FPGA architecture and implement it using a "C-like" programming language called "OpenCL" (open computing language) [16]. Therefore, we can use the proposed accelerator for different applications and boundary conditions by just changing the software code. Moreover, OpenCL provides a complete framework for system design that includes not only the FPGA accelerator design, but also the device drivers and API to control and transfer data between the accelerator and the host [17]. According to the experimental results, we achieved over 3.3 and 1.5 times higher processing speeds compared to those of the CPUs and GPUs, respectively. Moreover, the proposed accelerator is more than 14 times faster compared to the recently proposed FPGA accelerators that are capable of handling complex boundary conditions.

2. Related Works

FPGA accelerators for FDTD computation with simple boundary conditions are already implemented in previous works [5–7]. Although those works use different design methods such as OpenCL [16], HDL, or MaxCompiler [18], the basic architecture is very similar. To explain the accelerator architecture, we consider a simple example of 2D stencil computation as shown in Figure 1. Note that FDTD method is also regarded as a stencil computation. Figure 1(a) shows the data streaming order in a 2D $n_x \times n_y$ grid. A grid-point is called a cell. Data of the cells are streamed from left-to-right along the i axis and bottom-to-top along the j axis. Figure 1(b) shows the computations of two consecutive iterations. To compute cell$(1, 1)$ in the iteration $t + 1$ (Cell$^{t+1}(1, 1)$), data of its surrounding cells belonging to the iteration t are required. When the computation of cell$(2, 2)$ is in progress in the iteration t (Cell$^t(2, 2)$), all the data required for the computation of cell$(1, 1)$ are available. Therefore, the computations of cell$(2, 2)$ in iteration t and cell$(1, 1)$ in iteration $t + 1$ can be done in parallel. We call this "iteration-parallel" computation. Detailed description of the iteration-parallel computation can be found in [19].

Figure 2 shows the flowchart of the whole computation. Computations of d iterations are done in parallel on FPGA. If the total number of iterations is larger than d (which is the usual case), the FPGA computation is done for "*total_iterations/d*" times. In this method, the global memory is read once in each d iteration. Iteration-parallel computation reduces the global memory access while allowing sufficient amount of parallel operations.

The works in [5–7] propose FPGA accelerators based on iteration-parallel computation. A high level design tool called MaxCompiler [18] is used in [5] to accelerate 3D FDTD computation. OpenCL is used in [6, 7] for 2D FDTD computation. Although these works use iteration-parallelism to increase the processing speed, they only support simple boundary conditions such as fixed boundaries where constants are used as the boundary data.

The works in [8–10] propose FPGA accelerators that support complex boundary conditions. Impedance boundary condition is used in [8]. In terms of computation, impedance boundary is more complex compared to a fixed boundary, since it requires more computations. In terms of data dependency, it is easy to implement since the outputs are produced in the same order of the input data stream. However, it can be used only for 2D FDTD and the computations are done in 32-bit fixed point. Therefore, the usage of such an accelerator is severely restricted. Absorbing boundary conditions are supported by the FPGA accelerator proposed in [9]. However, it has not considered the periodic boundary conditions. The work in [10] is one the very few works that proposes an FPGA accelerator to compute both absorbing and periodic boundary conditions. The boundary-related data streamed out from the FPGA to the CPU through the PCI express bus. They are processed in the CPU and streamed into the FPGA after the computation of the core area is finished. In this method, the frequent data transfers and synchronizations between CPU and FPGA reduce the performance. Although the accelerators in [8–10] process boundary conditions, they have not used the iteration-parallel computation which is the most efficient way on FPGAs to increase the processing speed. Since the boundary conditions distort the regularity of the data flow, it is usually difficult to implement the iteration-parallelism.

3. FPGA Accelerator for 3D FDTD Computation

3.1. 3D FDTD with Periodic Boundary Conditions. In this section, we explain the FPGA acceleration for 3D FDTD computation when there are periodic and absorbing boundary conditions. Figure 3 shows the simulation area. Simulating very large grids could take enormous amount of processing time. Instead, we divide the grid into multiple boxes and consider that the same unit-box is replicated. We use periodic boundary conditions to correctly update the box. Using this method, we can reduce the computation amount significantly. This method is used for real-world FDTD simulations in many works such as [20–22].

Figure 4 shows the 3D computation domain of the unit-box. It contains six boundaries and the core. A cell in this 3D domain is denoted by the coordinates i, j, and k. The electric fields E_x, E_y, and E_z belonging to three directions are computed in each cell. The computations are classified into the core area and the boundary area computations. Absorbing boundary conditions are used to compute the top and the bottom boundaries (ij boundaries), while periodic boundary conditions are used for the other four boundaries (ik and

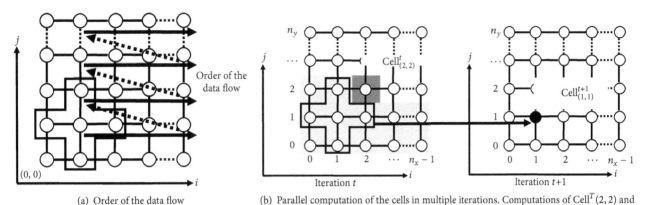

(a) Order of the data flow

(b) Parallel computation of the cells in multiple iterations. Computations of Cell$^T(2, 2)$ and Cell$^{T+1}(1, 1)$ can be done in parallel

FIGURE 1: 2D stencil computation using $n_x \times n_y$ grid. Iterations t and $t + 1$ are computed in parallel.

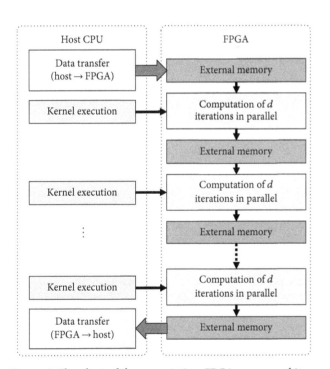

FIGURE 2: Flowchart of the computation. FPGA processes d iterations in parallel.

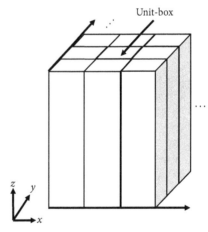

FIGURE 3: Simulation area and unit-box.

jk boundaries). Figure 5 shows a cross section of the computation domain that represents one ij plane. To compute the electric fields of cell$(0, j, k)$, we need the data of the cell$(n_x - 2, j, k)$ of the same iteration. Therefore, the cell$(n_x - 2, j, k)$ must be computed before computing the cell$(0, j, k)$. This is against the order of the input data stream shown in Figure 1(a).

Figure 6 shows the flowchart of the 3D FDTD algorithm. In usual Yee's FDTD algorithm [1], both the first-order differential equations of electric and magnetic fields are calculated. However, if we are interested only in electric field, we can simply substitute the magnetic field terms by equations that only contain electric field terms. The details of this method

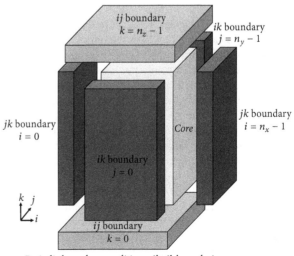

Periodic boundary conditions: ik, jk boundaries
Absorbing boundary conditions: ij boundaries

FIGURE 4: 3D computation domain of a unit-box.

$$E^{t+1}(0, y, z) = f(E^{t+1}(n_x - 2, y, z))$$
$$E^{t+1}(n_x - 1, y, z) = f(E^{t+1}(1, y, z))$$

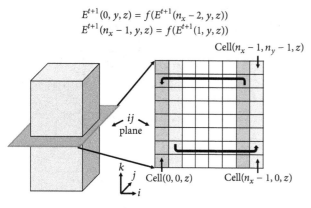

FIGURE 5: Data dependency on the boundaries.

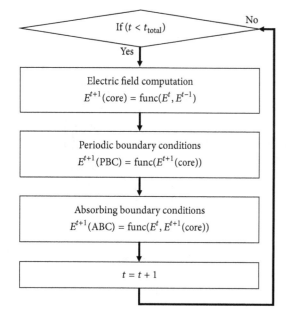

FIGURE 6: Flowchart of the 3D FDTD algorithm.

are available in [23, chapter 2]. Since the same equations are used, the physical model and the numerical values are the same as Yee's algorithm. However, we need the electric field data of the current and the previous iteration to compute the next iteration. In each iteration, both periodic and absorbing boundary data are computed. The periodic boundary data of iteration $t + 1$ are computed using the electric field data of the same iteration. The absorbing boundary data are computed using the electric field data of the iterations t and $t + 1$. Since the boundary computations require the data of the core cells, data dependencies exist among different cells of the same iteration. Therefore, the computations of the current iteration must be completed before starting the computations of the next iteration. Due to this problem, we cannot use the existing methods that are based on the iteration-parallel computation.

The computation of the electric field in x direction at time step $t + 1$ (E_x^{t+1}) is shown in (1). To compute E_x^{t+1}, we need the electric field data at the time steps t and $t - 1$. We also need the electric field data in y and z directions at the time step t

and also some constants such as $R_1 \sim R_4$ and ssn. Note that the computations of E_y and E_z are also done similar to

$$
\begin{aligned}
E_x^{t+1}&\left(i + \frac{1}{2}, j, k\right) = 2E_x^t\left(i + \frac{1}{2}, j, k\right) - E_x^{t-1}\left(i + \frac{1}{2}, j,\right. \\
&\left. k\right) + \text{ssn}\left(i + \frac{1}{2}, j, k\right) \times \left\{ R_1 \times \left\{ E_x^t\left(i + \frac{1}{2}, j + 1, k\right)\right.\right. \\
&\left.\left. - 2E_x^t\left(i + \frac{1}{2}, j, k\right) + E_x^t\left(i + \frac{1}{2}, j - 1, k\right)\right\} + R_2 \right. \\
&\times \left\{ E_x^t\left(i + \frac{1}{2}, j, k + 1\right) - 2E_x^t\left(i + \frac{1}{2}, j, k\right)\right. \\
&\left. + E_x^t\left(i + \frac{1}{2}, j, k - 1\right)\right\} - R_3 \times \left\{ E_y^t\left(i + 1, j + \frac{1}{2}, k\right) \right. \quad (1) \\
&\left. - E_y^t\left(i + 1, j - \frac{1}{2}, k\right) + E_y^t\left(i, j - \frac{1}{2}, k\right)\right. \\
&\left. - E_y^t\left(i + \frac{1}{2}, j, k\right)\right\} - R_4 \times \left\{ E_z^t\left(i + 1, j, k + \frac{1}{2}\right)\right. \\
&\left. - E_z^t\left(i + 1, j, k - \frac{1}{2}\right) + E_z^t\left(i, j, k - \frac{1}{2}\right)\right. \\
&\left.\left. - E_z^t\left(i, j, k + \frac{1}{2}\right)\right\}\right\}.
\end{aligned}
$$

Constant data set ssn contains wave impedance and refractive index data. It is given by

$$s = \text{CFL} \times s_{\min},$$
$$\text{ssn}(i, j, k) = \frac{s_{\min}^2}{r(i, j, k)^2}. \quad (2)$$

Note that $r(i, j, k)$ is the refractive index data for each coordinate, and it is given initially as an input data file. The minimum value of the refractive index data is given by $s_{\min}$. The stability constant is given by CFL and we use the value 0.99. The values of s and $\text{ssn}(i, j, k)$ do not change with iterations. Those are constants for all iterations. Therefore, we can compute those on CPU and the processing time required for this computation is very small, compared to the processing time of the whole FDTD computation.

3.2. Data Flow Regulation. Our goal in the proposed implementation is to maintain the regularity of the input and output data streams even when there are boundary conditions. However, as explained in Section 3.1, the order of the computations is different from that of the input data stream. To solve this problem, we regulate the output data stream by reordering the computed data. For example, let us consider the ij-plane shown in Figure 5 and assume that $n_x = 8$ and $k = m$. We consider the computations of the cells$(0, 1, m)$ to $(7, 1, m)$ when $j = 1$ on ij-plane. In this example, the data of the core cell$(6, 1, m)$ are required to compute the boundary cell$(0, 1, m)$. Let us assume that the data of cell$(6, 1, m)$ is computed at the clock cycle T. Using the data of the cell$(6, 1, m)$ as the input, we can compute the boundary cell$(0, 1, m)$ at the clock cycle $T + 1$. To maintain the regularity of the output

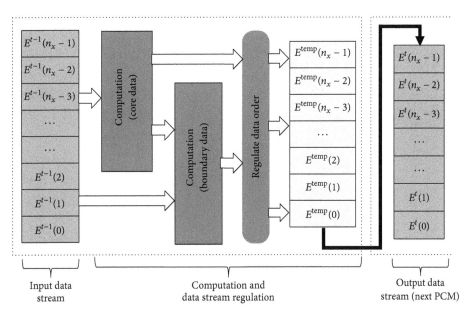

FIGURE 7: Proposed pipelined computation module (PCM). Computed data are arranged in the correct order to preserve the regularity of the data flow.

data stream, the output data should be in the order of cells $(0, 1, m), (1, 1, m), (2, 1, m), \ldots, (6, 1, m)$. If the data of the cell $(0, 1, m)$ is released to the output data stream at the clock cycle $T + 1$, the data of the cell $(6, 1, m)$ must be released at the clock cycle $T + 7$ and even it was computed before the cell $(0, 1, m)$. That is, the data of the cell $(6, 1, m)$ must be stored for 7 clock cycles before being released to the output data stream. Similarly, the core data of the cells $(1, 1, m), \ldots, (5, 1, m)$ also have to be delayed for 7 cycles each.

Figure 7 shows the proposed pipelined computation module (PCM) of our FPGA accelerator. It contains modules to compute core and the boundary data and a shift-register array to store the computed data. The input data streamed into the PCM in a regular pattern. The computation of the core starts before the boundaries. The computed data are written to the appropriate locations of the shift-register array. The locations of the shift-register array are calculated in such a way to preserve the data order. According to the example in Figure 5, the data of the cell $(6, 1, m)$ is stored in seven places after the data of the cell $(0, 1, m)$, irrespective of the order of the computation. After the data area is arranged in the correct order, they are released to the output stream.

Figure 8 shows the overall architecture. It consists of d PCMs where each of which processes one iteration. This architecture is very similar to the one discussed in [5–7]. The difference is the structure of a PCM which can process both core and boundary data and also produces a regular output data stream. To compute the electric field of the next iteration, we need the data of the current and the previous iterations. Fortunately, they are already available in the shift-registers of the current and the previous PCMs. For example, if we have 3 PCMs, the initial data of the iteration $t - 1$ and the data of three iterations $t, t + 1$ and $t + 2$ are available simultaneously. Therefore, d PCMs and an additional shift-register array are

sufficient to compute d iterations in parallel as shown in Figure 8.

However, there are a few disadvantages in this method. Since we have to use shift-registers to temporally store the computed data, the area of a PCM is increased. As a result, the number of PCMs can be decreased so that the processing time can be increased. The computed data have to be stored for several clock cycles until they are arranged correctly. This increases the latency and also the processing time.

3.3. OpenCL-Based Implementation and Optimization. This section explained how to implement and optimize the proposed FPGA accelerator using OpenCL [16]. OpenCL is a framework to write programs to execute across a heterogeneous parallel platform that consists of a host and devices. "Intel FPGA SDK for OpenCL" [24] is used for FPGA and CPU based systems, where the CPU is the host and the FPGA is the device. The "kernels" are the functions executed on FPGA and they are implemented using OpenCL. The inputs for the kernels are transferred from the host, and the outputs are transferred back to the host.

Listing 1 shows an extract of a C-program used to compute the electric field in x direction according to (1). Arrays *Efx*, *Enx*, and *Epx* are used to store the data of the electric fields in iterations $t + 1$, t, and $t - 1$, respectively. The electric fields at the coordinates $E_x^t(i + 1/2, j, k)$ and $E_x^t(i - 1/2, j, k)$ are represented by array indexes Enx[i][j][k] and Enx[i-1][j][k], respectively. Similar method is used to compute electric fields in y and z directions. Note that (i, j, k) notation is used for the cell coordinates in equations, and [i][j][k] notation is used to show the data array indexes used in the C-program.

Since E_x is defined at cell $(i + 1/2, j, k)$ as shown in (1), we have to use the average of ssn[i+1][j][k] and

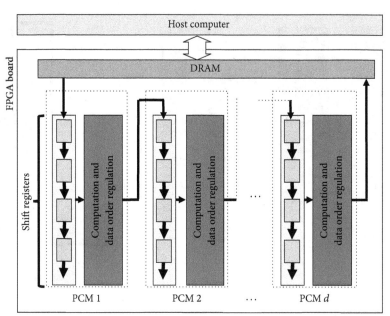

FIGURE 8: Architecture of the proposed FPGA accelerator. Iteration-parallel computation is achieved by processing d iterations in parallel.

ssn[i][j][k] to determine ssn at x direction (ssnx). Similar process is applied to compute ssny and ssnz also, as shown in Listing 2. Note that arrays ssnx, ssny, and ssnz are used in the C-program to store the data of ssn$_x$, ssn$_y$, and ssn$_z$, respectively. Constants ssn$_x$, ssn$_y$, and ssn$_z$ are the ssn values of x, y, and z directions, respectively.

To calculate the electric fields E_x, E_y, and E_z of a cell, we have to load nine data values that include electric field data of the present and the previous iterations of all three directions (Enx,Epx,Eny,Epy,Enz,Epz) and constants (ssnx,ssny,ssnz).

If all the data are stored in different off-sets in the global memory, we require at least 9 "load transactions." To reduce the amount of transactions, we use an array-of-structure in the global memory to store the data. Each element in the array has the data of the present and the previous electric fields and the constants. Therefore, one array element provides all the data necessary to compute one cell. One array element contains 36 bytes ($9 \times size\ of\ (float)$) in single precision and 72 bytes in double precision. On the other hand, one memory load/store transaction accesses 64 bytes from the global memory. If the data are not aligned, one or two transactions are required to access an array element. If the data are aligned to 64-byte boundary, only one transaction is required. Similarly, two memory transactions are required to load one array element in double precision for aligned data and more than two are required for nonaligned data.

To reduce the amount of memory transactions, we have to reduce the data amount of one array element. To reduce the data amount, we compute the constant in the FPGA instead of loading the already computed ones from the memory. For example, if we compute ssnx and ssny on FPGA, we have to load only ssn and ssnz from the memory. This reduces 4 bytes per cell. If we reduce the size of an array element to 32 bytes, we can load two array elements in one transaction. The computations of the constants can be done in parallel to

the computations of the electric fields. However, it requires additional computation units and increases the logic area of the FPGA.

Algorithm 1 shows the pseudo code of the computation kernel of the accelerator. The inputs and outputs of the kernel are represented by the array-of-structures in line (1). After an array element is read, the current and the previous electric field data of all three directions and constants are stored in the shift-registers. Shift-registers are included in each PCM to store the data of its inputs from the previous PCM. Shift-registers are defined using two-dimensional arrays as shown from line (2) in Algorithm 1. One array dimension represents the number of PCMs and the other represents the lifetime of the data. The lifetime represents the number of steps that one data value should be stored in the FPGA until it is no longer required for any further computation. Note that the lifetime is quite large since the output of one iteration is used in next two iterations. We also need another set of shift-registers to temporally store the computed data in order to regulate the data order. Those shift-registers are shown from line (5). The lifetime of the data stored in those shift-registers is small since the data are used in the same iteration. The behaviors of the shift-registers are coded from lines (8) to (29).

The computations of the cells in the core and the boundary are shown from line (37). Note that the computed data are temporary stored in the shift-registers to regulate the output data stream. The locations the shift-registers are determined by processing some conditional branches as shown from line 37. After the output data are available and the order is fixed, data are written to the shift-registers of the next PCM. If it is the last PCM, data are written back to the global memory.

4. Evaluation

For the evaluation, we use two FPGA boards, two GPUs, and two multicore CPUs. The FPGA boards are DE5 [25] and

```
(1)  _kernel FDTD (global struct *din, global struct *dout)
(2)      E_x[d + 1][lifetime]
(3)      E_y[d + 1][lifetime]
(4)      ⋯
(5)      E_x^{tmp}[d][tmptime]
(6)      ⋯
(7)      while count ≠ Loop iterations do
(8)          #pragma unroll
(9)          for  i = (lifetime − 1) → i = 1 do
(10)             #pragma unroll
(11)             for  j = 0 → j = d do
(12)                 E_x[j][i] = E_x[j][i − 1]
(13)                 E_y[j][i] = E_y[j][i − 1]
(14)                 ⋯;
(15)             end
(16)         end
(17)         #pragma unroll
(18)         for  i = (tmptime − 1) → i = 1 do
(19)             #pragma unroll
(20)             for  j = 0 → j = d − 1 do
(21)                 E_x^{tmp}[j][i] = E_x^{tmp}[j][i − 1]
(22)                 E_y^{tmp}[j][i] = E_y^{tmp}[j][i − 1]
(23)                 ⋯;
(24)             end
(25)         end
(26)         E_x[0][0] = din[count] · E_x^{prev};
(27)         ⋯;
(28)         E_x[1][0] = din[count] · E_x^{curr};
(29)         ⋯;
(30)         #pragma unroll
(31)         for  j = 0 → j = (d − 1) do
(32)             //compute the temporary storage locations
(33)             condition 1: (adr_a, …, adr_p, …)
(34)             condition 2: (adr_a, …, adr_p, …)
(35)             ⋯
(36)             //Computation of the core data
(37)             E_x^{tmp}[j][adr_a] = func(E_x[j][·], E_x[j + 1][·])
(38)             ⋯
(39)             //Computation of the boundary data
(40)             E_x^{tmp}[j][adr_p] = func(E_x^{tmp}[j][·])
(41)             ⋯
(42)             if count > j × latency then
(43)                 if  j == d then
(44)                     dout[adrs] · E_x^{prev} = E_x[j][·];
(45)                     ⋯;
(46)                     dout[adrs] · E_x^{curr} = E_x^{tmp}[j][·];
(47)                     ⋯
(48)                 else
(49)                     E_x[j + 2][0] = E_x^{tmp}[j][·];
(50)                     ⋯
(51)                 end
(52)             end
(53)         end
(54)         count + +;
(55)     end
(56) end
```

ALGORITHM 1: Pseudo code of the stencil computation kernel.

```
E2 = Enx[i][j][k]+Enx[i][j][k];
Efx[i][j][k]= E2-Epx[i][j][k]+ssnx[i][j][k]*
(R[0]*(Enx[i][j+1][k]-E2+Enx[i][j-1][k])
+R[1]*(Enx[i][j][k+1]-E2+Enx[i][j][k-1])
-R[2]*(Eny[i+1][j][k]-Eny[i+1][j-1][k]+
Eny[i][j-1][k]-Eny[i][j][k])
-R[3]*(Enz[i+1][j][k]-Enz[i+1][j][k-1]+
Enz[i][j][k-1]-Enz[i][j][k]));
```

LISTING 1: Extract of a C-program that shows the computation of E_x.

```
ssnx[i][j][k]=(ssn[i][j][k]+ssn[i+1][j][k])/2
ssny[i][j][k]=(ssn[i][j][k]+ssn[i][j+1][k])/2
ssnz[i][j][k]=(ssn[i][j][k]+ssn[i][j][k+1])/2
```

LISTING 2: Computation of constants.

395-D8 [26]. FPGAs are configured using Quartus 16.0 with SDK for OpenCL. The CPU code is written in C language with OpenMP directives and compiled using Intel C compiler 2016 (Intel Parallel Studio XE 2016) with relevant optimization options. GPU code is written in CUDA C code considering multithreaded data-parallel computation. GPUs are programmed using CUDA 7.5 compiler. The operating system is CentOS 6.7. We use a unit-box that has a periodic structure for the simulation. It is 960 nm × 960 nm × 9,540 nm long in x, y, and z dimensions, respectively. The objective of the simulation is to find various optical phenomena such as guided-mode resonance, at the wavelength range of 1,000 nm~2,000 nm. To simulate such resonance phenomena, a fine spatial mesh is needed. Thus, we set the grid division as 20 nm for each direction. This leads to a grid of 48 × 48 × 477 in each i, j, and k axis, respectively. Note that the grid size is given by parameters in the OpenCL code, and we can use a different grid by changing the values of the parameters. Computation is done for 8,192 iterations.

Table 1 shows the comparisons of the accelerators with different data access methods. We used DE5 board that contains Stratix V 5SGXEA7N2F45C2 FPGA. The computations are done in single-precision floating point. Method (1) uses "noncoalesced" memory access since it loads 9 data values from different locations in the global memory. Therefore, nine memory transactions are required for the computation of a cell. Since one transaction loads 64 bytes of data, the computations of the neighboring cells can be done by accessing the cache instead of the global memory. Memory access is coalesced in method (2) by using an array-of-structures. An array element contains 36 bytes so that the data are not aligned to the 64-byte boundary of a transaction. As a result, multiple transactions are required to access array elements, and the processing time is increased compared to method (1). This problem is easily solved in method (3) by aligning the data to the 64-byte boundary. After the data are aligned, only a single transaction is required to access an array element.

Moreover, the clock frequency is also improved due to the simplicity of the data access. As shown in Table 1, the processing time is reduced significantly compared to method (2). In method (4), the memory access is further reduced by decreasing the input data amount. It is done by computing the constants ssnx and ssny inside the FPGA in every cycle, instead of loading precalculated constants from the memory. Using this method, we reduce the size of an array element to 32 bytes so that two array elements can be read in a single transaction. The clock frequency is improved and the processing time is reduced significantly compared to method (3). In method (5), the size of an array element is further reduced to 28 bytes by computing all constants (ssnx,ssny,ssnz) on FPGA. However, this has increased the number of access points to ssn as shown in Listing 2. Moreover, the logic area is increased compared to method (4). Some of these reasons could be the cause for the processing time increase and clock frequency reduction. The best balance of the computation and the memory access is achieved in method (4) and it is the fastest implementation.

Table 2 shows the comparisons against the CPU and GPU based implementations. In this comparison, we used single-precision floating-point computation. The processing speed using DE5 FPGA board is 3.3 times and 1.5 times higher compared to those of the CPUs and GPUs, respectively. The processing speed using 395-D8 FPGA board is also higher than those of the CPUs and GPUs. The performances of GPUs are very sensitive to the memory bandwidth. Recent high-end GPU such as K40 with 288 GB/s bandwidth could provide better performance compared to this work. However, we believe that our evaluation using GTX680 (192.2 GB/s bandwidth) is a reasonable one, since it has a similar bandwidth compared to the high-end K20 GPU. In addition, it would be fair to compare devices such as Stratix V and GTX680, which are available in the same era. Despite having lower bandwidth and peak performance, DE5 FPGA gives the highest processing speed. Note that the peak performance of the FPGAs is calculated according to [27]. Unlike CPUs and GPUs, FPGAs are reconfigurable devices, and we can design the most suitable architecture for a given application considering its operations. We can use the resources efficiently by designing computing units that do only the required computation.

The comparison using double-precision floating-point computations is shown in Table 3. Although FPGAs give better performance compared to CPUs, they cannot beat the performances of the GPUs. Double-precision performance on FPGA is around 25% of the single-precision performance. The current generation FPGAs (Stratix V series) do not have dedicated floating-point units. Multiplications are done in DSPs and the additions are done using logic blocks. Due to the large logic block requirement for double-precision computation, the performances are decreased. However, the next-generation FPGAs such as Aria 10 and Stratix 10 devices contain dedicated floating-point units. Therefore, we can expect a significant reduction of the logic area and increase of the processing speed.

TABLE 1: Comparison of the FPGA accelerators with different data access methods using DE5 board.

| Method | Processing time (s) | Area (%) | | | | | Frequency (MHz) |
		ALMs	Registers	Memory (kByte)	DSPs	RAM blocks	
(1) Noncoalesced (36 bytes/cell)	8.01	179,925 (77)	368,483 (39)	2,911 (45)	114 (45)	2,050 (80)	205.6
(2) Coalesced (36 bytes/cell, nonaligned)	14.75	176,370 (75)	357,220 (38)	3,012 (47)	114 (45)	1,953 (76)	206.7
(3) Coalesced (36 bytes/cell, aligned)	9.42	170,692 (73)	349,960 (37)	2,958 (45)	114 (45)	1,879 (73)	217.8
(4) Coalesced (32 bytes/cell, aligned)	6.31	175,032 (75)	357,283 (38)	2,595 (41)	114 (45)	1,750 (68)	260.0
(5) Coalesced (28 bytes/cell, aligned)	6.69	176,637 (75)	359,472 (38)	2,363 (36)	114 (45)	1,618 (63)	243.6

TABLE 2: Comparison with GPUs and CPUs using single-precision floating-point computation.

| | FPGA | | GPU | | Multicore CPU | |
	DE5	395-D8	GTX680	GTX750Ti	i7-4960x	E5-1650 v3
Number of cores[1]	—	—	1152	1024	6	6
Core clock frequency (MHz)	260	193	980	1127	3600	3500
Memory bandwidth (GB/s)	25.6	34.1	192.2	86.4	51.2	59.7
Peak performance (Gflop/s)	193	1502.9	3090	1305	345.6	672
Processing time (s)	6.31	7.36	9.39	10.71	23.63	20.84

[1]GPU: CUDA cores; multicore CPU: CPU cores.

Table 4 shows the comparisons with other recent works that propose FPGA accelerators for 3D FDTD. All computations are done in single-precision floating point. The accelerator proposed in [9] provides 1000 mega cell/s processing speed using absorbing boundary conditions. However, it has not used periodic boundary conditions. Accelerators proposed in [5, 10] provide 325 and 1,820 mega cell/s processing speeds, respectively, for fixed boundary conditions. When absorbing boundaries are used, the performance of [10] is reduced to 65.5%. When periodic boundary conditions are used, the performance is reduced to just 5.5% and 8.4%, respectively, comparing with the ones that use fixed and absorbing boundary conditions. The accelerator proposed in this paper provides 1,427 mega cells/s processing speed on a single FPGA even using both absorbing and periodic boundary conditions together. This is a 14.2 times improvement compared to [10]. Since we used a single FPGA compared to four FPGAs in [10], our achievement is significant.

Memory bandwidths of the method in [10] are 26.8 GB/s and 29.9 GB/s when using fixed and absorbing boundaries, respectively. MAX3 board with Virtex-6 FPGAs used in [10] has a theoretical memory bandwidth of 38.6 GB/s, so that the accelerator is not memory bound. The theoretical memory bandwidth of the DE5 board used in this work is 25.6 GB/s. If the method in [10] is implemented on the DE5 board, it will become memory bound and would perform worse compared to the implementation on MAX3. On the other hand, our method uses only 13.4 GB/s bandwidth so that it is not memory bound in either of the FPGA boards. We use a single but very deep pipeline so that the application does not become memory bound. However, [10] uses multiple but shorter pipelines in parallel, and that requires reasonably large bandwidth. When [10] uses both absorbing and periodic boundaries, the boundary data are processed in the host CPU. This

requires frequent data transfers between host and FPGA. Such transfers depend on the PCIe bandwidth, and it is much lower than the memory bandwidth. Moreover, there could be some control overheads, synchronizing overheads, and so on that slow down the computation.

Table 5 shows the performance comparison against FPGA accelerators that use simple boundary conditions. All the implementations are done on DE5 FPGA board using single-precision floating-point computation. The 2D FDTD computation with fixed boundaries can be regarded as one of the simplest FDTD computations. The most recent and the fastest implementation of the 2D FDTD computation is proposed in [7]. It produces 150.3 Gflop/s of processing speed. We also measured the performance of the 3D FDTD computation with absorbing boundaries. It produces 98.5 Gflop/s of processing speed. The proposed 3D FDTD computation with absorbing and periodic boundary conditions produces 89.9 Gflop/s of processing speed. The performance of the proposed method is slightly small compared to the 3D FDTD implementation with only absorbing boundaries. However, the performance is reduced to nearly 60% compared to the 2D FDTD with fixed boundaries. Despite this reduction, we believe that retaining nearly 60% of the processing speed of the simplest 2D FDTD and yet processing the complex boundary conditions is a significant achievement.

We may improve the performance using manual HDL-based designs. However, we believe that the gap between the performances of OpenCL-based and HDL-based designs is getting narrower. In our earlier work in [7], we found that OpenCL-based design provides 76% of the FPGA peak performance for 2D FDTD with fixed boundaries. In this paper, we achieved over 51% of the peak performance for 3D FDTD with absorbing boundary and 46% of the peak performance with both absorbing and periodic boundaries. Moreover, the

TABLE 3: Comparison with GPUs and CPUs using double-precision floating-point computation.

	FPGA		GPU		Multicore CPU	
	DE5	395-D8	GTX680	GTX750Ti	i7-4960x	E5-1650 v3
Core clock frequency (MHz)	252	209	980	1127	3600	3500
Processing time (s)	28.09	25.24	14.44	20.61	69.45	62.13

TABLE 4: Comparison with other FPGA accelerators for 3D FDTD with boundary conditions.

Method	Boundary conditions	FPGA	Performance mega cell/s	Clock frequency MHz	Achieved throughput (maximum bandwidth) GB/s
Work in [9]	ABC	n/a	1,000	50	n/a
Work in [5]	fixed	Xilinx Virtex-6 XC6VSX475T	325	100	n/a
Work in [10]	fixed	Xilinx Virtex-6 XC6VSX475T × 4	1,820	100	26.8 (38.6)
	fixed and ABC		1,193		29.9 (38.6)
	ABC and PBC		100		n/a
This paper	ABC and PBC	Altera Stratix-V 5SGXEA7N2F45C2	1,427	260	13.4 (25.6)

n/a: not available.

TABLE 5: Performance comparison against FPGA accelerators that use simple boundary conditions.

Method	Boundary conditions	Performance (Gflop/s)	Frequency (MHz)
2D FDTD [6]	fixed	150.3	291
3D FDTD	ABC	98.5	261
3D FDTD (this paper)	ABC and PBC	89.9	260

work in [28] reports that, although HDL-based designs use less resources compared to OpenCL-based designs, there is not much difference in the clock frequency and performance.

5. Conclusion

We have proposed an FPGA accelerator for 3D FDTD that efficiently supports absorbing and periodic boundary conditions. The data flow is regulated in a PCM after the computation of the boundary data. This allows data streaming between multiple PCMs, so that we can implement iteration-parallel computation. The FPGA architecture is implemented using OpenCL. Therefore, we can use it for different applications and boundary conditions by just changing the software code. Since OpenCL is a system design method, we can implement the proposed accelerator on any system that contains an OpenCL-capable FPGA. According to the experimental results, we achieved over 3.3 times and 1.5 times higher processing speeds compared to the CPUs and GPUs, respectively. Moreover, the proposed accelerator is more than 14 times faster compared to the recently proposed FPGA

accelerators that are capable of handling boundary conditions.

References

[1] K. S. Yee, "Numerical solution of initial boundary value problems involving Maxwell's equations in isotropic media," *IEEE Transactions on Antennas and Propagation*, vol. 14, no. 3, pp. 302–307, 1966.

[2] F. Zepparelli, P. Mezzanotte, F. Alimenti et al., "Rigorous analysis of 3D optical and optoelectronic devices by the Compact-2D-FDTD method," *Optical and Quantum Electronics*, vol. 31, no. 9, pp. 827–841, 1999.

[3] M. A. Jensen and Y. Rahmat-Samii, "Performance analysis of antennas for hand-held transceivers using FDTD," *IEEE Transactions on Antennas and Propagation*, vol. 42, no. 8, pp. 1106–1113, 1994.

[4] Y. Takei, H. M. Waidyasooriya, M. Hariyama, and M. Kameyama, "FPGA-oriented design of an FDTD accelerator based on overlapped tiling," in *Proceedings of the International Conference on Parallel and Distributed Processing Techniques and Applications (PDPTA '15)*, pp. 72–77, Las Vegas, Nev, USA, 2015.

[5] K. Okina, R. Soejima, K. Fukumoto, Y. Shibata, and K. Oguri, "Power performance profiling of 3-D stencil computation on an FPGA accelerator for efficient pipeline optimization," *ACM SIGARCH Computer Architecture News*, vol. 43, no. 4, pp. 9–14, 2016.

[6] H. M. Waidyasooriya and M. Hariyama, "FPGA-based deep-pipelined architecture for FDTD acceleration using OpenCL," in *Proceedings of the IEEE/ACIS 15th International Conference on Computer and Information Science (ICIS '16)*, pp. 109–114, Okayama, Japan, June 2016.

[7] H. M. Waidyasooriya, Y. Takei, S. Tatsumi, and M. Hariyama, "OpenCL-based FPGA-platform for stencil computation and its optimization methodology," *IEEE Transactions on Parallel and Distributed Systems*, vol. 28, no. 5, pp. 1390–1402, 2017.

[8] R. Takasu, Y. Tomioka, Y. Ishigaki et al., "An FPGA implementation of the two-dimensional FDTD method and its performance comparison with GPGPU," *IEICE Transactions on Electronics*, vol. E97-C, no. 7, pp. 697–706, 2014.

[9] H. Kawaguchi and S.-S. Matsuoka, "Conceptual design of 3-D FDTD dedicated computer with dataflow architecture for high performance microwave simulation," *IEEE Transactions on Magnetics*, vol. 51, no. 3, pp. 1–4, 2015.

[10] H. Giefers, C. Plessl, and J. Förstner, "Accelerating finite difference time domain simulations with reconfigurable dataflow computers," *ACM SIGARCH Computer Architecture News*, vol. 41, no. 5, pp. 65–70, 2014.

[11] S. Williams, A. Waterman, and D. Patterson, "Roofline: an insightful visual performance model for multicore architectures," *Communications of the ACM*, vol. 52, no. 4, pp. 65–76, 2009.

[12] Y. Ohtera, "Calculating the complex photonic band structure by the finite-difference time-domain based method," *Japanese Journal of Applied Physics*, vol. 47, no. 6, pp. 4827–4834, 2008.

[13] Y. Ohtera, S. Iijima, and H. Yamada, "Cylindrical resonator utilizing a curved resonant grating as a cavity wall," *Micromachines*, vol. 3, no. 1, pp. 101–113, 2012.

[14] Y. Ohtera, "Design and simulation of planar chiral meta-surface for the application to NIR multi-patterned band-pass filters," in *Proceedings of the Progress in Electromagnetic Research Symposium (PIERS '16)*, pp. 2302–2302, Shanghai, China, August 2016.

[15] H. M. Waidyasooriya, M. Hariyama, and Y. Ohtera, "FPGA architecture for 3-D FDTD acceleration using open CL," in *Proceedings of the Progress in Electromagnetic Research Symposium (PIERS '16)*, pp. 4719–4719, Shanghai, China, August 2016.

[16] "The open standard for parallel programming of heterogeneous systems," 2015, https://www.khronos.org/opencl/.

[17] T. S. Czajkowski, D. Neto, M. Kinsner et al., "OpenCL for FPGAs: prototyping a compiler," in *Proceedings of the International Conference on Engineering of Reconfigurable Systems and Algorithms (ERSA '12)*, pp. 3–12, Las Vegas, Nev, USA, 2012.

[18] MaxCompiler, https://www.maxeler.com.

[19] K. Sano, Y. Hatsuda, and S. Yamamoto, "Multi-FPGA accelerator for scalable stencil computation with constant memory bandwidth," *IEEE Transactions on Parallel and Distributed Systems*, vol. 25, no. 3, pp. 695–705, 2014.

[20] T. Vallius, K. Jefimovs, J. Turunen, P. Vahimaa, and Y. Svirko, "Optical activity in subwavelength-period arrays of chiral metallic particles," *Applied Physics Letters*, vol. 83, no. 2, pp. 234–236, 2003.

[21] W. Zhang, A. Potts, D. M. Bagnall, and B. R. Davidson, "Large area all-dielectric planar chiral metamaterials by electron beam lithography," *Journal of Vacuum Science and Technology B: Microelectronics and Nanometer Structures*, vol. 24, no. 3, pp. 1455–1459, 2006.

[22] X. Meng, B. Bai, P. Karvinen et al., "Experimental realization of all-dielectric planar chiral metamaterials with large optical activity in direct transmission," *Thin Solid Films*, vol. 516, no. 23, pp. 8745–8748, 2008.

[23] A. Taflove and S. C. Hagness, *Computational Electrodynamics: The Finite-Difference Time-Domain Method*, Artech House, 3rd edition, 2005.

[24] Intel FPGA SDK for OpenCL, 2016, https://www.altera.com/products/design-software/embedded-software-developers/opencl/overview.html.

[25] Altera development and education boards, https://www.altera.com/support/training/university/boards.html#de5.

[26] Nallatech 395 with stratix V D8, http://www.nallatech.com/store/uncategorized/395-d8/.

[27] "Achieving One TeraFLOPS with 28-nm FPGAs," 2010, https://www.altera.com/content/dam/altera-www/global/zh_CN/pdfs/literature/wp/wp-01142-teraflops.pdf.

[28] K. Hill, S. Craciun, A. George, and H. Lam, "Comparative analysis of OpenCL vs. HDL with image-processing kernels on Stratix-V FPGA," in *Proceedings of the 26th IEEE International Conference on Application-Specific Systems, Architectures and Processors (ASAP '15)*, pp. 189–193, July 2015.

8

Exploring Shared SRAM Tables in FPGAs for Larger LUTs and Higher Degree of Sharing

Ali Asghar,[1] Muhammad Mazher Iqbal,[1] Waqar Ahmed,[1] Mujahid Ali,[1] Husain Parvez,[1] and Muhammad Rashid[2]

[1]*Karachi Institute of Economics and Technology, Karachi, Pakistan*
[2]*Umm Al-Qura University, Makkah, Saudi Arabia*

Correspondence should be addressed to Ali Asghar; aliasghar89@gmail.com

Academic Editor: Seda Ogrenci-Memik

In modern SRAM based Field Programmable Gate Arrays, a Look-Up Table (LUT) is the principal constituent logic element which can realize every possible Boolean function. However, this flexibility of LUTs comes with a heavy area penalty. A part of this area overhead comes from the increased amount of configuration memory which rises exponentially as the LUT size increases. In this paper, we first present a detailed analysis of a previously proposed FPGA architecture which allows sharing of LUTs memory (SRAM) tables among NPN-equivalent functions, to reduce the area as well as the number of configuration bits. We then propose several methods to improve the existing architecture. A new clustering technique has been proposed which packs NPN-equivalent functions together inside a Configurable Logic Block (CLB). We also make use of a recently proposed high performance Boolean matching algorithm to perform NPN classification. To enhance area savings further, we evaluate the feasibility of more than two LUTs sharing the same SRAM table. Consequently, this work explores the SRAM table sharing approach for a range of LUT sizes (4–7), while varying the cluster sizes (4–16). Experimental results on MCNC benchmark circuits set show an overall area reduction of ~7% while maintaining the same critical path delay.

1. Introduction

Look-Up Tables (LUTs) in an FPGA offer generous flexibility in implementing logic functions. LUT is an $N : 1$ multiplexer (MUX) with an N-bit memory [1]. Since MUX is a universal logic block; a k-input LUT can implement any k-variable Boolean function. Several LUTs are grouped together to form larger aggregates called Configurable Logic Blocks (CLBs) or simply clusters. LUTs inside a CLB are connected via intra-clustering routing network, while CLBs are connected with each other through a configurable routing network. However, this flexibility in an FPGA comes at the expense of area and performance overheads [2] when compared with their Application Specific Integrated Circuits (ASICs) counterparts, which are highly optimized for a certain class of applications. Hence, the very feature of FPGAs that makes them special is also responsible for their inferior performance to ASICs.

To bridge this gap between FPGAs and ASICs, FPGA architectures have been under continuous overhaul, ever since their inception. Previously published articles such as [3–6] attempt to explore the optimum values for coarser architecture level details such as cluster size (N), the number of inputs to a cluster (I), and the cross-bar topologies [7, 8]. FPGA's reconfigurable routing network, its switch box, and connection boxes have also been explored in detail.

In the past few years, some research has been focused towards exploring innovative logic blocks for FPGA, such as [9–11], which can compromise flexibility in favor of improving area and performance. The logic block architectures proposed in these works [9–12] replace legacy LUTs with innovative high coverage logic elements derived from frequently appearing logic functions. The idea is based on the fact that not all logic functions appear with the same frequency in digital circuits [9, 12].

All of the architectures discussed above utilize the concept of NPN-class equivalence [13] to characterize the frequency with which logic functions occur in a circuit.

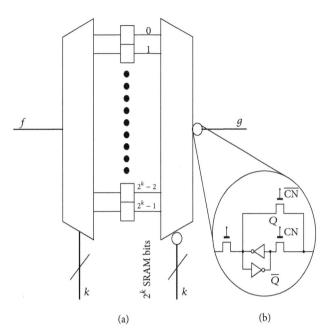

FIGURE 1: (a) LUTs with shared SRAM vectors and (b) CN logic.

The use of NPN-equivalent classes removes the redundancy (because of LUTs) inherent to FPGAs with some compact high coverage logic blocks. Other researchers have attempted to optimize FPGA logic blocks on a coarser architecture level which include [14, 15]. An SRAM table sharing based CLB [15] shares a single SRAM table between two or more LUTs, where all the LUTs sharing a single SRAM table map NPN-equivalent functions. The novel SRAM table sharing based CLB proposed in [15] has been improved and further explored in this research work.

The main drawback of the logic blocks proposed in [9–11] is that they are derived on the basis of NPN-equivalent classes for a particular benchmark suite; hence, they offer high-end efficiency only for the circuits from which their NPN classes were derived. For example, the logic blocks of [9] perform remarkably for the MCNC benchmarks, while for the VPR benchmark suite they fail to provide coverage for most of the frequently appearing logic functions. However, the SRAM table sharing based CLB is generic enough to provide area benefits for any set of benchmark circuits.

Meanwhile, a lot of research has also been directed towards architectures with reduced number of configuration memory cells. Architectures such as [14–17] fall in this category. The work in [17] utilizes the concept of Shannon Decomposition to trim down a larger k input function into two smaller ones, where one of the partial functions has less than $k - 1$ variables. The logic blocks (termed as Extended-LUT) used to map these functions require a smaller number of configuration memory bits than the conventional LUTs. The authors of [17] estimate improvements in area-depth product, without performing the place and route experiments. Hence, the efficiency of their proposed Extended-LUT [17] remains vague. Also the proposed logic cells are not fully permutable, which may result in routing

overheads. Another study [16] introduces the Scalable Logic Module (SLM) architecture which like [17] makes use of the Shannon Decomposition to find NPN-equivalent interconvertible partial functions, which can allow the sharing of their memory tables. The results show that a high percentage of functions with input size of 5–7 can be decomposed into interconvertible partial functions.

Kimura et al. [14] proposed function folding to reduce the number of configuration memory bits. The truth table of a function is divided into 2 parts; the whole truth table is then reconstructed using only a single part, while the other half is extracted using NOT, bit-wise OR, or any other suitable operation. However, [14] does not include delay results.

This work employs a novel CLB [15] to reduce the number of configuration memory bits. The reduction in configuration memory bits will reduce not only the area of the FPGA architecture, but also the configuration time and the size of the external memory used to store the bitstream. The CLB proposed in [15] allows sharing of memory vectors between 2 LUTs (as shown in Figure 1) on which NPN-equivalent functions are mapped. To realize NPN equivalence on hardware level, the inputs and output of one of the two shared LUTs are negated with the help of conditional negation (CN) block, as shown in Figure 1(b). To allow sharing of SRAM tables between two NPN-equivalent functions, an additional circuitry, conditional negation (CN) logic is added to the I/Os of one of the two shared LUTs which share their SRAM vectors.

The experiments in [15] were performed for LUT sized 4 ($k = 4$), while varying the cluster size (4–16) and the number of shared LUT pairs (2–4). The results show an estimated ~2% reduction in total FPGA (logic + routing) area. In this article, we investigate the feasibility of architecture presented in [15] for a range of input ($k = 4$–7) and cluster ($N = 4$, 10, 16) sizes. We have also performed experimentations with a much higher number of shared LUT pairs (i.e., 2–5 and 2–8, for N = 10 and 16, resp.). We have performed all the experimentation on the newer VTR exploration environment [18] with single driver unidirectional [19] routing network. On the contrary, the work done by [15] employed the older VPR with bidirectional routing network. We also propose a new clustering technique which attempts to pack the NPN-equivalent LUTs together inside the same CLB and present a comparison of our proposed technique with the one implemented in [15]. To find the NPN-equivalence among logic functions, we make use of an extremely efficient, high performance Boolean matching algorithm [20] instead of the brute-force approach employed in [15].

In an earlier work [21], we showed the feasibility of this architecture by obtaining an area gain of ~3.7%, for degree of sharing 2, that is, 2 LUTs sharing the same SRAM table. In this paper we attempt to enhance the area savings further, by exploring the possibility of CLBs with a higher degree of sharing (i.e., 3 or more LUTs sharing the same SRAM table).

The remainder of this paper is organized as follows. Section 2 covers the implementation and CAD flow details. The results are discussed in Section 3, while Section 4 presents the conclusion.

2. Implementation Details

This section describes the steps involved in mapping NPN-equivalent functions to LUTs with shared SRAM tables.

2.1. Finding NPN-Equivalent Classes. Two functions, say f and g, are NPN equivalent, if one can be derived from the other by negating (N) and/or permuting (P) some/all of the inputs and/or by negating (N) the outputs. If f and g are NPN equivalent they belong to the same NPN class.

For n-inputs, there are $2\exp(2^n)$ distinct possible functions. Hence, the Boolean space grows very rapidly as the number of inputs increase. However, this space can be compressed to a much smaller number of unique functions using the concept of NPN-equivalent classes. For example, for n = 4, there are $2\exp(2^n)$ = 65536 possible functions while there are only 222 distinct NPN-equivalent classes [13]. The task of Boolean matching (which involves pruning the logic space to find equivalent functions) becomes much simpler for the NPN-equivalence space compared to the humongous $2\exp(2^n)$ possible logic functions.

In [15], a brute-force method has been used to find NPN equivalence among logic functions. However, this approach is not scalable as the number of inputs increases. Hence, in this paper we make use of a recently proposed state-of-the-art Boolean matching algorithm [20], which has been integrated into the ABC framework [22] for finding NPN-equivalent classes.

2.2. Clustering NPN-Equivalent Classes. After finding the equivalent classes, LUTs are clustered using T-VPACk algorithm [23] with an emphasis on packing NPN-equivalent functions in such a way that LUTs with shared SRAM tables employ functions which belong to the same NPN class. For

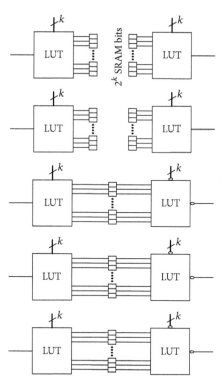

FIGURE 2: A CLB with 10 LUTs (N = 10) and 3 shared pairs (P = 3).

example, consider a CLB (shown in Figure 2) with 10 LUTs (N = 10), having 3 shared LUT pairs, that is, 3 LUT pairs sharing their SRAM tables (p = 3); hence, there will be a total of 7 SRAM vectors for 10 LUTs.

We employ two clustering approaches which attempt to map NPN-equivalent functions on these shared pairs. The one used in [15] (Algorithm 1) and its modified version (Algorithm 2) are proposed in this work. The first step of the two clustering methods is the same as both algorithms start by filling one of the two LUTs sharing their SRAM tables, with the LUTs present in the priority queue generated by the T-VPACK [23] algorithm. However, it is the second part in which the two clustering methods change course. To fill the second of the two LUTs in each pair, the method presented in [15] performs NPN-equivalence checks with only a single pair out of the possible p shared pairs. On the other hand, our clustering approach is far more flexible as it performs equivalence checks for all the possible p shared pairs. Hence, our proposed method offers flexibility at the expense of $p - 1$ more equivalence checks as compared to [15].

A comparative analysis of the two approaches has also been performed which will be discussed in Section 3.2. We have not made any changes to the priority queue generated by the T-VPACK [23] to ensure the optimal packing results. Finally, placement and routing results were obtained using VTR [18] with default settings. This modified CAD flow is shown in Figure 3.

2.3. Architecture Details. All the architecture files we have used for experimentation extract their parameters from the iFAR (*intelligent FPGA architecture repository*). The iFAR

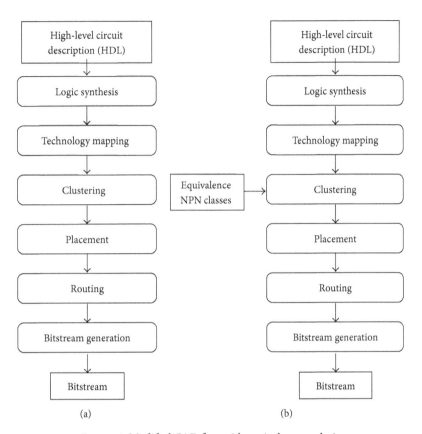

FIGURE 3: Modified CAD flow with equivalence analysis.

repository [24] has a wide variety of architecture files for different input and cluster sizes. It also contains architecture files for four different technology nodes (45 nm, 65 nm, 90 nm, and 130 nm) which extract parameters from *Predictive Technology Model* (PTM) [25]. The PDK available to us to estimate the delay of CN logic (discussed in Section 1) is on 150 nm process. Hence, the delay estimated using the PDK available to us, that is, 150 nm, would best correlate with the delay results for architecture files based on 130 nm technology node. We do not expect the delay values to vary much in moving from 150 nm to 130 nm process. Therefore, all the parameters for the architecture files used in our simulations have been obtained from the iFAR repository architecture files for 130 nm.

The number of inputs to the cluster (I) has been calculated using this well-established relation [26]:

$$I = \frac{K}{2} * (N + 1).   \tag{1}$$

Table 1 lists some of the most important architecture file parameters which affect the final results.

2.4. Configuration Bits Analysis. Since k input LUT requires 2^k configuration memory bits, hence, for every shared SRAM pair 2^k memory bits are saved. Xilinx [27] uses 5-transistor-based 5T SRAM cell as a configuration memory bit for its FPGA families. VPR [18] employs a 6T SRAM cell for LUT configuration and for the overall architecture. The paper [15]

TABLE 1: Architecture file parameters.

Parameter	Value
RMinWidth NMOS	2800
Switch block type	Wilton
Switch type	MUX
Segment length	4
RMinWidthPMOS	7077
Fs	3
Switch delay	103 ps
Segment type	Unidir.

uses an 8T SRAM cell, while the [16] architecture utilizes latch as configuration memory cells. Naturally, larger memory cells (in terms of transistor count) result in greater area savings for an FPGA. Since we have obtained the entire place and route results using VPR, we use a 6T SRAM cell to get a true picture of the overall area savings for an FPGA.

2.5. Area Savings. The model employed in VPR to perform area estimation is known as Minimum Width Transistor Area Model (MWTM) [1]. MWTA is simply the layout area occupied by the smallest possible transistor that can be contacted in a process, plus the spacing to other transistors above and to its right. Using MWTA, the calculated area for a 6T SRAM cell is 6 MWTAs (6 minimum width transistor areas). The CN logic block presented in [15] consists of a 5T

SRAM cell and two pass-transistors which overall requires 7 MWTAs. For the remainder of this paper, we will use these values to perform area calculations.

For a k input LUT, the number of shared pairs equals p. The number of transistors removed from a CLB can be given as

$$\text{No. of Transistors Removed} = p * \left(6 * 2^k - 7 * m\right), \quad (2)$$

where $m = k + 1$ represents the number of CN logic cells required to realize a k input LUT pair with shared SRAM vectors.

Since, for a k input function, an SRAM vector has 2^k, 6T SRAM cells, therefore, for p shared pairs, $p * (6 * 2^k)$ transistors are removed from each CLB, while the term $7 * (m * p)$ in (2) accounts for the transistor overhead required to implement the CN logic appearing at $k + 1$ I/Os. Consequently, the area saved (in terms of transistors count) resulting from the reduction of SRAM configuration cells over the entire FPGA can be calculated by simply multiplying (2) by the FPGA grid size:

$$\text{Area Savings} = \left(6 * 2^k * p * \text{Grid Size}\right)$$
$$- \left(7 * m * p * \text{Grid Size}\right). \quad (3)$$

2.6. Delay Analysis with CN Logic Cells. The LUTs whose I/Os are appended with CN logic cells will incur an additional delay in their look-up times. To estimate this delay, we simulated the CN logic cell in Cadence Virtuoso 6.1.5 using 150 nm process. The propagation delay is the average value for rise and fall transitions. The propagation delay of the CN logic (ε) was found to be ~15 psec, which is a small fraction of the overall time (τ) required to look up a value from the SRAM table. The value of (τ) for LUT-4 (as reported in the iFAR [24] repository files) is ~294 psec. It increases as the number of inputs of an LUT increases. Hence, the total delay through an LUT with CN logic cells at both input and output should be $\tau + 2\varepsilon$.

3. Results

To evaluate the performance of the CLBs with shared SRAM tables, we have performed rigorous testing on a variety of architectures by varying k, N, and p.

In this section, we present our observations for the following set of results:

(1) Number of NPN-equivalence classes as a function of input size

(2) Comparison of the two clustering methods (discussed in Section 2.2)

(3) Effects of varying the number of shared pairs (p)

(4) Effects of varying the degree of sharing (d); number of LUTs sharing the same SRAM vector

(5) Impact of modified clustering on routability

(6) Channel width, critical path, logic area, and total FPGA area for cluster sized $N = 10$ and 16

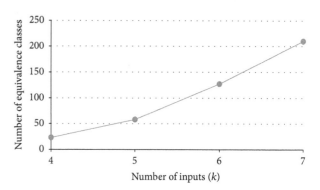

FIGURE 4: Number of used NPN-equivalence classes for input size k = 4–7.

3.1. Number of NPN-Equivalence Classes as a Function of Input Size. NPN-Equivalence analysis is performed for an input circuit after it is synthesized as shown in Figure 3. As discussed earlier, for n inputs there are $2 \exp(2^n)$ possible Boolean functions. These Boolean functions can be mapped upon a limited set of NPN-equivalent classes. For example, for $K = 4$, there can be a total of 222 NPN-equivalent classes. However, a given input circuit does not utilize all of the NPN-equivalent classes. As the number of inputs increases the Boolean space grows exponentially. A direct consequence of this behavior is the quick rise in the number of NPN-equivalent classes used. Figure 4 which shows the average number of NPN-equivalence classes, for input sizes $k = 4$ to 7, over the 20 MCNC benchmark circuits, depicts this behavior very clearly. The NPN-class size grows from ~23 for $k = 4$ to ~210 for $k = 7$. Therefore, as the number of inputs increases the probability of mapping two NPN-equivalent classes on a shared LUT pair decreases and vice versa.

3.2. Comparison of the Two Clustering Methods. In Section 2.2, we discussed two clustering methods (Algorithm 1 and 2). The CLB, shown in Figure 2, contains a mix of LUTs, those that could share their SRAM tables and others which do not share their tables. Hence, both the clustering approaches (discussed in Algorithms 1 and 2) pay attention to this detail while packing CLBs. If a packing algorithm fails to map NPN-equivalent functions on a LUT pair with shared SRAM vectors, then the LUT with CN logic at its I/Os is left vacant. As a result, the CLB does not get fully packed, if this happens for a large number of shared LUT pairs, then the number of utilized CLBs in the FPGA architecture would rise which will affect the final place and route results and may eventually increase the FPGA grid size.

Hence, to evaluate performance of the two methods, we observed the number of CLBs required to implement the whole circuit. The number of required CLBs serves as a measure of relative efficiency; the clustering approach which requires more CLBs is not well-suited to map NPN-equivalent functions on LUTs which allow sharing their SRAM tables. Also an increase in the number of CLBs affects the final place and route results like critical path delay and routing channel width.

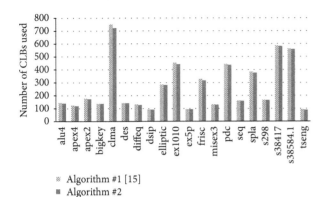

FIGURE 5: Comparison of the clustering methods for $N = 10$.

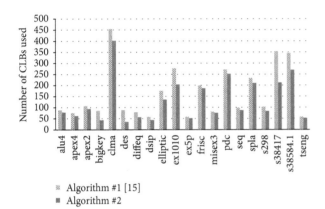

FIGURE 6: Comparison of the clustering methods for $N = 16$.

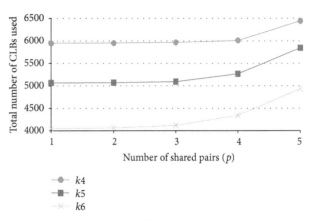

FIGURE 7: Number of CLBs utilized for cluster size of $N = 10$ and $p = 1$–5.

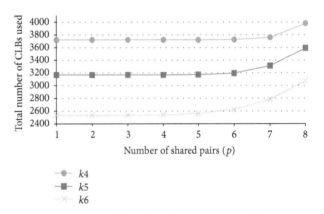

FIGURE 8: Number of CLBs utilized for cluster size of $N = 16$ and $p = 1$–8.

In Figures 5 and 6, we present the performance of the two algorithms for $k = 4$ and 5, with a cluster size of $N = 10$ and 16, respectively, and number of shared pairs $p = 3$. As seen from the results in Figures 5 and 6, our proposed method outperforms the other approach for both the architectures $k4N10$ and $k5N10$, over the entire MCNC benchmark suite. The reason for this improved performance is the flexibility (at the expense of more equivalence checks) of our clustering approach (Algorithm 2) compared to the one presented in [15]. Since Algorithm 2 is better suited to map NPN-equivalent functions on a shared LUT pair, we will use the results obtained from it for the remainder of this section.

3.3. Effects of Varying the Number of Shared Pairs. The area and configuration memory savings are directly related to the number of shared SRAM tables in a CLB. For example, in a CLB with cluster size $N = 10$ and $p = 5$, there are 5 SRAM tables which are shared between 10 LUTs resulting in exactly 50% reduction in configuration memory. For $p = 4$ and 3, the memory savings reduce by 40% and 30%, respectively. Hence, greater are the numbers of shared pairs greater are the configuration memory savings, which result in more area savings.

Although a high value of p seems ideal for the CLBs under exploration, there is an issue which restricts setting arbitrarily high values for p. Since a high value of p means that a large number of LUTs with shared memory vectors should

be mapped with NPN-equivalent functions, as the input size increases the number of NPN-equivalent classes grows rapidly (discussed in Section 3.1). As a result, it becomes increasingly difficult to map all the LUTs (with shared SRAM vectors) with NPN-equivalent functions.

Figures 7 and 8 depict this behavior with a high degree of clarity. The figures show the sum of the number of CLBs utilized to implement the entire MCNC benchmark suite, by varying the number of shared LUT pairs (p) from 1 to 5, for $N = 10$ and $p = 1$–8, for $N = 16$. The results obtained are concordant with our earlier observations that a high value of k or p makes it difficult to map all the shared LUT pairs with NPN-equivalent functions. The results in Figures 7 and 8 show a trend similar to a switching behavior; that is, for a particular value of k, the number of shared LUT pairs (p) can be increased up to a certain limit, after which the number of CLBs required to implement a circuit grows rapidly. For $k = 4$, this switching threshold is at $p = 4$ and $p = 6$, for cluster sizes $N = 10$ and 16, respectively. However, for $k = 6$, these values drop down to $p = 2$ and 4, for $N = 10$ and 16, respectively.

3.4. Effect of Varying the Degree of Sharing. The idea of LUT pair sharing a memory vector can be extended to 3 or more

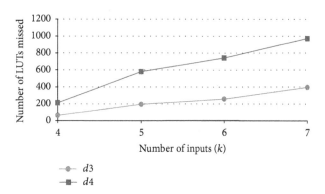

FIGURE 9: Number of LUTs missed for cluster size $N = 16$ and $p = 3$ for $d = 3$ and 4.

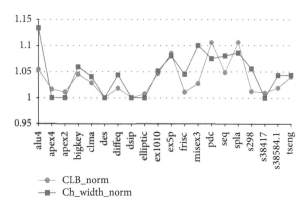

FIGURE 10: Impact of high CLB usage on channel width.

LUTs, if all the LUTs have been mapped with the same NPN class. In this article, we extend the degree of sharing (d) of SRAM tables from 2 to 3 and 4 LUTs sharing the same SRAM vector. Naturally, a high value of d means greater area savings because now a larger number of LUTs are sharing the same configuration bits. To account for the increased value of d, we have augmented the relationship for area savings presented in (3) with a new term ($d - 1$)

$$\text{Area Savings} = \left(6 * 2^k * p * (d - 1) * \text{Grid Size}\right)$$
$$- \left(7 * m * p * \text{Grid Size}\right). \tag{4}$$

However, similar to the number of shared pairs (p), the value of d cannot be made arbitrarily high. A high value of d means a large number of LUTs should be mapped with the same NPN class. This will happen only when there is high percentage of functions in the priority queue belonging to the same NPN class. For small input sizes ($k = 4$ or 5) the chances of finding such functions are pretty high, as the number of equivalent classes for functions with smaller inputs is usually low.

To depict this behavior we plot the number of LUTs left empty during clustering due to the lack of NPN-equivalent classes in the priority queue against the varying input size (k). Figure 9 shows the number of unmapped LUTs for $d = 3$ and 4 for the architecture having $p = 3$ and $N = 16$.

3.5. Impact of Modified Clustering on Routability. In Sections 3.3 and 3.4, we showed that high values of p and d make it very difficult to map all the shared LUTs with equivalent classes. As a result, the number of CLBs required to implement the whole circuit goes up, which may affect the final place and route results. Figure 8 shows the number of CLBs used to implement the entire MCNC benchmark suite for cluster size $N = 16$ and by varying the number of shared pairs (p) from 1 to 8. The results show a slight increase in the number of required CLBs for $k = 6$ and $p = 6$.

To analyze the impact of greater CLB usage on the circuits routability, we normalize the number of CLBs and channel widths required to implement the entire MCNC benchmark circuits using the modified architecture $k6N16$ (with $p = 6$ and $d = 2$) with the number of CLBs and channel widths

required using the default $k6N16$ architecture. The results in Figure 10 show a clear trend; as the number of utilized CLBs goes above the default value, the channel width required to route the circuit increases accordingly.

3.6. Cluster Size $N = 10$. We first consider the CLBs with cluster size $N = 10$. The results obtained for the 20 MCNC benchmark circuits have been presented in Figures 11 and 12. All the results have been obtained by running VPR in the default mode of operation. In the default mode, VPR attempts to place the circuit on the minimum possible number of logical resources and for routing employs a binary-search algorithm which repetitively searches for the minimum value of channel width for which the circuit becomes routable. We compare our results with the default cluster size $N = 10$ architecture, without any shared LUT pairs.

For the experimentation with cluster size $N = 10$, we set the number of shared pairs equal to 3 ($p = 3$), while for the degree of sharing ($d = 3$ and 4) p was set to a value of 2. As can be seen from Figure 7, for input sizes $k = 4$, 5, and 6; the number of utilized CLBs stays relatively constant up to $p = 3$, after which they start growing rapidly. As mentioned in Section 3.3, the higher the value of p or d, the more difficult it becomes for the clustering algorithm to map NPN-equivalent functions to a large number of LUTs with shared SRAM vectors. Moreover, large values of k further exacerbate this problem, as the size of NPN-equivalence class grows rapidly with the increasing input size (as shown in Figure 4), which results in a wide variety of NPN-equivalence classes in the priority queue, making it difficult for the clustering algorithm to find NPN-equivalent functions for a large number of shared LUT pairs, resulting in higher CLB utilization (as discussed in Section 3.2).

The results in Figure 11 show the average (over the 20 MCNC benchmark circuits) savings in the total FPGA area, as the number of inputs and degree of sharing increase. The results in Figure 11 show a progressive increase in the total area savings with the increasing input size and degree of sharing from ~0.8% for $k = 4$ and $d = 2$ to ~3.9% for $k = 7$ and $d = 4$. The behavior depicted by the results in Figure 11 is in agreement with (4), according to which the progressive area gains can be attributed to the rapidly growing 2^k term.

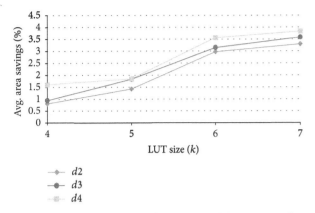

FIGURE 11: Average area savings for $N = 10$ and $k = 4–7$ over the 20 MCNC benchmark circuits.

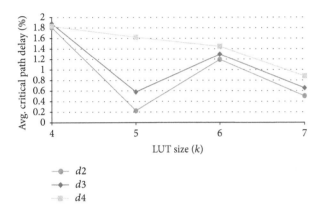

FIGURE 12: Average critical path for $N = 10$, $k = 4–7$, and $d = 2–4$ over the 20 MCNC benchmark circuits.

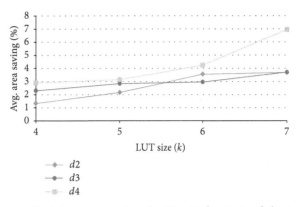

FIGURE 13: Average area savings for $N = 16$, $k = 4–7$, and $d = 2–4$ over the 20 MCNC benchmark circuits.

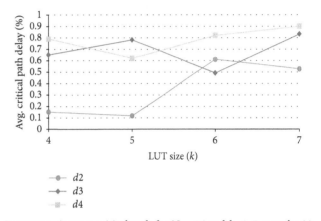

FIGURE 14: Average critical path for $N = 16$ and $k=4–7$ over the 20 MCNC benchmark circuits.

On the other hand, the results for the average (over the entire MCNC benchmark suite) critical path (shown in Figure 12) show a consistent behavior, with the average delay values staying within 2% of the results obtained for the conventional cluster size $N = 10$ architecture without any shared LUT pairs.

3.7. Cluster Size $N = 16$. The results obtained for the cluster size $N = 16$, for the 20 MCNC benchmark circuits, have been presented in Figures 13 and 14. The results have been compared with the default cluster size $N = 16$ architecture, without any shared LUT pairs. For the experimentation with cluster size $N = 16$, we set the number of shared pairs equal to 5 ($p = 5$), while for the degree of sharing ($d = 3$ and 4) p was set to values 4 and 3, respectively. Based on the observations from Figure 8, it is clear that, for input sizes $k = 4$, 5, and 6, the number of utilized CLBs stays relatively constant up to $p = 5$, after which they start growing rapidly. The reason for decreasing the value of p has been discussed in Section 3.6.

The results in Figure 13 show the average savings in the total FPGA area, as the number of inputs and degree of sharing increase. Similar to the trend observed in Figure 11, the area savings for cluster size $N = 16$ increase progressively as the input size and degree of sharing grow from $k = 4–7$,

from ~1.32% for $k = 4$ and $d = 2$, to ~7% for $k = 7$ and $d = 4$. Also the results for the average critical path delay (shown in Figure 14) follow a similar consistent pattern (as seen in Figure 12, for cluster size $N = 10$), staying within 1% of the results obtained for the conventional cluster size $N = 10$ architecture without any shared LUT pairs.

4. Conclusion

Most of the recently proposed FPGA architectures focus on replacing legacy LUTs with innovative, high coverage logic blocks. Although such logic blocks offer high area and performance gains for a particular benchmark suite, they are not generic enough to maintain quality of results over a wide range of circuits. In this paper, we have explored a novel FPGA architecture which allows sharing LUTs SRAM vectors between NPN-equivalent functions. To find NPN equivalence, a very high speed state-of-the-art Boolean matching algorithm has been employed. Furthermore, an efficient packing technique has also been introduced to cluster NPN-equivalent functions together inside a CLB. By using CLBs with shared LUTs (for cluster size $N = 16$, $k = 7$, $p = 3$, and $d = 4$), the configuration memory cells of logic blocks were reduced by ~56% which resulted in area savings of up to ~7%, with a negligible penalty on the critical path delay (<1%).

Acknowledgments

This project is funded by NSTIP, Saudi Arabia. The authors acknowledge the support of STU (Science and Technology Unit), Umm Al-Qura University, Saudi Arabia.

References

[1] V. Betz, J. Rose, and A. Marquardt, "Architecture and CAD for Deep-Submicron FPGAs," Kluwer Academic Publishers, Norwell, MA, USA, 1999.

[2] I. Kuon and J. Rose, *Quantifying and Exploring the Gap between FPGAs and ASICs*, Springer Science and Business Media, 2010.

[3] V. Betz and J. Rose, "How much logic should go in an FPGA logic block," *Design & Test of Computers, IEEE*, vol. 15, no. 1, pp. 10–15, 1998.

[4] E. Ahmed and J. Rose, "The effect of LUT and cluster size on deep-submicron FPGA performance and density," in *Proceedings of the ACM/SIGDA 8th International Symposium on FPGAs*, 2000.

[5] A. DeHon, "Balancing Interconnect and Computation in a Reconfigurable Computing Array (or, why you do not really want 100% LUT utilization)," in *Proceedings of the ACM/SIGDA 7th International Symposium on FPGAs*, Montery, CA, USA, 1999.

[6] A. Marquardt, V. Betz, and J. Rose, "Using Cluster-Based Logic blocks to improve FPGA Speed and Density," in *Proceedings of the ACM/SIGDA 7th International Symposium on FPGAs*, pp. 203–213, Monterey, CA, USA, 2000.

[7] J. Rose and S. Brown, "Flexibility of interconnection structures in field-programmable gate arrays," *IEEE Journal of Solid State Circuit*, vol. 26, no. 3, 1991.

[8] G. Lemieux and D. Lewis, "Using sparse crossbars within LUT," in *Proceedings of the 2001 ACM/SIGDA ninth international symposium on Field programmable gate arrays*, 2001.

[9] Y. Okamoto, Y. Ichinomiya, M. Amagasaki, M. Iida, and T. Sueyoshi, "COGRE: a configuration memory reduced reconfigurable logic cell architecture for area minimization," *Field Programmable Logic and Applications (FPL)*, pp. 304–309, 2010.

[10] B. K. I. Ahmadpour and H. Asadi, "An efficient reconfigurable architecture by characterizing most frequent logic functions," *Field Programmable Logic and Applications (FPL)*, 2015.

[11] Z. Zilic and Z. Vranesic, "Using decision diagrams to design ULMs for FPGAs," *IEEE Transactions on Computers*, vol. 47, no. 9, pp. 971–982, 1998.

[12] A. Ahari, B. Khaleghi, Z. Ebrahimi, H. Asadi, and M. B. Tahoori, "Towards dark silicon era in FPGAs using complementary hard logic design," *Field Programmable Logic and Applications (FPL)*, pp. 1–6, 2014.

[13] V. P. Correia and A. I. Reis, "Classifying n-input Boolean functions," *VII Workshop Iberchip*, 2001.

[14] S. Kimura, T. Horiyama, M. Nakanishi, and H. Kajihara, "Folding of logic functions and its application to look up table compaction," in *Proceedings of the IEEE/ACM International Conference on Computer-Aided Design (ICCAD '02)*, pp. 694–697, San Jose, CA, USA, 2002.

[15] J. Meyer and F. Kocan, "Sharing of SRAM tables among NPN-equivalent LUTs in SRAM-based FPGAs," *IEEE Transactions on Very Large Scale Integration Systems (VLSI)*, vol. 15, p. 15, 2007.

[16] Q. Zhao, K. Yanagida, M. Amagasaki, M. Iida, M. Kuga, and T. Sueyoshi, "A logic cell architecture exploiting the shannon expansion for the reduction of configuration memory," *Field Programmable Logic and Applications (FPL)*, pp. 1–6, 2014.

[17] J. H. Anderson and Q. Wang, "Area-efficient FPGA logic elements: Architecture and synthesis," in *Proceedings of the 16th Asia and South Pacific Design Automation Conference*, pp. 369–375, Yokohama, Japan, 2011.

[18] J. Luu, J. Goeders, M. Wainberg et al., "VTR 7.0: Next generation architecture and CAD system for FPGAs," *ACM Transactions on Reconfigurable Technology and Systems (TRETS)*, vol. 7, no. 2, 2014.

[19] G. Lemieux, E. Lee, M. Tom et al., "Directional and single-driver wires in FPGA interconnect," in *Proceedings of the International Conference on Field Programmable Technology (ICFPT)*, pp. 41–48, Brisbane, NSW, Australia, 2004.

[20] Z. Huang, L. Wang, Y. Nasikovskiy et al., "Fast Boolean matching based on NPN classification," in *Proceedings of the International Conference on Field Programmable Technology (ICFPT)*, pp. 310–313, Kyoto, Japan, 2013.

[21] A. Asghar, M. M. Iqbal, W. Ahmed et al., "Exploring shared SRAM tables among NPN equivalent large LUTs in SRAM-based FPGAs," in *International Conference on Field Programmable Technology (ICFPT)*, pp. 229–232, Xi'an, China, 2016.

[22] Berkeley Logic Synthesis and Verification Group, ABC: System for Sequential Synthesis and Verification, http://www-cad.eecs.berkeley.edu/alanmi/abc.

[23] Y. Marquardt, V. Betz, and J. Rose, "Using cluster-based logic blocks and timing-driven packing to improve FPGA speed and density," in *Proceedings of the ACM/SIGDA International Symposium on Field Programmable Gate Arrays*, 1999.

[24] Intelligent FPGA Architecture Repository (iFAR), http://www.eecg.toronto.edu/vpr/architectures.

[25] Predictive Technology Model (PTM), http://www.eas.asu.edu/ptm.

[26] E. Ahmed and J. Rose, "The Effect of LUT and Cluster Size on Deep-Submicron FPGA Performance and Density," *IEEE Transactions on Very Large Scale Integration Systems (VLSI)*, vol. 12, no. 3, 2004.

[27] Xilinx Inc., Programmable Logic Data Book, 1996.

9

Challenges in Clock Synchronization for On-Site Coding Digital Beamformer

Satheesh Bojja Venkatakrishnan, Elias A. Alwan, and John L. Volakis

Department of Electrical and Computer Engineering, Florida International University, Miami, FL 33174, USA

Correspondence should be addressed to Satheesh Bojja Venkatakrishnan; bojjavenkatakrishnan.1@osu.edu

Academic Editor: John Kalomiros

Typical radio frequency (RF) digital beamformers can be highly complex. In addition to a suitable antenna array, they require numerous receiver chains, demodulators, data converter arrays, and digital signal processors. To recover and reconstruct the received signal, synchronization is required since the analog-to-digital converters (ADCs), digital-to-analog converters (DACs), field programmable gate arrays (FPGAs), and local oscillators are all clocked at different frequencies. In this article, we present a clock synchronization topology for a multichannel on-site coding receiver (OSCR) using the FPGA as a master clock to drive all RF blocks. This approach reduces synchronization errors by a factor of 8, when compared to conventional digital beamformer.

1. Introduction

Synchronization techniques are required for reliable high data rate communications to avoid phase mismatches and jitter [1, 2]. For complex RF systems involving data converter arrays, different frequencies may be required implying that components are clocked at different frequencies as well. Synchronization then requires different clocking architectures depending on the system configuration [3, 4].

In complex systems, the number of clock signals can rapidly increase from just a few to hundreds. Quite often, in large scale systems, a single external clock circuit may not have enough outputs to drive all branches. To overcome this issue, various clock tree topologies are used to synchronize multiple parts, devices, or systems [5]. However, each level in the tree introduces a delay component that is fixed or undetermined. Although fixed delays can be compensated with additional effort, it is highly challenging to eliminate the undetermined delays. Further, these delays may be affected by external factors like voltage and temperature changes and device-specific variations. Altogether, inaccuracies result in intolerable timing variations in analog-to-digital converters

(ADCs) and digital-to-analog converters (DACs) that affect the clocking [3, 4].

For transceivers where the devices and components are located in proximity, sharing a common timing signal is generally the easiest and most accurate method for synchronization [5–7]. This is the case with on-site coding receiver (OSCR) [8, 9] that combines several of signals into a single ADC using coding technique, as shown in Figure 1. Since a single ADC is used to handle several antennas/paths, errors due to ADC-FPGA synchronization, interchannel skews, and variations within ADCs can be reduced. Specifically, in OSCR architecture [9–11], all the components are enclosed within a single block making synchronization easier and less prone to errors. Further, using a single FPGA as a master source for synchronization removes the clock skew errors [12]. However, to highlight the implementation challenges using different topologies, we have included the analysis of clock synchronization implementation using external distribution circuit. Preliminary work has already been presented in [13]. In this article, we present a clock synchronization implementation for an 8-channel OSCR digital beamformer using an FPGA,

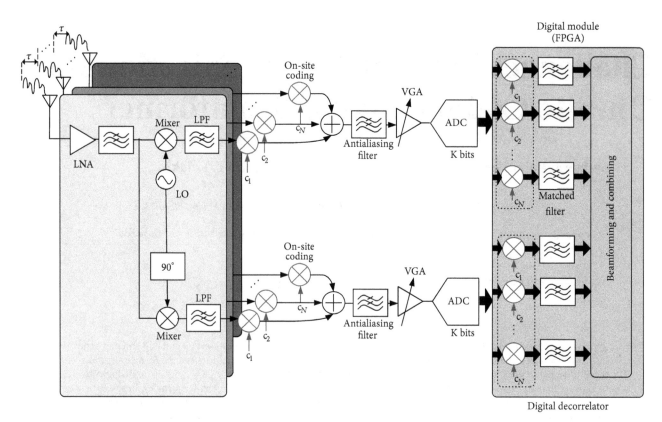

FIGURE 1: Block diagram representation of OSCR system [8, 9].

an ADC, an in-house built encoder board, and RF transceiver boards.

2. Clock Synchronization Implementation

2.1. FPGA Controlled Distribution Circuit. A general description of realized OSCR is given in [9–11]. The 8-channel OSCR employs 8 RF boards that require 8 clock signals operating at 38.4 MHz and an encoder board with 8 differential (16 signals) orthogonal codes, perfectly synchronized with each other. Also, a dual-channel ADC sampling at 256 MSPS, requiring a clock of 256 MHz is included. Thus, for an 8-channel OSCR 25 signals (8 RF clocks + 8 differential codes + 1 ADC clock) must be synchronized. To keep the jitter low and reliability high, the total number of components used for synchronization must be minimized. With this in mind, FPGA platform was chosen as a good compromise between performance and flexibility. Figure 2 shows the FPGA used to provide timing signals to all devices. Notably, using a single FPGA to generate clock signals at different rates becomes a significant design challenge. An additional complexity is that most RF front-end units rely on serial interfaces to the transmission/receive blocks, requiring that data and clock be embedded/deembedded by a digital processor or FPGA.

As can be seen from Figure 2, clock synchronization was implemented using Xilinx VC707 FPGA running ISE software. VHDL was used for programming and the "clocking wizard" IP from Xilinx was used to generate and distribute

the required clocks. To do so, a low phase noise reference signal of 12.8 MHz was fed to the FPGA. The phase noise at 10 KHz offset was found to be −80 dBc/Hz and at 1 KHz offset was −102 dBC/Hz. This clock frequency was chosen to reduce output jitter and clock skew. Using this clocking wizard, the 12.8 MHz reference clock was used to generate output clock frequencies of 38.4 MHz for the RF boards, 256 MHz for the ADC clock, and 64 MHz to be used by the FPGA for generating orthogonal codes whose maximum frequency component is 32 MHz. It should be noted that, for ADCs with high sampling rate, the sampling clock should be sharp. High phase noise will lead to degradation in signal-to-noise ratio (SNR) performance [14].

Having determined the clock frequencies, a next step is to program the clock signal assignments and code generation using VHDL. After an error free execution of the program, module level simulation was performed. Figure 3 shows the simulated output generated by the FPGA. There are 8 different orthogonal codes each synchronously triggered with reference to the rising edge of the 64 MHz internal FPGA clock. We note that each of the 8 signals represents a 16-bit orthogonal code used for encoding/decoding, as shown in Figure 1. From the simulations in Figure 3, we observe that the FPGA generates clocks and codes with perfect synchronization. This has been verified using lab measurements as presented in the later sections. From the measured lab result, it was seen that the system exhibits mesosynchronization with constant delay or phase shift between signals.

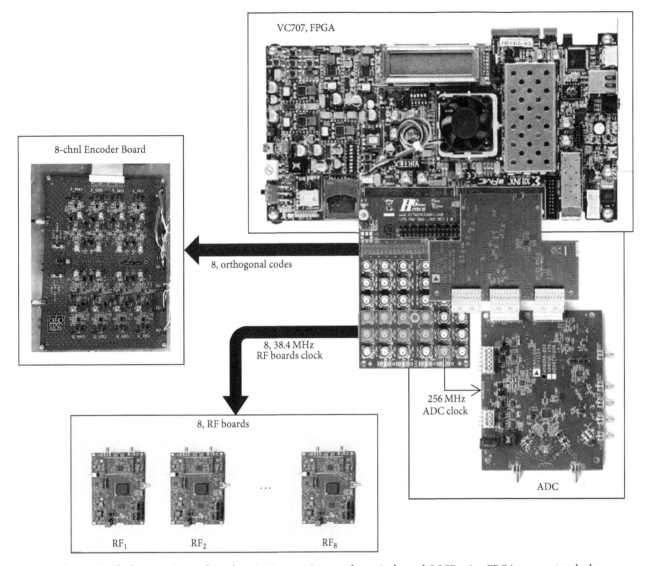

FIGURE 2: Clock generation and synchronization requirement for an 8-channel OSCR using FPGA as a master clock.

The 25 signals of the OSCR must be rerouted within the FPGA to the output pins of the VC707 board. These signals are taken from the debug card connected to the FPGA using the FPGA Mezzanine Card (FMC). FMC houses 400 pins and hence 200 signals can be generated at any time from the fully populated debug card. In the present scenario, pin placement was performed following the interface constraints. Also, like signals were placed within close proximity to reduce mismatch in the path lengths of these signal.

It is necessary to generate all 25 signals with proper logic levels. For example, to generate high-speed orthogonal code signals and still keep jitter low, a low voltage differential signaling (LVDS) output buffer was used for the FPGA outputs. Mapping is then performed after converting the register-transistor logic (RTL) description into a netlist of basic elements (BELs). This takes care of the packaging and signal placement. Subsequently, we perform routing of the signals to specified user pins. As a final step, timing analysis is

performed to ensure all signals have comparable path delays. This timing analysis considers the location of the output pins and is hence more realistic in determining the propagation delay of each signal. Timing analysis was performed only for 8 orthogonal codes and 8 RF board clocks and had to be perfectly synchronized for realizing digital beamforming. Timing analysis for ADC clock was ignored. Propagation delays for RF board clock signals and orthogonal codes are given in Figures 4(a) and 4(b), respectively. It should be noted that for OSCR, mesochronous synchronization is also considered to be perfectly synchronized, since the phase difference between signals is constant without skews and can be corrected in post processing.

From Figure 4(a), we can infer that the propagation delays of the clock sources decrease uniformly. This is due to the way the clock outputs were routed. The path taken by clock is controlled by the slices location and output pins in the floor plan of the FPGA. That is, even though all 8 clock outputs

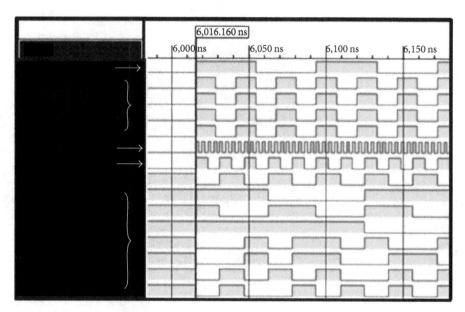

FIGURE 3: Simulated signal waveforms as required by the 8-channel OSCR system.

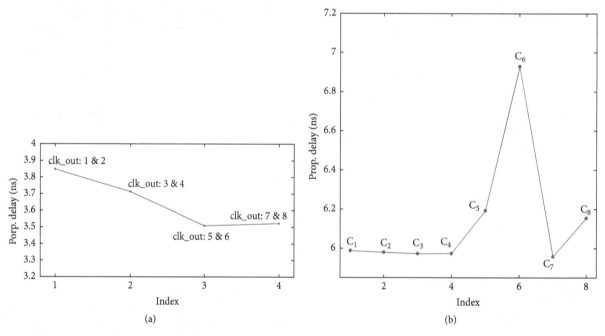

FIGURE 4: Simulated propagation delay of signals based on timing analysis. (a) Propagation delay of 8 RF board clock signals at 38.4 MHz and (b) Propagation delay of 8 orthogonal codes.

are at the same frequency of 38.4 MHz, their signal paths are different and hence they experience different propagation delays. Clock outputs 1, 2, 3, and 4 have a longer propagation path and clock outputs 5, 6, 7, and 8 have shorter paths. Therefore, longer propagation delays were associated with clock outputs 1 and 2. Similarly, for the orthogonal code signals, 7 sets of codes were placed within close proximity of each other except for the code pair 6. As a result, propagation delays of this code were higher as compared to the others (see Figure 4(b)). It should be noted that the mismatch in the paths is due to design constraint of the OSCR architecture.

Generally, the propagation delays between the board and the FPGA paths are in "ns" range. Correspondingly, the delay differences among the clock signals are in the "ps" range. Similarly, from the analysis of the orthogonal code signals, the worst-case scenario arises when we compare code 6 (C6) with code 4 (C4). The propagation delay difference between C6 and C4 is approximately 0.9 ns. These delays can be corrected within the FPGA. The reason is that VC707 can generate signals up to 933 MHz and corresponding clock of 1.07 ps. Hence, any clock signal with time period greater than 1.07 ps can be easily synthesized. Consequently, delays

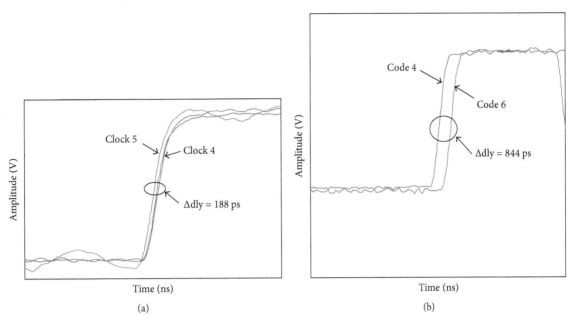

FIGURE 5: Generated signals by the FPGA measured using oscilloscope. (a) Generated clock signals (Clock 4 and Clock 5) and (b) Generated codes (C4 and C6).

also of the order "ps" can be synthesized and accounted within the FPGA using VHDL coding. Notably, differences of this magnitude have minimum effect on the on-site coding performance.

Figure 5(a) shows the captured clock signals on an oscilloscope for clock outputs 4 and 5. Similarly, Figure 5(b) shows the captured codes of C4 and C6 generated by the FPGA. We note that the reason for considering these specific signals is because they exhibited the largest delay. As can be seen from Figures 5(a) and 5(b), the maximum delay between clock signals used for triggering the RF boards is ~188 ps and the maximum delay between codes is ~844 ps.

For the direction of arrival application using current OSCR system, the RF boards are clocked at 38.4 MHz or 26.04 ns. Since the maximum delay between these clock signals is 0.188 ns, which falls within the rise time/fall time of the specification of the clock generator chip, the delay has no significant impact on the system performance. Similarly, the maximum delay for the codes is ~0.9 ns. It should be noted that the same codes generated by the FPGA are used for encoding and decoding. Hence, by delaying the digitized coded signals for processing within the FPGA, it is possible for us to compensate for the delay caused by the codes. Alternatively, the FPGA has the capability to generate delays as low as 1.07 ps. Hence, corresponding delays between codes can be generated and corrected within the FPGA itself before encoding.

Using the above synchronization topology, OSCR performance was measured and it was found that there is no overall degradation in OSCR performance due to synchronization issues, as detailed in [9, 10, 15]. Using the above synchronization scheme, bit error rate (BER) and SNR was simulated. Based on the results in [9, 10, 15], it can be concluded that

above synchronization scheme results in no performance degradation.

2.2. Clock Synchronization Using External Distribution Circuit. It is also imperative to analyze the clock synchronization implementation using an external distribution clock. In complex systems involving multiple components to be synchronized, a single external clock generation integrated circuits may not have enough outputs to drive all branches. This problem can be overcome using clock tree topology to synchronize multiple devices [4]. However, in such topologies each level of distribution introduces a delay component that is the result of fixed and undetermined delays that are also affected by external factors. The inaccuracies add up causing intolerable timing variations which drastically affect the high frequency components clocking. Although it is relatively easy to compensate for fixed delays, undetermined delays cannot be corrected for within the system [4]. In addition to these constraints, the tree structure should be accommodating when the number of branches is increased.

Despite these drawbacks, analysis was performed for 8-element OSCR clock synchronization using external source and distribution circuit to compare it with our proposed synchronization method using FPGA for clock distribution. In order to do so, the clock tree should have at least 10 clock outputs (8 for RF boards, 1 for ADC, and 1 for FPGA), as shown in Figure 6. Commercially off-the-shelf (COTS) components were considered for this case. AD9576 by analog devices was the right choice providing up to 11 clock outputs and also has the capability to generate clocks. It has built-in dividers that enable generation of multiple frequencies. Despite the capability of the evaluation board (AD9576) to generate low jitter clock signals over wide frequency range,

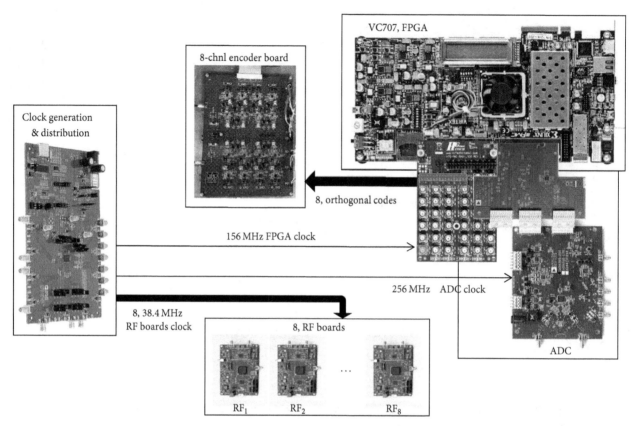

FIGURE 6: Clock generation and synchronization requirement for an 8-channel OSCR using external source.

it still is not desirable for synchronization implementation in OSCR. By employing external distribution circuit, the hardware requirement increases, thus defeating the novelty of OSCR [8–11]. Further, the existing FPGA generates signals which results in the required synchronization without any performance degradation.

Nevertheless, referring to the block diagram in Figure 6, an external source can be used to achieve clock synchronization. This evaluation board has a maximum jitter of up to 50 ps which is better than the previous architecture discussed. The output signaling modes may be changed by software control independent from each other, which gives the option of trade-off between power consumption and drive strength versus frequency. The clock signals generated by the COTS evaluation board suffered from overshoot at high frequencies. When sampled at incorrect instance, this leads to significant synchronization error.

Orthogonal codes used for encoding/decoding had to be generated using FPGA. Hence, it was imperative to employ FPGA in any clocking architecture [8–11]. Further, multiple AD9576 distribution boards are required to achieve clock synchronization for a 64-element OSCR system. Apart from increased implementation complexity, this also requires synchronization of the distribution circuit. It should be noted that OSCR would behave in a similar manner if external clock synchronization scheme is implemented. Doing so will lead to increased power and cost, thus defeating the sole purpose of OSCR. It also should be noted that the scope of this paper

was to prove that clock synchronization was in fact possible without any additional components. Hence, this architecture is not suited for OSCR, since the drawbacks outweigh its low jitter performance.

2.3. Measurements and Results. Using the setup in Figure 7, various multibeam and multifrequency measurements are performed in the anechoic chamber using the constructed 8 channels [9, 15]. For the measurement, 8 RF boards were used as receivers and an encoder board was employed for performing on-site coding. A single ADC was used for digitization and the FPGA employed at the digital backend for post processing. For the setup shown in Figure 7, all the digital components are synchronized using the initial scheme. The measurements in the anechoic chamber included five different test cases, namely, $(\Theta_{s1,in}, \Theta_{s2,in}) = (0°, 50°), (-10°, 40°),$ $(-20°, 30°), (-30°, 20°),$ and $(-40°, 10°)$ at frequencies $f_1 = 1350$ MHz and $f_2 = 1800$ MHz and SNR of 22 dB. The main goal of the measurement is to verify the faithful recovery of the signal phase after on-site coding/decoding. That is, OSCR was experimentally verified by accurately estimating location of two beams simultaneously and performing digital beamforming.

Table 1 gives the measured angle of incidence $(\Theta_{s,in})$ and decoded angles $(\Theta_{s,out})$ for various cases. For evaluating the OSCR, phases were estimated for two different incoming beams at different frequencies. To evaluate the accuracy of our approach, we computed the maximum phase error

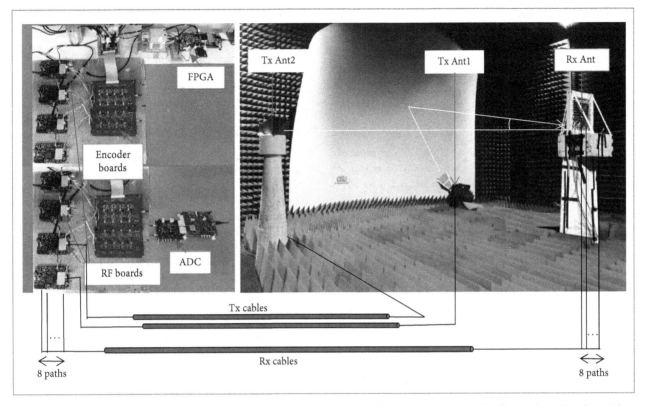

FIGURE 7: Eight-channel OSCR on the workstation outside the chamber. Also shown is the setup inside the anechoic chamber with two transmitting horn antennas at different locations and 64-element receiver array mounted on a rotating foam column.

TABLE 1: Angle estimation.

Cases	Incident angle		Measured angle		Max error
	$\Theta_{s1,in}$	$\Theta_{s2,in}$	$\Theta_{s1,out}$	$\Theta_{s2,out}$	$\Theta_{s,err}$
1	0°	50°	0°	50°	0°
2	−10°	40°	−9.8°	41.8°	1.8°
3	−20°	30°	−19.6°	31.4°	1.4°
4	−30°	20°	−29.1°	20.4°	0.9°
5	−40°	10°	−38.1°	10.4°	1.9°

($\Theta_{s,err}$) defined as the maximum of $|\Theta_{s,in} - \Theta_{s,out}|$. Thus from Table 1, the maximum computed phase error using 8-channel OSCR is $\Theta_{s,err} = 1.9°$. This error is mostly attributed to system hardware component nonidealities and hence can be removed via calibration. Also, it should be noted that multiple measurements were performed for repeatability and OSCR performance remained the same.

Further, from the phase distribution plot shown in Figure 8, phase variance (σ_φ) can be estimated. The latter is used to compute the SNR using [11],

$$SNR = \frac{1}{\sigma_\varphi^2}. \tag{1}$$

Based on the decoded data, the phase variance was found to be 0.083 rad, which corresponds to SNR of 21.6 dB. This

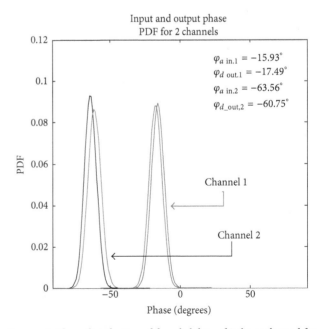

FIGURE 8: Phase distribution of decoded data of 2 channels used for quantifying the performance of OSCR.

results in 0.4 dB degradation as compared with the input SNR of 22 dB. As stated earlier, this degradation could be attributed to the hardware component nonidealities.

Due to hardware limitations of our OSCR system, BER was computed indirectly from the estimated SNR using,

$$\frac{E_b}{N_0} = \text{SNR} \times \frac{1}{\log_2 M}, \qquad (2)$$

where E_b is the energy per bit, N_0 is the noise spectral density, and $M = 4$ for QPSK. Hence, BER for the corresponding E_b/N_0 can be estimated from the theoretical AWGN BER graph. From the theoretical BER plot for QPSK [9, 11], the BER is estimated to be ~$5e-7$ for the computed E_b/N_0 of 10.8 dB. Thus, it can be concluded that with the above synchronization scheme, OSCR performance was not degraded.

3. Conclusion

Utilizing state-of-the-art FPGA circuits, we designed a purely digital clock synchronization system, without analog components (i.e., delay lines) that would require a time-consuming calibration and lead to increasing jitter for long delay ranges. Thus, the entire functionality, such as selecting trigger and clock source, defining trigger threshold level, setting delay, and defining the polarity and width of the output, is programmed using VHDL. Clock synchronization was implemented using the above setup for 8-channel OSCR system and various measurements and performance analysis were conducted. It was observed that system worked in a perfect synchronous manner and signals were detected and decoded with no synchronization errors. Alternatively, in this article we showed that implementing clock synchronization using COTS distribution board suffers from many drawbacks as compared to FPGA distribution. Further, when expanding OSCR to 64 channels, establishing clock synchronization using the above approach leads to more complex problems. It can be concluded that using FPGA as a master source for synchronization proves to be a better choice owing to its performance and the flexibility it offers.

Acknowledgments

This work was supported by the Office of Naval Research, Arlington, VA, USA, under Grant no. N00014-16-1-2253.

References

[1] A. A. Nasir, S. Durrani, H. Mehrpouyan, S. D. Blostein, and R. A. Kennedy, "Timing and carrier synchronization in wireless communication systems: a survey and classification of research in the last 5 years," *EURASIP Journal on Wireless Communications and Networking*, vol. 2016, no. 1, article 180, 2016.

[2] C. Winstead and M. E. Hamoui, "Reducing clock jitter by using Muller-C elements," *IEEE Electronics Letters*, vol. 45, no. 3, pp. 150-151, 2009.

[3] P. Poshala and P. Shetty, "Synchronizing the giga-sample ADCs interfaced with multiple FPGAs," Application Report SLAA643, Texas Instruments, Dallas, Tex, USA, 2014.

[4] K. Pekar and A. Oz, "Synchronizing sample clocks of a data converter array," Technical Article, Analog Devices, Norwood, Mass, USA, http://www.analog.com/en/technical-articles/synchronizing-sample-clocks-of-a-data-converter-array.html.

[5] J. Dedić, A. Hasanović, D. Golob, and M. Pleško, "Extremely low-jitter FPGA based synchronization timing system," in *Proceedings of the IEEE Particle Accelerator Conference (PAC '07)*, pp. 296–298, Albuquerque, NM, USA, June 2007.

[6] C. Y. Wu, J. Chen, K. H. Hu et al., "RF reference distribution and timing system for the taiwan photon source," in *Proceedings of the 10th European Workshop on Beam Diagnostics and Instrumentation for Particle Accelerators (DIPAC '11)*, Hamburg, Germany, May 2011.

[7] S. Li, W. Wan, and L. Pan, "A practical method of clock synchronization in 2-out-of-3 system," in *Proceedings of the IET International Communication Conference on Wireless Mobile and Computing (CCWMC '11)*, pp. 304–306, Shanghai, China, November 2011.

[8] E. A. Alwan, A. A. Akhiyat, W. Khalil, and J. L. Volakis, "Analytical and experimental evaluation of a novel wideband digital beamformer with on-site coding," *Journal of Electromagnetic Waves and Applications*, vol. 28, no. 12, pp. 1401–1429, 2014.

[9] S. B. Venkatakrishnan, D. K. Papantonis, A. A. Akhiyat, E. A. Alwan, and J. L. Volakis, "Experimental validation of on-site coding digital beamformer with ultra-wideband antenna arrays," *IEEE Transactions on Microwave Theory and Techniques*, vol. 99, pp. 1–10, 2017.

[10] S. B. Venkatakrishnan, A. A. Akhiyat, E. A. Alwan, and J. L. Volakis, "Dual-band validation of on-site coding receiver using ultra-wideband antenna array at C, X and Ku-bands," in *Proceedings of the 2016 IEEE Antennas and Propagation Society International Symposium (APSURSI '16)*, pp. 1655-1656, Fajardo, Puerto Rico, July 2016.

[11] E. A. Alwan, S. B. Venkatakrishnan, A. A. Akhiyat, W. Khalil, and J. L. Volakis, "Phase error evaluation in a two-path receiver front-end with on-site coding," *IEEE Access*, vol. 3, pp. 55–63, 2015.

[12] J. M. Castillo-Secilla, F. León, J. Olivares, and J. M. Palomares, "Multiplicative composition of clock-skew components for improving time synchronisation," *IEEE Electronics Letters*, vol. 51, no. 13, pp. 991–993, 2015.

[13] S. B. Venkatakrishnan, E. A. Alwan, and J. L. Volakis, "Clock synchronization challenges for on-site coding digital beamformer," in *Proceedings of the 2017 IEEE International Symposium on Antennas and Propagation (APSURSI '17)*, San Diego, Calif, USA, July 2017.

[14] W. Kester, "Converting oscillator phase noise to time jitter," Tutorial MT-008, Analog Devices, Norwood, Mass, USA, http://www.analog.com/media/en/training-seminars/tutorials/MT-008.pdf.

[15] S. B. Venkatakrishnan, A. Akhiyat, E. A. Alwan, and J. L. Volakis, "Multiband and multibeam direction of arrival estimation using on-site coding digital beamformer," *IEEE Antennas and Wireless Propagation Letters*, vol. 16, pp. 2332–2335, 2017.

10

FPGA-Based Real-Time Moving Target Detection System for Unmanned Aerial Vehicle Application

Jia Wei Tang, Nasir Shaikh-Husin, Usman Ullah Sheikh, and M. N. Marsono

Faculty of Electrical Engineering, Universiti Teknologi Malaysia (UTM), 81310 Skudai, Johor Bahru, Malaysia

Correspondence should be addressed to Nasir Shaikh-Husin; nasirsh@fke.utm.my

Academic Editor: João Cardoso

Moving target detection is the most common task for Unmanned Aerial Vehicle (UAV) to find and track object of interest from a bird's eye view in mobile aerial surveillance for civilian applications such as search and rescue operation. The complex detection algorithm can be implemented in a real-time embedded system using Field Programmable Gate Array (FPGA). This paper presents the development of real-time moving target detection System-on-Chip (SoC) using FPGA for deployment on a UAV. The detection algorithm utilizes area-based image registration technique which includes motion estimation and object segmentation processes. The moving target detection system has been prototyped on a low-cost Terasic DE2-115 board mounted with TRDB-D5M camera. The system consists of Nios II processor and stream-oriented dedicated hardware accelerators running at 100 MHz clock rate, achieving 30-frame per second processing speed for 640×480 pixels' resolution greyscale videos.

1. Introduction

Unmanned Aerial Vehicle (UAV) plays an important role in mobile aerial monitoring operations and has been widely applied in diverse applications such as aerial surveillance, border patrol, resource exploration, and combat and military applications. Due to its mobility, UAV has also been deployed for search and rescue operation [1] by acquiring high-resolution images in disaster area. Apart from that, several researches [2, 3] have also been done on traffic monitoring using UAV. As most monitoring systems require detection and tracking object of interest, moving target detection is a typical process in UAV monitoring system [4].

Moving target detection is the process of locating moving objects (foreground) residing in the static scene (background) from a series of visual images captured from a camera. As displacement of object in subsequent video frames defines its movement, at least two successive video frames are required for processing. An object is defined as a moving target if it is located in two different positions corresponding to the background from two selected frames taken at different time intervals. Thus, a background model is required to represent the static scene from incoming video frames prior to the segmentation of moving object.

Background model can be categorized based on the type of camera movement [5], including stationary camera, pan-tilt-zoom camera, free camera motion with planar scene, and free camera motion with complex scene geometry. Detection and segmentation of moving objects in stationary background (static camera) can be performed easily using background subtraction technique [6–11], while image registration technique is required in moving background (moving camera) involving ego-motion (camera motion) estimation and compensation to align the backgrounds of selected video frames prior to object segmentation. The scene in aerial imagery in UAV video is assumed to be planar [12]. The ego-motion estimation for planar scene can be estimated using homography transformation such as affine model. Hence, moving object can be detected by registering the video frame to the estimated model and employing the background subtraction with this registered model. This approach does not consider the scene with significant depth variations as it causes incorrect registrations due to parallax.

Due to the complexity of computer vision algorithm, moving target detection in aerial imagery is a time consuming process. It is also not practical to rely on a ground processing station via radio link as video quality will greatly depend on the wireless communication speed and stability. In addition, full autonomous UAV is desirable as it can operate and react towards detected target with minimal human intervention [13]. Thus, an autonomous UAV demands a system with high mobility and high computing capability to perform detection on the platform itself. The use of Field Programmable Gate Array (FPGA) will satisfy the low power consumption, high computing power, and small circuitry requirements of a UAV system. FPGA-based system is a good solution in real-time computer vision problem for mobile platform [14] and can be reconfigured to handle different tasks according to desired applications.

This paper presents a FPGA implementation of real-time moving target detection system for UAV applications. The detection algorithm utilizes image registration technique which first estimates the ego-motion from two subsequent frames using block matching (area-based matching) and Random Sample Consensus (RANSAC) algorithm. After compensating the ego-motion, frame differencing, median filtering, and morphological process are utilized to segment the moving object. The contributions of this paper are as follows:

(i) Development of real-time moving target detection in a System-on-Chip (SoC), attaining 30 frames per second (fps) processing rate for 640 × 480 pixels' video.

(ii) Prototyping of the proposed system in a low-cost FPGA board (Terasic DE2-115) mounted with a 5 megapixels' camera (TRDB-D5M), occupying only 13% of total combinational function and 13% of total memory bits.

(iii) Partitioning and pipeline scheduling of the detection algorithm in a hardware/software (HW/SW) codesign for maximum processing throughput.

(iv) Stream-oriented hardware accelerators including block matching and object segmentation module which are able to operate in one cycle per pixel.

(v) Analyzing detection performance with different density of area-based ego-motion estimation and frame differencing threshold.

The rest of the paper is as follows. Section 2 discusses the literatures in moving target detection. Section 3 discusses the moving target detection algorithm while Section 4 describes the SoC development and the specialized hardware architecture of moving target detection. Section 5 presents the detection result from the complete prototype. Section 6 concludes this paper.

2. Related Work

Moving target detection targeting for aerial videos or UAV applications has been widely researched in the past few decades. A framework consisting of ego-motion compensation, motion detection, and object tracking was developed in [15]. The authors used combination of feature and gradient-based techniques to compensate ego-motion while utilizing accumulative frame differencing and background subtraction

TABLE 1: Comparison between related works on FPGA-based object detection system for different applications with proposed system.

Related work	Camera platform	Detection technique and application
[6–11]	Static camera	(i) Background subtraction (ii) Using GMM, ViBE, and so forth
[23]	Moving robot	(i) Detecting moving object using (ii) Optical flow and frame differencing
[24]	UAV	(i) Detecting and tracking object feature
[13]	UAV	(i) Car detection (ii) Based on shape, size, and colour
[25]	UAV	(i) Detecting moving object (ii) Using regional phase correlation (iii) Does not prototype the complete system
[26]	UAV	(i) Real-time ego-motion estimation
Proposed	UAV	(i) Moving target detection (ii) Using area-based image registration (iii) Prototyping the complete system

to detect moving vehicle in aerial videos. The research in [16] presented two different approaches to detect and track moving vehicle and person using a Hierarchy of Gradient (HoG) based classifier. The work in [17] has proposed a moving target detection method that performs motion compensation, motion detection, and tracking in parallel by including data capture and collaboration control modules. Multiple target detection algorithm was proposed in [18], catering for large number of moving targets in wide area surveillance application. Moving target detection and tracking for different altitude were presented and demonstrated on UAV-captured videos in [19]. Feature-based image registration technique was proposed in [20] to detect moving object in UAV video. The authors utilized corner points in subsequent video frames as features to perform ego-motion estimation and compensation. In [21], a multimodel estimation for aerial video was proposed to detect moving objects in complex background that is able to remove buildings, trees, and other false alarms in detection. As these literature works focused on improving the detection algorithm for different cases and did not consider autonomous UAV deployment, they developed their system in a common desktop computer [17, 19–21] or Graphic Processing Unit (GPU) accelerated [22] environment.

In the context of FPGA-based object detection system, most works in the literature were targeted for static camera [6–11] as illustrated in Table 1. They utilized background subtraction techniques such as Gaussian Mixture Model (GMM) and ViBE (Visual Background Extractor) to perform foreground object segmentation in static background video. The work in [23] has proposed FPGA-based moving object detection for a walking robot. They implemented ego-motion estimation using optical flow technique and frame differencing in hardware/software codesign system.

There are also several literatures proposing FPGA-based detection for UAV applications. The research in [24] has proposed a hardware/software codesign using FPGA for feature detection and tracking in UAV applications. The authors implemented Harris feature detector in dedicated hardware to extract object features from aerial video while tracking of object based on the features is executed in software. Implementation of real-time object detection for UAV is described in [13] to detect cars based on their shape, size, and colour. However, both works in [13, 24] performed detection and tracking based on object features and did not focus on moving targets. A suitable moving target detection algorithm for FPGA targeting sense and avoid system in UAV has been proposed in [25] by using regional phase correlation technique but the authors did not prototype the complete system in FPGA device. In addition, research in [26] also presented the hardware design and architecture of real-time ego-motion estimation for UAV video. Hence, there are limited numbers of works in the literature focusing on the development of a complete prototype to perform real-time moving target detection for UAV applications using FPGA.

3. Moving Target Detection Algorithm

As UAV is a moving platform, the proposed moving target detection algorithm employs image registration technique to compensate the ego-motion prior to object segmentation. Image registration algorithms can be classified into feature-based and area-based (intensity-based) methods [27, 28].

In feature-based method, detected features such as corners [29, 30] or SURF [31] from two subsequent frames are cross-correlated to find the motion of each feature from one frame to another. Feature-based image registration is reported to have faster computation in software implementation as it uses only a small number of points for feature matching regardless of the number of pixels. The number of detected features is unpredictable as it depends on the captured scene of the frames, thus having unpredictable amount of computation and memory resource, making it difficult to be implemented in highly parallel hardware. Number of features can be reduced to a predictable constant with an additional step of selecting strongest features based on their score (i.e., feature strength) by sorting or priority queuing [24]. However, it presents some limitations as only pixels of the highly textured areas would be selected while neglecting the homogeneous area [32]. Moreover, feature-based method requires irregular access of memory which is not suitable for streaming hardware.

On the contrary, area-based technique construct point-to-point correspondence between frames by finding the most similar texture of a block (area) from one frame to another. It is suitable for parallelism and stream processing as it offers several benefits for hardware implementation:

(i) It has highly parallel operations that make it suitable for parallel processing in hardware implementation.

(ii) It allows simple control-flow and does not require irregular accessing of image pixels.

(iii) It has predictable memory requirement with fixed size of computation data.

The overall flow of the proposed algorithm is illustrated in Figure 1. It consists of two main processes, which are

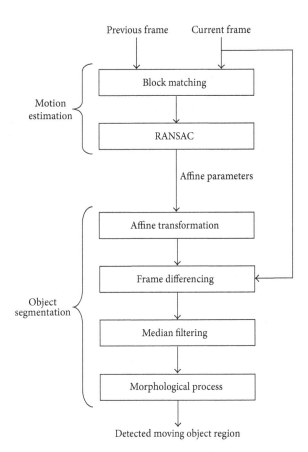

FIGURE 1: Overall algorithm of moving target detection using image registration technique.

motion estimation and object segmentation. Area-based image registration is utilized in this work. The inputs to the system are two consecutive greyscale video frames, which are the current and the previous frames. First, block matching is performed on these two frames to produce point-to-point motion between frames. As aerial imagery in UAV video is assumed to have free camera motion with planar scene [5], affine model is employed to estimate the ego-motion. RANSAC is then used to remove insignificant motion (outliers) among all points, resulting in the ego-motion in terms of affine transformation matrix.

After the previous frame is aligned with current frame using parameters in the affine transformation matrix, frame differencing can be performed with pixel-by-pixel subtraction on both aligned frames, followed by thresholding to produce a binary image. Median filtering and morphological processes are done on the binary image to remove noises, resulting in only the detected moving target.

The proposed algorithm is intended for SoC implementation consisting of a Nios II embedded software processor running at 100 MHz. However, most processes running on Nios II are slow and insufficient to achieve real-time capability. In order to realize a real-time moving target detection system, all processes in this work are implemented in fully dedicated hardware accelerators except RANSAC, which is partially accelerated in hardware.

3.1. Block Matching. Block matching involves two steps: extraction and matching, where two consecutive frames are required. Extraction process will store several blocks or patches of image pixels from one frame as template, while matching process will find their most similar blocks in the second frame. By considering the center points of blocks as reference, this algorithm will yield numerous pairs of corresponding points which indicate the point-to-point motion (movement of the pixels) between two consecutive frames. The paired points from these two frames will be used in RANSAC to estimate the ego-motion.

Block extraction is the process of storing numerous blocks of 9×9 pixels from a predefined location from a video frame. These blocks will be used as templates in the matching process. The positions of the template blocks are distributed evenly over the image. There is no mathematical computation in the extraction process as it involves only direct copying of image patches from video stream into temporary memory.

Matching process plays the role of finding the most similar blocks from current frame for every extracted template block from the previous frame. This is done by correlating the template blocks with next frame to find their corresponding position based on similarity measure. Due to simplicity of hardware implementation, Sum of Absolute Difference (SAD) is chosen as the matching criterion for the correlation process. SAD will generate a similarity error rating of pixel-to-pixel correlation between each template block (from previous frame) and matching block (from current frame). SAD will yield zero result if both blocks are pixel-by-pixel identical.

Block matching is computation intensive as each template block has to search for its most similar pair by performing SAD with each block within its search region. Several search techniques had been proposed in the literatures to reduce the computation by minimizing the search region such as Three-Step Search Technique [33, 34], Four-Step Search Technique [35], and Diamond Search [36]. However, most of these techniques are targeted for general purpose processor which reads image in irregular way and are not suitable for streaming hardware architecture. This work uses traditional full search technique [37] as it is efficient to be performed in stream-oriented hardware due to its regular accessing of image.

The number of required matching computations is proportional to the number of blocks (density) and their corresponding search areas. Higher density of block matching provides more points for ego-motion estimation to reduce image registration error but with higher hardware cost requirement (number of hardware computation units). To reduce hardware cost, this work employs only a low density block (area-based) matching and does not estimate frame-to-frame motion of every pixel.

To further optimize hardware resources in stream-oriented architecture, best-fit and nonoverlapping search areas are utilized to ensure only one SAD computation is performed for each incoming pixel. For a number of row blocks, m, and a number of column blocks, n, search areas are evenly distributed for each block with $s_m \times s_n$ pixels, formulated in

$$
\begin{aligned}
s_m &= \left\lfloor \frac{W}{m} \right\rfloor, \\
s_n &= \left\lfloor \frac{H}{n} \right\rfloor,
\end{aligned} \tag{1}
$$

where W and H represent image width and image height, respectively.

The template block positions (blue) and their corresponding search areas (green) are illustrated in Figure 2. In each clock cycle, only one template block is matched with one block from its corresponding search area. As each template block will only search in its dedicated search area without intruding other regions, the whole block matching process shares only one SAD computation unit for processing the whole image, allowing m and n to be context-switched in runtime.

The proposed approach is able to perform different densities of area-based registration using the same hardware cost. However, higher density reduces the search areas of each block, thus limiting the flow displacement (travel distance of each point). The displacement limitations in horizontal d_m and vertical d_n are given as $d_m = \pm W/2m$ and $d_m = \pm H/2n$, respectively. As the position and movement of UAV (height, velocity, etc.) as well as frame rate of captured aerial video affect the point-to-point displacement between two successive frames, the proposed technique will produce wrong image registration result if the point-to-point displacement between frames exceeds d_m in horizontal or/and d_n in vertical.

3.2. RANSAC. After the block matching stage, a set of point pairs (point-to-point motion) from two successive frames are identified. Based on these point pairs, ego-motion estimation can be performed. As outliers (inconsistent motions) usually appear in these point pairs, RANSAC algorithm is applied to remove outliers from the data. RANSAC is an iterative algorithm to find the affine model that best describes the transformation of the two subsequent frames. Unlike the conventional RANSAC [38], this work uses an upper bound time to terminate RANSAC computation (similar to [39]) regardless of the number of iterations due to the real-time constraint as illustrated in Algorithm 1.

At each iteration, RANSAC algorithm chooses three distinct point pairs randomly as samples. Hypothesis model of affine transformation is then generated from the selected samples based on

$$
\begin{bmatrix} x'_1 & x'_2 & x'_3 \\ y'_1 & y'_2 & y'_3 \\ 1 & 1 & 1 \end{bmatrix} = \begin{bmatrix} h_0 & h_1 & h_2 \\ h_3 & h_4 & h_5 \\ 0 & 0 & 1 \end{bmatrix} \begin{bmatrix} x_1 & x_2 & x_3 \\ y_1 & y_2 & y_3 \\ 1 & 1 & 1 \end{bmatrix}, \tag{2}
$$

where h_i denote the parameters of the affine model to be estimated, x_i and y_i are the coordinates of chosen sample points, and x'_i and y'_i represent their corresponding point pairs.

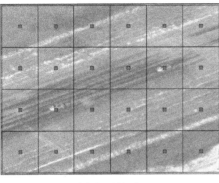

(a) 6×4 blocks

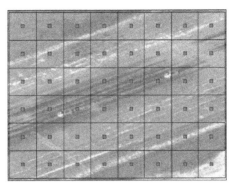

(b) 8×6 blocks

FIGURE 2: Positions of template blocks (blue) and search areas (green) in video frame for different densities ($m \times n$) of block matching with same hardware cost.

---

while time taken < upper bound time **do**
    (1) Randomly select 3 distinct point pairs as samples.
    (2) Generate hypothesis model (affine parameters) based
    on the chosen samples.
    (3) Apply $T_{d,d}$ test on the hypothesis model.
    (4) Calculate the fitness score of the model.
    (5) Update and store best scored parameters.
end while

ALGORITHM 1: RANSAC algorithm.

---

fitness score = 0
for all data$_i$ **do**
    asub$x$ = abs($x_{2i} - (x_{1i} \cdot H_0 + y_{1i} \cdot H_1 + H_2)$)
    asub$y$ = abs($y_{2i} - (x_{1i} \cdot H_3 + y_{1i} \cdot H_4 + H_5)$)
    score = min((asubx^2 + asuby^2), th$_{\text{dist}}^2$)
    fitnessscore = fitnessscore + score
end for
Where:
Each data$_i$ contains a point pair ($x_{1i}, x_{2i}, y_{1i},$ and y_{2i})
$H_0, H_1, H_2, H_3, H_4, H_5$ are affine parameters of hypothesis
model.
th$_{\text{dist}}^2$ is the predefined distance threshold.

ALGORITHM 2: Fitness scoring in RANSAC algorithm.

$T_{d,d}$ test proposed in [40] is applied in the algorithm to speed up RANSAC computation by skipping the following steps (step (4) and (5)) if the hypothesis model is far from the truth. Fitness of the hypothesis is then evaluated and scored by fitting its parameters to all point pairs. The best hypothesis model is constantly updated in each iteration and emerges as the final result when the RANSAC is terminated upon reaching an upper bound time. As RANSAC has the least computation among overall moving target detection algorithms, it is implemented as software program with only the fitness scoring step (step (4)) being hardware accelerated. Fitness scoring is the calculation of the fitness for a hypothesis model towards all input data (point pairs from block matching), as described in Algorithm 2.

Each data is considered as an inlier if its fitting error is smaller than a predefined distance threshold, th$_{\text{dist}}$ or vice versa. Inlier fitness score is its fitting error while outlier score is fixed to th$_{\text{dist}}$ as a constant penalty. The total fitness score is calculated by accumulating all individual scores for each data where a perfect fit will have zero fitness score. As fitness scoring is an iterative process for all data, the number of computations increases with size of data. As RANSAC is a stochastic algorithm, it may not produce the best-fit affine model when given limited iteration.

3.3. Object Segmentation. After estimating ego-motion, the camera movement between two successive frames is to be compensated prior to object foreground detection. The

previous frame is transformed and mosaic with current frame using the estimated affine parameters from RANSAC algorithm. Reverse mapping technique is applied by calculating the corresponding location in the source image based on the destination pixel location. The equation of affine transformation is shown in

$$
\begin{bmatrix} x_i' \\ y_i' \\ 1 \end{bmatrix} = \begin{bmatrix} h_0 & h_1 & h_2 \\ h_3 & h_4 & h_5 \\ 0 & 0 & 1 \end{bmatrix} \begin{bmatrix} x_i \\ y_i \\ 1 \end{bmatrix}, \tag{3}
$$

where x_i and y_i are the pixel coordinates of destination image, x_i' and y_i' denote the corresponding pixel coordinates in source image, and h_i are best-fit affine parameters from RANSAC.

As the transformation may produce fractional result, nearest neighbour interpolation is utilized due to its efficiency in hardware design. The ego-motion compensation is performed pixel-by-pixel in raster scan, generating a stream of the transformed previous frame to the next process.

Frame differencing is executed on the current frame and the transformed (ego-motion compensated) previous frame by pixel-to-pixel absolute subtraction of both frames. The pixels in the resultant image are threshold with constant

TABLE 2: Pipeline scheduling for processing subsequent frames.

Processes	Processing frame at frame period, t_i						
	t_0	t_1	t_2	t_3	t_4	$\cdots$	t_i
Motion estimation							
(i) Block matching	F_0	$F_1 \leftarrow F_0$	$F_2 \leftarrow F_1$	$F_3 \leftarrow F_2$	$F_4 \leftarrow F_3$	$\cdots$	$F_i \leftarrow F_{i-1}$
(ii) RANSAC	—	—	$F_1 \leftarrow F_0$	$F_2 \leftarrow F_1$	$F_3 \leftarrow F_2$	$\cdots$	$F_{i-1} \leftarrow F_{i-2}$
Object segmentation							
(i) Affine transformation							
(ii) Frame differencing	—	—	—	$F_1 \leftarrow F_0$	$F_2 \leftarrow F_1$	$\cdots$	$F_{i-2} \leftarrow F_{i-3}$
(iii) Median filtering							
(iv) Morphological							

$F_i \leftarrow F_j$ is detection of moving object from jth frame to ith frame.

value of $\mathrm{th_{fd}}$ to produce binary image. Lower value of $\mathrm{th_{fd}}$ may induce more false alarm in detection while higher value causes the miss detection. Both subtraction and thresholding processes can be done as soon as two pixels for the same coordinate from these frames are obtained to yield one binary pixel for the next process. Lastly, 7×7 binary median filter and dilation processes are performed on the binary image to remove noise and improve the detected region of moving target.

3.4. Pipeline Scheduling. In order to establish a real-time moving target detection system for streaming video, proper pipeline scheduling is utilized to fully maximize the overall system throughput. The algorithm is split into several subprocesses with each hardware accelerator working on different frames independently, transferring the intermediate result from one process to another until the end of the detection cycle. Hence, the system will always produce output every time after a fixed latency. The overall process is divided into four stages of pipeline as shown in Table 2.

Due to data dependencies of the streaming algorithm, all processes must be done sequentially to produce one detection result. Block matching requires two successive video frames for computation. The first frame is streamed in for block extraction process and stored into frame buffer. Block matching is performed after the next frame is obtained with the extracted block of previous frame. RANSAC can only begin its computation after block matching has finished processing on the entire frame. Lastly, two original frames (F_{i-2} and F_{i-3}) are read from frame buffer for object segmentation to produce the final result. Object segmentation computation can be performed in stream without further frame buffering. The overall pipeline processing of the streaming system has four frames' latency. Hence, at least four frames (F_{i-3} to F_i) must be stored in frame buffer at all time for a complete moving target detection process.

4. Proposed Moving Target Detection SoC

The moving target detection SoC is developed and prototyped in Terasic DE2-115 board with Altera Cyclone IV FPGA device. The system consists of hardware/software codesign of the algorithm of where the hardware computation is executed in dedicated accelerator coded in Verilog Hardware Description Language (HDL) while software program is performed using a soft-core Nios II processor with SDRAM as software memory. The system architecture of the proposed moving target detection SoC is illustrated in Figure 3.

Camera interface handles the image acquisition tasks to provide the raw image for processing, while VGA interface manages video displaying task. Apart from being a software memory, part of SDRAM is also reserved as video display buffer. Thus, Direct Memory Access (DMA) technique is applied to read and write the displaying frame in SDRAM to ensure the high throughput image transfer.

As multiple frames are required at the same time to detect moving target, frame buffer is required to temporarily store the frames for processing. Hence, SRAM is utilized as frame buffer due to its low latency access. Since most computations are performed in the dedicated hardware, Nios II handles only RANSAC process (except fitness scoring step as described in Section 3.2) and auxiliary firmware controls. USB controller is included in the SoC to enable data transfer with USB mass storage device for verification and debugging purposes. In addition, embedded operating system (Nios2-linux) is booted in the system to provide file system and drivers support.

The real-time video is streamed directly into the moving target detector for processing. Both Nios II and hardware accelerator modules compute the result as a hardware/software codesign system and transfer the output frame to SDRAM via DMA. VGA interface constantly reads and displays the output frame in SDRAM. All operations are able to be performed in real-time, attaining a 30 fps moving target detection system.

4.1. Moving Target Detection Hardware Accelerator. The hardware architecture of the moving target detector is shown in Figure 4. It is composed of motion estimation core, object segmentation core, frame grabber, and other interfaces. The overall moving target detection is performed according to the following sequences:

(1) Frame grabber receives the input video stream and stores four most recent frames (F_{i-3} to F_i) into frame buffer through its interface. At the same time frame

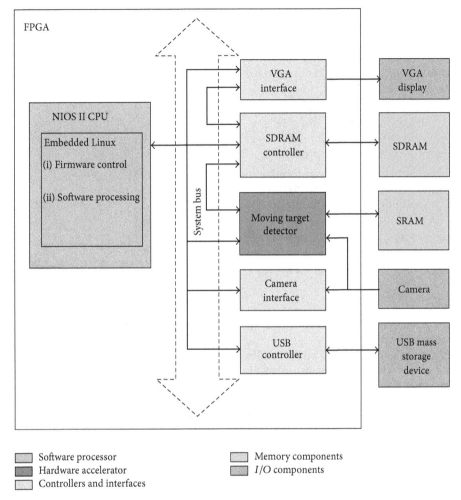

FIGURE 3: System architecture of moving target detection.

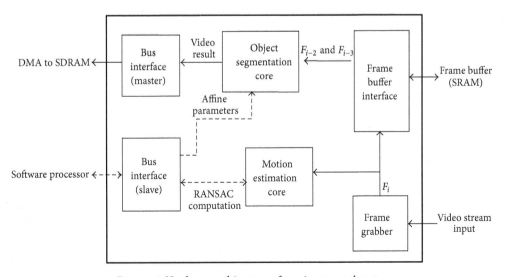

FIGURE 4: Hardware architecture of moving target detector.

grabber also provides the current frame (F_i) to motion estimation core.

(2) Motion estimation core performs block matching and RANSAC computation. Since RANSAC is computed in both hardware and software, software processor is constantly accessing this core via system bus interface to calculate the affine parameters.

(3) After RANSAC, the affine parameters are transferred from software to object segmentation core. Two previous frames (F_{i-2} and F_{i-3}) are read from the frame buffer by object segmentation core for processing.

(4) Several processes involving affine transformation, frame differencing, median filter, and dilation are then performed on both frames, resulting in the detected moving target.

(5) Lastly, the bus interface (master) provides DMA access for object segmentation core to transfer the end result into SDRAM for displaying and verification purposes.

As the frame buffer (SRAM) is a single port 16-bit memory, frame grabber concatenates two neighbouring 8-bit greyscale pixels to store in one memory location. Since frame grabber and object segmentation core share the frame buffer to write and read frames, respectively, frame buffer interface provides priority arbitration and gives frame grabber the highest priority, granting every write request. However, frame buffer may be busy for a couple of clock cycles due to read operation of SRAM by other modules; a small FIFO with depth of 4 is utilized in frame grabber to temporarily buffer the incoming image pixels.

4.2. Motion Estimation Hardware Accelerator. Motion estimation core consists of block matching and RANSAC hardware accelerators. Since RANSAC requires the entire data of point pairs provided by block matching to begin its computation, additional buffers are needed to temporarily store the corresponding point pairs for every two subsequent frames. The hardware architecture for motion estimation process is shown in Figure 5.

To enable high throughput data (point pairs) sharing for both block matching and RANSAC, double buffering technique is applied by using two buffers (Buffer 1 and Buffer 2) as data storage. For any instance, one buffer is written by block matching while the other is used for computation by RANSAC. Buffer controller swaps the roles of these two buffers for each incoming new frame, therefore ensuring both processes to be pipelined by reading and writing on each buffer subsequently. Buffer swapping is initiated at each completion of block matching modules while RANSAC is performed during the time gap between each swap and is terminated before the next swap.

4.2.1. Block Matching Hardware Accelerator. Figure 7 shows the architecture of the proposed block matching hardware accelerator, performing template blocks extraction from one frame and matching of these template blocks in their corresponding search areas from next frame. The overall

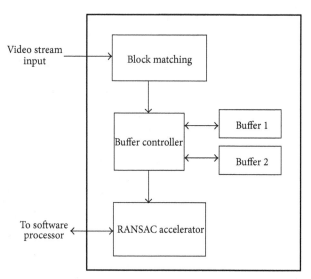

FIGURE 5: Hardware architecture of motion estimation core.

process can be completed in stream to yield the point-to-point motion (point pairs) of two subsequent frames without buffering an entire frame.

As 9×9 block size is utilized in block matching, a 9-tap line buffer is designed in such a way that 9×9 pixels of moving window can be obtained in every clock cycle. These 9×9 pixels are shared for both block extraction and matching processes and are read one by one in pipeline from the line buffer at each valid cycle, resulting in a total of 81 cycles to obtain a complete window.

The block extractor keeps track of the coordinate of current pixel in video stream as a reference for extraction process. Template blocks from incoming frames are extracted and stored temporarily into block memory. As each block is extracted line-by-line in raster scan, block memory is divided into nine-row memories as illustrated in Figure 6(a) with each of which being used to store one pixel row in template blocks. When video stream reaches the block position, each pixel row is loaded into each row memory from the corresponding tap of the line buffer. Block coordinates are also stored in a separate FIFO to keep track of its position.

Since only one SAD processor is used for matching $m \times n$ blocks as mentioned in Section 3.1, the template block has to be swapped according to the corresponding search area during raster scan. Hence, row memory is constructed with two FIFOs, upper and lower FIFO as illustrated in Figure 6(b), to enable block swapping during matching process. Template blocks are stored into upper FIFO during extraction process. During matching process, each line of raster scan enters eight different search areas to match eight different template blocks, respectively. Hence, one row of template blocks is cached in lower FIFO and is repeatedly used until the end of their search areas (reaching next row of search areas). Upon reaching each new row of search areas, template blocks in lower FIFO are replaced with new row of template blocks from upper FIFO. At the last line of raster scan, the lower FIFO is flushed to prevent overflow.

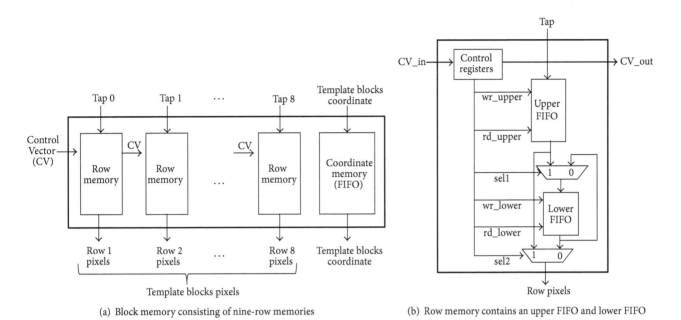

(a) Block memory consisting of nine-row memories

(b) Row memory contains an upper FIFO and lower FIFO

FIGURE 6: Block memory architecture for storing template blocks.

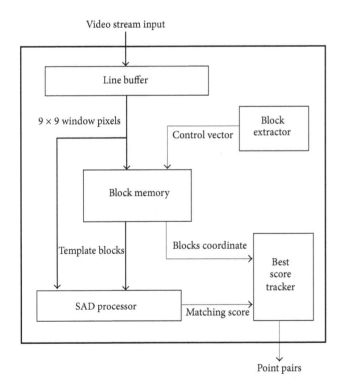

FIGURE 7: Stream-oriented hardware architecture of block matching.

TABLE 3: Control Vector (CV) for different read and write operations of block memory.

Position of raster scan	Write, upper	Read, upper	Write, lower	Read, lower	sel1	sel2
Entering template block position	1	x	x	x	x	x
Entering first search area row	x	1	1	0	1	1
Entering next search area row	x	1	1	1	1	1
Reentering same search area row	x	0	1	1	0	0
Leaving last search area row	x	0	0	1	0	0

In order to efficiently extract and match all blocks, different Control Vector (CV) as illustrated in Table 3 is sent to perform different reading and writing operations in block memory based on the current position in raster scan. Both reads and writes are independent of each other and are able to be executed at the same time. Pixels are processed one by one in 81 cycles to complete a window. Both writing and reading processes require 9 cycles for each row memory, passing CV from the first row memory to the next row memory until the end to complete a 81-pixel write or read operation of a template block.

SAD processor performs the correlation of the template blocks from previous frame with all possible blocks from current frame according to the search area. Extracted block pixels are read from block memory, while window pixels in search areas are provided from the taps of the line buffer. The total number of required PEs is the total number of pixels in a window. The process is pipelined such that each pixel is computed in each PE as soon as it is obtained from the line buffer. Matching score of each window can be obtained in every cycle after a fixed latency.

Lastly, the best score tracker constantly stores and updates the best matching score for each template block within its corresponding search area. The matching score is compared

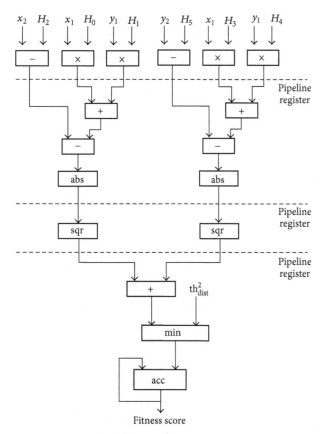

FIGURE 8: Hardware datapath of fitness scoring in RANSAC accelerator.

TABLE 4: Fixed point precision of fitness scoring inputs.

Parameter	Number of bits		Number range
	Integer	Fraction	
x_1, y_1, x_2, y_2	11	0	$[-1024, 1024)$
H_0, H_1, H_3, H_4	4	12	$[-8, 8)$
H_2, H_5	11	5	$[-1024, 1024)$

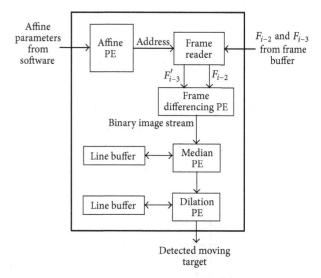

FIGURE 9: Hardware architecture for object segmentation.

among the same search area and the coordinates of the best-scored blocks are preserved. At the end of each search area, the coordinates of the best pairs (template blocks and their best-scored blocks) are sent to RANSAC module for next processing. Hence, the proposed block matching hardware is able to produce point-to-point motion (point pairs) of every two successive frames in streaming video at line rate.

4.2.2. RANSAC Hardware Accelerator. RANSAC hardware design in [39] is utilized in this work, which accelerates only fitness scoring step. As described in Algorithm 2, fitness scoring is an iterative process which performs similar computation to all data samples based on hypothesis model. Hence, this data intensive process is executed in pipelined datapath as illustrated in Figure 8. A control unit is utilized to read input data provided by block matching from buffer and stream these inputs to the datapath unit at every clock cycle.

The datapath unit utilizes three stages of pipeline with the aim of isolating multiplication processes, thus allowing faster clock rate. The first stage pipeline registers are located right after the first multiplication, while the other two stages of pipeline registers enclose the squaring processes. The individual score is accumulated in the last stage, producing total final fitness score. The accumulator is reset on each new set of hypothesis. Thus, the total number of cycles required

for fitness score computation is the number of overall data plus the four-cycle latency.

Although fitness scoring could require floating point computations, the datapath unit uses suitable fixed point precision for each stage. Since Nios II is a 32-bit processor, the affine parameters in hypothesis model (H_0 to H_6) are properly scaled to different precision of 16-bit fixed points as described in Table 4 so that two affine parameters can be assigned in a single 32-bit write instruction. As this system is targeted for 640×480 pixels' video, all input coordinates (x_1, y_1, x_2, and y_2) are scaled to 11 bits.

4.3. Object Segmentation Hardware Architecture. As object segmentation can be performed in one raster scan, a stream-oriented architecture is proposed as illustrated in Figure 9. All subprocesses are executed in pipeline on the streaming video without additional frame buffering. Object segmentation process is initiated by software processor after providing the affine parameters from RANSAC to affine PE. Two frames (F_{i-2} and F_{i-3} as described in Table 2) from frame buffer (SRAM) are required to segment the moving target.

Based on the affine parameters from RANSAC, affine PE uses reverse mapping technique to find each pixel location in previous frame (F_{i-3}) using (3) and generates their addresses in frame buffer (SRAM). Frame readers fetch the previous frame (F_{i-3}) pixel-by-pixel according to the generated addresses from frame buffer, thus constructing a stream of transformed frame, which is denoted as F'_{i-3}.

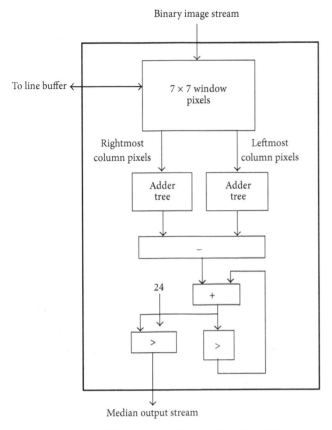

FIGURE 10: Hardware architecture of median PE.

By synchronizing the streams of both frames, frame differencing can be executed in pipeline as soon as one pixel from each frame is obtained. Hence, one pixel in current frame (F_{i-2}) and one pixel in transformed frame (F'_{i-3}) are fetched alternatively from their corresponding memory locations by frame reader, constructing two synchronized streams of F_{i-2} and F'_{i-3} frames. Frame differencing PE performs pixel-to-pixel absolute subtraction and thresholding on the streams. The frame differencing PE is able to compute in one cycle per pixel. A configurable threshold value, th_{fd}, is used after the subtraction, yielding a stream of binary image without buffering the whole frame.

After frame differencing the binary image is streamed into 7×7 median filtering. Seven lines of the image are buffered in the line buffer, providing 7×7 pixels window for the median PE to perform the median computation. Median computation can be performed in one clock cycle for each processing window due to short propagation delay as only binary pixels are involved. Figure 10 shows the hardware logic design of median PE.

Median filtering can be computed by counting the number of asserted (binary 1) pixels in the window. If more than half the pixels in the window (24 pixels) are asserted, the resultant pixel is "1," or "0" otherwise. Since processing window will move only one pixel to the right for each computation during raster scan, current pixel count is computed by adding the previous pixel count and rightmost column pixels in the current window while subtracting the leftmost column pixels in the previous window. Final binary output pixel is produced by thresholding the current pixel count with 24 (half of window size).

As dilation is also a 7×7 window-based processing, it uses similar line buffering technique as median filtering. However, only simple logical OR operation is performed on all window pixels. Due to its simplicity, dilation PE can also be computed in one clock cycle, resulting in the stream of binary image with detected region of moving targets.

5. Experimental Results

5.1. Verification of Proposed SoC. The proposed moving target detection SoC is verified in offline detection mode using the database in [41]. Test videos are 640×480 pixels in size and are greyscaled prior to the verification process. The test videos are transferred to the system for computation via a USB mass storage device. After performing the detection in SoC, the image results are displayed on VGA and also stored on USB drive for verification. Figure 11 shows the moving target detection result from the proposed SoC using different sample videos. The detected regions (red) are overlaid on the input frame. In most cases, the proposed SoC is able to detect the moving target in consecutive frames.

However, there are several limitations in this work. Block matching may not give a good motion estimation result if the extracted blocks do not have texture (the pixels intensity are similar). Moreover, the detected region of moving target may appear in cavity or multiple split of smaller regions as only simple frame differencing is applied in the proposed system. Additional postprocessing to produce better detected blob by merging split regions is out of the scope in this work.

As the stochastic RANSAC algorithm is terminated after a constant time step for each frame, image registration error may occur which produces incorrect ego-motion estimation. This could be mitigated by accelerating RANSAC algorithm to ensure more iterations using dedicated hardware or high performance general purpose processor.

5.2. Performance Evaluation of Detection Algorithm. The performance evaluation of the implemented detection algorithm uses the Mathematical Performance Metric in [42] that involves several parameters as follows:

(i) True positive, TP: the detected moving object.

(ii) False positive, FP: detected regions that do not correspond to any moving object.

(iii) False negative, FN: the nondetected moving object.

(iv) Detection rate, DR: the ratio of TP with the combination of TP and FN, as formulated in

$$DR = \frac{TP}{TP + FN}. \tag{4}$$

(v) False alarm rate, FAR: the ratio between FP in all positive detection, as defined in

$$FAR = \frac{FP}{TP + FP}. \tag{5}$$

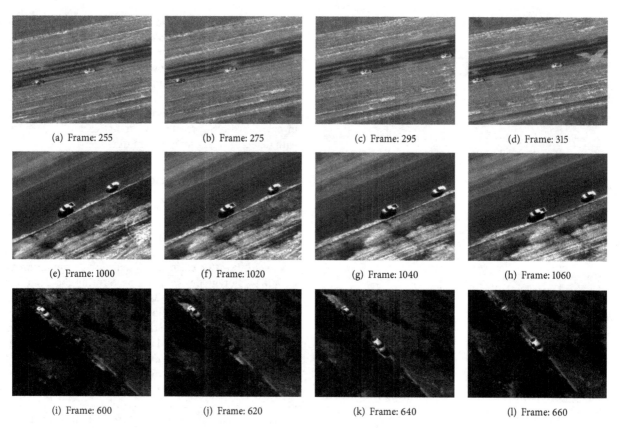

FIGURE 11: Detected regions from the proposed moving target detection SoC on different sample videos in [41]. Video numbers (a)–(d): V3V100003_004, video numbers (e)–(h): V3V100004_003, and video numbers (i)–(l): V4V100007_017.

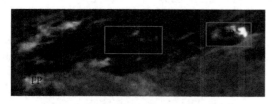

FIGURE 12: Evaluation of performance metrics TP, FP, and FN based on ground truth boxes (blue) and the detected region (red).

To obtain the performance metrics, ground truth regions are manually labelled in several frames of test videos. A bounding box is drawn across each moving object to indicate the ground truth region of every frame as depicted in Figure 12. A simple postprocessing is performed on the detected region by filtering out the detected region smaller than 15 pixels' width or 15 pixels' height prior to the evaluation. A detected moving object (TP) has detected regions in its bounded ground truth area, while a nondetected moving object (FN) has no detected region overlapping with its ground truth area. Detected region that does not overlapp with any ground truth region is considered as false positive (FP).

The detection performance is evaluated on different parameters configuration. The DR and FAR for 1000 test frames using different number of blocks (density in ego-motion estimation), $m \times n$, in area-based registration and

frame differencing threshold, th_{fd}, are depicted in Table 5 and Figure 13.

The experiment results show that DR is almost similar for different density of ego-motion estimation but decreases with th_{fd}. Although higher density in the proposed work has lower displacement limitation, d_m and d_n as discussed in Section 3.1, most of the point-to-point displacements do not exceed the limitation due to slow UAV movement in the most frames of the test dataset. On the contrary, higher value of th_{fd} may filter out the moving object if the differences in intensity of the object pixels and background pixels are almost similar.

FAR decreases with density in ego-motion estimation due to the higher quality in image registration process but increases if most frames exceed the displacement limitation, d_m and d_n. However, false registration due to displacement limitation results in a huge blob of foreground but does not greatly increase FAR. Although higher values of th_{fd} decrease the false detection rate, they also produce smaller foreground area for all detected moving objects as pixels almost similar intensity with background will be thresholded.

5.3. Speed Comparison with Full Software Implementation. The computation speed of the proposed moving target detection SoC is compared with software computation in different platforms, including modern CPU (Intel Core i5) in desktop computer and embedded processor (ARM). Table 6 illustrates the comparison of computation frame rate and hardware

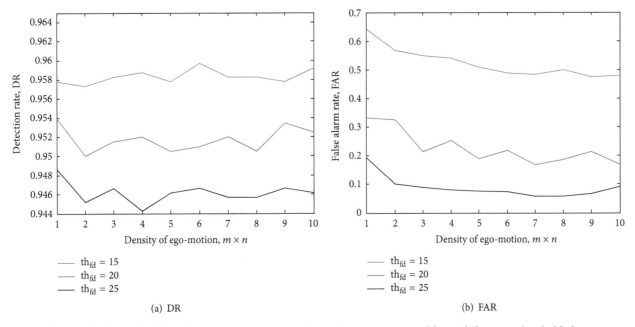

(a) DR

(b) FAR

FIGURE 13: DR and FAR for different density in ego-motion estimation, $m \times n$, and frame differencing threshold, th_{fd}.

TABLE 5: Performance evaluation in terms of DR and FAR for 1000 frames using different density in ego-motion estimation, $m \times n$, and frame differencing threshold, th_{fd}.

$m \times n$	th_{fd}	DR	FAR
12	15	0.958	0.643
12	20	0.954	0.331
12	25	0.949	0.194
24	15	0.957	0.568
24	20	0.950	0.324
24	25	0.945	0.101
35	15	0.958	0.548
35	20	0.952	0.215
35	25	0.947	0.090
48	15	0.959	0.539
48	20	0.952	0.253
48	25	0.944	0.079
70	15	0.958	0.509
70	20	0.951	0.188
70	25	0.946	0.075
88	15	0.960	0.489
88	20	0.951	0.219
88	25	0.947	0.074
108	15	0.958	0.483
108	20	0.952	0.168
108	25	0.946	0.058
140	15	0.958	0.499
140	20	0.951	0.187
140	25	0.946	0.059
165	15	0.958	0.474
165	20	0.953	0.214
165	25	0.947	0.068
192	15	0.959	0.478
192	20	0.952	0.169
192	25	0.946	0.092

TABLE 6: Computation speed comparison of the proposed system with different software implementation using area-based and feature-based registrations.

Platform	Frequency	Registration technique	Frame rate	Hardware speed-up
Proposed SoC	100 MHz	Area-based	30	1
Intel Core i5-4210U	1.70 GHz	Area-based	4.26	7.04
		Feature-based	13.11	2.29
ARM1176JZF	700 MHz	Area-based	0.20	150
		Feature-based	0.56	53.57

speed-up between the proposed system and other software implementations using test videos in [41].

As feature-based image registration has faster computation in software implementation comparing to area-based registration, speed performance of feature-based method is also included for comparison. In feature-based implementation, features are first detected in each frame. The detected features from current frame are cross-correlated with features with previous frame while RANSAC algorithm is used to estimate the ego-motion between frames. After compensating the ego-motion, segmentation of moving object uses the same processes with the proposed system. To further optimize the software implementation in terms of speed performance, a fast feature detection algorithm [30] is utilized. As the number of features will affect the computation time in feature matching step, only 100 strongest features in each frame are selected for processing. However, the performance evaluation does not consider multithreaded software execution.

TABLE 7: Resources usage of the proposed moving target detection SoC.

	Logic units	Utilization (%)
Total combinational function	15161	13%
Total registers	10803	9%
Total memory bits	521054	13%
Embedded multiplier	27	5%
FPGA device	Altera Cyclone IV	

Based on experimental result, the speed performance of the proposed moving target detection SoC surpasses optimized software computation by 2.29 times and 53.57 times compared with implementations in modern CPU and embedded CPU, respectively. The software computation (RANSAC) in HW/SW codesign of the proposed system creates speed bottleneck, thus limiting the maximum throughput to 30 fps. The processing frame rate of the proposed system can be further improved by using fully dedicated hardware.

5.4. Resource Utilization. The overall hardware resources utilization of the complete system is illustrated in Table 7. This prototype of real-time moving object detection system utilizes only less than 20 percent of total resources in Altera Cyclone IV FPGA device. As the proposed system uses off-chip memory components for frame buffering, FPGA on-chip memory is utilized only for line buffering in streaming process (e.g., block matching and median filtering) and storing intermediate results (e.g., point pairs after block matching). Thus, the low resource usage of the proposed system provides abundant hardware space for other processes such as target tracking or classification to be developed in future.

6. Conclusions

Moving target detection is a crucial step in most computer vision problem especially for UAV applications. On-chip detection without the need of real-time video transmission to ground will provide immense benefit to diverse applications such as military, surveillance, and resource exploration. In order to perform this complex embedded video processing on-chip, FPGA-based system is desirable due to the potential parallelism of the algorithm.

This paper proposed a moving target detection system using FPGA to enable autonomous UAV which is able to perform the computer vision algorithm on the flying platform. The proposed system is prototyped using Altera Cyclone IV FPGA device on Terasic DE2-115 development board mounted with a TRDB-D5M camera. This system is developed as a HW/SW codesign using dedicated hardware with Nios II software processor (booted with embedded Linux) running at 100 MHz clock rate. As stream-oriented hardware with pipeline processing is utilized, the proposed system achieves real-time capability with 30 frames per second processing speed on 640 × 480 live video. Experimental result shows that the proposed SoC performs 2.29 times and 53.57 times faster than optimized software computation on modern

desktop computer (Intel Core i5) and embedded processor (ARM). In addition, the proposed moving target detection uses only less than 20 percent of total resources in the FPGA device, allowing other hardware accelerators to be implemented in future.

Competing Interests

The authors declare that they have no competing interests.

Acknowledgments

The authors would like to express their gratitude to Universiti Teknologi Malaysia (UTM) and the Ministry of Science, Technology and Innovation (MOSTI), Malaysia, for supporting this research work under research Grants 01-01-06-SF1197 and 01-01-06-SF1229.

References

[1] A. Ahmed, M. Nagai, C. Tianen, and R. Shibasaki, "Uav based monitoring system and object detection technique development for a disaster area," *International Archives of Photogrammetry, Remote Sensing and Spatial Information Sciences*, vol. 37, pp. 373–377, 2008.

[2] B. Coifman, M. McCord, R. Mishalani, M. Iswalt, and Y. Ji, "Roadway traffic monitoring from an unmanned aerial vehicle," *IEE Proceedings-Intelligent Transport Systems*, vol. 153, no. 1, pp. 11–20, 2006.

[3] K. Kanistras, G. Martins, M. J. Rutherford, and K. P. Valavanis, "Survey of unmanned aerial vehicles (uavs) for traffic monitoring," in *Handbook of Unmanned Aerial Vehicles*, pp. 2643–2666, Springer, 2015.

[4] K. Nordberg, P. Doherty, G. Farnebäck et al., "Vision for a UAV helicopter," in *Proceedings of the International Conference on Intelligent Robots and Systems (IROS '02), Workshop on Aerial Robotics*, pp. 29–34, Lausanne, Switzerland, October 2002.

[5] D. Zamalieva and A. Yilmaz, "Background subtraction for the moving camera: a geometric approach," *Computer Vision and Image Understanding*, vol. 127, pp. 73–85, 2014.

[6] M. Genovese and E. Napoli, "ASIC and FPGA implementation of the Gaussian mixture model algorithm for real-time segmentation of high definition video," *IEEE Transactions on Very Large Scale Integration (VLSI) Systems*, vol. 22, no. 3, pp. 537–547, 2014.

[7] F. Kristensen, H. Hedberg, H. Jiang, P. Nilsson, and V. Öwall, "An embedded real-time surveillance system: implementation and evaluation," *Journal of Signal Processing Systems*, vol. 52, no. 1, pp. 75–94, 2008.

[8] H. Jiang, H. Ardö, and V. Öwall, "A hardware architecture for real-time video segmentation utilizing memory reduction techniques," *IEEE Transactions on Circuits and Systems for Video Technology*, vol. 19, no. 2, pp. 226–236, 2009.

[9] M. Genovese and E. Napoli, "FPGA-based architecture for real time segmentation and denoising of HD video," *Journal of Real-Time Image Processing*, vol. 8, no. 4, pp. 389–401, 2013.

[10] A. Lopez-Bravo, J. Diaz-Carmona, A. Ramirez-Agundis, A. Padilla-Medina, and J. Prado-Olivarez, "FPGA-based video system for real time moving object detection," in *Proceedings*

of the 23rd International Conference on Electronics, Communications and Computing (CONIELECOMP '13), pp. 92–97, IEEE, Cholula, Mexico, March 2013.

[11] T. Kryjak, M. Komorkiewicz, and M. Gorgon, "Real-time moving object detection for video surveillance system in FPGA," in Proceedings of the Conference on Design and Architectures for Signal and Image Processing (DASIP '11), pp. 1–8, IEEE, Tampere, Finland, November 2011.

[12] A. Mittal and D. Huttenlocher, "Scene modeling for wide area surveillance and image synthesis," in Proceedings of the IEEE Conference on Computer Vision and Pattern Recognition, vol. 2, pp. 160–167, IEEE, June 2000.

[13] A. Price, J. Pyke, D. Ashiri, and T. Cornall, "Real time object detection for an unmanned aerial vehicle using an FPGA based vision system," in Proceedings of the IEEE International Conference on Robotics and Automation (ICRA '06), pp. 2854–2859, IEEE, Orlando, Fla, USA, May 2006.

[14] G. J. García, C. A. Jara, J. Pomares, A. Alabdo, L. M. Poggi, and F. Torres, "A survey on FPGA-based sensor systems: towards intelligent and reconfigurable low-power sensors for computer vision, control and signal processing," Sensors, vol. 14, no. 4, pp. 6247–6278, 2014.

[15] S. Ali and M. Shah, "Cocoa: tracking in aerial imagery," in Airborne Intelligence, Surveillance, Reconnaissance (ISR) Systems and Applications III, vol. 6209 of Proceedings of SPIE, Orlando, Fla, USA, April 2006.

[16] J. Xiao, C. Yang, F. Han, and H. Cheng, "Vehicle and person tracking in aerial videos," in Multimodal Technologies for Perception of Humans, pp. 203–214, Springer, 2008.

[17] W. Yu, X. Yu, P. Zhang, and J. Zhou, "A new framework of moving target detection and tracking for uav video application," in Proceedings of the International Archives of the Photogrammetry, Remote Sensing and Spatial Information Science, vol. 37, Beijing, China, 2008.

[18] V. Reilly, H. Idrees, and M. Shah, "Detection and tracking of large number of targets in wide area surveillance," in Computer Vision—ECCV 2010: 11th European Conference on Computer Vision, Heraklion, Crete, Greece, September 5–11, 2010, Proceedings, Part III, vol. 6313 of Lecture Notes in Computer Science, pp. 186–199, Springer, Berlin, Germany, 2010.

[19] J. Wang, Y. Zhang, J. Lu, and W. Xu, "A framework for moving target detection, recognition and tracking in UAV videos," in Affective Computing and Intelligent Interaction, vol. 137 of Advances in Intelligent and Soft Computing, pp. 69–76, Springer, Berlin, Germany, 2012.

[20] S. A. Cheraghi and U. U. Sheikh, "Moving object detection using image registration for a moving camera platform," in Proceedings of the IEEE International Conference on Control System, Computing and Engineering (ICCSCE '12), pp. 355–359, IEEE, Penang, Malaysia, November 2012.

[21] Y. Zhang, X. Tong, T. Yang, and W. Ma, "Multi-model estimation based moving object detection for aerial video," Sensors, vol. 15, no. 4, pp. 8214–8231, 2015.

[22] Q. Yu and G. Medioni, "A GPU-based implementation of motion detection from a moving platform," in Proceedings of the IEEE Computer Society Conference on Computer Vision and Pattern Recognition Workshops (CVPR '08), pp. 1–6, Anchorage, Alaska, USA, June 2008.

[23] A. Laika, J. Paul, C. Claus, W. Stechele, A. E. S. Auf, and E. Maehle, "FPGA-based real-time moving object detection for walking robots," in Proceedings of the 8th IEEE International Workshop on Safety, Security, and Rescue Robotics (SSRR '10), pp. 1–8, IEEE, Bremen, Germany, July 2010.

[24] B. Tippetts, S. Fowers, K. Lillywhite, D.-J. Lee, and J. Archibald, "FPGA implementation of a feature detection and tracking algorithm for real-time applications," in Advances in Visual Computing, pp. 682–691, Springer, 2007.

[25] K. May and N. Krouglicof, "Moving target detection for sense and avoid using regional phase correlation," in Proceedings of the IEEE International Conference on Robotics and Automation (ICRA '13), pp. 4767–4772, IEEE, Karlsruhe, Germany, May 2013.

[26] M. E. Angelopoulou and C.-S. Bouganis, "Vision-based ego-motion estimation on FPGA for unmanned aerial vehicle navigation," IEEE Transactions on Circuits and Systems for Video Technology, vol. 24, no. 6, pp. 1070–1083, 2014.

[27] I. M. El-Emary and M. M. A. El-Kareem, "On the application of genetic algorithms in finger prints registration," World Applied Sciences Journal, vol. 5, no. 3, pp. 276–281, 2008.

[28] A. A. Goshtasby, 2-D and 3-D Image Registration: for Medical, Remote Sensing, and Industrial Applications, John Wiley & Sons, New York, NY, USA, 2005.

[29] C. Harris and M. Stephens, "A combined corner and edge detector," in Proceedings of the 4th Alvey Vision Conference, vol. 15, pp. 147–151, 1988.

[30] E. Rosten and T. Drummond, "Machine learning for high-speed corner detection," in Computer Vision—ECCV 2006, pp. 430–443, Springer, 2006.

[31] H. Bay, T. Tuytelaars, and L. Van Gool, "SURF: speeded up robust features," in Computer Vision—ECCV 2006, A. Leonardis, H. Bischof, and A. Pinz, Eds., vol. 3951 of Lecture Notes in Computer Science, pp. 404–417, Springer, 2006.

[32] G. R. Rodríguez-Canosa, S. Thomas, J. del Cerro, A. Barrientos, and B. MacDonald, "A real-time method to detect and track moving objects (DATMO) from unmanned aerial vehicles (UAVs) using a single camera," Remote Sensing, vol. 4, no. 4, pp. 1090–1111, 2012.

[33] B. Liu and A. Zaccarin, "New fast algorithms for the estimation of block motion vectors," IEEE Transactions on Circuits and Systems for Video Technology, vol. 3, no. 2, pp. 148–157, 1993.

[34] R. Li, B. Zeng, and M. L. Liou, "New three-step search algorithm for block motion estimation," IEEE Transactions on Circuits and Systems for Video Technology, vol. 4, no. 4, pp. 438–442, 1994.

[35] L.-M. Po and W.-C. Ma, "A novel four-step search algorithm for fast block motion estimation," IEEE Transactions on Circuits and Systems for Video Technology, vol. 6, no. 3, pp. 313–317, 1996.

[36] S. Zhu and K.-K. Ma, "A new diamond search algorithm for fast block-matching motion estimation," IEEE Transactions on Image Processing, vol. 9, no. 2, pp. 287–290, 2000.

[37] L. De Vos and M. Stegherr, "Parameterizable VLSI architectures for the full-search block-matching algorithm," IEEE Transactions on Circuits and Systems, vol. 36, no. 10, pp. 1309–1316, 1989.

[38] M. A. Fischler and R. C. Bolles, "Random sample consensus: a paradigm for model fitting with applications to image analysis and automated cartography," Communications of the ACM, vol. 24, no. 6, pp. 381–395, 1981.

[39] J. W. Tang, N. Shaikh-Husin, and U. U. Sheikh, "FPGA implementation of RANSAC algorithm for real-time image geometry

estimation," in *Proceedings of the 11th IEEE Student Conference on Research and Development (SCOReD '13)*, pp. 290–294, IEEE, Putrajaya, Malaysia, December 2013.

[40] O. Chum and J. Matas, "Randomized ransac with $T_{d,d}$ test," in *Proceedings of the British Machine Vision Conference*, vol. 2, pp. 448–457, September 2002.

[41] DARPA, SDMS Public Web Site, 2003, https://www.sdms.afrl.af .mil.

[42] A. F. M. S. Saif, A. S. Prabuwono, and Z. R. Mahayuddin, "Motion analysis for moving object detection from UAV aerial images: a review," in *Proceedings of the International Conference on Informatics, Electronics and Vision (ICIEV '14)*, pp. 1–6, IEEE, Dhaka, Bangladesh, May 2014.

11

Efficient Realization of BCD Multipliers using FPGAs

Shuli Gao,[1] Dhamin Al-Khalili,[1] J. M. Pierre Langlois,[2] and Noureddine Chabini[1]

[1]*Department of Electrical and Computer Engineering, Royal Military College of Canada, Kingston, ON, Canada*
[2]*Department of Computer Engineering, École Polytechnique de Montréal, Montréal, QC, Canada*

Correspondence should be addressed to Dhamin Al-Khalili; alkhalili-d@rmc.ca

Academic Editor: Seda Ogrenci-Memik

In this paper, a novel BCD multiplier approach is proposed. The main highlight of the proposed architecture is the generation of the partial products and parallel binary operations based on 2-digit columns. 1×1-digit multipliers used for the partial product generation are implemented directly by 4-bit binary multipliers without any code conversion. The binary results of the 1×1-digit multiplications are organized according to their two-digit positions to generate the 2-digit column-based partial products. A binary-decimal compressor structure is developed and used for partial product reduction. These reduced partial products are added in optimized 6-LUT BCD adders. The parallel binary operations and the improved BCD addition result in improved performance and reduced resource usage. The proposed approach was implemented on Xilinx Virtex-5 and Virtex-6 FPGAs with emphasis on the critical path delay reduction. Pipelined BCD multipliers were implemented for 4×4, 8×8, and 16×16-digit multipliers. Our realizations achieve an increase in speed by up to 22% and a reduction of LUT count by up to 14% over previously reported results.

1. Introduction

The traditional approach of using binary number system based operations in a decimal system requires frontend and backend conversion. These conversions can take a significant amount of processing time and consume large area. A more important problem with fractional decimal numbers expressed in a binary format may result in lack of accuracy. This can have major impact in finance and commercial applications. To solve these problems, interest in hardware design of decimal arithmetic is growing. This has led to the incorporation of specifications of decimal arithmetic in the IEEE-754 2008 standard for floating-point arithmetic [1]. The development of decimal operations in hardwired designs with high performance and low resource usage is expected to facilitate the implementation of various applications [2].

Multiplication is a complex operation among decimal computations. To speed up this operation, early decimal multipliers were designed at the gate level targeting ASICs. The authors in [3] proposed an improved iterative decimal multiplier approach to reduce the number of iteration cycles. To avoid a large number of decimal to binary conversions, a two-digit stage was used as the basic block for the iterative Binary Coded Decimal (BCD) multiplier. To further speed up the multiplication, parallel decimal multipliers were proposed. Binary multiplier and binary to BCD conversion were utilized to implement 1×1-digit multipliers, and different binary compressors were employed for the result of the multiplier [4–6]. To avoid the binary to decimal conversion, recoding methods were used to generate the partial products of the BCD multiplier [7, 8]. A Radix10 combinational multiplier was introduced in [7] and Radix4 and Radix5 recoding methods were presented in [8]. In [9], Radix5 recoding was combined with BCD code converters using BCD4221 and BCD5211 codes to simplify the partial product generation and reduction. In the recent two years, some ASIC-based designs for the realization of decimal multiplication were proposed in [10–14]. The recoding methods and BCD code conversions were used in these designs for efficient implementation in ASIC.

Although there are a number of approaches to implement decimal multipliers in ASICs, utilizing the same methods in FPGA devices is not necessarily efficient. With recent advancements in FPGA technology, enhanced architectures, and availability of various hardware resources, the FPGA platform is recognized as a viable alternative to ASICs in many cases. To make efficient use of FPGA resources in the implementation of decimal multiplication, new algorithms and approaches have been developed. The authors in [15] implemented decimal multipliers using embedded binary multiplier blocks in FPGAs. The binary-BCD conversion was implemented using base-1000 as an intermediate base, and the result was converted to BCD using a shift-add-3 algorithm. In [16], the authors presented a double-digit decimal multiplier technique that performs 2-digit multiplications simultaneously in one clock cycle; then the overall multiplication was performed serially. In [17, 18], a 1×1-digit multiplier was designed directly with BCD inputs/outputs and implemented using 6-input or 4-input LUTs. To sum the results of 1×1-digit multipliers, a fast carry-chain decimal adder was also proposed in [18]. These decimal-operation-based approaches avoided the conversions but also impacted the speed. Vázquez and De Dinechin implemented a BCD multiplier using a recoding technique [19]. Signed-Digit (SD) Radix5 was employed to recode one of the input operands of the multiplier for the generation of the partial products. 6-input LUTs and fast carry chains in Xilinx FPGAs were used to generate the building blocks and the decimal adders. To increase the performance, the authors in [20] implemented a parallel decimal multiplier based on Karatsuba-Ofman algorithm. The building blocks used in Karatsuba-Ofman algorithm were deigned based on the approach proposed in [19]. Another SD-based decimal multiplier approach was proposed in [21]. The recoding was based on SD Radix10. BCD4221, 5211, and 5421 converters were used for the partial product generation. BCD4221-based compressors and adders were utilized in this approach. Although the BCD4221-based operations are similar to binary operation, the recoding and the different code conversions still lead to delay and resource cost.

In this paper, we propose a new parallel binary-operation-based decimal multiplier approach. Binary operations are performed for the 1×1-digit multiplication and the partial product reduction based on the columns with two digits in each column. The operations for all columns are processed in parallel. After the column-based binary operations, binary to decimal conversions are required but the bit sizes of the operands to be converted are limited based on the columns. In this paper, an improved 6-LUT-based BCD adder and a 2-digit column-based binary-decimal compressor are also presented. Our proposed approach was implemented in Xilinx Virtex-5 and Virtex-6 FPGAs. The results are compared with Radix-recoding-based approaches using a BCD4221 coding scheme. The proposed approach achieves improved FPGA performance in part because of the parallel binary operations and small size conversions.

The organization of this paper is as follows. Section 2 presents optimized building blocks required by the BCD multiplication. The proposed multiplier architecture and the schemes of the partial product generation and reduction are presented in Section 3. The implementation results of $n \times n$-digit BCD multipliers are depicted in Section 4. Conclusions are given in Section 5.

2. Proposed Building Blocks for the Realization of BCD Multiplication

In this section, proposed schemes for an improved 6-input LUTs-based BCD adder and a mixed binary-decimal compressor are presented. These schemes will be utilized as the basic building blocks to construct our proposed BCD multipliers presented in Section 3.

2.1. 6-Input LUTs-Based 1-Digit BCD Adder. The 6-input LUTs-based 1-digit BCD adder is based on the use of 6-input LUTs and MUX-XOR networks in FPGAs. It is an improved version of the architecture presented in [19].

Assume that the input operands of the adder are $A = [a_3\ a_2\ a_1\ a_0]$ and $B = [b_3\ b_2\ b_1\ b_0]$ in BCD8421 format. The input operands are decomposed as

$$A = [a_3\ a_2\ a_1] \times 2 + a_0 = A_1 \times 2 + a_0,$$
$$B = [b_3\ b_2\ b_1] \times 2 + b_0 = B_1 \times 2 + b_0. \quad (1)$$

Then, the addition is presented as

$$A + B + C_{in} = (A_1 \times 2 + a_0) + (B_1 \times 2 + b_0) + C_{in}$$
$$= (A_1 + B_1) \times 2 + (a_0 + b_0 + C_{in}) \quad (2)$$
$$= [F_4\ F_3\ F_2\ F_1] \times 2 + [C_0 \times 2 + S_0].$$

In (2), A_1 or B_1 has the binary set $\{000, 001, 010, 011, 100\}$, and the full adder $[a_0 + b_0 + C_{in}]$ has two outputs, the carry C_0 and the sum S_0. The function $F = [F_4\ F_3\ F_2\ F_1]$ is a three-bit adder with the add-3 correction merged, which can be expressed as

$$F = [F_4\ F_3\ F_2\ F_1] = \begin{cases} A_1 + B_1 & \text{if } A_1 + B_1 < 5, \\ A_1 + B_1 + 3 & \text{if } A_1 + B_1 \geqslant 5. \end{cases} \quad (3)$$

In (3), the F cannot be $[0101]_2$, $[0110]_2$, or $[0111]_2$ because of the +3 correction. Also, since the maximal value of A_1 and B_1 is $[100]_2$, the maximal value of F is $[1011]_2$. The function F has 6 inputs; therefore, it can be efficiently mapped in a single level of 6-input LUTs.

To calculate the final result in BCD format, the carry C_0 of the full adder must be added to F. As a special case, an add-3 correction must be considered if $F = 4$ and $C_0 = 1$ to achieve a correct final result. Table 1 is the truth table for the final correction.

Therefore, the proposed scheme requires the following steps:

(i) Decompose the addition as two adders: one is a full adder for adding the two least significant bits of the input operands with the incoming carry, and another is a 3-bit adder with add-3 correction merged for the remaining bits. This function decomposition is presented in (2).

(ii) Implement the full adder and the 3-bit adder merged with an add-3 correction as presented in (3).

TABLE 1: Final correction for the BCD adder.

$F = F_4\ F_3\ F_2\ F_1$	$C_0 = 0$ $C_{out}\ S_3\ S_2\ S_1$	$C_0 = 1$ $C_{out}\ S_3\ S_2\ S_1$	Comments
0 0 0 0	0 0 0 0	0 0 0 1	"+3" is not required
0 0 0 1	0 0 0 1	0 0 1 0	"+3" is not required
0 0 1 0	0 0 1 0	0 0 1 1	"+3" is not required
0 0 1 1	0 0 1 1	0 1 0 0	"+3" is not required
0 1 0 0	0 1 0 0	1 0 0 0	at $C_0 = 1$, "+3" is required
0 1 0 1	x x x x	x x x x	
0 1 1 0	x x x x	x x x x	
0 1 1 1	x x x x	x x x x	
1 0 0 0	1 0 0 0	1 0 0 1	"+3" has been performed
1 0 0 1	1 0 0 1	1 0 1 0	"+3" has been performed
1 0 1 0	1 0 1 0	1 0 1 1	"+3" has been performed
1 0 1 1	1 0 1 1	1 1 0 0	"+3" has been performed
1 1 0 0	x x x x	x x x x	
1 1 0 1	x x x x	x x x x	
1 1 1 0	x x x x	x x x x	
1 1 1 1	x x x x	x x x x	

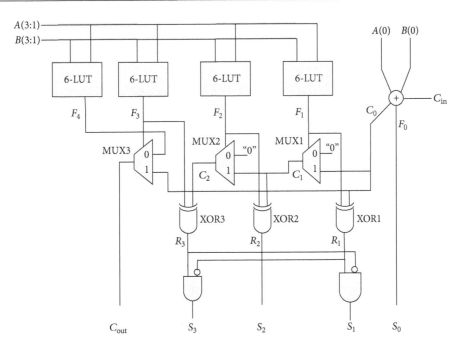

FIGURE 1: Improved 1-digit BCD adder using 6-LUTs and MUX-XOR network in FPGA.

(iii) Add the carry of the full adder with the output of the 3-bit adder using MUX-XOR networks. The multiplexers generate the propagated carries and the XOR gates output the sum bits.

(iv) Perform a final correction for the case of the carry of the full adder equal to "1" and the sum of the 3-bit adder equal to "4" to obtain the final result.

Figure 1 shows the architecture of this approach.

In this design, if the carry of the full adder, C_0, is "0"; there is no change to the result of the 3-bit adder and no carry is propagated. The output of the BCD adder is the same as that of the 3-bit adder, which is $[C_{out}\ S_3\ S_2\ S_1] = [F_4\ F_3\ F_2\ F_1]$. However, if C_0 is "1," the carry must be added to the result of the 3-bit adder. First, XOR_1 and MUX_1 add C_0 to F_1 and generate the sum $R_1 = (F_1\ XOR\ C_0)$ and the carry $C_1 = (F_1\ AND\ C_0)$. If $C_0 = 1$ and $F_1 = 0$, the sum R_1 is equal to "1" and no carry ($C_1 = 0$) is propagated. However, if $C_0 = 1$ and $F_1 = 1$, the sum R_1 is equal to "0," and the carry is propagated to C_1. The same procedure applies to XOR_2 and MUX_2. For MUX_3, it produces the output carry, C_{out}. Based on the truth table listed in Table 1, the output carry C_{out} is the same as F_4 when $F_3 = 0$ and the same as C_0 when $F_3 = 1$, which is realized by MUX_3. In this case, propagating C_0 from the output of the

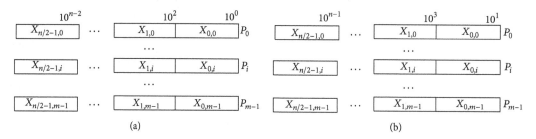

FIGURE 2: Two-group operands with the mixed binary-decimal format.

TABLE 2: Comparison of the implementation results for the BCD adders.

Improved 6-LUT		Reference [19]	
Delay (ns)	LUTs	Delay (ns)	LUTs
1.372	10	1.397	10

full adder directly to the input of MUX_3 reduces this critical path delay. This has a significant performance impact on large size BCD ripple adders required by BCD multipliers.

To achieve a correct final result, a final correction in the cases of $C_0 = 1$ and $F = 4$ must be performed to the sum. Since, before the final correction, the sum of the adder is equal to

$$
\begin{aligned}
\left([F_4\ F_3\ F_2\ F_1] + C_0\right) \times 2 + F_0 &= (0100 + 1) \times 2 + F_0 \\
&= (101\ F_0)_2 = (R_3\ R_2\ R_1\ F_0)_2,
\end{aligned} \tag{4}
$$

therefore under the condition of $C_0 = 1$ and $F = 4$, the final add-3 correction is performed to $(R_3\ R_2\ R_1)$, and the final result is equal to

$$
[C_{out}\ S_3\ S_2\ S_1\ F_0] = (1\ 000\ F_0)_{BCD}. \tag{5}
$$

In this case, the outputs, S_3 and S_1, have to be forced to "0." Otherwise, S_3 and S_1 are the same as R_3 and R_1, respectively. Thus, the final correction performed to S_3 and S_1 is equal to

$$
\begin{aligned}
S_3 &= R_3 \cdot \overline{R_3 \cdot R_1} = R_3 \cdot \overline{R_1}, \\
S_1 &= R_1 \cdot \overline{R_3 \cdot R_1} = R_3 \cdot \overline{R_1}.
\end{aligned} \tag{6}
$$

The proposed 1-digit BCD adder was coded in VHDL and implemented in a Virtex-6 6vlx75tff784 Xilinx FPGA with a −3 speed grade using ISE13.1 [23]. The results are compared with the carry-ripple BCD adder approach proposed in [19] using the same FPGA. The delays were extracted from Postplacement-and-Routing Static Timing Report and the LUTs usage was obtained from Place-and-Routing Report. Table 2 lists the implementation results.

Table 2 shows that the improved 6-LUT-based BCD adder approach achieves better performance compared with the reference BCD adder. Although the improvement in delay is approximately 2%, for large size adders the cumulative effect can be significant.

2.2. Binary-Decimal Compression. The binary-decimal (BD) compression performs 2-digit column-based binary operations and binary to decimal conversions. The input operands of the BD compression are the results of 1×1-digit BCD multipliers presented in binary format, and the output of the BD compression is in BCD format. Since a 1×1-digit BCD multiplier results in a 2-digit decimal number, the binary inputs are based on 2-digit decimal positions. The input operands of the BD compression are

$$
P_i = \sum_{k=0}^{n/2-1} X_{k,i} \times 10^{2k} \quad \text{for } i = 0, 1, 2, \ldots, m-1 \tag{7}
$$

or

$$
P_i = \sum_{k=0}^{n/2-1} X_{k,i} \times 10^{2k+1} \quad \text{for } i = 0, 1, 2, \ldots, m-1, \tag{8}
$$

where m is the number of operands to be compressed, and n is the number of digits in each operand. The variable $X_{k,i}$ is expressed in a binary format but placed in a 2-digit decimal position. Since $X_{k,i}$ is the result of a 1×1-digit BCD multiplier, it has 7 binary bits. Figure 2 illustrates these two-group operands, where (a) and (b) correspond to (7) and (8), respectively. The difference between Figures 2(a) and 2(b) is the decimal positions of the columns.

The binary-decimal compression performs the following steps:

(i) Aligning the input operands based on 2-digit decimal position. All operands in the same column should have the same 2-digit decimal position

(ii) Compressing all operands in each of the columns using binary compressors

(iii) Adding the compressed binary operands in each column using binary adders

(iv) For each column, converting the binary sum to decimal with two digits as the sum and other digits as the carry

(v) Saving the decimal sums and carries in carry-save format for all columns based on their decimal positions

As an example, Figure 3 illustrates the BD compression with m input operands for the case presented in Figure 2(a). This procedure can also be used for the case in Figure 2(b).

In this case, the BD compression first compresses the m binary operands to one binary sum using binary compressors

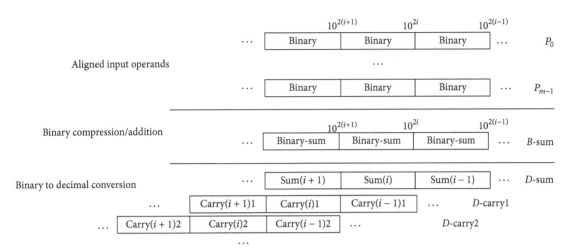

FIGURE 3: Binary-decimal compression.

and binary adders. In this step, the binary compressors reduce m binary operands to $k = (\lfloor \log_2 m \rfloor + 1)$ operands; then the binary adders add these k operands to produce a binary sum.

Then, the binary sum is converted to a decimal number. The decimal number has a two-digit decimal sum, $D\text{-sum}(i)$, and the decimal carries, $D\text{-carry}(i)_t$ (for $t = 1, 2, \ldots$). Each of the decimal sums or decimal carries takes two-digit position. The $D\text{-sum}(i)$ is located at the 10^{2i} column and the carries are located at the columns of 10^{2i+1}, 10^{2i+2}, and so on. Then, the decimal sum and carries for each column are saved as carry-save format based on their digit positions. Therefore, only $(t + 1)$ decimal operands are generated after the BD compression. The value of t is dependent on the value of m. If m is between 2 and 123, the maximal decimal result in each column is $81 \times 123 = 9963$, for which $D\text{-sum} = 63$ and $D\text{-carry} = 99$. In this case, only t ($=1$) decimal carry is generated. Thus, 123 such binary operands can be compressed to two decimal operands, one for the D-sum and the other for the D-carry. This arrangement results in a fast way to reduce the number of partial products for a BCD multiplier.

3. Proposed BCD Multiplier Approach

In this section, we present a binary-decimal compression (BDC) based BCD multiplier. The proposed approach consists of 1×1-digit binary multiplication, partial product generation, binary-decimal compression, and decimal addition. Figure 4 shows a block diagram which captures all the steps for this approach.

3.1. 1×1-Digit Binary Multipliers.
The 1×1-digit binary multiplier receives two 1-digit BCD operands and outputs a binary result. The maximal output is $9 \times 9 = 81 = [1010001]_2$, which is a 7-bit binary number. Since 1-digit 8421BCD number is the same as a 4-bit binary number, a 4×4-bit binary multiplier is used to perform the 1×1-digit binary multiplier. In our approach, the 4×4-bit binary multiplier is simply coded as $X \times Y$, where X and Y are 1-digit 8421BCD numbers.

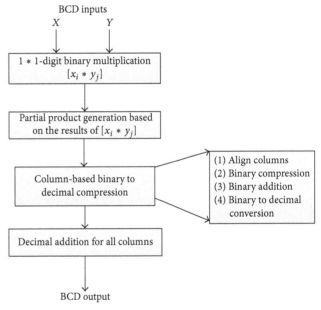

FIGURE 4: Block diagram of the proposed BDC-based BCD multiplier.

3.2. Partial Product Generation (PPG).
The partial product generation is based on 1×1-digit binary multipliers. These binary outputs of the 1×1-digit binary multipliers are grouped according to their decimal positions. A triangular organization of the partial products is used for the BCD multiplier, which is similar to our previous work proposed in [24] for a binary multiplier. For the BCD multiplication, let us assume that the input operands of the multiplier are X and Y. They are in BCD format and can be expressed as

$$X = \sum_{i=0}^{n-1} X_i \times 10^i,$$

$$Y = \sum_{j=0}^{n-1} Y_j \times 10^j. \tag{9}$$

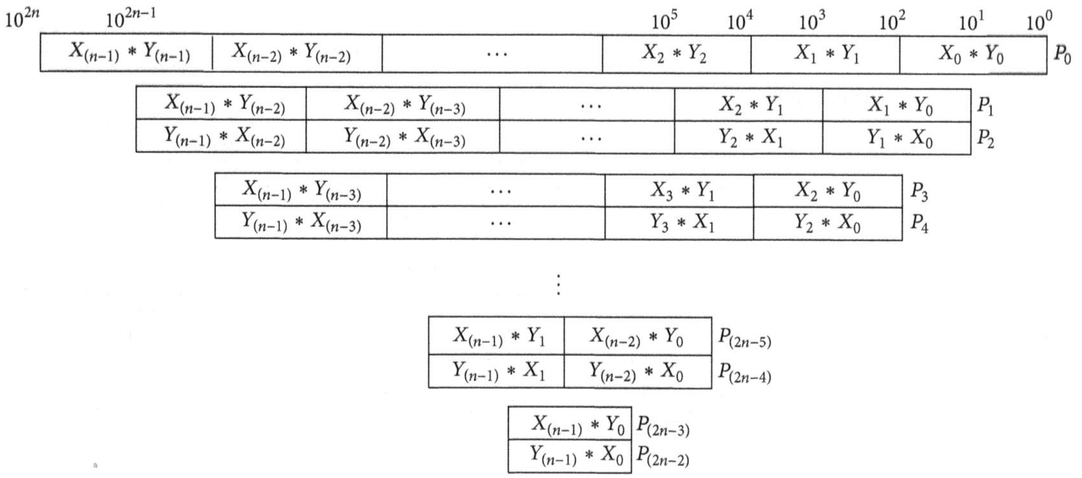

10^{2n}	10^{2n-1}				10^5	10^4	10^3	10^2	10^1	10^0	
$X_{(n-1)} * Y_{(n-1)}$	$X_{(n-2)} * Y_{(n-2)}$		$\cdots$			$X_2 * Y_2$		$X_1 * Y_1$		$X_0 * Y_0$	P_0

	$X_{(n-1)} * Y_{(n-2)}$	$X_{(n-2)} * Y_{(n-3)}$	$\cdots$	$X_2 * Y_1$	$X_1 * Y_0$	P_1
	$Y_{(n-1)} * X_{(n-2)}$	$Y_{(n-2)} * X_{(n-3)}$	$\cdots$	$Y_2 * X_1$	$Y_1 * X_0$	P_2

	$X_{(n-1)} * Y_{(n-3)}$	$\cdots$	$X_3 * Y_1$	$X_2 * Y_0$	P_3
	$Y_{(n-1)} * X_{(n-3)}$	$\cdots$	$Y_3 * X_1$	$Y_2 * X_0$	P_4

$$\vdots$$

$X_{(n-1)} * Y_1$	$X_{(n-2)} * Y_0$	$P_{(2n-5)}$
$Y_{(n-1)} * X_1$	$Y_{(n-2)} * X_0$	$P_{(2n-4)}$

$X_{(n-1)} * Y_0$	$P_{(2n-3)}$
$Y_{(n-1)} * X_0$	$P_{(2n-2)}$

FIGURE 5: Triangular organization of the partial products of the BCD multiplier.

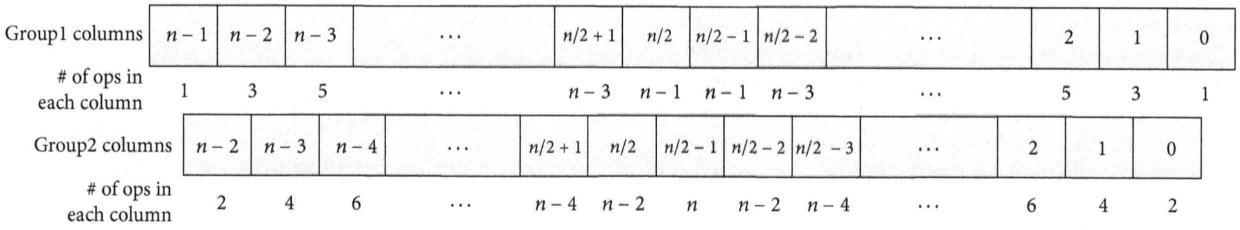

Group1 columns	$n-1$	$n-2$	$n-3$	$\cdots$	$n/2+1$	$n/2$	$n/2-1$	$n/2-2$	$\cdots$	2	1	0
# of ops in each column	1	3	5	$\cdots$	$n-3$	$n-1$	$n-1$	$n-3$	$\cdots$	5	3	1
Group2 columns	$n-2$	$n-3$	$n-4$	$\cdots$	$n/2+1$	$n/2$	$n/2-1$	$n/2-2$	$n/2-3$	$\cdots$	2	1	0
# of ops in each column	2	4	6	$\cdots$	$n-4$	$n-2$	n	$n-2$	$n-4$	$\cdots$	6	4	2

FIGURE 6: Number of operands in each of the columns.

By multiplying X and Y in (9), the product becomes

$$Z = X \times Y = \left(\sum_{i=0}^{n-1} X_i \times 10^i \right) \times \left(\sum_{j=0}^{n-1} Y_j \times 10^j \right)$$

$$= \sum_{i=0}^{n-1} X_i \times Y_i \times 10^{2i}$$

$$+ \sum_{i=1}^{n-1} \left(\sum_{j=0}^{n-1-i} X_{i+j} \times Y_j \times 10^{(i+2j)} \right)$$

$$+ \sum_{i=1}^{n-1} \left(\sum_{j=0}^{n-1-i} Y_{i+j} \times X_j \times 10^{(i+2j)} \right),$$

(10)

where $X_i \times Y_i$, $X_{i+j} \times Y_j$, and $Y_{i+j} \times X_j$ are the products from 1×1-digit binary multipliers. These 1×1-digit binary multipliers are organized based on their decimal positions, and the architecture of the BCD multiplier is shown in Figure 5.

Based on the decimal positions of the results of 1×1-digit binary multipliers, these partial products are separated into two groups. The first group is composed of $P_0, P_3, P_4, \ldots, P_{(2n-3)}$ and $P_{(2n-2)}$. The second group is composed of P_1 and $P_2, \ldots, P_{(2n-5)}$ and $P_{(2n-4)}$. The number of operands in each of the columns is shown in Figure 6. The maximal number of operands in the first group is $(n-1)$ that is located at the column $(n/2)$ and column $(n/2-1)$. The maximal number of operands in the second group is n that is located at the column $(n/2-1)$.

As an example, Figure 7 shows the organization of a 4×4-digit BCD multiplier. In this example, the operands in group 1 are located at the decimal positions 10^{2i} with $i = 0, 1, 2, 3$, and the number of operands in each column is 1, 3, 3, and 1, respectively. The operands in group 2 are located at the decimal positions 10^{2i+1} with $i = 0, 1, 2$, and the number of operands in each column is 2, 4, and 2.

3.3. Partial Product Reduction. Based on the architecture of the BCD multiplier, the partial products are in mixed binary-decimal format. To reduce the number of partial products, two steps are performed: partial product compression and partial product conversion.

Partial Product Compression. The partial product compression performs $(m : 1)$ compression for the binary operands in each column using efficient binary compression and addition methods. The binary compressors first reduce $m = (2^k$ to $2^{k+1} - 1)$ binary operands to $(k + 1)$ binary operands in each column. For example, for $k = 3$ the number of operands to be compressed is $m = (8$ to $15)$. After the compression, 4 binary operands are generated.

Then, these binary operands after the compression are added in binary to obtain a binary sum. Thus, the m operands are compressed to a single one for all columns.

Partial Product Conversion. The partial product conversion converts the binary sum to decimal operands. Double-Dabble (DD) converters [25] can be used in this step. Since the

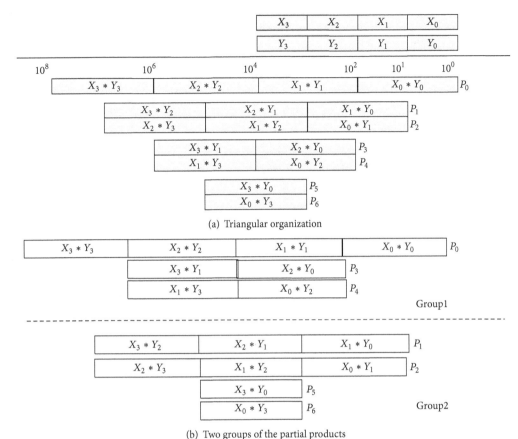

(a) Triangular organization

(b) Two groups of the partial products

FIGURE 7: A 4×4-digit BCD multiplier.

column-based operations produce limited size binary sums in each column, the conversions introduce only a small delay overhead.

After the binary to decimal conversion, normally only 3 or 4 decimal operands are generated. If there are 12 binary operands or less in one column, the maximal sum is $81 \times 12 = 972$, which is a 3-digit decimal number. Thus, the decimal sum has two digits and the decimal carry has only one digit. Moreover, the decimal carries in two groups are located at different digital positions. Therefore, the carries can be combined as one decimal operand. Figure 8 illustrates this situation for the 4×4-digit BCD multiplier example. Only three decimal operands are generated after the partial product reduction.

However, if there are more than 12 operands in one column, at least four digits are required in this column because $81 \times 13 = 1053$. Thus, the decimal carry has two digits. In this case, 4 decimal operands will be generated after the partial product reduction. For example, based on the number of operands in each column for a 16×16-digit BCD multiplier, as shown in Figure 9(a), the columns at 6, 7, 8, and 9 in the first group create 4-digit decimals for each column, and the columns at 6, 7, and 8 in the second group also generate 4-digit decimals for each column. The decimal operands after the conversion are shown in Figure 9(b), where DS_1 and C_1 are the decimal sum and carry for group 1 and DS_2 and C_2 are the

decimal sum and carry for group 2. By combining the decimal carries in two groups, Figure 9(c) shows the decimal operand organization. CC_1 combines the first digit of the carries for all columns, and CC_2 combines the second digit of the carries for the related columns. After partial product reduction, four decimal operands are generated for the 16×16-digit BCD multiplier as shown in Figure 9(c).

3.4. Final Decimal Addition (FDA). To obtain the final result of the BCD multiplier, the decimal operands generated after the partial product reduction must be added to decimal adders. BCD ripple adders are used in our approach. These BCD ripple adders are built using our improved 6-LUTs-based BCD adders. Since only 3 or 4 decimal operands need to be added, two-level BCD ripple adders are required. Figure 10 shows the final addition of the BCD multiplication. If there are only three decimal operands to be added, the BCD adder2 in this figure is removed.

3.5. Pipelined Multipliers. Based on the architecture of the BCD multiplier, a 4-stage pipelined BCD multiplier is illustrated in Figure 11.

In this pipelined multiplier, the 1×1-digit (4×4-bit) binary multiplication and binary compression and addition are combined in the first stage. In this stage, all operations in each column are in binary format. The second stage

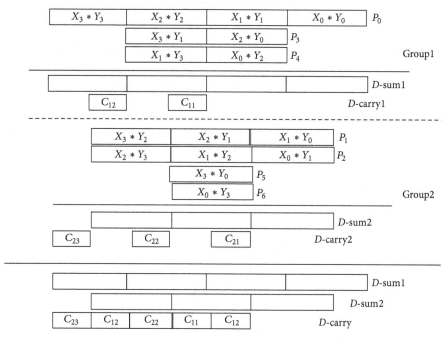

FIGURE 8: Partial product reduction for a 4×4-digit BCD multiplier.

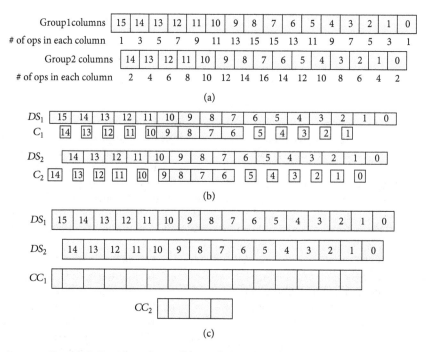

FIGURE 9: Partial product reduction for a 16×16-digit BCD multiplier.

converts the binary numbers to decimal using the Double-Dabble (DD) converter [25]. Since the input operand of the conversion is based on each column, the number of bits in the input operands is limited. Therefore, the delay for the conversions is relatively small. After the binary to decimal conversion, 3 or 4 decimal operands are generated and need to be added. To add these decimal operands, two levels of additions are performed. For a larger size multiplier, more

pipeline stages may be required. Figure 12 shows an 8-stage pipeline strategy.

4. Implementation Results

The proposed BCD multiplier approach was implemented in Xilinx Virtex-5 and Virtex-6 FPGAs for 4×4, 8×8, and 16×16-digit pipelined BCD multipliers. The ISE 13.4 tool

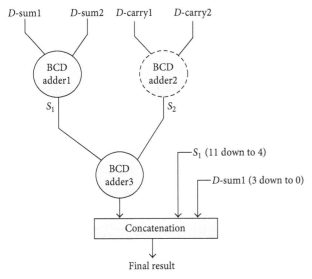

FIGURE 10: The final addition for a BCD multiplier.

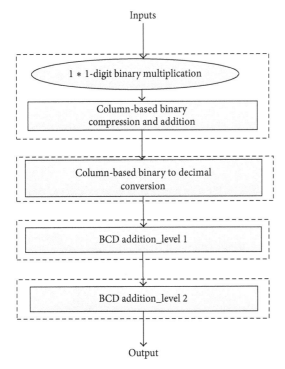

FIGURE 11: 4-stage pipelined BCD multiplier.

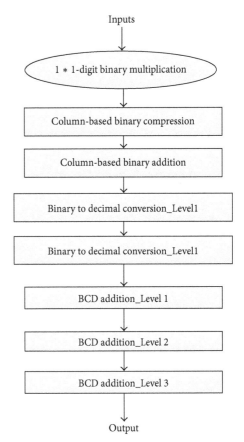

FIGURE 12: An 8-stage pipeline multiplier.

suite [23] was used for the synthesis and implementation. 4 × 4-bit binary multipliers were used for the partial products generation. The mixed binary-decimal compressors were employed for partial product reduction. The improved 6-LUTs-based BCD adders were connected as ripple adders and used to sum the compressed partial products and generate the final result. Our multipliers were implemented targeting Xilinx xc5vlx330ff1760-2 and xc6vlx760ff1760-2 FPGA devices. The results of the total delay and number of LUTs usage were extracted after the synthesis and implementation and compared with those of the multipliers proposed in [21, 22].

Figures 13 and 14 illustrate timing information and LUTs utilized for 4 × 4, 8 × 8, and 16 × 16-digit pipelined BCD multipliers based on our proposed approach and on the architecture presented in [21]. The implementation targeted Virtex-5 and Virtex-6 FPGAs, which are the exact same devices used in [21]. The number of pipeline stages was selected based on the best implementation result for each of the multipliers. The total delay, clock cycle time, and LUT usage were depicted in these two figures labeled as (a), (b), and (c), respectively.

Compared with the results presented in [21], our proposed approach achieves improvements in all cases as shown in these figures. On average, the total delay reductions are 22.5% and 14.3% with 14.6% and 16.6% LUT savings when targeting Virtex-5 and Virtex-6 FPGAs, respectively.

The 16 × 16-digit multiplier with 5, 6, and 7 pipeline stages was implemented targeting Virtex-5 FPGA. The results were compared with the architecture in [22] and presented in Table 3. The total delay of all pipeline stages and the worst-case clock cycle for one pipelined stage were extracted and used for speed comparison.

Compared with the result proposed in [22], our approach achieves faster performance in terms of the total delay and worst-case minimum clock period. On average, the improvement in total delay reduction is 20.2% and in clock cycle reduction is 21.0%, with 8.7% LUTs penalty.

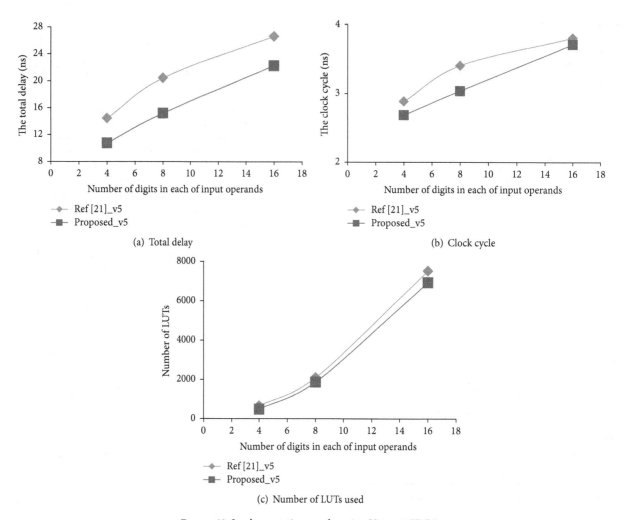

(a) Total delay

(b) Clock cycle

(c) Number of LUTs used

FIGURE 13: Implementation results using Virtex-5 FPGA.

TABLE 3: Results compared with [22] for the 16 × 16-digit pipelined multiplier.

# of pipeline stages	[22]			Proposed			Comparison		
	Total delay (ns)	Clock cycle (ns)	#LUTs	Total delay (ns)	Clock cycle (ns)	#LUTs	Delay reduction (%)	Clock cycle time reduction (ns)	# of LUT saving (%)
5	27.400	5.480	6438	19.025	3.805	6843	30.57	30.57	−6.29
6	28.740	4.830	6664	22.242	3.707	6918	22.61	23.25	−3.81
7	30.660	4.460	5992	28.392	4.056	6953	7.40	9.06	−16.04

Thus, our approach compares favorably with the architectures in [21, 22]. The improvement comes in part from the use of parallel and binary operations, as well as our fast BCD additions. By using 1 × 1-digit binary multipliers and the 2-column-based binary-decimal compressors, fast parallel operations are performed with small size binary numbers. These binary-decimal compressors efficiently reduce the number of partial products to 3 or 4 decimal operands, which simplifies the decimal additions required by the multiplication. Moreover, in the decimal addition, our fast BCD adder

decreases the propagation delay for BCD ripple adders. All these lead to superior multiplier architecture.

5. Conclusions

In this paper, a new $n \times n$-digit BCD multiplier approach was proposed. This approach uses 1 × 1-digit binary multipliers for the partial product generation. 2-digit column-based binary operations are used for partial product reduction. This proposed binary-decimal compression scheme makes

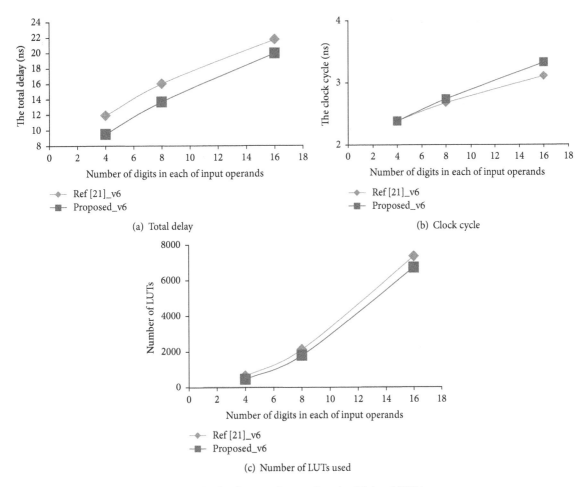

(a) Total delay

(b) Clock cycle

(c) Number of LUTs used

FIGURE 14: Implementation results using Virtex-6 FPGA.

efficient use of a parallel strategy and of fast binary operation schemes to reduce the number of partial products of the multiplier. After the binary-decimal compression, only 3 or 4 operands in general need to be added in decimal to receive the final result of a BCD multiplier. To perform the decimal additions, a fast 6-LUTs-based BCD adder was proposed to realize BCD ripple adders required for the multiplication. The proposed BCD multipliers were pipelined and implemented on Xilinx Virtex-5 and Virtex-6 FPGAs. Compared with existing architectures, improved results have been achieved.

Competing Interests

The authors declare that they have no competing interests.

References

[1] IEEE Computer Society, "IEEE 754-2008 Standard for Floating-Point Arithmetic," August 2008 http://ieeexplore.ieee.org/stamp/stamp.jsp?tp=&arnumber=4610935.

[2] B. Hickmann, M. Schulte, and M. Erle, "Improved combined Binary/Decimal Fixed-Point multipliers," in *Proceedings of the 26th IEEE International Conference on Computer Design (ICCD '08)*, pp. 87–94, Lake Tahoe, Calif, USA, October 2008.

[3] R. D. Kenney, M. J. Schulte, and M. A. Erle, "A high-frequency decimal multiplier," in *Proceedings of the IEEE International Conference on Computer Design: VLSI in Computers and Processors (ICCD '04)*, pp. 26–29, October 2004.

[4] J. Bhattacharya, A. Gupta, and A. Singh, "A high performance Binary to BCD converter for decimal multiplication," in *Proceedings of the IEEE International Symposium on VLSI Design Automation and Test (VLSI-DAT '10)*, pp. 315–318, Hyderabad, India, 2010.

[5] G. Jaberipur and A. Kaivani, "Binary-coded decimal digit multipliers," *IET Computers and Digital Techniques*, vol. 1, no. 4, pp. 377–381, 2007.

[6] G. Jaberipur and A. Kaivani, "Improving the speed of parallel decimal multiplication," *IEEE Transactions on Computers*, vol. 58, no. 11, pp. 1539–1552, 2009.

[7] T. Lang and A. Nannarelli, "A radix-10 combinational multiplier," in *Proceedings of the 40th Asilomar Conference on Signals, Systems, and Computers (ACSSC '06)*, pp. 313–317, November 2006.

[8] A. Vázquez, E. Antelo, and P. Montuschi, "A new family of high—performance parallel decimal multipliers," in *Proceedings of the 18th IEEE Symposium on Computer Arithmetic (ARITH '07)*, pp. 195–204, Montpellier, France, June 2007.

[9] A. Vázquez, E. Antelo, and P. Montuschi, "Improved design of high-performance parallel decimal multipliers," *IEEE Transactions on Computers*, vol. 59, no. 5, pp. 679–693, 2010.

[10] A. Vazquez, E. Antelo, and J. D. Bruguera, "Fast radix-10 multiplication using redundant BCD codes," *IEEE Transactions on Computers*, vol. 63, no. 8, pp. 1902–1914, 2014.

[11] A. Kaivani, L. Han, and S.-B. Ko, "Improved design of high-frequency sequential decimal multipliers," *Electronics Letters*, vol. 50, no. 7, pp. 558–560, 2014.

[12] M. Zhu, A. M. Baker, and Y. Jiang, "On a parallel decimal multiplier based on hybrid 8421-5421 BCD recoding," in *Proceedings of the IEEE 56th International Midwest Symposium on Circuits and Systems (MWSCAS '13)*, pp. 1391–1394, IEEE, Columbus, Ohio, USA, August 2013.

[13] M. Zhu and Y. Jiang, "An area-time efficient architecture for 16 x 16 decimal multiplications," in *Proceedings of the 10th International Conference on Information Technology: New Generations (ITNG '13)*, pp. 210–216, April 2013.

[14] L. Han and S.-B. Ko, "High-speed parallel decimal multiplication with redundant internal encodings," *Institute of Electrical and Electronics Engineers. Transactions on Computers*, vol. 62, no. 5, pp. 956–968, 2013.

[15] H. C. Neto and M. P. Véstias, "Decimal multiplier on FPGA using embedded binary multipliers," in *Proceedings of the International Conference on Field Programmable Logic and Applications (FPL '08)*, pp. 197–202, September 2008.

[16] R. K. James, K. P. Jacob, and S. Sasi, "Performance analysis of double digit decimal multiplier on various FPGA logic families," in *Proceedings of the 5th Southern Conference on Programmable Logic (SPL '09)*, pp. 165–170, IEEE, São Carlos, Brazil, April 2009.

[17] O. D. Al-Khaleel, N. H. Tulić, and K. M. Mhaidat, "FPGA implementation of binary coded decimal digit adders and multipliers," in *Proceedings of the 8th International Symposium on Mechatronics and its Applications (ISMA '12)*, Sharjah, United Arab Emirates, April 2012.

[18] G. Sutter, E. Todorovich, G. Bioul, M. Vazquez, and J.-P. Deschamps, "FPGA implementations of BCD multipliers," in *Proceedings of the International Conference on ReConFigurable Computing and FPGAs (ReConFig '09)*, pp. 36–41, Quintana Roo, Mexico, December 2009.

[19] Á. Vázquez and F. De Dinechin, "Efficient implementation of parallel BCD multiplication in LUT-6 FPGAs," in *Proceedings of the International Conference on Field-Programmable Technology (FPT '10)*, pp. 126–133, December 2010.

[20] M. Véstias and H. Neto, "Parallel decimal multipliers and squarers using Karatsuba-Ofman's algorithm," in *Proceedings of the 15th Euromicro Conference on Digital System Design (DSD '12)*, pp. 782–788, Izmir, Turkey, September 2012.

[21] C. E. M. Guardia, "Implementation of a fully pipelined BCD multiplier in FPGA," in *Proceedings of the 8th Southern Programmable Logic Conference (SPL '12)*, pp. 1–6, March 2012.

[22] M. Baesler, S.-O. Voigt, and T. Teufel, "An IEEE 754-2008 decimal parallel and pipelined FPGA floating-point multiplier," in *Proceedings of the 20th International Conference on Field Programmable Logic and Applications (FPL '10)*, pp. 489–495, Milano, Italy, September 2010.

[23] Xilinx Inc, "Virtex-6 User Guide," February 2012, http://www.xilinx.com/support/documentation/user_guides/ug364.pdf.

[24] S. Gao, D. Al-Khalili, and N. Chabini, "FPGA realization of high performance large size computational functions: multipliers and applications," *Analog Integrated Circuits and Signal Processing*, vol. 70, no. 2, pp. 165–179, 2012.

[25] Binary-to-BCD Converter, Double-Dabble Binary-to-BCD Conversion Algorithm, http://www.tkt.cs.tut.fi/kurssit/1426/S12/Ex/ex4/Binary2BCD.pdf.

12

Real-Time Control System for Improved Precision and Throughput in an Ultrafast Carbon Fiber Placement Robot using a SoC FPGA Extended Processing Platform

Gilberto Ochoa-Ruiz,[1] **Romain Bevan,**[2] **Florent de Lamotte,**[2]
Jean-Philippe Diguet,[2] **and Cheng-Cong Bao**[3]

[1]*CONACYT-Universidad Autonoma de Guadalajara, Guadalajara, JAL, Mexico*
[2]*Lab-STICC-CNRS/ComposiTIC, Lorient, France*
[3]*Coriolis Composites, Lorient, France*

Correspondence should be addressed to Gilberto Ochoa-Ruiz; gilberto.ochoa@edu.uag.mx

Academic Editor: Bibhu P. Panigrahi

We present an architecture for accelerating the processing and execution of control commands in an ultrafast fiber placement robot. The system consists of a robotic arm designed by Coriolis Composites whose purpose is to move along a surface, on which composite fibers are deposed, via an independently controlled head. In first system implementation, the control commands were sent via Profibus by a PLC, limiting the reaction time and thus the precision of the fiber placement and the maximum throughput. Therefore, a custom real-time solution was imperative in order to ameliorate the performance and to meet the stringent requirements of the target industry (avionics, aeronautical systems). The solution presented in this paper is based on the use of a SoC FPGA processing platform running a real-time operating system (FreeRTOS), which has enabled an improved comamnd retrieval mechanism. The system's placement precision was improved by a factor of 20 (from 1 mm to 0.05 mm), while the maximum achievable throughput was 1 m/s, compared to the average 30 cm/s provided by the original solution, enabling fabricating more complex and larger pieces in a significant fraction of the time.

1. Introduction

Given the continuous advances in communication networks and the increasing sophistication of embedded systems, there has been a widespread interest in recent years in the creation of distributed control systems (DCS) based on novel architectural paradigms [1]. In particular, distribution and reconfiguration are considered essential features for such new devices, typically known as intelligent electronic devices (IED). Such capabilities are indispensable in today's increasingly and ever-changing manufacturing settings for enabling fast prototyping and quick adaptation to emerging needs at the plant level [2].

Such DCS rely heavily on various industrial fieldbuses and protocols, and thus the performance of the IEDs and the correct behavior of the overall application strongly depend on the networking and processing capabilities integrated in the control, measurement, and I/O devices. However, real-time constraints limit the applicability of many solutions, due principally to the stringent time constraints inherent to the most demanding applications in which they are to be integrated [3].

Therefore, in order to be viable, modern DCS need to meet these demanding real-time capabilities and support event-based execution policies [4], which are difficult to attain due to nondeterministic latencies in the communication networks and, to a great extent, due to the computational capabilities of today's programmable devices (PLCs), which still rely on the sequential processing paradigm [5].

This problem has been recognized by the academia and the industry at large, which have tackled the problem by proposing new programming and architectural paradigms aiming at improving the performance of automation and manufacturing processes, as well as their resilience and adaptability and the distribution of various complex control algorithms over several nodes to improve the data efficiency. Many of these approaches point towards the introduction of specialized processing units, in the form of microprocessors [6], and increasingly as customized computing machines implemented in FPGAs [7].

In this manner, the more demanding components of the application can be decentralized, improving the performance and reliability of the subprocesses, while decreasing the computational load in the main PLCs and the communication bandwidth requirements of the overall system. Moreover, the complexity of the verification process can be significantly reduced due to an improved separation of concerns, leading to more dependable, fault-tolerant, and maintainable systems [8].

In this paper, we present a case study of a DCS in the context of an advanced fiber placement platform. Such a system encompasses a large number of physically distant subcomponents due to the dimensions of the controlled plant (the robot is used for 3D print large pieces for avionics and nautical applications) and for safety reasons. The original system made use of a decentralized architecture, consisting of several PLCs for controlling the fiber feeding subsystem, the robot itself, and a very large number of I/Os integrated in the robot's head, which severely limited the attainable performance of the system.

These limitations stemmed from the manner in which the control commands were sent to the ultrafast fiber placement head (via Profibus-DP by the main PLC), thus limiting the reaction time and, in consequence, the precision of the fiber placement and the maximum attainable deposition throughput. In this paper, we present a novel, custom real-time, and distributed solution, which has been integrated directly in the robot head to accelerate the control of very fast actuators and is based on novel SoC FPGA devices.

The rest of this paper is organized as follows: in the next section, we provide more ample motivations for the implementation of IEDs, as well as other Industrial Process Measurement and Control Systems (IPMCS) using reconfigurable devices, based on the limitations of current DCS design approaches and programming paradigms. In Section 3, we delve into discussion of the successful application of FPGA devices for implementing IMPCS platforms, which will serve as the stepping stone for the rest of the article. Subsequently, we embark into a description of the application context and, in particular, of the specific challenges for the design of a novel control system for the robotized fiber placement unit at the heart of the article. Thereafter, in Section 5, we embark in the description of the proposed architecture and we discuss the rationale behind the use of SoC FPGAs and the real-time operating system solution. Finally, in Section 6, we compare the proposed solution with the original PLC-based implementation and with a second MCU-based embedded system in terms of the achieved precision, performance, and response time, as well as the attainable fabrication time.

2. Context and Motivation

Today's fast-changing manufacturing markets are forcing a paradigm shift in the associated fabrication processes. These tight demands are leading to an increased complexity of the industrial environments and associated equipment as well as a shift in the conception of the underlying control settings. Hence, in order to cope with these emerging necessities (i.e., improved fault-tolerance, online monitoring, and prognosis), new manufacturing infrastructures, production facilities, and operation/control methods are very much required, accompanied by new standards and devices to support them.

Therefore, in recent years, a great deal of research has been conducted to improve the capabilities of the manufacturing control systems, mainly based on the concept of distributed intelligent control, which aims at bridging the gap among different domain practices, with special emphasis on improving systems integration and coordination. The resulting automation models are underpinned by wide networks of devices, known as distributed control systems (DCS), interconnected through field area networks and industrial fieldbuses, as depicted in Figure 1. Such systems of systems are encompassed by heterogeneous sensors, actuators, and local regulators/controllers, typically attached to a locally central unit, implementing one or a set of control/monitoring algorithms.

These subsystems are typically known as Remote Terminal Units, which might exchange information with other controllers over the network (i.e., Programmable Logic Controllers, PLC) in order to synchronize their operations and carry out a complex process. The possibility of implementing DCS with local intelligence and distributed control, enabling fully monitoring a plant, is becoming more attractive but increases exponentially the complexity of such systems. For instance, DCS pose very specific requirements in terms of the latency, reliability, and availability of the control system. Moreover, a distributed architecture must deal with safety issues such as redundancy, data validation, fault isolation, and tolerance [9].

It has been difficult to meet the aforementioned requirements with existing technologies, which are based on traditional sequential controllers, limiting the response time and their deployment in many demanding applications. Thus, control engineers have sought new manners to implement high-performance systems, often based on devices such as FPGAs [10], especially in niche areas such as motion control and voltage regulators and also in the creation of intelligent sensors and other intelligent electronic devices [11]. Moreover, the introduction of new technological features, such as the extended embedded platforms (with offers from all FPGAs vendors), containing high-end processors and reconfigurable logic, seems like the next logical step for the creation of plants-on-a-chip [12].

In this paper, we posit that such SoC FPGA platforms represent an excellent technological choice for implementing heterogeneous, customizable, scalable, and reconfigurable DCS, a fact that has been widely recognized in the industrial community [13]. Moreover, reconfigurable devices have the added benefit of fostering interoperability by easily customizing the supported fieldbus protocols on the field and remotely

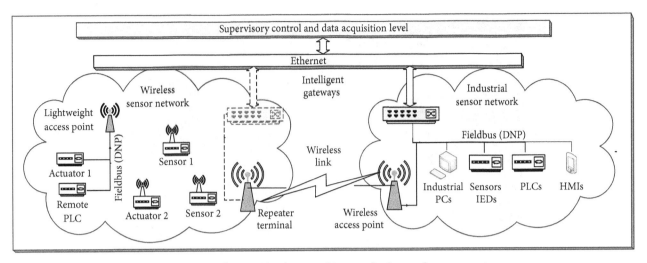

FIGURE 1: Typical IPMCS hardware architecture for factory floor automation.

with the possibility of using partial reconfiguration techniques, being even promoted as intelligent and upgradeable gateways, seeking to harmonize the current limitation in the industrial ecosystem [14]. In the next section, we analyze some of the current efforts in the creation of intelligent electronic devices and control subsystems in reconfigurable platforms for a variety of applications; some emphasis is given at the end of the section as well not only to the substitution of PLC devices by FPGAs [15] but also to more general applications as digital controllers for a variety of industrial applications.

Furthermore, we analyze the current divide between the existing literature and the need for actual, interconnected, and distributed IEDs and controllers, which we argue could be alleviated through the use of SoC FPGA devices and the associated resources. For this purpose, in Section 4, we present a case study for a distributed control system based on Xilinx Zynq Extended Processing Platform, which has been deployed in industrial environment for 3D printing and fiber carbon reinforcement.

3. Use of FPGAs in Industrial Applications

In this section, we discuss some of the limitations of the current approaches for distributed control systems. Afterwards, we briefly describe some successful uses of FPGA in the implementation of IEDs and various types of control algorithms. In the same vein, some initial efforts for the integration of PLC-like type of functionalities within the programmable fabric will be addressed. Finally, in the last subsection, we will discuss how more advanced type of reconfigurable devices (such as SoC FPGAs) could help bridge the gap between the endeavors carried out within the control and automation domain and embedded design communities.

3.1. Limitations of Current DCS Paradigms. Most of the current process automation and control platforms, globally known as Industrial Process Measurement and Control Systems (IPMCS), are built around traditional PLC architectures,

which are generally oriented towards centralized applications, in which several nodes retrieve data from the plant and react to external events according to a main application running on a central controller. These solutions are not well suited for implementing complex DCS for many reasons, the most important being that existing approaches are designed under the execution constraints imposed by the cycle-scan nature of the PLCs [16]. The performance of such solutions is rather limited in very demanding applications, such as highly dynamic and ultrafast processes (such as electronic drives and ultrafast robotics), as depicted in Figure 2. Thus, practitioners in the domain have been looking for effective manners to respond to these heterogeneous and stringent constraints.

In recent years, there has been a trend towards the use of intelligent electronic field devices (IEDs) or Intelligent Mechatronic Components (IMCs) [17], which contain a certain amount of embedded computing power, in tandem with communication and monitoring capabilities. Complex algorithms can be distributed over such smart devices, resulting in the reduction of the computing load for the main PLCs and of the required communication bandwidth of the overall application.

The use of such intelligent components promises essential benefits for the design and reconfiguration of automated production systems due to encapsulation and reuse of a great deal of intellectual property modules. However, the design patterns promoted by current programming and architectural standards (such as the IEC 61131-3 [18]) do not conceptually support the capabilities that are necessary to fulfill those promises [19]. Moreover, the design of control systems by the practitioners is still very much linked to a PLC-programming mindset, which, as discussed above, does not lend very well to the implementation of more sophisticated decentralized applications.

Some initial efforts towards a more varied ecosystem have been observed in recent years, with an increased inclusion of various types of microcontroller units (MCUs) into IEDs, as well as their deployment as the technology of choice for new developments in the automation domain, as

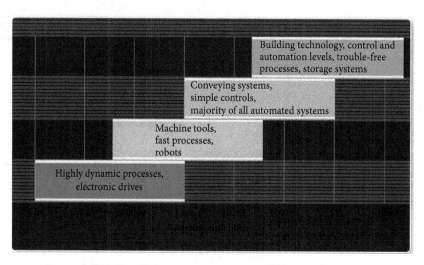

FIGURE 2: Real-time classes and application areas (IAONA classification).

those represented by the IEC 61499 standard for distributed control systems [20], which is based on an event-driven approach. However, the existing development tools and the supported architectures do not fully implement the standard as originally intended and are still very much bounded by the sequential cycle-scan of the underlying platforms.

3.2. Trends in the Use of FPGAs for Implementing IEDs. In recent years, researchers and industry have been looking for means to overcome the aforementioned limitations. For instance, the study of the possibilities of FPGAs for implementing IEDs and PLC-based platforms has been a very active area of research [21]. The most important benefits of using FPGAs for implementing complex control systems are related to performance in terms of the execution speeds that can be attained by massively parallel architectures, in tandem with significantly larger I/O processing capabilities.

Reconfigurable devices could enable improved control systems, where designers can combine one or several RISC processors with dedicated computing hardware accelerators [10] implementing control algorithms, while enabling the integration of communication blocks (to support the fieldbus protocols) and other specialized peripherals. On the other hand, designers can also design custom hardware architectures for stringent applications in terms of performance, which when coupled with the embedded processors could help harness IP reuse and product diversification [7]. Furthermore, other advantages of FPGAs over competing technologies are their programmability on the field, customization through programmable logic, and the ability to tailor the communication protocols to a particular system configuration, among others.

A good introduction to the advantages of the use of FPGAs in industrial settings can be found in [5], where an account and analysis of the benefits of using these devices are presented. As noted by the authors, industrial robot control systems in particular represent an especially interesting application scenario, given that such systems have evolved

from open-loop to closed-loop, adaptive controlled systems. This evolution entails a dramatic technological shift from relatively simple architectures to more complex platforms integrating DSP functions, ADC/DAC converters, along with Pulse Width Modulation (PWM) generators and the underlying logic resources of the FPGA for implementing the computation for the control algorithms. The next generation of control systems needs to be able to cope with increasingly faster real-time responses, and thus FPGAs are regarded as ideal candidates for implementing these demanding applications [12].

It has been argued that, when compared with their analogue counterparts, a digital system that could execute quasi-instantaneously a control algorithm should be of great interest by cumulating the advantages of both worlds [22]. This has led to a third category of control devices: the quasi-analog controllers by digital means. FPGA devices represent a good choice for this new category of controllers, since they incorporate various heterogeneous resources (i.e., BRAM and DSP blocks) within the reconfigurable fabric, along with the necessary logic for implementing a great variety of algorithms. Moreover, FPGAs enable integrating not only traditional control algorithms but also other more PLC-oriented functions that can coexist in the same device [23], offering a very high level of integration and computational heterogeneity.

It is not the goal of this section to delve into a detailed state of the art of this area, which has been profusely done in the papers cited above. However, we can briefly mention some successful applications of FPGA devices, for instance, as power conversion controllers (as pulse width-modulation (PWM) inverters [24, 25] and multilevel converters [26, 27]). Uses can also be found in the control of electrical machines and in robotics applications (induction machine drives [28, 29] and motion control [30, 31]). More recently, reconfigurable devices have been increasingly finding applications as means for implementing hardware-in-the-loop platforms [32, 33] for debugging purposes principally but increasingly as a means to emulate subcomponents of larger systems.

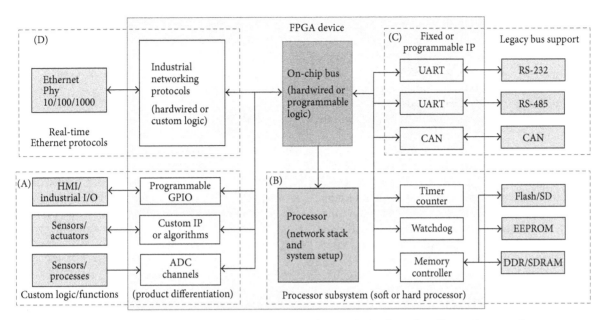

FIGURE 3: A possible architecture for a SoC FPGA-based networked industrial intelligent electronic device.

3.3. Trends in the Use of FPGAs for Implementing IEDs. In the industrial control domain, there are a number of reasons for the use and integration of novel architectures and industrial-optimized semiconductor devices. In the first place, there is a shift from point-to-point data communication towards network-based solutions, as profusely discussed in Section 2.

Second, in many application domains, this allows system integrators to build larger, scalable, upgradeable, and more cost-effective systems. Factory automation and control systems could benefit from the expandability that network communication and control offer, such as easily adding and upgrading equipment that is connected using standardized protocols [34].

Third, another major trend is represented by a shift towards the miniaturization of the application processing systems. Many factory equipment suppliers have learned that, by incorporating sophisticated motor-control algorithms, they can use low-cost motors, while reducing power consumption and improving reliability and safety. The same applies for many of the applications and control algorithms briefly described above: indeed, many of the applications described at the end of the previous section have clearly shown that parallel implementation of many control algorithms can attain significantly greater performances compared with other competing approaches, such as MCU and DSP devices [35].

These major trends have been driven by a need for high-performance, Ethernet-ready, low-power semiconductor devices to control the next generation of industrial machines. In particular, low cost is an important priority in many very specific and high-end applications; FPGAs and SoC FPGAs address this need by enabling differentiation via custom algorithms and functions tightly integrated in a single device, reducing BOM costs by integrating specialized ASIC components, DSP processors, and industrial buses and protocols into a single device, as depicted in Figure 3.

Features and functions supported by an FPGA can be updated long after deployment [36]. In areas such as industrial networking, where the protocols and standards are shifting and changing, the programmability of FPGAs versus fixed-logic devices (e.g., ASICs and ASSPs) saves migration costs and makes the solutions easier to maintain and scale. The same applies for the control algorithms as well, which can be updated when needed, taking advantage of the fast-prototyping capabilities afforded by reconfigurable devices, minimizing the cost and the time to market. As depicted in block (A) of Figure 3, the vast majority of today's FPGAs and SoC FPGAs incorporate programmable ADC channels, which in tandem with logic, memory, and DSP resources present in the reconfigurable fabric enable implementing complete custom functionalities, such as those described in the previous section. In the same vein, FPGAs integrate up to hundreds of programmable and customizable general-purpose I/O pins, which could be used to interface an FPGA-based IED and the associated custom functions with other industrial sensors and actuators.

Moreover, the possibility of integrating embedded processors (block (B) in the figure) within the device fosters improved HW/SW partitioning design strategies, helping designers to achieve a better compromise in the implementation of the constituent blocks of a control algorithm. The use of control functions into tightly integrated SoC FPGA-based IED entails many other benefits as well, which will be described as follows. First and foremost, the algorithms described before cannot function in isolation: an IED must be capable of performing system setup and managerial and monitoring operations in order to guarantee the correct operation of the controlled plant or process. These tasks are typically catered by a tightly coupled embedded processor, which either can be implemented in the FPGA resources or be a hardwired CPU. Secondly, the processor takes care as well of scheduling the execution and the communication among cooperating control functions, making the implementation of the control easier to maintain and validate at each stage of the development process. Finally, the performance of the control algorithms as well as the communication among the various control modules, sensors, and actuators is drastically reduced due to shortest response times of the underlying hardware implementation.

Process level communication is facilitated as well by the use of the embedded MCUs, which are responsible for federating peer-to-peer communication, both at the device level and among IEDs and other equipment. This communication is achieved through legacy buses (block (C)), which can either be present in the device or specifically mapped for a given application, taking advantage of the available logic resources and programmable GPIO. The FPGA can act as a bridge between industrial Ethernet protocols to RS-232, RS-485, and CAN, still widely used by many vendors for actuators and sensors alike. The main benefit of using FPGAs in this regard is that system can be tailored for the specific needs of the application, mapping only the required IP modules for supporting a given legacy protocol, saving valuable resources, and reducing the footprint of the hardware solution in a cost-effective manner.

In the same vein, the highest level of communication is the use of Ethernet, which provides the largest data bandwidth and distance to provide communication between various factory sites. Fieldbus communications employ RS-485, RS-422, and RS-232 as the physical layer interface, with protocols specified by the IEC 61158 standard, for example, DeviceNet, CANopen, and Profibus. However, as Ethernet matures in the SCADA segment, many fieldbus installations are being replaced or redesigned with real-time Ethernet protocols augmented with deterministic communication profiles and mechanisms. In order to meet the real time, low latency, and the deterministic capabilities required for industrial applications, many of these Ethernet protocols use specialized Ethernet Media Access Control (MAC) modules (hardware accelerators present in the FPGA, Block (D)), in tandem with specialized data packaging stacks for high-speed encoding and decoding. Reconfigurable devices support many of these protocols, which can be mapped onto the programmable logic and easily accessed and controlled by the processor through a lightweight IP stack or be present as hardened modules.

As briefly discussed at the end of Section 1, in this paper, we present the development of IED for controlling, in real time, the deposition of fibers by Automated Fiber Placement Robot to be discussed in the next section. The proposed solution had a set of constraints that were especially well suited for implementation in an embedded device: the available space was reduced, it had to meet real-time constraints, at both the control and communication levels, in order to maximize the attainable throughput and achievable precision, and, finally, it needed to be adaptable to any protocol changes in the rest of the DCS platform where it is to be integrated. Some implementation choices were initially explored, finally settling into a SoC FPGA from Xilinx (the Zynq EPP 7000),

which enables many of the features described above, as we will discuss in a subsequent section.

4. Application Context: The Control AFP Robot

Composite materials are increasingly used by the automotive, aerospace, and nautical industries to manufacture complex structures in terms of shape and also with the aim of addressing stringent requirements such as to lighten the weight of the vehicles while maintaining other properties such as resistance and reliability. Today, it is beyond dispute that three-dimensional (3D) fabric preforms can produce high-performance composite parts in sizes ranging from small to gigantic.

But, for high-volume industries, such as the automotive sector, 3D preforming processes have been, thus far, too time-consuming and, therefore, too expensive to be a serious materials/process option for producing cars. However, these limitations have been steadily overcome in recent years with the introduction of emerging technologies that offer the opportunity to automate the time-consuming and labor-intensive hand layup of 3D preforms, based on robotized fiber placement systems.

Robots have long been used to perform a variety of manufacturing tasks, but their use in the field of composites has been limited. In some cases, end-of-arm equipment has been used for water-jet cutting, drilling and tapping, material-handling, assembly, and fiber-placement applications [37]. Lasers have assisted greatly in verifying material location and orientation for manual layup and water-jet systems can generate holes and cutouts after layup is complete and the part is cured. Moreover, significant improvements in X-Y cutting systems and associated software have expedited material profiling [38].

Robotized Automated Tape Laying (ATL) and Automated Fiber Placement (AFP) are two emerging technologies for the production of a large variety of composites parts in the aeronautic industry. Their advantage towards fabric or large tape manual layup consists mainly of the ability to place consistently the fiber at the right place with the correct orientation in order to achieve the mechanical characteristics demanded by primary load-bearing structures [39].

Automation also promotes consistency in the quality of the produced parts, often obtained in a fraction of the time, compared to manual methods. The possibility of producing larger components, such as aircraft fuselages, is another advantage of these methods together with the ability to achieve near net-shape preforms, reducing material wastage and, hence, costs.

All these aspects make ATL and AFP ideal candidates for the production of helicopter panels and blades, tail cones, components for business jets, short and long range civil aircraft, military aircraft, engine nacelles, fan blades, and components for the automotive industry. However, such systems have some limitations regarding the speed and precision at which the fibers can be deposed, as we will see in the following subsections.

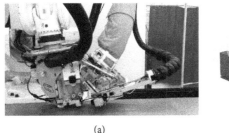 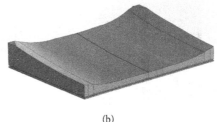

(a)   (b)

FIGURE 4: (a) An example of a fiber placement robot and (b) of a piece for the automotive industry.

4.1. The Fiber Placement Robot. The need for flexibility and modularity has led to the development of new systems mostly based on polyarticulated robots, which are able to be adapted or reprogrammed to different processes and different applications. These units are able to handle a variety of raw materials and to provide high production rates while working on complex and challenging structures.

Nowadays, these standard off-the-shelf polyarticulated robots are widely developed and have been produced for many years for the requirements of the automotive industry. They have reached a very high level of reliability and appear to be ideally suited for use within an AFP system able to satisfy all the requirements listed above. These polyarticulated robots have payloads ranging from 6 kg to 1 ton and can be combined with linear axis up to 60 m and spindle axis up to 40 m.

The AFP system deployed in our application (Figure 4(a), created by Coriolis Composites) uses the 6 motion axes of the polyarticulated robot (supplied either by ABB or by KUKA) plus two external units: a mould guiding unit and a robot positioning axis; therefore, the complete cell has 8 degrees of freedom. The robot, as well as the whole cell, complies with aeronautic specifications in terms of fiber placement and cutting accuracy as well as the repeatability of the process [40].

This flexible, compact, and versatile AFP system adapts easily to different geometries and ranges, making it suitable for manufacturing of complex parts and adaptable to any industrial settings as well as for applications in research centers, an is the case of the system presented herein. Its reliable and robust design meets the requirements of series production maintenance and high production levels are ensured through the speed of its movements. Precision and repeatability (basic criteria for the aeronautic market) are assured through a light maneuverable layup head, as shown in Figure 4(a).

4.2. Fiber Placement Real-Time Requirements. The AFP robot integrates an advanced fiber deposition head, a complex system in charge of feeding the carbon fibers to the deposition subsystem (where an array of actuators reside), using a roller system to move the fiber from a gantry to the mould, as depicted in Figure 5(a). The number of controllable actuators in the edge of the head determines the size and attainable throughput in the fabrication process, which involves depositing fibers over a prefabricated mould. This process is akin

to 3D printing, with the main difference that the positioning process involves a stitching fibers in layups instead of melting plastics such PLA to produce the piece (see Figure 4(b)).

As discussed before, the fibers are fed to the head subsystem from the creel using a pulley system in order to avoid the burden of the extra payload and complexity in the head, thus limiting the speed and the accuracy of the process. Therefore, a mechanism to depose fibers of different sizes in a controlled manner is implemented in the robot head, as depicted in Figure 5(a); each of the fibers in the head subsystem requires 3 actuators for feeding (via a roller), clamping, and cutting individual fibers, permitting a fine-grained deposition.

These actions need to be performed while the robot head is moving along the mould in an ultrafast, precise, and synchronized manner, which entails that the trigger time needs to be very short for all the actuators (very low jitter and skew). The Profibus communication proved to be a major bottleneck for real-time performances as the number of fibers augmented, producing accumulative positioning errors as depicted in Figure 5(b). In order to attain much lower response times, the communication bottleneck had to be eliminated by distributing the real-time functionalities of the BoxPC controller, integrating a rapid action processing system in close proximity to the actuators.

This issue stems from the fact that the Profibus link limited the speed at which the triggers could operate, forcing the system to decelerate in order to wait for new commands. Therefore, a reduced response time was deemed necessary to alleviate the above-mentioned issues, leading to a higher-performance solution (in terms of the deposition precision), which could potentially help in attaining higher fabrication throughput.

A distributed and networked IED implementation for managing this process seemed like the most viable choice, since this could be optimized for coping with the real-time requirements of the application directly into the robot head, discharging the main PLC from some of the time-consuming duties and enabling a higher degree of intelligence and data efficiency.

A more detailed description of the initial distributed control architecture will be provided in the next section, pointing at its limitations and outlining the requirements for the IEC control system in more detail, in order to gain greater understanding of the benefits of using reconfigurable devices in this industrial application. Particularly, we discuss how the features of SoC FPGA described in Section 3.3 were deployed.

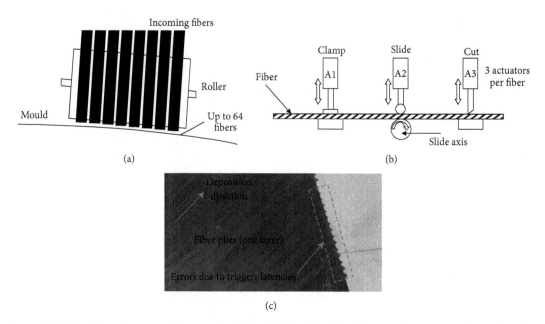

FIGURE 5: (a) The fiber placement subsystems in the head of the robot. (b) Actions and actuators per incoming fiber.

4.3. Distributed Control System Architecture. The AFP system is composed, apart from the robotic arm, of a placement head, a creel, and a tube for feeding the fibers. The creel provides all the necessary functions for unwinding the composite fiber bobbins at very high speeds with low tension and enables swift loading and unloading of the bobbins. The flexible pipes feed each fiber from the creel to the layup head, avoiding risks for twisting or damage. The system is compatible not only with preimpregnated thermoset material certified by the aeronautic industry but also with materials "of the future" such as dry fibers and preimpregnated thermoplastics.

This adaptation is made possible by a rapid change of the heating system. The unwinding, guiding, and laying up system are already adapted to these three families of materials. The entire system is controlled by a complex DCS split among different components due to the use of different vendor and proprietary subsystems. However, the fiber feeding system mounted in the robot is of paramount importance in the successful deployment of ADFP in ultrafast fabrication processes, and thus we concentrate on the specific issues of this subcomponent. In what follows, we will provide a general description of how the AFP robot is deployed within the DCS application to provide the reader with a glimpse of its complexity and of the limitations addressed in this work.

The initial DCS architecture is depicted in Figure 6, where the AFP robot (1) is the central component of the distributed system. The robot is tightly connected to Automatic Spool Frame (2), which contains the various types of fibers to manufacture a given piece and is controlled, along with the robot, by the AFP Robot Controller PLC. This PLC contains the general fiber placement software, generating the necessary commands to control the 6 axes and position the robot's head in the required coordinates. The control program, in the BoxPC (4), constantly monitors the speed

and position of the robot via a high-precision encoder in order to determine at which points a set of actions over the fibers need to take place. Whenever an action has to be undertaken, the appropriate command (5) is sent to the deposition head by a real-time BoxPC (a WinAC RTX [41]) via a Profibus link.

These events (referred to as triggers thereafter) control the Head Electronic-Pneumatic (6) subsystem (containing internally a very large number of actuators (7)) used for deposing the fiber over a surface (typically a mould (8)), using the mechanism of Figure 5(a). In order to attain the highest possible throughput, while maintaining a high precision (and low jitter) in the actions, the response time between the trigger and the action must be as short as possible, typically in the order of microseconds, positioning the system in the scale of the most demanding applications depicted in Figure 2. Apart from the stringent execution requirements needed for attaining the necessary processing capabilities, the solution should meet some other requirements, which are described as follows.

(1) Real-Time Ethernet Connectivity. The solution needs to be able to interact with the main PLC and the associated HMI software in order to upload the deposition program over real-time Ethernet connections. Manual command settings should also be possible through the HMI for debugging purposes. The proposed solution must then implement a lightweight TCP/IP stack and client for such purposes.

(2) Remote Storage of the Deposition Program. In order to minimize the data transfer delays associated with the previous solution, it is desirable to be able to store large control programs, which trigger the actions of the electropneumatic actuators in the head. The program needs to be stored either

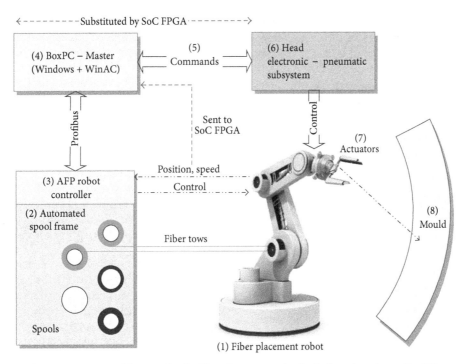

FIGURE 6: Previous system architecture for the fiber placement robotic platform based on a BoxPC controller.

temporally (for test purposes or small fabrication batches) or in a more long-term basis (using internal flash memory or SD cards).

(3) Act over a Large Number of I/O in a Scalable Manner. In order to be of any use, the system should be capable of dealing with a large number of actuators so that larger draping patterns can be handled. However, the amount of actuators for a given phase in the fabrication process changes and, thus, the system should be able to be seamlessly configured for different configurations (i.e., 8, 16, 32, and 64 tapes).

(4) Calculate the Position and Speed Independently. As we will see in the next section, the deposition program includes information about the precise moment at which the rolling, clamping, and cutting operations must be performed. The latter two are especially important, since they determine the precision that can be attained. Therefore, position and speed calculations should be available in real time so that triggers are activated at the optimal time, while avoiding the latencies associated with the original implementation.

(5) Backward Compatibility and Upgradeability. The proposed solution should be capable of interacting with existing infrastructure and equipment, as well as supporting legacy communication protocols. For instance, a previous development made use of SPI communications for the GPIO voltage scaling, as well as for interacting with visualization and storage devices.

In the next section, we will present the proposed solution, based on a SoC FPGA (Xilinx's Zynq Extended Processing Platform [42]), which enabled us to meet the constraints and requirements discussed above, in a cost-effective manner.

5. Proposed Real-Time Architecture Based on SoC FPGA

The PLC and BoxPC solution for controlling the deposing of fibers in the AFP robot was not able to meet the ever-increasing stringent requirements that such an application requires. For this reason, it was decided that an intelligent electronic device, closer to the deposing head, could accelerate the actuator triggering process, as well as the precision in the actions, by introducing a higher degree of intelligence and reducing the signal latency (see the dotted square on the top of Figure 6).

A first, proof of concept system was created, based on a small microcontroller running a real-time operating system (FreeRTOS [43]), which, in tandem with a Modbus stack, addressed the communication bottleneck and, furthermore, accelerated the command processing itself by storing large numbers of actions (even complete manufacturing sequences) directly in flash memory. In this manner, the main PLC was discharged of the significant computational and communication loads, while eliminating the use of the BoxPC PLC.

As we will see later in the article, this solution provided a significant speed-up over the PLC-based solution, but it quickly proved to be of limited use for systems which required deposing more than 16 fibers, as the number of signals the MCU could control is limited. This shortcoming severely limited the scalability of the deposing system, in which it is desirable to be able to program the number of fibers in real time and to be able to depose up to 48 fibers (which entails controlling $3 \times 48 = 132$ actuators). Therefore, it was decided to move to FPGA implementation to take advantage of the very large number of programmable I/Os FPGAs provide, as well as to leverage the field-programmability of this technology to accommodate future developments and upgrades. In order to make this passage more straightforward, a SoC FPGA has been chosen (the Zynq EPP 7000) in order to port the FreeR-TOS implementation previously developed while gaining in customization capabilities using programmable logic and the increased number of I/Os.

In the next subsections, we will first briefly discuss the benefits of using SoC FPGAs. Then, we will detail the proposed architecture and software implementation of the real-time control system. Finally, we will discuss initial tests performed using a mechatronic platform for validating the design before moving to the actual system. Then, in the next section, a comparison between the various systems will be carried out.

5.1. An Introduction to SoC FPGA Heterogeneous Platforms. The design of FPGA-based Systems-on-Chip has typically revolved around a hardware-centric view of system design, which has been deemed as too complex and technology-specific by nonspecialists, making the use of FPGA difficult beyond some niche applications in which their full potential has already been demonstrated.

Moreover, to make matters worse, the implementation of the management processing unit (MPU) of many of platforms (i.e., SoC, ASSP, or intelligent control devices) has been often carried out using the so-called soft-processors, which are mapped to the reconfigurable logic of the FPGA and usually do not have enough processing power for the most demanding applications. Furthermore, FPGA vendors have struggled to gain traction beyond some niche markets, since nonexperts regard the development flow as too complex.

For tackling the technological shortcomings briefly discussed above, the main FPGA vendors have made some major strides in adapting to the needs of the markets by introducing new capabilities, both technological and methodological [44]. Examples of the former are the increased integration of specialized functions such as Digital Signal Processing (DSP) blocks, distributed and configurable memory blocks (i.e., distributed BRAMs), and, more recently, large memory banks for data intensive applications, as well as the support of a plethora of communication protocols for moving large amounts of data.

On the other hand, and in order to address the hardware/software divide typically associated with FPGA-based SoCs, FPGA vendors have made major strides in introducing application grade processors, such as the ARM Cortex A9, capable of running full operating systems such as Linux, with the aim of simplifying the specification, implementation, and validation of heterogeneous embedded systems. This new kind of devices (which can be dubbed SoC FPGAs and depicted in Figure 7) couples a pair of high-performance ARM processors with a programmable logic extension block to promote a software-centric approach first and foremost.

Following this rationale, these Extensible Processing Platforms (as Xilinx has named their Zynq devices [42]) take a processor-first approach, in which the ARM processor

development flow is emphasized over the traditional FPGA-based design approaches. This entails that software designers can start developing new applications right away, using the well-known and well-regarded ARM Cortex architecture, taking advantage of a fixed number of standards modules and interfaces, which were briefly discussed in Section 3.3 and shown in Figure 3.

In many instances, when developing a new product or project, the first step entails developing a proof of concept. Thus, the designers are thus less concerned about customizing the system requirements for specific customer or niche market. The most important concern at this phase is to have the maximum amount of flexibility to determine which functions are needed for the basic prototype in terms of the constituent components required for the embedded application.

Then, in a second phase, the design team can fine-tune the application to meet specific constraints (i.e., power consumption and real-time performance) by using profiling tools, which can help them to decide whether any segments of the applications can be sped up exploiting hardware implementation, discharging the main processor of some time-consuming processes. SoC FPFAs like the Zynq integrate a tightly coupled programmable logic extension block that allows designers to partition their hardware and software functions based on system requirements and to customize the device for a given application scenario [45]. They can implement functions in the programmable logic extension block to create their own application-specific, highly optimized Systems-on-Chips (SoCs), with the additional advantages of reducing chip-count and the complexity of the circuit board, as well as avoiding signal integrity issues.

It is at this hardware specialization phase that the methodological aspects hinted above come to the fore. In order to accelerate the integration of complex SoC and simplify the design process for nonexperts, FPGA vendors offer nowadays a variety of means for translating and implementing application-specific functions into hardware accelerated functions. The functions can be written using Hardware Description Languages (HDLs) or translated to RTL using High-Level Synthesis (HLS) techniques and then wrapped by bus interfaces for promoting IP reuse and taking advantage of the HW/SW interface and associated application-programming interface (API), which makes the call and use of the function easier from the application development perspective [46].

In order to make the communication between the processor and the programmable logic more efficient, the architecture of SoC FPGAs such as the Zynq is completed by industry standard AXI interfaces, which provide high-bandwidth, low-latency connections between the two parts of the device. This means that the processor and logic can each be used for what they do best, without the overhead of interfacing between two physically separate devices.

In this paper, we leverage the capabilities of these newly introduced heterogeneous Extended Processing Platforms for implementing the control system described in Section 4 and depicted in Figure 6. The main goal of this hardware implementation is to overcome the limitations of the previous

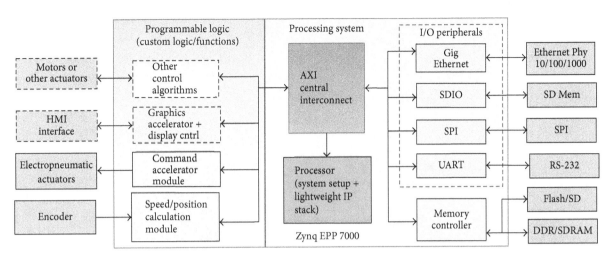

FIGURE 7: Architecture of the implemented SoC FPGA-based industrial intelligent electronic device.

PLC and MCU-based solutions and to meet the stringent constraints and capabilities introduced in the previous section.

5.2. Intelligent Electronic Controller for Fiber Placement. In this section, we introduce the proposed architecture (Figure 7) for speeding up the deposition of carbon fibers in the system described above, as well as the integration of the solution in the overall design chain of Coriolis Composites. The main rationale of the proposed architecture is to overcome as much as possible the communication bottleneck of the original PLC-based architecture, while maintaining compatibility with the CAD tools deployed for generating the fiber placement control commands and fostering the upgradeability of the system.

The bottleneck created by the use of the BoxPC has been circumvented by implementing a TCP/IP client using a lightweight IP stack, using the Ethernet MAC module integrated in the SoC FPGA for transferring the entire control program to the IED controller. The fiber deposition path is generated using a couple of pieces of software, CATFiber and CADFiber, which in tandem produce CAD data for a workpiece. This code is encompassed, on one hand, by the orientations of the carbon plies for each layer and, on the other hand, by the actions to be performed upon each fiber (Figure 5).

The CAD tools enable importing and visualizing surface and geometry information of the manufacturing tools and jigs, allowing the generation of ply sequences (defined by their contour and a reference curve or ply direction). Moreover, the tools are tightly coupled with quality assessment analyses of draped laminated complex surfaces and augmented with fiber covering simulation tools, which cater for fiber angle deviation and steering. If necessary, a ply can be cut automatically into smaller sections in order to fulfill maximum angle deviations.

On the other hand, the Composites Manufacturing Module of the CAD tools allows the automatic generation actions for the tapes, that is, bands of several fibers that are deposed over the surface in a computer-controlled manner.

Premanufacturing checks can be performed thanks to various analysis tools including fiber compaction, roller crush, and tool path viewing.

The design process for a given piece is as follows: (i) a laminate piece is designed with the required number of plies and orientations, (ii) subsequently, plies are generated for a mould surface based on the CAD data from the piece, (iii) afterwards, a deposition program for the tapes is generated depending on the number of fibers to be used for a particular scenario (current systems support 16 fibers simultaneously), and finally (iv) tool paths are created in Kuka Robot Language (KRL) as a succession of linear movements or spline based displacements.

Once a piece has been created and simulated, the program is stored in an XML format and the program is executed by the BoxPC module described in Section 4.3 (Figure 6). As discussed above, the control for the robot is independent of that for the pneumatic actuators in the deposing head: the main PLC caters for positioning the robot along the trajectories generated by CADFiber, while a real-time OS running on the BoxPC controls the actions associated with the fiber deposing subsystem, introducing the previously discussed performance bottleneck.

Indeed, in spite of the capabilities of the BoxPC, a control loop encompassed by the position and speed signals coming from the robot limited the attainable speed at which the robot head could react, since this information is vital to trigger the control signals for the actuators in the head (Figure 5(a)). This is because the code generated by CADFiber for triggering the actuators in the head is dependent upon the robot position information, and in order to improve the accuracy of the finished pieces, all the encompassing actuators per fiber have to react very fast in a highly synchronized and repeatable manner. Additionally, the internal calculations by the BoxPC and the latencies introduced by the Profibus link only made matters worse.

Therefore, it was decided early on to substitute the BoxPC with a dedicated real-time embedded controller, which could satisfy the requirements briefly discussed at the end of Section 4.3. First, real-time connectivity is achieved by

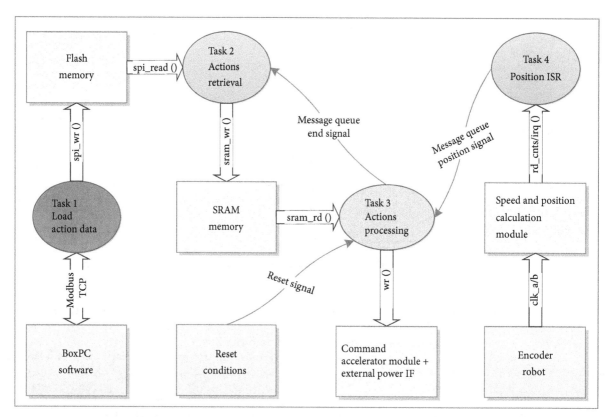

FIGURE 8: Architecture of the real-time control application based on FreeRTOS.

implementing an Ethernet client on the hybrid reconfigurable device, taking advantage of the integrated MAC controller. In this manner, we are able to communicate order to the deposing system, but the totality of the program resides now in the embedded platform, reducing the communication latency. The program can be remotely sent by the PLC via Modbus and stored in internal flash memory or controlled from the HMI for testing purposes by modifying sections of a Modbus stack. A real-time operating system (FreeRTOS) running on the ARM processor caters for the timely execution of the various components in the application (which is shown in Figure 8) and fosters reuse and maintainability of the developed code, which can be easily migrated to other platforms as well. We harness as well the capabilities of the Zynq heterogeneous platform for maintaining back compatibility with previous solutions by supporting legacy buses such as I2C, SPI, and RS-232, but the main advantages are the increased I/O capabilities and customization afforded by using the programmable section of the device.

As can be seen in the left side of Figure 7, the programmable logic of the heterogeneous platform has been used to move some of the functionalities that were missing in the BoxPC implementation, while overcoming the limitations of more constrained embedded devices (i.e., microcontroller units or MCUs). First of all, a specialized circuit has been implemented for decoding the quadrature encoder signals (a pulse detection circuit) and for computing the position and speed of the robot in real time without the intervention of

the MPU. Secondly, a configurable expansion port is used for configuring the number of fibers to be deposed at any given point, according to the specifications of the CAD program stored in the internal memory; since this module has been mapped to the programmable logic, it can be upgraded to accommodate future developments.

The programmable section of the hybrid device contains enough resources to accommodate extra functionalities as can be observed in the top left corner of Figure 7.

Such functionalities could include an independent controller and graphics accelerator for implementing an HMI for monitoring and testing purposes (i.e., using a customized programmable accelerator, such as the Xylon IP). Furthermore, as we will discuss in Section 6.1, the proposed architecture has been first integrated in a test bench platform before moving to the final implementation in the actual robot; the test bench platform incorporates a motor that is currently controlled separately, complicating the testing process. Incorporating the control algorithms and electronic drive for the motor directly in the device could make a seamless demonstration and learning tool.

5.3. Hardware/Software Architecture: RTOS and Custom IPs. In this section, we will briefly discuss how the real-time embedded application has been conceived and implemented in the ARM processor integrated in the heterogeneous all programmable Zynq platform. As described before, such platforms foster a processor-first approach, in which the

ARM boots first, performing subsequently duties such as system initialization and configuration. Afterwards, the processor retrieves the configuration data for bootstrapping the programmable configurable logic, effectively fostering fail-safe strategies and avoiding some of the pitfalls of reconfigurable devices in control systems. Once the device and peripherals are up and running, the ARM processor takes a more managerial role, federating the proper execution of the overall application, catered in this case by a real-time operating system (RTOS). We have chosen FreeRTOS for a number of reasons: the code is open source and widely used and documented. Furthermore, the RTOS supports a wide range of microcontrollers and MPUs and has been especially designed for medium range devices, albeit consuming a very small memory footprint.

The task diagram for the application as implemented using FreeRTOS is shown in Figure 8. The RTOS performs the following actions for a given deposition program.

Task 1. The application can start by receiving a write request from the TCP/IP server (main PLC), in which case a task called *Load Action Data* retrieves the program data for the actuators, stored temporally into a Modbus table, using a tailored lightweight TCP/IP stack running on the ARM processor.

Task 2. The deposition program can then move to nonvolatile memory (i.e., SD or flash) through an *Actions Retrieval* task. Once the program has been stored, the system waits for an initialization signal from the main PLC to start execution.

The system can operate in two modes: in normal and in force/debug modes. The latter case is used for writing commands directly to a Modbus table, interacting directly with an external Human Machine Interface that enables testing arbitrary patterns monitoring any problems with the system. In the former case, the RTOS allocates portions of the program onto SDRAM memory using DMA for faster processing and uses the position and speed information from the system to execute these commands generated by CADFiber.

Task 3. In normal operating mode, once the program execution is triggered by the main PLC, the commands are retrieved from the SDRAM memory (running the Actions Processing) software task in the ARM processor, which basically places the initial memory address for a given command and amount of actions to be performed. This information is then sent as a burst to custom hardware accelerator, labeled *Command Accelerator Module* (CAM) in Figure 8.

The CAM module is a hardware accelerated function wrapped using an AXI Intellectual Property Interface module, as depicted in Figure 9(a). This module resides in the programmable logic section of the device and has been implemented in such a manner that the number of actuators can be automatically selected by the application, enabling seamlessly modifying the external interface without undergoing any hardware modifications in the rest of the system. The module was implemented in VHDL using Xilinx ISE, functionally verified and subsequently wrapped with the AXI IPIF using the IP creation infrastructure provided by Vivado.

This CAM module permits as well the interaction between the *Actions Processing* task at the RTOS level and the controlled plant via the HW/SW interface that translates the logical actions in the control program into electrical signals that drive the external electropneumatic controller that is in charge of actually triggering the pneumatic actuators in the robot's head, as depicted on the left side of Figure 7. The module acts basically as a processor-configurable demultiplexer: depending on the head configuration, the module can control 16, 32, and 64 fibers, and, as such, the CAM controls how the data bursts are mapped from memory to the outputs, using a configuration register, a set of multiplexers, and a state machine that controls the shown datapath.

Nonetheless, the capabilities of the Zynq platform foster backward compatibility through the use of QUAD SPI IPs that can be used with previous versions of the electropneumatic control system. This previous version, based on a microcontroller, used an SPI port and I/O expander to control up to 16 actuators; in the Zynq, several of these ports can be mapped in the PL section and control various sets of fiber bundles, but there is an associated timing penalty, as will be discussed in the next section.

Task 4. In order to trigger the actions at the correct time stamps, the processor subsystem has been extended with a *Speed and Position Calculation Module* (SPCM) (shown in Figure 9(b)). This hardware accelerator, also implemented in the PL section of the Zynq, is responsible for calculating the position and speed of the robot using the signals from the quadrature encoder in tandem with the circuitry integrated in the AXI IP shown in the figure.

As with the CAM module, the circuitry was described and functionally validated using Xilinx ISE and then exported to Vivado for creating a customized AXI-based hardware accelerator, which can be accessed by the processor via the HW/SW interface provided by the RTOS. In particular, the RTOS retrieves the next position at which a command is to be executed next and stores it into an internal register of the SPCM IP.

This value is compared with the position calculated by the SPCM and, depending upon the current speed, it can anticipate when the next command should be sent to the CAM IP, which is signaled to the RTOS via a message queue, triggered by an interrupt from the IP and captured by the *Action Processing* task, as depicted in Figure 8.

On the other hand, the *Action Processing* task notifies the *Actions Retrieval* task whether it requires more data, so commands are always available for streaming. The processor can then buffer the data corresponding to the next section of the program onto the CAM internal FIFO, effectively eliminating unnecessary waiting times and thus increasing the attainable deposition throughput. It must be noted that these tasks are run cyclically by the FreeRTOS scheduler, which is generated automatically during the compilation of the operation, making the application easier to maintain and scale.

In the following subsection, we will briefly show how the system has been put together using Vivado and discuss aspects related to hardware resources utilization and the performance of the solution.

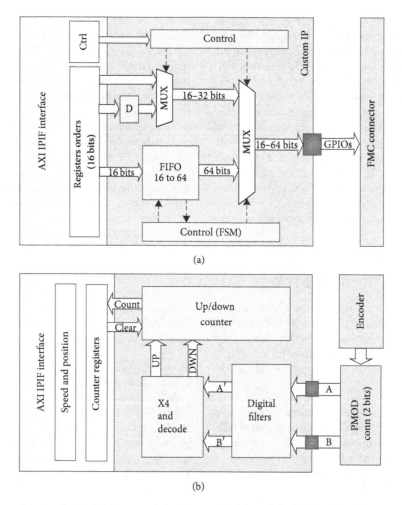

(a)

(b)

FIGURE 9: Hardware accelerators for the (a) Command Accelerator Module and the (b) Speed and Position Calculation Module.

5.4. Implementation Results in the Zynq-7000 Platform. As described in the previous section, the CAM and SPCM HDL descriptions have been integrated as AXI-based hardware accelerators so they can be integrated into the proposed SoC platform, using Vivado IP integrator. Furthermore, the IPIF interface enables the application engineer to interact with the underlying hardware modules via the HW/SW interfaces via a simplified API and to exploit their functionalities by encapsulating them as FreeRTOS tasks. The SoC platform introduced in Section 5.2 (and depicted in Figure 7) was thus created using Vivado, targeting the ZedBoard (which integrates the Zynq-7010 EPP, with a bus clock of 100 MHz), as depicted in Figure 10.

The synthesis results showing the resource utilization for each of the modules are summarized in Table 1. The table compares the resource utilization of the CAM and SPCM modules with that of a single instance of the QUAD SPI, the means of communication of the MCU-based implementation.

On the other hand, the overall resource utilization of the modules in the PL region of the Zynq device is summarized in Table 2. The resource utilization, including other modules for putting the SoC together, accounts for 7.4% (LUT) and

TABLE 1: Hardware resource utilization of each of the modules.

Module	LUT	FF	BRAM/DSP
QUAD SPI	339	539	0
CAM	104	220	0
SPCM	93	186	0

TABLE 2: Overall resource utilization for the modules in the PL section.

Resource type	Usage	Total available resources	Utilization (%)
LUT	1297	17,600	7.40%
FF	1716	35,200	4.90%

4.9% (FF). No BRAM or DSP blocks have been used, leaving ample resources for implementing other modules or control algorithms, as shown in Figure 7.

The platform description was then exported to SDK, where the application was put together using the FreeRTOS Zynq port and associated files. The design was then programmed onto the device to carry out the tests, first in the mechatronic testbed to be presented in Section 6.1 and,

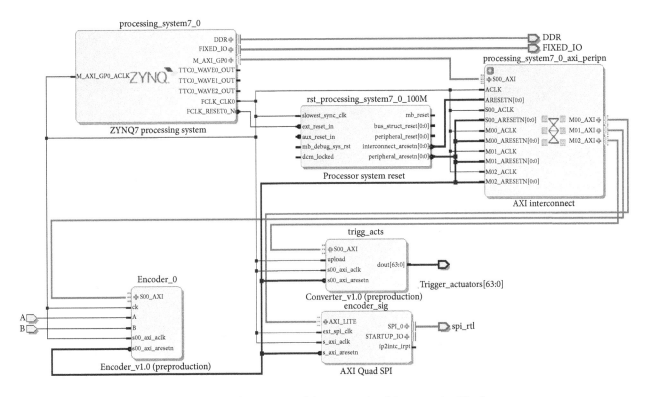

FIGURE 10: Implementation of the proposed architecture using Vivado.

once validated, in the actual AFP robot in the ComposiTIC facilities.

6. Experimental Results and Validation of the Solution

In this section, we briefly discuss how the proposed platform has been initially tested in order to experimentally validate the correctness of the software application and to assess the performance gains that were expected using FPGAs in this particular context, deploying initially a custom mechatronic testbed to validate the solution in a safe setting. Subsequently, we delve into experimental tests carried in the real robot and how the proposed SoC FPGA-based solutions have enabled us to speed up the fiber deposition process in the AFP robot while increasing the precision in the overall process.

6.1. A Mechatronic Platform for Fast-Prototyping Purposes. The main rationale for using a mechatronic testbed was to emulate the fiber deposition process (which is essentially performed in a single axis) by moving a deposition head with the aid of one-axis actuator. This one-axis mechatronic system is driven by SIMODRIVE POSMO A motor (from Siemens), which is controlled by SIMATIC Box PC (IPC 827C) running a real-time operating system (WinAC RTX) and enables the control of the motor via Profibus DP.

The control architecture was created using the Total Integrated Architecture (TIA) software module by Siemens, as depicted in Figure 11(a). This software enables creating the control interface between the SIMATIC Box PC and

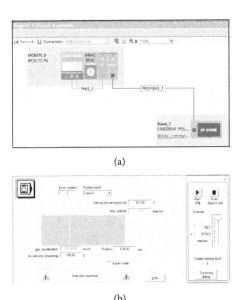

(a)

(b)

FIGURE 11: Architecture interface of the Siements Sysmatic motor controller.

the motor and setting configuration parameters such as the motor rotational speed, max acceleration, and the desired position, as depicted in Figure 11(b). This architecture enabled us to control the speed and acceleration of the overall system and to test response time of the proposed solution.

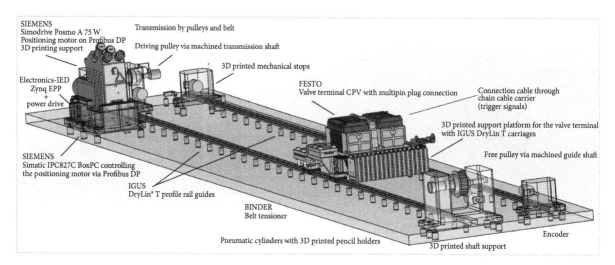

FIGURE 12: Reconfigurable mechatronic testbed platform and one axis actuator for fast-prototyping and experimental purposes.

The mechatronic testbed or fast-prototyping platform is depicted in Figure 12. It integrates a Siemens SIMODRIVE POSMO A [47] motor (controlled using the WinAC RTX OS running in SIMATIC Box PC, model IPC 827C), the Zynq-based intelligent electronic device controller, and, finally, the FESTO electropneumatic head, with several internal mechanical actuators that emulate the behavior in the actual robot head.

The mechatronic system has been conceived as a one-axis deposition system, as we are solely interested in the response time of the actuators in the robot head as it moves along a deposition trajectory. The FESTO air distribution system, driven electronically by the proposed IED, is fixed to a base plate attached to a rail system on the bottom and attached to a motor and a shaft support in the other end which enables free movement in a single axis, using a BINDER belt tensiometer.

It must be noted that the deposition head deployed in the testbed mechatronic system is not necessarily identical to the one in the actual AFP robot, since at this stage we were not interested in implementing the behavior of each actuator independently but more in the overall response time. Indeed, the main rationale for the FPGA-based implementation presented in this paper is to test the response time of the actuators in the AFP deposition head (see Figure 5(b)). Nonetheless, the response time for actuators responsible for the fiber cutting is the most sensible and we concentrated our efforts on characterizing and testing the limits of these in order to push the limits of the original platform.

Therefore, for the experiments performed with the aid of the mechatronic testbed, the programs generated using CAD-Fiber were preprocessed in order to include only commands associated with the fiber rolling and cutting actuators, which were then sent to the embedded IED, either as complete programs or applied directly using the HMI client. As mentioned previously, a TCP/IP server has been implemented using a lwIP stack running in the Zynq EPP 7000, which has been conceived in such a way that the actuators in the dummy robot head can be controlled using the Command Accelerator

FIGURE 13: IED control system for the head (pneumatic valve actuator terminal).

Module in the programmable logic section of the SoC FPGA device.

For this purpose, a ZedBoard platform integrating a Zynq EPP 7000 device has been extended with a custom board to interface the IED with external signals, as depicted in Figure 13. For instance, the FMC connector in the board has been used to connect the processor subsystem in the device, via the customized hardware accelerator in the programmable logic section of the Zynq, with the power electronics in charge of driving an arrangement of Siemens electropneumatic valves. The latter subcomponent acts as the bridge between the electronic control systems and the actual mechanical action and represents thus the most important component of the system.

Furthermore, other components and sensors have been integrated in the mechatronic platform and interfaced with the IED. For instance, a quadrature pulse decoder has been integrated in the same axes of the Siemens SIMODRIVE POSMO A motor (through a mechanical coupling and the belt tensiometer) to provide information about the position of dummy deposition head, which is fed to the Speed and Position Calculation module in the programmable section of the SoC FPGA through an external port.

It must be emphasized that the use of the Zynq EPP has enabled us to seamlessly move from an initial standalone

Table 3: Performance comparisons between the different solutions.

Metrics/solution	Cutting speed	Cutting precision	Response time
BoxPC-based solution	400 mm/s	1 mm	2.5 ms/cycle
MCU-based solution	1000 mm/s	0.1 mm	250 us/cycle
Proposed solution	1500 mm/s	0.05 mm	50 us/cycle
Gain in performance	3.75x	20x	50x

prototype to a fully functional proof-of-concept mechatronic system and, finally, to its deployment in the actual AFP robot. Preliminary results obtained using the testbed as well as actual tests in the robot will be detailed in the next section.

6.2. Experimental Results and Performed Tests. For testing the increased processing capabilities of the proposed architecture, tailored test patterns were generated using CADFiber and tested using three different solutions for benchmarking purposes: the original BoxPC-based solution, a platform based on a Renesas microcontroller running FreeRTOS, and, finally, the SoC FPGA-based Zynq implementation, as depicted in Table 1.

Several design patterns, customly designed to trigger the cutting sequences in the deposition program were first generated and tested in the mechatronic subsystem presented in Section 6.1. These patterns needed to be tested over a distance of one meter, given the geometric limitations of the one-axis actuator; the required acceleration and nominal speed of the system were remotely controlled via Profibus DP using the SimoCom A software (as depicted in Figure 11).

As thoroughly discussed in the article, the main goal of the MCU and SoC FPGA-based implementation was to speed up the command processing and triggering process in order to attain a higher response time in the overall deposition process.

Additionally, the control system needs to constantly calculate the current speed and position of the head in order to anticipate any upcoming commands (i.e., triggers) accordingly. The original PLC-based implementation relied on a feedback loop, which introduced a significant delay and hindered the entire deposition process; this issue has been overcome in the two subsequent solutions by integrating this computation directly in the embedded system.

Several tests were carried out to compare the performance of the various solutions outlined above, which are summarized in Table 3 and discussed as follows. As stated previously, the maximum deposition speed attainable by the PLC-based solution was 400 mm/s, which leads to a response time of 2.5 ms per cycle. The MCU-based IED solution fares much better in this regard, attaining a response time of 250 us per cycle (10x), which enabled us to depose complex patterns at over 1000 mm/s.

Nonetheless, the response time is not the only limiting factor. Despite of the gain in response time obtained by using the MCU-based solution, the number of actuators that can be triggered at once was rather limited, imposing a constraint in the fabrication time, as shown in Figure 14.

Due to confidentiality issues, we concentrate here only on relatively simple test pieces, as depicted in Figures 14(a) and 14(b), respectively. As the results in the analysis of the figure show, the increased deposition afforded by the SoC FPGA solution (1500 mm/s, with a 50x response time over the PLC-based solution), in tandem with a larger number of available triggers, has enabled us to significantly reduce the fabrication throughput.

The results in Figure 14(c) show a reduction in the fabrication process of 12%, 15%, and 55%, respectively, over the original implementation. Nonetheless, it must be noted that this reduction is greatly dependent on the geometry of the piece and on the frequency and number of rolling and cutting commands and thus requires further investigation.

7. Conclusions

The Industrial Internet of Things (IIoT), the idea that all systems should be connected on a global scale in order to share information, is quickly becoming a reality. Today, a growing number of companies, especially in the industrial equipment markets, are taking IIoT one step further by creating complex systems that integrate sensors, processing capabilities, and adaptable communications protocols to form intelligent factories, smart energy grids, and even smart cities.

In this paper, we have presented the implementation of a SoC FPGA-based intelligent electronic device, which has been seamlessly integrated into a previously existing infrastructure for an advanced fiber placement system. In this sense, the implementation proposed here can be subscribed to the smart factories paradigm, since the overall platform is in fact a distributed control system, which relies on complex industrial communication network to properly operate. Furthermore, some of the most demanding aspects of the original application have been migrated to a SoC FPGA to add a higher degree of intelligence and flexibility in the control of the deposition subsystem, which can accommodate future developments as well.

The very specific requirements of the application, which demanded not only very low response times but also flexibility in terms of reconfiguration of the deposition head and the control hardware and software, made a strong case for the use of FPGAs. The application necessitated a real-time and low-latency Ethernet communication, remote configuration and storage of the deposition programs, and the availability and customization of a large number of I/Os. Moreover, it also had to be backward compatible and to accommodate future developments (i.e., new industrial protocols for any-to-any connectivity approaches and also more intelligence and/or on-board processing on the edge).

Indeed, in order to maximize profitability, factories seek more flexibility in their layouts, more information about the process and manufactured products, more intelligence in the processing of this data, and an effective integration of the human experience/interaction (HMIs). However, as new technologies are introduced into the factory sector, those creating them need to overcome several constraints. The first and the most important is that production cannot stop.

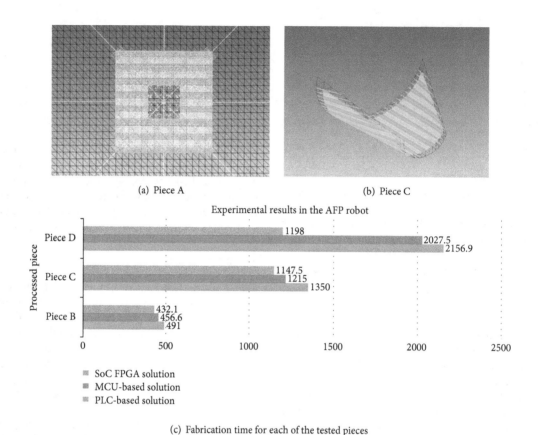

(a) Piece A

(b) Piece C

(c) Fabrication time for each of the tested pieces

FIGURE 14: ((a) and (b)) Two examples of pieces used to test the capabilities of the proposed solution. (c) Deposition times for three pieces using the SoC FPGA-based solution, the MCU-based solution, and the original PLC-based solution.

New technologies must be compatible with old systems and interoperability among vendors should be facilitated. This has been achieved in our implementation by deploying reconfigurable devices, which have been demonstrated to be an exceptional rapid prototyping tool over the years, as well as a means to close the gap between hardware and software development, promoting as well important aspects as customization and upgradeability in the field, potentially reducing the costs associated with production downtimes.

Furthermore, modern industrial solutions should provide the means for taking the next step in automation, leading to more autonomous or decentralized analytics. In this sense, recent strides in reconfigurable devices (in particular, the introduction of Extended Processing Platforms such as the Zynq EPP 7000m) are making this convergence more likely, and the incorporation of such devices in the automation domain seems quite logical to us. In this sense, we envision the incorporation of prognosis approaches in the control loop in order to determine, predict, and prevent possible wear-out in the actuators, which would severely affect the performance of the fiber deposition head.

In the particular context of the application presented here, the use of SoC FPGAs enabled not only improving over the original implementation of the system in terms of performance but also migrating the two previous solutions in a seamless manner, while respecting the constraints cited

above. In order to make this passage more straightforward, a SoC FPGA was chosen (the Zynq EPP 7000) in order to port the FreeRTOS implementation previously developed while gaining in customization capabilities through programmable logic and the extended number of I/Os.

As thoroughly discussed in this article, the SoC FPGA-based implementation of the fiber deposition control system introduced significant speed-up over the original PLC-based and MCU-based solutions, this done by overcoming the communication bottleneck of the former solution, while increasing the number of actuators that could be controlled by the latter. Furthermore, the hardware accelerators in the reconfigurable logic section of the device and the reduced latency in the communication gained through the increased integration have improved the real-time performance of the application. We have performed several experimental tests, first in a mechatronic testbed and subsequently in the actual robot, with various synthetic programs and later with actual pieces, showing a significant improvement in the attainable precision at higher speeds and, thus, improved throughput in the fabrication process.

Acknowledgments

The authors wish to acknowledge Coriolis Composites for the support during the duration of this project. In the same vein, they express their most sincere gratitude to the ComposiTIC research center for the support and access to its facilities. They also acknowledge Xilinx and Digilent for their generous donation of the ZedBoard platforms used in this study.

References

[1] V. Vyatkin, "Intelligent mechatronic components: Control system engineering using an open distributed architecture," in *Proceedings of the 2003 IEEE Conference on Emerging Technologies and Factory Automation, ETFA 2003*, pp. 277–284, prt, September 2003.

[2] G. Morel, P. Valckenaers, J.-M. Faure, C. E. Pereira, and C. Diedrich, "Manufacturing plant control challenges and issues," *Control Engineering Practice*, vol. 15, no. 11, pp. 1321–1331, 2007, Special Issue on Manufacturing Plant Control: Challenges and Issues INCOM 2004 11th IFAC INCOM'04 Symposium on Information Control Problems in Manufacturing.

[3] K. Thramboulidis, "Challenges in the development of mechatronic systems: The Mechatronic Component," in *Proceedings of the 13th IEEE International Conference on Emerging Technologies and Factory Automation, ETFA 2008*, pp. 624–631, deu, September 2008.

[4] M. N. Rooker, G. Ebenhofer, and T. Strasser, "Reconfigurable control in distributed automation systems," in *Proceedings of the 2009 ASME/IFToMM International Conference on Reconfigurable Mechanisms and Robots, ReMAR 2009*, pp. 705–714, gbr, June 2009.

[5] C. Paiz and M. Porrmann, "The utilization of reconfigurable hardware to implement digital controllers: a review," in *Proceedings of the 2007 IEEE International Symposium on Industrial Electronics, ISIE 2007*, pp. 2380–2385, June 2007.

[6] C. E. Pereira and L. Carro, "Distributed real-time embedded systems: Recent advances, future trends and their impact on manufacturing plant control," *Annual Reviews in Control*, vol. 31, no. 1, pp. 81–92, 2007.

[7] S. Z. Ahmed, G. Sassatelli, L. Torres, and L. Rougé, "Survey of new trends in industry for programmable hardware: FPGAs, MPPAs, MPSoCs, structured ASICs, eFPGAs and new wave of innovation in FPGAs," in *Proceedings of the 20th International Conference on Field Programmable Logic and Applications, FPL 2010*, pp. 291–297, September 2010.

[8] C.-H. Yang and V. Vyatkin, "Design and validation of distributed control with decentralized intelligence in process industries: a survey," in *Proceedings of the IEEE INDIN 2008: 6th IEEE International Conference on Industrial Informatics*, pp. 1395–1400, kor, July 2008.

[9] A. Zoitl, T. Strasser, K. Hall, R. Staron, C. Sunder, and B. Favre-Bulle, "The past, present, and future of iec 61499," in *Holonic and Multi-Agent Systems for Manufacturing*, vol. 4659 of *Lecture Notes in Computer Science*, pp. 1–14, Springer Berlin Heidelberg, Berlin, Heidelberg, 2007.

[10] E. Monmasson, L. Idkhajine, and M. W. Naouar, "FPGA-based controllers," *IEEE Industrial Electronics Magazine*, vol. 5, no. 1, pp. 14–26, 2011.

[11] A. de la Piedra, A. Braeken, and A. Touhafi, "Sensor systems based on FPGAs and their applications: a survey," *Sensors*, vol. 12, no. 9, pp. 12235–12264, 2012.

[12] L. Gomes, E. Monmasson, M. Cirstea, and J. J. Rodriguez-Andina, "Industrial electronic control: FPGAs and embedded systems solutions," in *Proceedings of the 39th Annual Conference of the IEEE Industrial Electronics Society, IECON 2013*, pp. 60–65, aut, November 2013.

[13] A. Chang, "Innovative platform-based design for the industrial internet of things," *Xilinx Xcell Journal*, vol. 92, pp. 32–37, 2015.

[14] A. Astarloa, "Intelligent gateways make a factory smarter," *Xilinx Xcell Journal*, vol. 94, pp. 14–21, 2016.

[15] A. Khamis, D. Zydek, G. Borowik, and D. S. Naidu, "Control System Design Based on Modern Embedded Systems," in *Computer Aided Systems Theory - EUROCAST 2013*, R. Moreno-Díaz, F. Pichler, and A. Quesada-Arencibia, Eds., vol. 8112 of *Lecture Notes in Computer Science*, pp. 491–498, Springer Berlin Heidelberg, Berlin, Heidelberg, 2013, ISBN 978-3-642-53861-2.

[16] S. Ichikawa, M. Akinaka, H. Hata, R. Ikeda, and H. Yamamoto, "An FPGA implementation of hard-wired sequence control system based on PLC software," *IEEJ Transactions on Electrical and Electronic Engineering*, vol. 6, no. 4, pp. 367–375, 2011.

[17] A. Lüder, L. H. M. Foehr, T. Holm, T. Wagner, and J.-J. Zaddach, "Manufacturing system engineering with mechatronical units," in *Proceedings of the 15th IEEE International Conference on Emerging Technologies and Factory Automation, ETFA 2010*, esp, September 2010.

[18] IEC, *Internaional Standard IEC 6113-3: Part 3: Programming Languages*, IEC, 1993.

[19] V. Vyatkin, "IEC 61499 as enabler of distributed and intelligent automation: State-of-the-art review," *IEEE Transactions on Industrial Informatics*, vol. 7, no. 4, pp. 768–781, 2011.

[20] IEC, *Internaional Standard IEC 61499-1: Function Blocks - Part 1: Architecture*, IEC, 2005.

[21] D. Du, X. Xu, and K. Yamazaki, "A study on the generation of silicon-based hardware Plc by means of the direct conversion of the ladder diagram to circuit design language," *International Journal of Advanced Manufacturing Technology*, vol. 49, no. 5-8, pp. 615–626, 2010.

[22] S. Simard, J. G. Mailloux, and R. Beguenane, "Prototyping advanced control systems on FPGA," *Eurasip Journal on Embedded Systems*, vol. 2009, no. 5, Article ID 897023, pp. 1–5, 2009.

[23] Z. Hajduk, B. Trybus, and J. Sadolewski, "Architecture of FPGA Embedded Multiprocessor Programmable Controller," *IEEE Transactions on Industrial Electronics*, vol. 62, no. 5, pp. 2952–2961, 2015.

[24] J. Álvarez, Ó. López, F. D. Freijedo, and J. Doval-Gandoy, "Digital parameterizable VHDL module for multilevel multiphase space vector PWM," *IEEE Transactions on Industrial Electronics*, vol. 58, no. 9, pp. 3946–3957, 2011.

[25] A. Sathyan, N. Milivojevic, Y.-J. Lee, M. Krishnamurthy, and A. Emadi, "An FPGA-based novel digital PWM control scheme for BLDC motor drives," *IEEE Transactions on Industrial Electronics*, vol. 56, no. 8, pp. 3040–3049, 2009.

[26] C. Buccella, C. Cecati, and H. Latafat, "Digital control of power converters—a survey," *IEEE Transactions on Industrial Informatics*, vol. 8, no. 3, pp. 437–447, 2012.

[27] M. Shahbazi, P. Poure, S. Saadate, and M. R. Zolghadri, "FPGA-based reconfigurable control for fault-tolerant back-to-back converter without redundancy," *IEEE Transactions on Industrial Electronics*, vol. 60, no. 8, pp. 3360–3371, 2013.

[28] X. Lin-Shi, F. Morel, A. M. Llor, B. Allard, and J.-M. Rétif, "Implementation of hybrid control for motor drives," *IEEE Transactions on Industrial Electronics*, vol. 54, no. 4, pp. 1946–1952, 2007.

[29] R. Dubey, P. Agarwal, and M. K. Vasantha, "Programmable logic devices for motion control - a review," *IEEE Transactions on Industrial Electronics*, vol. 54, no. 1, pp. 559–566, 2007.

[30] L. Zhang, P. Slaets, and H. Bruyninckx, "An open embedded hardware and software architecture applied to industrial robot control," in *Proceedings of the 2012 9th IEEE International Conference on Mechatronics and Automation, ICMA 2012*, pp. 1822–1828, chn, August 2012.

[31] T. Sutikno, N. R. N. Idris, A. Jidin, and M. N. Cirstea, "An improved FPGA implementation of direct torque control for induction machines," *IEEE Transactions on Industrial Informatics*, vol. 9, no. 3, pp. 1280–1290, 2013.

[32] M. Bacic, "On hardware-in-the-loop simulation," in *Proceedings of the 44th IEEE Conference on Decision and Control, and the European Control Conference, CDC-ECC '05*, pp. 3194–3198, esp, December 2005.

[33] A. Sanchez, A. De Castro, and J. Garrido, "A comparison of simulation and hardware-in-the-loop alternatives for digital control of power converters," *IEEE Transactions on Industrial Informatics*, vol. 8, no. 3, pp. 491–500, 2012.

[34] R. Dubey, *Embedded System Design Using Field Programmable Gate Arrays*, Springer, 1st edition, 2009.

[35] R. Woods, J. McAllister, G. Lightbody, and Y. Yi, *FPGA-based Implementation of Signal Processing Systems*, Wiley, 1st edition, 2008.

[36] I. Kuon and R. Rose, *Quantifying and Exploring the Gap Between FPGAs and ASICs*, Springer, 2010.

[37] D. Groppe, *Robots take on composite layup, machine design*, 2003, http://www.machinedesign.com.

[38] J. Sloan, *Atl and afp: Signs of evolution in machine process control. high-performance composites, composites world*, 2008, http://www.compositesworld.com.

[39] P. Maitani, *Rapid layup: New 3-d preform technology, composites world*, 2012, http://www.compositesworld.com.

[40] G. Dell'Anno, I. Partridge, D. Cartié et al., "Automated manufacture of 3D reinforced aerospace composite structures," *International Journal of Structural Integrity*, vol. 3, no. 1, pp. 22–40, 2012.

[41] Siemens, "Simatic winac rtx the simatic s7 as software controller," http://w3.siemens.com/mcms/programmable-logic-controller/en/software-controller/software-plc-simatic-winac/simatic-winac-rtx/pages/default.aspx, 2016.

[42] Xilinx, "Ds190 - zynq-7000 all programmable soc overview," https://www.xilinx.com/support/documentation/data_sheets/ds190-Zynq-7000-Overview.pdf.

[43] R. Barry, *Using the FreeRTOS Real Time Kernel*, FreeRTOS Tutorial Books, 2010.

[44] M. Santarini, "Xilinx architects arm-based processor-first, processor-centric device," *Xilinx Xcell Journal*, vol. 71, pp. 6–11, 2010.

[45] Xilinx, *Zynq-7000 all programmable soc technical reference manual*, 2016, https://www.xilinx.com/support/documentation/user_guides/ug585-Zynq-7000-TRM.pdf.

[46] Crocket and Steward, *The Zynq Book*, The University of Strathclyde, 1st edition, 2015.

[47] Siemens, "Simidrive posmo a -distributed positioning motor on profibus dp - user manual," https://cache.industry.siemens.com/dl/files/007/78797007/att_46305/v1/SIMODRIVE_POSMO_A_BHB_A0813_us.pdf, 2016.

13

FPGA-Based Channel Coding Architectures for 5G Wireless using High-Level Synthesis

Swapnil Mhaske,[1] Hojin Kee,[2] Tai Ly,[2] Ahsan Aziz,[2] and Predrag Spasojevic[1]

[1]*Wireless Information Networking Laboratory, Rutgers University, New Brunswick, NJ 08902, USA*
[2]*National Instruments Corporation, Austin, TX 78759, USA*

Correspondence should be addressed to Swapnil Mhaske; swapnil.mhaske@rutgers.edu

Academic Editor: João Cardoso

We propose strategies to achieve a high-throughput FPGA architecture for quasi-cyclic low-density parity-check codes based on circulant-1 identity matrix construction. By splitting the node processing operation in the min-sum approximation algorithm, we achieve pipelining in the layered decoding schedule without utilizing additional hardware resources. High-level synthesis compilation is used to design and develop the architecture on the FPGA hardware platform. To validate this architecture, an *IEEE 802.11n* compliant 608 Mb/s decoder is implemented on the *Xilinx Kintex-7* FPGA using the *LabVIEW FPGA Compiler* in the *LabVIEW Communication System Design Suite*. Architecture scalability was leveraged to accomplish a 2.48 Gb/s decoder on a single *Xilinx Kintex-7* FPGA. Further, we present rapidly prototyped experimentation of an *IEEE 802.16* compliant hybrid automatic repeat request system based on the efficient decoder architecture developed. In spite of the *mixed* nature of data processing—digital signal processing and finite-state machines—*LabVIEW FPGA Compiler* significantly reduced time to explore the system parameter space and to optimize in terms of error performance and resource utilization. A 4x improvement in the system throughput, relative to a CPU-based implementation, was achieved to measure the error-rate performance of the system over large, realistic data sets using accelerated, in-hardware simulation.

1. Introduction

The year 2020 is slated to witness the first commercial deployment of the 5th generation of wireless technology. 5G is expected to deliver a uniform Quality of Service (QoS) of 100 Mb/s and peak data rates of up to 20 Gb/s, with over-the-air latency of less than 1 ms [1]. All of this is with the energy consumption of contemporary cellular systems. Channel coding is crucial to achieve good performance in a communication system. Near-capacity performing codes such as Turbo codes [2] and Low-Density Parity-Check (LDPC) codes [3] typically require high-complexity encoding and decoding methods. Today, the standardization efforts towards realizing 5G cellular systems have already begun [4]. The suitability of a particular channel coding scheme is being discussed; and for a system realization of the size of 5G, the evolution of requirements pertaining to channel coding is naturally expected. In our effort to study and design channel codes based on areas ranging from theoretical performance

evaluation up to implementation complexity analysis, we have identified two main requirements in the development process. The first one is *flexibility for future modifications*. To facilitate this, we choose the reconfigurable FPGA platform. Moreover, for this evolving architecture, we aim to observe not only the theoretical complexity versus performance trade-off, but also the implementation complexity versus performance trade-off. This brings us to the second major requirement, which is *real-world rapid prototyping* of our methods. Figure 1 summarizes our research methodology. Even though theoretical simulations validate a novel idea, they fail to comprehensively assess its real-world impact. In an effort towards designing and developing a hardware architecture for channel coding, it is crucial to monitor the performance of the system in real-time, on actual state-of-the-art hardware. This helps us keep track of parameters such as throughput, latency, and resource utilization of the system, each time a modification is done. We would also like to emphasize that *rapid prototyping* can be used not only

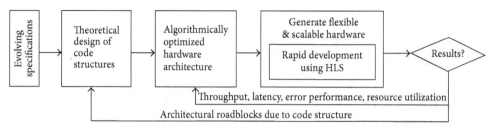

FIGURE 1: Illustration of our research methodology for the design and development of the channel coding architecture.

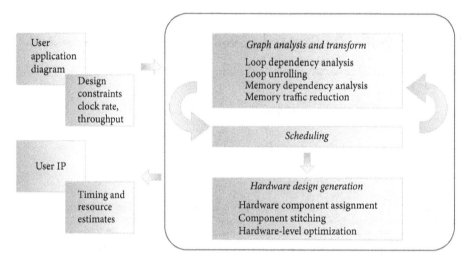

FIGURE 2: Illustration of the HLS compile flow.

for validating the design on real-world hardware platforms (Sections 5.1 and 5.2), but also for speedup of theoretical simulations (Section 5.3).

To accomplish this, in addition to the use of FPGA-based implementation, we use a High-Level Synthesis (HLS) compiler built in *LabVIEW*, namely, the *LabVIEW FPGA Compiler* [5–9] the details of which (relevant to this work) are given in Section 3. One of the main contributions of this work is the state-of-the-art HLS technology that offers an automated and systematic compilation flow, which generates an optimized hardware implementation from a user's algorithm and design requirements. This methodology empowers domain experts with minimum hardware knowledge to leverage FPGA technology in exploring, prototyping, and verifying their complex domain-specific applications. As shown in Figure 2, our compilation flow takes an application diagram as well as high-level design requirements, such as clock rate and throughput, and produces an optimized implementation with resource and timing estimates. By simply modifying application parameters and design requirements, designers can quickly get new hardware implementations with updated estimates. High-level design (user) requests and estimates enable designers to easily evaluate the current model and requirements and plan further algorithmic exploration. This rapid design process paves the way for domain experts to successfully accomplish the optimized design solution with significant time and cost savings.

QC-LDPC codes or their variants (such as accumulator-based codes [10]) that can be decoded (suboptimally) using Belief Propagation (BP) are highly likely candidates for 5G systems [4]. Insightful work on high-throughput (order of Gb/s) BP-based QC-LDPC decoders is available; however, most of such works focus on an application-specific integrated circuit (ASIC) design [11, 12] which usually requires intricate customizations at the register-transfer level (RTL) and expert knowledge of very-large-scale integration (VLSI) design. A sizeable subset of the above-mentioned work caters to fully-parallel [13] or code-specific [14] architectures. From the point of view of an evolving research solution, this is not an attractive option for rapid prototyping. In the relatively less explored area of FPGA-based implementation, impressive results have recently been presented in works such as [15–17]. However, these are based on fully-parallel architectures which lack flexibility (code-specific) and are limited to small block sizes (primarily due to the inhibiting routing congestion) as discussed in the informative overview in [18]. Since our case study is based on fully automated generation of the hardware description language (HDL), we compare our results with some recent HLS-based state-of-the-art implementations [19–22] in Section 6. The main contributions of this work are as follows. In this work, we present a high-throughput FPGA-based *IEEE 802.11n* standard compliant QC-LDPC channel decoder. With the architectural technique of splitting of the node processing, we achieve the said degree of pipelining without utilizing additional hardware resources. To demonstrate the scalability of the architecture, we present its application to a massively-parallel 2.48 Gb/s USRP-based decoder implementation (also demonstrated on the exhibit floor in the *2014 IEEE GLOBE-COM* conference [23]). The final contribution is a method to rapidly prototype the experimentation of a HARQ system based on the efficient decoder architecture developed, using the *IEEE 802.16* standard compliant QC-LDPC code. The system not only comprises digital signal processing (DSP), but also finite-state machines (FSM). In spite of such *mixed* nature of data processing, *LabVIEW FPGA Compiler* was able to significantly reduce the time to explore the overall system parameter space and to optimize resource utilization for the error-rate performance achieved.

The remainder of this article is organized as follows. Section 2 provides a succinct introduction to the QC-LDPC code structure and the corresponding decoding algorithm considered for the architecture. The strategies for achieving high-throughput for the stand-alone QC-LDPC decoder are explained in Section 4. The case studies for the high-throughput decoder, its application demonstrating scalability, and the rapidly prototyped HARQ experiment are detailed in Section 5. A survey of recent state-of-the-art solutions is provided in Section 6. Section 7 concludes the article.

2. Quasi-Cyclic LDPC Codes

LDPC codes are a class of linear block codes that have been shown to achieve near-capacity performance on a broad range of channels. Invented by Gallager [3] in 1962, they are characterized by a Low-Density (sparse) Parity-Check Matrix (PCM) representation. Mathematically, an LDPC code is a null-space of its $m \times n$ PCM **H**, where m denotes the number of parity-check equations or parity-bits and n denotes the number of variable nodes or code bits [24]. In other words, for a rank m PCM **H**, m is the number of redundant bits added to the k information bits, which together form the codeword of length $n = k + m$. An example of a Tanner graph representation (due to Tanner [25] who introduced a graphical representation) is shown in Figure 3. Here, the PCM **H** is the incidence matrix of a bipartite Tanner graph comprising two sets: the check node (CN) set of m parity-check equations and the variable node (VN) set of n variable or bit nodes; the ith CN is connected to the jth VN if $\mathbf{H}(i, j) = 1$. The column weight $d_c \ll m$ and the row weight $d_r \ll n$, where row weight and column weight are defined as the number of 1s along a row and a column, respectively. An LDPC code is called a regular code if each CN has a degree d_r and each VN has a degree d_c and is called an irregular LDPC code otherwise.

2.1. Parity-Check Matrix. The first LDPC codes by Gallager [3] are random, which complicate the decoder implementation, mainly because a random interconnect pattern between the VNs and CNs directly translates to a complex wire routing circuit on hardware. QC-LDPC codes [26] belong to the class

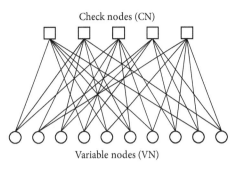

FIGURE 3: A Tanner graph where the variable nodes (VN), representing the code bits, are shown as circles and the check nodes (CN), representing the parity-check equations, are shown as squares. Each edge in the graph corresponds to a nonzero entry (1 for binary LDPC codes) in the PCM **H**.

of structured codes that do not significantly compromise performance relative to randomly constructed LDPC codes.

The construction of QC-LDPC codes relies on an $m_b \times n_b$ matrix $\mathbf{H}_b$, sometimes called the *base matrix* which comprises cyclically right-shifted identity and zero submatrices both of size $z \times z$, where, $z \in \mathbb{Z}^+$, $0 \le i_b \le (m_b - 1)$ and $0 \le j_b \le (n_b - 1)$, the shift value,

$$s = \mathbf{H}_b\left(i_b, j_b\right) \in \mathscr{S} = \{-1\} \cup \{0, \dots, z - 1\}. \tag{1}$$

The PCM matrix **H** is obtained by *expanding* $\mathbf{H}_b$ using the mapping,

$$s \longrightarrow \begin{cases} \mathbf{I}_s, & s \in \mathscr{S} \setminus \{-1\}, \\ \mathbf{0}, & s \in \{-1\}, \end{cases} \tag{2}$$

where $\mathbf{I}_s$ is an identity matrix of size z which is cyclically right-shifted by $s = \mathbf{H}_b(i_b, j_b)$ and $\mathbf{0}$ is the all-zero matrix of size $z \times z$. As **H** comprises the submatrices $\mathbf{I}_s$ and $\mathbf{0}$, it has $m = m_b \cdot z$ rows and $n = n_b \cdot z$ columns. The *base matrix* for the *IEEE 802.11n (2012)* standard [27] with $z = 81$ is shown in Table 1.

2.2. Scaled Min-Sum Approximation Decoding. LDPC codes can be suboptimally decoded using the BP method [3, 28] on the sparse bipartite Tanner graph where the CNs and VNs communicate with each other, successively passing revised estimates of the log-likelihood ratio (LLR) associated in every decoding iteration. In this work, we have employed the efficient decoding algorithm presented in [29], with a pipelining schedule based on the row-layered decoding technique [30], detailed in Section 4.3.

Definition 1. For $1 \le i \le m$ and $1 \le j \le n$, let v_j denote the jth bit in the length n codeword and $y_j = v_j + n_j$ denote the corresponding received value from the channel corrupted by the noise sample n_j. Let the variable-to-check (VTC) message from VN j to CN i be q_{ij} and let the check-to-variable (CTV) message from CN i to VN j be r_{ij}. Let the a posteriori probability ratio for variable node j be denoted as p_j.

TABLE 1: Base matrix $\mathbf{H}_b$ for $z = 81$ specified in the IEEE 802.11n (2012) standard used in the case study (see Section 5.1). L_1–L_{12} are the layers and B_1–B_{24} are the block columns (see Section 4.3). Valid blocks (see Section 4.3) are bold.

Layers ↓	Blocks →																							
	B_1	B_2	B_3	B_4	B_5	B_6	B_7	B_8	B_9	B_{10}	B_{11}	B_{12}	B_{13}	B_{14}	B_{15}	B_{16}	B_{17}	B_{18}	B_{19}	B_{20}	B_{21}	B_{22}	B_{23}	B_{24}
L_1	**57**	−	−	−	**50**	−	**11**	−	**50**	−	**79**	−	**1**	**0**	−	−	−	−	−	−	−	−	−	−
L_2	**3**	−	**28**	−	**0**	−	−	−	**55**	**7**	−	−	−	**0**	**0**	**0**	−	−	−	−	−	−	−	−
L_3	**30**	−	−	−	**24**	**37**	−	−	**56**	**14**	−	−	−	−	**0**	**0**	**0**	−	−	−	−	−	−	−
L_4	**62**	**53**	−	−	**53**	−	−	**3**	**35**	−	−	−	−	−	−	**0**	**0**	**0**	−	−	−	−	−	−
L_5	**40**	−	−	**20**	**66**	−	−	**22**	**28**	−	−	−	−	−	−	−	**0**	**0**	**0**	−	−	−	−	−
L_6	**0**	−	−	−	**8**	−	**42**	−	**50**	−	−	**8**	−	−	−	−	−	**0**	**0**	**0**	−	−	−	−
L_7	**69**	**79**	**79**	−	−	−	**56**	−	**52**	−	−	−	**0**	−	−	−	−	−	**0**	**0**	**0**	−	−	−
L_8	**65**	−	−	−	**38**	**57**	−	−	**72**	−	**27**	−	−	−	−	−	−	−	−	**0**	**0**	**0**	−	−
L_9	**64**	−	−	−	**14**	**52**	−	−	**30**	−	−	**32**	−	−	−	−	−	−	−	−	**0**	**0**	**0**	−
L_{10}	−	**45**	−	**70**	**0**	−	−	−	**77**	**9**	−	−	−	−	−	−	−	−	−	−	−	**0**	**0**	**0**
L_{11}	**2**	**56**	−	**57**	**35**	−	−	−	−	−	**12**	−	−	−	−	−	−	−	−	−	−	−	**0**	**0**
L_{12}	**24**	−	**61**	−	**60**	−	−	**27**	**51**	−	−	**16**	**1**	−	−	−	−	−	−	−	−	−	−	**0**

The steps of the scaled-MSA are given below.

(1) Initialization. The a posteriori probability p_j for the VN j and the CTV messages are initialized as

$$p_j^{(0)} = \ln \left\{ \frac{P\left(v_j = 0 \mid y_j\right)}{P\left(v_j = 1 \mid y_j\right)} \right\}, \quad 1 \le j \le n, \tag{3}$$

$$r_{ij}^{(0)} = 0, \quad 1 \le i \le m, \ 1 \le j \le n.$$

(2) Iterative Process. During the tth decoding iteration,

$$q_{ij}^{(t)} = p_j^{(t-1)} - r_{ij}^{(t-1)}, \tag{4}$$

$$r_{ij}^{(t)} = a \cdot \prod_{k \in \mathcal{N}(i) \backslash \{j\}} \text{sign}\left(q_{ik}^{(t)}\right) \cdot \min_{k \in \mathcal{N}(i) \backslash \{j\}} \left\{ \left| q_{ik}^{(t)} \right| \right\}, \tag{5}$$

$$p_j^{(t)} = q_{ij}^{(t)} + r_{ij}^{(t)}, \tag{6}$$

where $1 \le i \le m$ and $k \in \mathcal{N}(i) \backslash \{j\}$ represents the set of the VN neighbors of CN i excluding VN j and a is the scaling factor used, the rationale behind which is explained below.

(3) Decision Rule. $1 \le i \le m$,

$$\widehat{v}_j = \begin{cases} 0, & p_j < 0, \\ 1, & p_j \ge 0. \end{cases} \tag{7}$$

(4) Stopping Criteria. If $\widehat{\mathbf{v}}\mathbf{H}^T = 0$ or $t = t_{\max}$ (maximum number of decoding iterations), declare $\widehat{\mathbf{v}}$ as the decoded codeword.

It is well known that since the MSA is an approximation of the sum-product algorithm (SPA) [3], the performance of the MSA is relatively worse than the SPA [24]. However, work such as [31] has shown that scaling the CTV messages r_{ij} can improve the performance of the MSA. Hence, we scale the CTV messages by a factor a (set to 0.75) to compensate for the performance loss due to the MSA approximation.

The standard BP algorithm is based on the so-called *flooding* or *two-phase* schedule where each decoding iteration comprises two phases. In the first phase, VTC messages for all the VNs are computed and, in the second phase, the CTV messages for all the CNs are computed, strictly in that order. Thus, message updates from one side of the graph propagate to the other side only in the next decoding iteration. In the algorithm given in [29] however, message updates can propagate across the graph in the same decoding iteration. This provides advantages such that a single processing unit is required for both CN and VN message updates, memory storage is reduced on account of the on-the-fly computation of the VTC messages q_{ij}, and the algorithm converges faster than the standard BP flooding schedule requiring fewer decoding iterations.

3. HLS with *LabVIEW FPGA Compiler*

The HLS compiler in *LabVIEW CSDS* [32], namely, *LabVIEW FPGA Compiler*, aims at identifying opportunities to efficiently parallelize in the application's algorithmic description, subject to requirements set by the user. Here, we briefly describe the main techniques [5] embedded into the *LabVIEW FPGA Compiler* toolset that enable efficient high-throughput translation of the algorithm into a VHDL description.

3.1. Memory Dependency Analysis. Loop unrolling on FPGA platforms is a well-known compiler optimization used to exploit parallelism [33]. However, in the presence of execution dependencies between loop iterations, loop unrolling may not contribute to throughput improvement. An example is shown in Figure 4(a) where an execution dependency restricts parallelization of unrolled loops. Although loops have been unrolled by a factor of two as shown in Figure 4(b), the first loop copy waits until the second loop copy execution is finished. Due to the serialized loop execution, the overall performance is the same as the original loop, however at the cost of more FPGA resources used by the new loop copies.

However, if unrolling is performed only when it improves throughput, a trade-off between throughput and resource consumption can be achieved in the implementation. An illustrative example is provided in Figure 5, where a feedback node defines a data dependency across consecutive diagram executions. A Read-After-Write (RAW) dependency between the current memory read operation R_i and a previous memory write operation W_{i-1} is shown in Figure 5(a). This dependency prevents the compiler from pipelining the diagram executions and becomes a bottleneck, restricting the overall throughput as shown in Figure 5(b). However, if the compiler can determine that R_i never reads a memory location that is updated by W_{i-1}, then the ith diagram execution can overlap with the $(i-1)$th execution and achieve better throughput as shown in Figure 5(c). Such an analysis is also applicable to relax WAR and WAW dependencies.

The memory access pattern analysis in *LabVIEW FPGA Compiler* mainly comprises two steps. In the first step, a periodic access pattern is determined by monitoring all the stateful nodes that contribute to each memory access pattern. In the second step, access patterns of memory accessor pairs are compared, and the pairwise worst iteration distance k is computed. This dependent iteration distance is used to create a relaxed interiteration dependency, thus allowing pipelined executions without any memory corruption.

3.2. Memory Access Traffic Relaxation. Loop unrolling may not be effective if the memory access speed cannot keep up with the data throughput request set by the user. This is particularly true for processing intensive applications like the ones studied and implemented in this work. *LabVIEW FPGA Compiler* uses the following techniques to reduce memory traffic such that the performance targets set by the user are met.

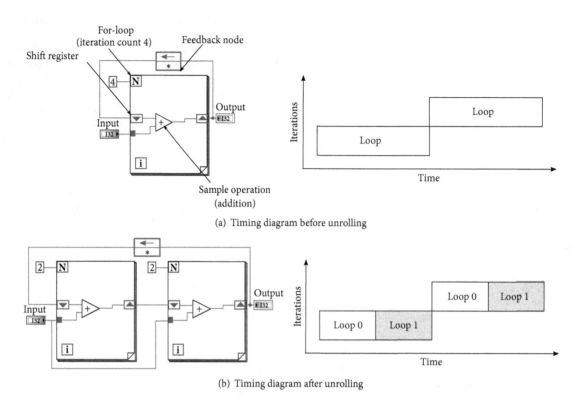

(a) Timing diagram before unrolling

(b) Timing diagram after unrolling

FIGURE 4: Ineffective loop unrolling. Shown on the left are representative schematics of the *LabVIEW* graphical programming virtual instruments (VI), and on the right are the corresponding timing diagrams.

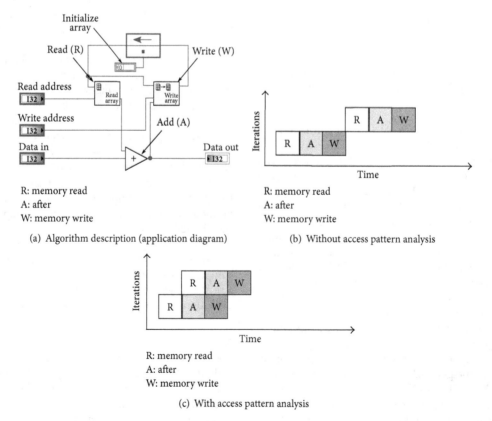

R: memory read
A: after
W: memory write

(a) Algorithm description (application diagram)

R: memory read
A: after
W: memory write

(b) Without access pattern analysis

R: memory read
A: after
W: memory write

(c) With access pattern analysis

FIGURE 5: Throughput improvement using access pattern analysis. Shown on (a) is the representative schematic of the *LabVIEW* graphical programming virtual instrument (VI), and on (b and c) are the corresponding timing diagrams.

3.2.1. Memory Partitioning. Memory blocks on modern FPGAs typically have only two ports, one of which is generally read-only. Implementing memories with more ports can become very resource intensive and can drastically reduce the clock rate of the design. The limited amount of memory ports often causes accesses to get serialized. These serialized memory access requests often make computational cores idle, thus resulting in a reduction of the system throughput [34]. Memory partitioning is the division of the original memory block into multiple smaller memory blocks. This partitioning effectively increases FPGA physical memory access ports to allow simultaneous memory read and write operations, thus minimizing the idle time of the computational cores. Memory accessors are grouped into sets, such that accessors within one set are guaranteed to have a nonoverlapping address space with members of another set, allowing the compiler to safely partition the single memory into a memory for each set of accessors. The size of each partition is the size of the address space for that set. The original memory is divided into small partitions based on min-max address ranges of memory accessor groups, and each group is mapped to a separate partition having the matched address range.

LabVIEW FPGA Compiler statically analyzes memory access patterns in a given application diagram and automatically relaxes the memory access bottleneck without impacting the execution of the high-level algorithmic description input to it. Memory traffic is thereby reduced linearly by the partitioning number at no additional memory space cost.

3.2.2. Memory Accessor Jamming. In many applications, memory access is sequential and predictive. When multiple accesses to a memory can be computed in parallel, the values can be accessed together in one clump rather than as many separate smaller accesses. We refer to this as *memory accessor jamming*. This method creates a memory accessor group such that accessor patterns are of the form,

$$i \cdot o_p, i \cdot o_p + 1, \ldots, i \cdot o_p + o_c, \tag{8}$$

where o_p is a periodic offset, i is a loop indexer, and o_c is a constant offset that is smaller than o_p. The multiple accessors in a group are jammed into a single accessor with a wide word length. This word length is the product of the original word length and the jamming factor value. Consequently, memory access traffic is decreased by the value of the jamming factor. Jamming modifies the memory layout by increasing the word length and reducing the address range by the jamming factor, but it does not need any additional memory space. Jamming is well suited for use with loop unrolling because any in-order memory access pattern inside the loop becomes a jammable access pattern after unrolling.

All of the above techniques have been successfully employed by *LabVIEW FPGA Compiler* without any manual intervention from the user. For instance, loop unrolling is primarily employed to process algorithmic metrics described in Section 2.2 for the technique of *z*-fold parallelization of node metric processing as described in Section 4.2. Here, memory access analysis captures relaxed memory dependencies and achieves the reported throughput without any application-specific compiler directives. Moreover, due to the graph-based iterative decoding nature of the application considered for this work, read-write patterns that lend themselves to memory accessor jamming have been identified by the tool and successfully exploited.

The authors would like to emphasize that the algorithmic compiler (*LabVIEW FPGA Compiler*) translates the application's high-level description to VHDL. The subsequent compilation of VHDL is performed by the *Xilinx Vivado* compiler, the details of which are beyond the scope of this work.

4. Techniques for High-Throughput

To understand the high-throughput requirements for LDPC decoding, let us first define the decoding throughput T of an iterative LDPC decoder.

Definition 2. Let F_c be the clock frequency, n be the code length, N_i be the number of decoding iterations, and N_c be the number of clock cycles per decoding iteration; then the throughput of the decoder is given by $T = (F_c \cdot n)/(N_i \cdot N_c)$ b/s.

Even though n and N_i are functions of the code and the decoding algorithm used, F_c and N_c are determined by the hardware architecture. Architectural optimization such as the ability to operate the decoder at higher clock rates with minimal latency between decoding iterations can help achieve higher throughput. We have employed the following techniques to increase the throughput given by Definition 2.

4.1. Linear Complexity Node Processing. As noted in Section 2.2, separate processing units for CNs and VNs are not required unlike that for the flooding schedule. The hardware elements that process (4)–(6) are collectively referred to as the Node Processing Unit (NPU).

Careful observation reveals that, among (4)–(6), processing the CTV messages r_{ij}, $1 \le i \le m$ and $1 \le j \le n$, is the most computationally intensive due to the calculation of the sign and the minimum value of the set of magnitudes of VTC messages q_{ik} received from VN j to CN i, where $k \in \mathcal{N}(i)\backslash\{j\}$. As the degree of CN i is d_{c_i}, the complexity of processing the minimum value (in terms of the comparisons required) is $\mathcal{O}(d_{c_i}^2)$. In a straightforward algorithmic description, this translates to two nested for-loops, an outer loop that executes d_{c_i} times and an inner loop that executes $(d_{c_i} - 1)$ times.

To achieve linear complexity $\mathcal{O}(d_{c_i})$ for the CN message update process in our implementation, the minimum value is computed in two phases or passes. In the first (global) pass, the two smallest values for the CN are computed. These are the first and the second minimum (the smallest value in the set excluding the minimum value of the set). Subsequently, for every incident edge on the said CN, the smallest VN message that does not correspond to the considered edge is selected. In other words, if the said incident edge (for which the CN to VN message is to be sent) has the smallest value (first min), then the second smallest value (second min) obtained in the global pass is sent over this edge, else, the second smallest value (second min) is sent. This pass is called the second (local) pass. A similar approach is found in [11, 35].

TABLE 2: Arbitrary submatrix $\mathbf{I}_s$ in $\mathbf{H}$, $0 \leq J \leq n_b - 1$, illustrating the opportunity to parallelize z NPUs.

	VN_{zJ}	$\cdots$	$VN_{zJ+\ell-1}$	VN_{zJ+l}	$VN_{zJ+\ell+1}$	$\cdots$	$VN_{z(J+1)-1}$
NPU_0	0	$\cdots$	0	1	0	$\cdots$	0
NPU_1	0	$\cdots$	0	0	1	$\cdots$	0
$\vdots$	$\vdots$						$\vdots$
NPU_{z-2}	0	$\cdots$	0	0	0	$\cdots$	0
NPU_{z-1}	0	$\cdots$	1	0	0	$\cdots$	0

In a straightforward algorithmic description, this translates to two separate for-loops in tandem: first loop executes $(d_{c_i} - 1)$ times computing the first and the second minimum for the set of VTC message values q_{ik} and the second loop executes $(d_{c_i} - 1)$ times assigning the overall minimum to each branch connecting CN i and VN k, where $1 \leq i \leq m$, $1 \leq j \leq n$, and $k \in \mathcal{N}(i) \setminus \{j\}$. Consequently, this reduces the complexity from $\mathcal{O}(d_{c_i}^2)$ to $\mathcal{O}(d_{c_i})$. Based on the functionality of the two passes, the NPU is divided into the Global NPU (GNPU) and the Local NPU (LNPU). The algorithm to accomplish this is as follows.

(1) Global Pass. The Global NPU (GNPU) processes this pass.

(i) Initialization: let ℓ denote the discrete time-steps such that $\ell \in \{0, 1, 2, \ldots, |\mathcal{N}(i) \setminus \{j\}|\}$ and let $f^{(\ell)}$ and $s^{(\ell)}$ denote the value of the first and the second minimum at time ℓ, respectively. The initial value at time $\ell = 0$ is

$$f^{(0)} = s^{(0)} = \infty. \quad (9)$$

(ii) Comparison: for $1 \leq i \leq m$, $1 \leq j \leq n$, and $k(\ell) \in \mathcal{N}(i) \setminus \{j\}$, note that the ordering of the set that ℓ belongs to is induced on the set that $k(\ell)$ belongs to.

$$f^{(\ell)} = \begin{cases} |q_{ik(\ell)}|, & |q_{ik(\ell)}| \leq f^{(\ell-1)}, \\ f^{(\ell-1)}, & \text{otherwise,} \end{cases} \quad (10)$$

$$s^{(\ell)} = \begin{cases} |q_{ik(\ell)}|, & f^{(\ell-1)} < |q_{ik(\ell)}| < s^{(\ell-1)}, \\ f^{(\ell-1)}, & |q_{ik(\ell)}| \leq f^{(\ell-1)}, \\ s^{(\ell-1)}, & \text{otherwise.} \end{cases} \quad (11)$$

(2) Local Pass. The Local NPU (LNPU) at time $\ell \in \{1, 2, \ldots, |\mathcal{N}(i) \setminus \{j\}|\}$ determines the actual minimum value for each VN $k(\ell)$, as per the equivalence relation:

$$\min_{k(\ell) \in \mathcal{N}(i) \setminus \{j\}} \{|q_{ik(\ell)}|\} \equiv \begin{cases} f^{(\ell_{\max})}, & |q_{ik(\ell)}| \neq f^{(\ell_{\max})}, \\ s^{(\ell_{\max})}, & \text{otherwise,} \end{cases} \quad (12)$$

where $\ell_{\max} = |\mathcal{N}(i) \setminus \{j\}|$. Thus, the computation of the minimum value is accomplished in linear complexity $\mathcal{O}(d_{c_i})$. It was rightly noted by one of the reviewers that initializing the variable $f^{(0)} = \infty$ is unnecessary, resulting in a redundant iteration in (10). However, we would like to note that the implementation was done based on (10) as given in the algorithm.

4.2. z-Fold Parallelization of NPUs. The CN message computation given by (5) is repeated m times in a decoding iteration, that is, once for each CN. A straightforward serial implementation of this kind is slow and undesirable. Instead, we apply a strategy based on the following understanding.

Fact 1. An arbitrary submatrix $\mathbf{I}_s$ in the PCM $\mathbf{H}$ corresponds to z CNs connected to z VNs on the bipartite graph, with strictly 1 edge between each CN and VN.

This implies that no CN in this set of z CNs given by $\mathbf{I}_s$ shares a VN with another CN in the same set. Table 2 illustrates such an arbitrary submatrix in $\mathbf{H}$. This presents us with an opportunity to operate z NPUs in parallel (hereafter referred to as an *NPU array*), resulting in a z-fold increase in throughput.

4.3. Layered Decoding. In the flooding schedule discussed in Section 2.2, *all* nodes on one side of the bipartite graph can be processed in parallel. Although such a *fully-parallel* implementation may seem as an attractive option for achieving high-throughput performance, it has its own drawbacks. Firstly, it becomes quickly intractable in hardware due to the complex interconnect pattern between the nodes of the bipartite graph. Secondly, such an implementation usually restricts itself to a specific code structure. Although the efficient scaled-MSA algorithm discussed in Section 2.2 is inherently serial in nature (as the messages are propagated across the bipartite graph more than once every decoding iteration), one can process multiple nodes at the same time if the following condition is satisfied.

Fact 2. From the perspective of CN processing, two or more CNs can be processed at the same time (i.e., they are independent of each other) if they do not have one or more VNs (code bits) in common.

The row-layering technique used in this work essentially relies on the condition in Fact 2 being satisfied. In terms of the PCM $\mathbf{H}$, an arbitrary subset of rows can be processed at the same time, provided that no two or more rows have a 1 in the same column of $\mathbf{H}$. This subset of rows is termed as a *row-layer* (hereafter referred to as a *layer*). In other words, given a set $\mathcal{L} = \{L_1, L_2, \ldots, L_I\}$ of I layers in $\mathbf{H}$, $\forall u \in \{1, 2, \ldots, I\}$ and $\forall i, i' \in L_u$, then, $\mathcal{N}(i) \cap \mathcal{N}(i') = \phi$.

Observing that $\sum_{u=1}^{I} |L_u| = m$, in general, L_u can be any subset of rows as long as the rows satisfy the condition specified by Fact 2, implying that $|L_u| \neq |L_{u'}|$, $\forall u, u' \in \{1, 2, \ldots, I\}$ is possible. Owing to the structure of QC-LDPC

TABLE 3: Illustration of message passing in row-layered decoding in a section of the PCM $\mathbf{H}_b$.

Layers ↓	...	B_2	B_3	B_4	...
			Blocks →		
L_1	...	↓	↓	↓	...
L_2	...	↓	28	↓	...
L_3	...	↓	↓	↓	...
L_4	...	53	↓	↓	...
L_5	...	↓	↓	20	...
L_6	...	↓	↓	↓	...
L_7	...	79	79	↓	...
L_8	...	↓	↓	↓	...
L_9	...	↓	↓	↓	...
L_{10}	...	45	↓	70	...
L_{11}	...	56	↓	57	...
L_{12}	...	↓	61	↓	...
		To L_4	To L_2	To L_5	

codes, the choice of $|L_u|$ (and hence I) becomes much obvious. Submatrices $\mathbf{I}_s$ in $\mathbf{H}_b$ (with row and column weight of 1) guarantee that, for the z CNs (rows corresponding to $\mathbf{I}_s$), condition in Fact 2 is always satisfied. Hence, in our work, we choose $|L_u| = |L_{u'}| = z$.

From the VN or column perspective, $|L_u| = z$, $\forall u = \{1, 2, \ldots, I\}$ implies that the columns of the PCM $\mathbf{H}$ are also divided into subsets of size z (called *block columns* from now on) given by the set $\mathscr{B} = \{B_1, B_2, \ldots, B_J\}$, $J = n/z = n_b$. The VNs belonging to a block column may participate in CN equations across several layers. We call the intersection of a layer and a block column as a *block*. Two or more layers $L_u, L_{u'}$ are said to be *dependent* with respect to the block column B_w if $\mathbf{H}_b(u, w) \neq -1$ and $\mathbf{H}_b(u', w) \neq -1$. This is observed in Table 3, where we can see that layers L_4, L_7, L_{10}, and L_{11} are dependent with respect to block column B_2. Assuming that the message update begins with layer L_1 and proceeds downward, the arrows represent the directional flow of message updates from one layer to another. For the block column B_2, for instance, layer L_7 cannot begin updating the VNs associated with block column B_2 before layer L_4 has finished updating messages for the same set of VNs and so on.

The idea of parallelizing z NPUs seen in Section 4.2 can be extended to layers, where z-sized arrays of NPUs can process message updates for multiple layers, provided they are independent with respect to the block column being processed. In Section 4.4, we discuss pipelining methods that allow us to overcome layer-to-layer dependency and maximize the throughput. Before we discuss the pipelined processing of layers implemented in our decoder, in this section, we present a novel compact (thus efficient) matrix representation leading to a significant improvement in throughput. We call $\mathbf{0}$ submatrices in $\mathbf{H}$ (corresponding to a -1 in $\mathbf{H}_b$) as *invalid* blocks, since there are no edges between the corresponding CNs and VNs. The other submatrices $\mathbf{I}_s$ are called *valid* blocks. In a conventional approach to scheduling, for example, in [12], message computation is done over all the valid and invalid blocks. To avoid processing invalid blocks, we propose an

alternate representation of $\mathbf{H}_b$ in the form of two matrices: $\boldsymbol{\beta}_I$, the block index matrix, and $\boldsymbol{\beta}_S$, the block shift matrix. $\boldsymbol{\beta}_I$ and $\boldsymbol{\beta}_S$ hold the index locations and the shift values (and hence the connections between the CNs and VNs) corresponding to *only* the valid blocks in $\mathbf{H}_b$, respectively. Construction of $\boldsymbol{\beta}_I$ is based on the following definition.

Definition 3. Construction of $\boldsymbol{\beta}_I$ is as follows.

$$\text{for } u = \{1, 2, \ldots, I\}$$
$$\quad \text{set } w = 0$$
$$\quad \text{for } j_b = \{1, 2, \ldots, n_b\}$$
$$\quad\quad \text{if } \mathbf{H}_b(u, j_b) \neq -1$$
$$\quad\quad\quad w = w+1; \boldsymbol{\beta}_I(u, w) = j_b; \boldsymbol{\beta}_S(u, w) = \mathbf{H}_b(u, j_b).$$

Let $\mathscr{V}_u$ denote the set of valid blocks for layer L_u, $\forall u = 1, 2, \ldots, I$.

$$\mathscr{V}_u = \{j_b : \mathbf{H}_b(u, j_b) \neq -1\}. \tag{13}$$

Let $J = \max_u |\mathscr{V}_u|$; then, $\forall w = \{1, 2, \ldots, J\}$, we define the block index matrix as

$$\boldsymbol{\beta}_I(u, w) = \begin{cases} j_b, & \mathbf{H}_b(u, j_b) \neq -1, \\ -1, & \text{otherwise.} \end{cases} \tag{14}$$

Similarly, we define $\boldsymbol{\beta}_S$ as

$$\boldsymbol{\beta}_S(u, w) = \begin{cases} \mathbf{H}_b(u, j_b), & \mathbf{H}_b(u, j_b) \neq -1, \\ -1, & \text{otherwise.} \end{cases} \tag{15}$$

The block index (shift) matrix $\boldsymbol{\beta}_I$ ($\boldsymbol{\beta}_S$) is shown in Table 4 (Table 5) for the case of the *IEEE 802.11n* rate-1/2 LDPC code. To observe the benefit of this alternate representation, let us define the following ratio.

Definition 4. Let λ denote the compaction ratio, which is the ratio of the number of columns of $\boldsymbol{\beta}_I$ (which is the same for $\boldsymbol{\beta}_S$) to the number of columns of $\mathbf{H}_b$. Hence, $\lambda = J/n_b$.

TABLE 4: Block index matrix $\boldsymbol{\beta}_{\mathrm{I}}$ showing the valid blocks (bold) to be processed.

Layers ↓	Blocks →							
	b_1	b_2	b_3	b_4	b_5	b_6	b_7	b_8
L_1	0	4	6	8	10	12	13	−1
L_2	0	2	4	8	9	13	14	−1
L_3	0	4	5	8	9	14	15	−1
L_4	0	1	4	7	8	15	16	−1
L_5	0	3	4	7	8	16	17	−1
L_6	0	4	6	8	11	17	18	−1
L_7	0	1	2	6	8	12	18	19
L_8	0	4	5	8	10	19	20	−1
L_9	0	4	5	8	11	20	21	−1
L_{10}	1	3	4	8	9	21	22	−1
L_{11}	0	1	3	4	10	22	23	−1
L_{12}	0	2	4	7	8	11	12	23

TABLE 5: Block shift matrix $\boldsymbol{\beta}_{\mathrm{S}}$ showing the right-shift values for the valid blocks to be processed.

Layers ↓	Blocks →							
	b_1	b_2	b_3	b_4	b_5	b_6	b_7	b_8
L_1	57	50	11	50	79	1	0	−1
L_2	3	28	0	55	7	0	0	−1
L_3	30	24	37	56	14	0	0	−1
L_4	62	53	53	3	35	0	0	−1
L_5	40	20	66	22	28	0	0	−1
L_6	0	8	42	50	8	0	0	−1
L_7	69	79	79	56	52	0	0	0
L_8	65	38	57	72	27	0	0	−1
L_9	64	14	52	30	32	0	0	−1
L_{10}	45	70	0	77	9	0	0	−1
L_{11}	2	56	57	35	12	0	0	−1
L_{12}	24	61	60	27	51	16	1	0

The compaction ratio λ is a measure of the compaction achieved by the alternate representation of H_b. Compared to the conventional approach to scheduling node processing based on $\mathbf{H}_b$ matrix, scheduling as per the $\boldsymbol{\beta}_I$ and $\boldsymbol{\beta}_S$ matrices improves throughput by $1/\lambda$ times. In our case study, $\lambda = 8/24 = 1/3$, thus providing a throughput gain of $1/\lambda = 3$.

Remark 5. In the QC-LDPC code in our case study, $|\mathscr{V}_u| = 7$ for all layers except layers L_7 and L_{12} where it is 8. With the aim of minimizing hardware complexity by maintaining a static memory-address generation pattern (does not change from layer-to-layer), our implementation assumes regularity in the code. The decoder processes 8 blocks for each layer of the $\boldsymbol{\beta}_I$ matrix resulting in some throughput penalty.

4.4. Area Efficient Pipelining Architecture. In Section 4.3, we saw how dependent layers for a block column cannot be processed in parallel. For instance, in the base matrix $\mathbf{H}_b$ in Table 1, VNs associated with the block column B_1 participate in CN equations associated with all the layers except layer L_{10}, suggesting that there is no scope of parallelization of layer processing at all. This situation is better observed in $\boldsymbol{\beta}_I$ shown in Table 4.

Fact 3. If a block column of $\boldsymbol{\beta}_I$ has a particular index value appearing in more than one layer, then the layers corresponding to that value are dependent.

Proof. It follows directly by applying Fact 2 to Definition 3. $\square$

In other words, $\forall u,\ u' \in \{1, 2, \ldots, I\}, \forall w \in \{1, 2, \ldots, J\}$, if $\boldsymbol{\beta}_{\mathrm{I}}(u, w) = \boldsymbol{\beta}_{\mathrm{I}}(u', w)$, then the layers L_u and $L_{u'}$ are dependent. It is obvious that, to process all layers in parallel (L_1 to L_{12} in Table 1), the condition

$$\boldsymbol{\beta}_{\mathrm{I}}(u, w) \neq \boldsymbol{\beta}_{\mathrm{I}}(u', w) \tag{16}$$

must hold $\forall u,\ u' \in \{1, 2, \ldots, I\}$. For the structure of $\boldsymbol{\beta}_I$ shown in Table 4 (by definition of the code), it is not possible to parallelize *all* the layers. However, a degree of parallelization can be achieved by making the layers independent with respect to a block column.

To accomplish this, we rearrange the $\boldsymbol{\beta}_I$ matrix elements from their original order with the following idea. If $\boldsymbol{\beta}_{\mathrm{I}}(u, w) = \boldsymbol{\beta}_{\mathrm{I}}(u', w)$, $u < u'$, then *stagger* the execution of $\boldsymbol{\beta}_{\mathrm{I}}(u', w)$ with respect to $\boldsymbol{\beta}_{\mathrm{I}}(u, w)$ by moving $\boldsymbol{\beta}_{\mathrm{I}}(u', w)$ to $\boldsymbol{\beta}'_{\mathrm{I}}(u', w')$,

TABLE 6: Rearranged block index matrix β'_I used for our work, showing the valid blocks (bold) to be processed.

Layers ↓	Blocks →							
	b_1	b_2	b_3	b_4	b_5	b_6	b_7	b_8
L_1	0	4	8	13	6	10	12	−1
L_2	9	0	4	8	13	14	2	−1
L_3	15	9	0	4	8	5	14	−1
L_4	7	15	16	0	4	8	1	−1
L_5	17	7	3	16	0	4	8	−1
L_6	6	17	18	11	−1	0	4	8
L_7	19	6	0	8	1	2	18	12
L_8	4	19	5	0	8	20	10	−1
L_9	21	4	11	5	0	8	20	−1
L_{10}	1	21	4	3	22	9	8	−1
L_{11}	0	1	23	4	3	22	10	−1
L_{12}	8	0	2	23	4	12	7	11

$w < w'$. Table 6 shows one such rearrangement of β_I (Table 4) for the QC-LDPC code for our case study. However, some dependencies still remain (shown in bold and italic in Table 6). Note that if we partition β'_I into two halves, L_1 to L_6 and L_7 to L_{12}, each half satisfies Fact 2 separately. In other words, $\forall u_f, u'_f \in \mathscr{L}_f = \{1, 2, \dots, 6\}$, $\forall w \in \{1, 2, \dots, 8\}$, $\beta_I(u_f, w) \neq \beta_I(u'_f, w)$, and $\forall u_s, u'_s \in \mathscr{L}_s = \{7, 8, \dots, 12\}$, $\forall w \in \{1, 2, \dots, 8\}$, $\beta_I(u_s, w) \neq \beta_I(u'_s, w)$.

We call the set of layers $\mathscr{L}$ satisfying Fact 2 a *superlayer*. Figure 6(a) shows the block-level view of the NPU timing diagram without the pipelining of layers. As seen in Section 4.1, the GNPU and LNPU operate in tandem and in that order, implying that the LNPU has to wait for the GNPU updates to finish. The layer-level picture is depicted in Figure 7(a). This idling of the GNPU and LNPU can be avoided by introducing pipelined processing of blocks given by the following lemma.

Lemma 6. *Within a superlayer, while the LNPU processes messages for the blocks $\beta'(u, w)$, the GNPU can process messages for the blocks $\beta'(u + 1, w)$, $u = \{1, 2, \dots, |\mathscr{L}| - 1\}$, and $w = \{1, 2, \dots, J\}$.*

Proof. It follows directly from the layer independence condition in Fact 2. □

Figure 6(c) illustrates the block-level view of this 2-layer pipelining scheme. It is important to note that the splitting of the NPU process into two parts, namely, the GNPU and the LNPU (that work in tandem), is a necessary condition for Lemma 6 to hold. However, at the boundary of the superlayer, Lemma 6 does not hold and pipelining has to be restarted for the next layer as seen in the layer-level view shown in Figure 7(c). This is the classical pipelining overhead.

Definition 7. Without loss of generality, the pipelining efficiency η_p is the number of layers processed per unit time per NPU array.

For the case of pipelining, two layers are shown in Figure 7(c):

$$\eta_p^{(2)} = \frac{|\mathscr{L}|}{|\mathscr{L}| + 1}. \tag{17}$$

Thus, we impose the following conditions on $|\mathscr{L}|$:

(1) Since two layers are processed in the pipeline at any given time,

$$|\mathscr{L}| \in \mathscr{F} = \{x : x \text{ is an even factor of } I\}. \tag{18}$$

(2) Given a QC-LDPC code, $|\mathscr{L}|$ is a constant. This is to facilitate a symmetric pipelining architecture which is a scalable solution.

(3) Choice of $|\mathscr{L}|$ should maximize pipelining efficiency η_p,

$$l^* = \arg \max_{|\mathscr{L}| \in \mathscr{F}} \eta_p. \tag{19}$$

In our work, $I = m_b = 12$, $\mathscr{F} = \{2, 4, 6\}$, and $l^* = \arg \max_{|\mathscr{L}| \in \mathscr{F}} \eta_p = 6$. The rearranged block index matrix β'_I is shown in Table 6 and the layer-level view of the pipeline timing diagram for the same is shown in Figure 7(d).

Remark 8.

Four-Layer Pipelining. For the case of the *IEEE 802.11n (2012)* QC-LDPC code chosen for this work, the pipelining of four layers might suggest an increase in the throughput; however, this is not the case as depicted in Figure 8. Due to the need for two NPU arrays, the pipelining efficiency of this scheme is

$$\eta_p^{(4)} = \frac{\eta_p^{(2)}}{2}. \tag{20}$$

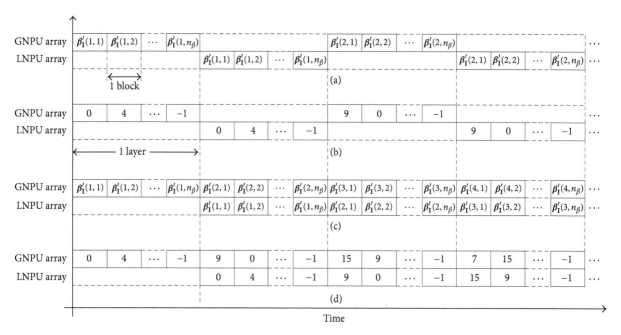

FIGURE 6: Block-level view of the pipeline timing diagram. (a) General case for a circulant-1 identity submatrix construction based QC-LDPC code (see Section 2) without pipelining. (b) Special case of the *IEEE 802.11n* QC-LDPC code used in this work without pipelining. (c) Pipelined processing of two layers for the general QC-LDPC code case in (a). (d) Pipelined processing of two layers for the *IEEE 802.11n* QC-LDPC code case in (b). This schedule is illustrated by the *block processing* loop in the high-level decoder architecture shown in Figure 9. Here, n_β represents the number of columns of $\boldsymbol{\beta}_I'$.

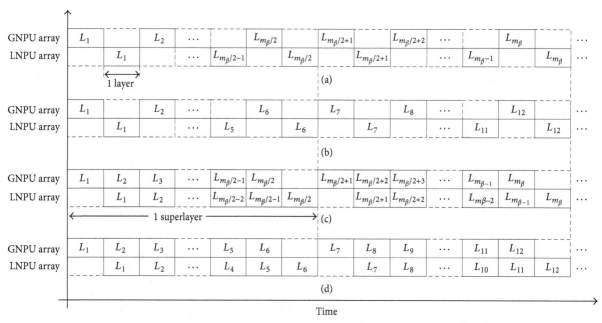

FIGURE 7: Layer-level view of the pipeline timing diagram. (a) General case for a circulant-1 identity submatrix construction based QC-LDPC code (see Section 2) without pipelining. (b) Special case of the *IEEE 802.11n* QC-LDPC code used in this work without pipelining. (c) Pipelined processing of two layers for the general QC-LDPC code case in (a). (d) Pipelined processing of two layers for the *IEEE 802.11n* QC-LDPC code case in (b). This schedule is illustrated by the *layer processing* loop in the high-level decoder architecture shown in Figure 9. Here, m_β represents the number of rows of $\boldsymbol{\beta}_I'$.

Hence, we limit ourselves to pipelined processing of two layers. To achieve further gains in throughput, without loss of generality, parallel processing of multiple blocks can be performed. For details on this approach of improving throughput, the reader is referred to Appendix B. From the perspective of memory access relaxation (Section 3.2) in *LabVIEW FPGA Compiler*, the proposed 2-layer pipelining is a suitable methodology for the FPGA internal memory with

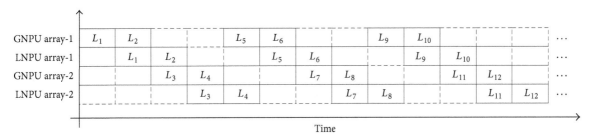

FIGURE 8: Layer-level view of the pipeline timing diagram for the GNPU and LNPU arrays when two NPU arrays are employed to process four layers. Due to the requirement of two NPU arrays, this method is inefficient compared to the two-layer pipelining method. Moreover, this method is not adopted for the implementation as the number of layers in a parallel run is limited by the number of ports in the shared memory.

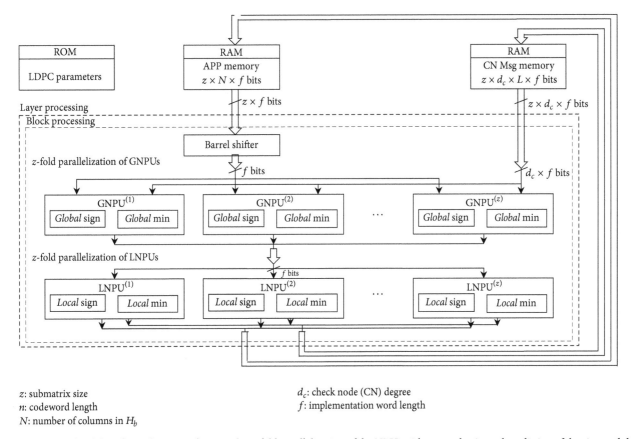

z: submatrix size
n: codeword length
N: number of columns in H_b

d_c: check node (CN) degree
f: implementation word length

FIGURE 9: High-level decoder architecture showing the z-fold parallelization of the NPUs with an emphasis on the splitting of the sign and the minimum computation given in (5). Note that, other computations in (3)–(6) are not shown for simplicity here. For both the pipelined and the nonpipelined versions, processing schedule for the inner block processing loop is as per Figure 6 and that for the outer layer processing loop is as per Figure 7.

a single pair of read/write port. This is because two layers running in parallel are timely assigned to a memory read and write port. Since this approach does not have any layer execution postponed due to a resource limitation, we can achieve the theoretical maximum throughput performance. Even if pipelining more than two layers was efficient, for such a method multiple layers need to be processed in parallel. However, the number of layers in a parallel run is limited by the number of ports in the shared memory. Any layers that need processing beyond the shared memory port number would be postponed, and this would prevent us from

achieving the theoretical maximum throughput. Deploying multiple decoding cores (as described in Section 5.2) is another way of improving throughput. The downside of this approach is that the memory requirement grows linearly with the number of parallel layers.

High-Level FPGA-Based Decoder Architecture. The high-level decoder architecture is shown in Figure 9. The read-only memory (ROM) holds the LDPC code parameters specified by $\boldsymbol{\beta}_I'$ and $\boldsymbol{\beta}_s'$ along with other code parameters such as the block length and the maximum number of decoding iterations. Initially, the a posteriori probability (APP) memory is set to the channel LLR values corresponding to all the VNs as per (3). The barrel shifter operates on blocks of VNs APP values of size $z \times f$, where f is the fixed-point word length used in the implementation for APP values. It circularly rotates the values in the APP block to the right by using the shift values from the β'_s matrix in the ROM, effectively implementing the connections between the CNs and VNs specified by the Tanner graph of the code. The cyclically shifted APP memory values and the corresponding CN message values for the block in question are fed to the array of z NPUs. Here, the GNPUs compute VN messages as per (4) and the LNPUs compute CN messages as per (5). These messages are then stored back at their respective locations in the random-access memory (RAM) for processing the next block. At the time of writing this paper, we have successfully implemented two versions of the decoder.

(1) 1x. As the name suggests, only one layer is processed at a time by the NPU array; in other words, there is no pipelining of layers. The block-level and the layer-level view of the pipelining are illustrated in Figures 6(b) and 7(b), respectively.

(2) 2x. This version is based on the 2-layer pipeline processing. Pipelining is done in software at the algorithmic description level. The block-level and layer-level views of the pipelined processing are shown in Figures 6(d) and 7(d), respectively. Due to the pipelining overhead, $\eta_p^{(2)} = 6/7 = 0.86$. Comparing this to the 1x version with $\eta = 6/12 = 0.5$, the 2x version is $\eta_p^{(2)}/\eta = 1.7$ times faster than the 1x version.

5. Case Studies

The techniques for improving throughput in an efficient manner, described in Section 4, are realized on hardware using an HLS compiler. The realization is divided into three case studies, namely, an efficiently pipelined *IEEE 802.11n* standard [27] compliant QC-LDPC decoder, an extension of this decoder that provides a throughput of 2.48 Gb/s, and an HARQ experimentation system based on the *IEEE 802.16* standard [36] QC-LDPC code. Each case study is detailed in the following Sections.

5.1. IEEE 802.11n Compliant LDPC Decoder. To evaluate the proposed strategies for achieving high-throughput, we have implemented the scaled-MSA based decoder for the QC-LDPC code in the *IEEE 802.11n (2012)*. For this code, $m_b \times n_b = 12 \times 24$, $z = 27, 54$, and 81 resulting in code lengths of $n = 24 \times z = 648, 1296$, and 1944 bits, respectively. Our implementation supports the submatrix size of $z = 81$ and is thus capable of supporting all the block lengths for the rate $R = 1/2$ code.

We represent the input LLRs from the channel and the CTV and VTC messages with 6 signed bits and 4 fractional bits. Figure 10 shows the bit-error-rate (BER) performance for the floating-point (FP) and the fixed-point (FxP) data representation with 8 decoding iterations. As expected, the

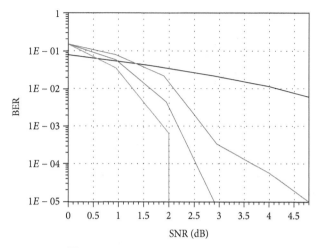

☐ Uncoded BPSK
☐ LDPC $R = 1/2$, 4 iter. (fixed-point)
☐ LDPC $R = 1/2$, 8 iter. (fixed-point)
☐ LDPC $R = 1/2$, 8 iter. (floating-point)

FIGURE 10: BER performance comparison between uncoded BPSK (rightmost), rate $= 1/2$ LDPC with 4 iterations using fixed-point data representation (second from right), rate $= 1/2$ LDPC with 8 iterations using fixed-point data representation (third from right), and rate $= 1/2$ LDPC with 8 iterations using floating-point data representation (leftmost).

TABLE 7: LDPC decoder IP FPGA resource utilization and throughput after mapping onto the Xilinx *Kintex-7 FPGA*.

	1x	2x
Device	*Kintex-7k410t*	*Kintex-7k410t*
Throughput (Mb/s)	337	608
FF (%)	9.1	5.3
BRAM (%)	4.7	6.4
DSP48 (%)	5.2	5.2
LUT (%)	8.7	8.2

fixed-point implementation suffers by about 0.5 dB compared to the floating-point version at a BER of 10^{-4}, and the gap widens for lower BER values. The decoder algorithm was described using the *LabVIEW CSDS* software. *LabVIEW FPGA Compiler* was then used to generate the very high speed integrated circuit (VHSIC) hardware description language (VHDL) code from the graphical dataflow description. The VHDL code was synthesized, placed, and routed using the *Xilinx Vivado* compiler on the *Xilinx Kintex-7* FPGA available on the *NI PXIe-7975R* FPGA board. The decoder achieves an overall throughput of 608 Mb/s at an operating frequency of 200 MHz and a latency of 5.7 μs at 4 decoding iterations with BER performance shown in Figure 10 (blue curve). Table 7 shows that the resource usage for the 2x version (almost twice as fast due to pipelining) is close to that of the 1x version. The *LabVIEW FPGA Compiler* chooses to use more flip-flops (FF) for data storage in the 1x version, while it uses more block RAM (BRAM) in the 2x version.

TABLE 8: Performance and resource utilization comparison, after mapping onto the FPGA, for versions with varying number of cores of the QC-LDPC decoder implemented on the *NI USRP-2953R* containing the Xilinx *Kintex-7 (410t)* FPGA.

Cores	1	2	4	5	6
Throughput (Mb/s)	420	830	1650	2060	2476
Clock rate (MHz)	200	200	200	200	200
Time to VHDL (min)	2.08	2.08	2.08	2.02	2.04
Total compile (min)	≈36	≈60	≈104	≈132	≈145
Total slice (%)	28	44	77	85	97
LUT (%)	18	28	51	62	73
FF (%)	10	16	28	33	39
DSP (%)	5	11	21	26	32
BRAM (%)	11	18	31	38	44

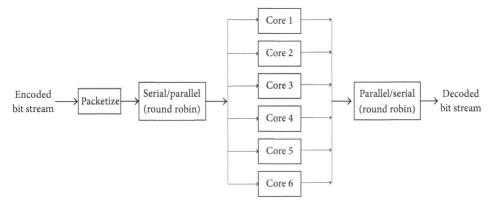

FIGURE 11: High-level system schematic illustrating the fixed latency, parallel processing of the decoder cores.

Remark 9. The clock rate selection in the HLS compiler generally determines pipeline stage depth of each primitive operation. For example, a higher target clock rate would result in a deeper pipeline stage. This requires more FPGA resources and a relatively longer compile time. Various *target* clock rates were tested, and the one offering the highest throughput in time with the most optimal resource utilization was chosen for the subsequent VHDL compile (e.g., 200 MHz for the compiles shown in Table 8). It is important to note that the HLS compiler provides an accurate throughput and resource estimation after it generates VHDL. This throughput and resource estimation time is short as recorded in the results tables (e.g., Table 8) as *Time to VHDL*. The user can easily find the optimal clock rate in terms of maximal throughput and optimized resource utilization.

5.2. Case Study: A 2.48 Gb/s QC-LDPC Decoder on the Xilinx Kintex-7 FPGA. On account of the scalability and reconfigurability of the decoder architecture in [37], it is possible to achieve high-throughput by employing multiple decoder cores in parallel as detailed in [38]. As shown in Figure 11, the encoded bit stream is packetized into frames of equal size and distributed for decoding in a round-robin manner to the cores operating in parallel. The main contribution of this approach is the elimination of a complicated buffering

and handshake mechanism which increases the development time and adds hardware overhead. This is mainly due to

(1) fixed latency of decoding the frames across all cores,

(2) time-staggered operation of cores,

(3) tightly controlled execution of the round-robin serial-parallel-serial conversion process.

To validate the multicore decoder architecture, in this case study, we chose the *IEEE 802.11n (2012)* QC-LDPC code for which $m_b \times n_b = 12 \times 24$, $z = 27, 54$, and 81 resulting in code lengths of $n = 24 \times z = 648, 1296$, and 1944 bits, respectively, and a code rate $R = 1/2$. The decoder *core* (described in Section 5.1) was compiled for a clock rate of 200 MHz and achieves a throughput of 420 Mb/s (first column in Table 8) with pipelining as described in Section 4.4.

The multicore decoder was developed in stages. The first stage is the aforementioned pipelined decoder core to which additional cores were added incrementally as per the scheme depicted in Figure 11. We have listed the resource utilization and the throughput performance for each stage in Table 8 for a qualitative comparison.

5.3. Rapid Prototyping of Hybrid-ARQ System. Hybrid-ARQ (HARQ) is a transmission technique that combines Forward Error Correction (FEC) with ARQ. In HARQ, a suitable FEC

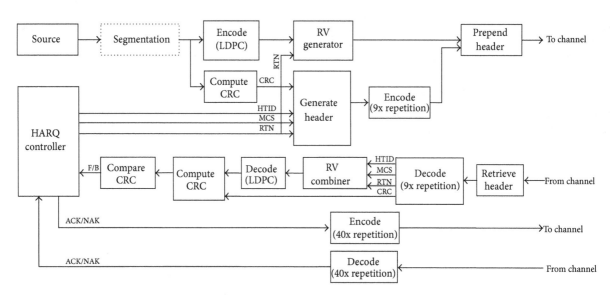

FIGURE 12: HARQ system schematic for one node. Overall, the system simulation uses two nodes (BS and UE).

code protects the data and error-detection code bits. In its simplest form, the FEC encoded packet—referred to as a Redundancy Version (RV) in this context—is transmitted as per the ARQ mechanism protocol. If the receiver is able to decode the data, it sends an acknowledgement (ACK) back to the transmitter. However, if it fails to recover the data, the receiver sends a negative acknowledgement (NAK) or retransmission request to the transmitter. In this scenario, the FEC simply increases the probability of successful transmission, thus reducing the average number of transmissions required in an ARQ scheme. HARQ has two modes of operation: Type-I and Type-II. In Type-I, a current retransmission is chase-combined [39] with a previously buffered (and failed) retransmission and then decoded. In Type-II HARQ, in the event of a decoding failure, additional code bits are transmitted in every subsequent retransmission. Since, in this mode, all code bits are not transmitted every retransmission, the efficiency of this scheme is higher. However, the complexity is also higher compared to Type-I.

To study the performance of the two HARQ schemes (Type-I and Type-II), we have implemented a baseband bidirectional link with two transceiver *nodes*. This can be compared to a downlink connection between a base station (BS) and user equipment (UE) with a data channel and a feedback channel. Each node is capable of running the HARQ protocol in its two modes. In our work, the BS (initiator of the transmission) operates in the *master* mode and the UE operates in the *slave mode*. A high-level description of the overall system with several subsystems is shown in Figure 12 and the media access control- (MAC-) level operation is described in Appendix A. At the initiator node, each data packet of length $k = 1152$ is encoded with an LDPC *mother* code of rate $R = 1/2$ and the Cyclic Redundancy Check (CRC) value for it is simultaneously computed. The RV generator selects bits from the encoded data to form RVs as per the code rate adaptation algorithm [40]. The header is encoded with a rate 1/9 repetition code. Finally, the RV is appended to the header and sent over the channel.

At the receiver node, header bits are decoded and the RV combiner uses the information in the header to combine the received signal values for Type-I mode or Type-II mode. CRC values from the header and the decoded data are compared to generate a feedback for the initiator node. The feedback (1-bit ACK/NAK) is coded with a rate 1/40 repetition code before sending over the channel. We assume an error-free feedback for this experiment, which is guaranteed by the rate 1/40 repetition code over the SNR range in consideration.

5.3.1. LabVIEW FPGA Compiler for Ease of Experimentation. The HARQ system comprises subsystems that can be classified into two main categories based on the nature of the processing they perform. The *bit-manipulation* subsystems—akin to digital signal processing (DSP)—follow a pattern of processing that does not change significantly on a per transmission basis. In other words, they are more or less stateless. The channel encoders and decoders are examples of this category. The *protocol-sensitive* subsystems on the other hand have to perform functions that are highly sensitive to the state of the system in a given transmission. For instance, the HARQ controller, the RV generator, and the RV combiner maintain a state [40]. With a few examples, this section highlights the ease of modification in a short time that *LabVIEW FPGA Compiler* provides across subsystems which is otherwise not possible for a purely HDL-based description.

Protocol-Sensitive Subsystem Modification. The HARQ controller is essentially a finite-state machine (FSM). For a reliable and an efficient implementation of an FSM on an FPGA, the designer needs to take care of issues such as clock and input signal timing, state encoding scheme, and the choice of the coding style [41]. Modification to the MAC-level protocol directly affects the FSM in our work. For details on the MAC-level operation of the HARQ protocol, the reader is referred to Appendix A. For instance, during experimentation, the frame structure is likely to undergo modifications. Any modification to the frame structure

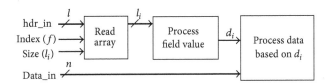

FIGURE 13: Realization of an example of *protocol-sensitive* subsystem using HLS.

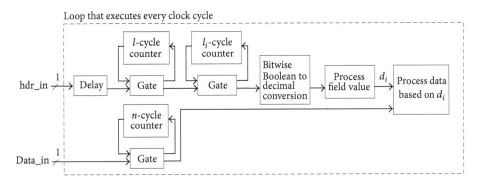

FIGURE 14: RTL block diagram: realization of an example of *protocol-sensitive* subsystem using HDL.

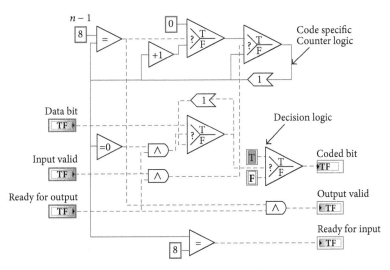

FIGURE 15: Schematic depiction of the description of a 9x repetition encoder in *LabVIEW FPGA* (subsequently compiled to *VHDL*). Note that the logic required is specific to the codeword size *n*.

affects nearly all subsystems. One such example is illustrated in Figures 13 and 14 where the ith field (of length l_i bits) of the header is read to process output d_i which is further used to process the data. The description in Figure 13 is agnostic to the modification at the HDL level and the designer can implement a change without HDL domain expertise, whereas in Figure 14 one can see that the description is specific to the subsystem in which the header is being used. Modifying the length of a field, for instance, requires modification of counter logic and adjustment of the delay value. This needs to be repeated for all subsystems that are affected by this change. In contrast, *LabVIEW FPGA Compiler* automatically generates the counter logic and delay values in Figure 14 by propagating the field-length values into the algorithm in Figure 13, allowing the same algorithmic description to be reused for different values of the field-length.

Bit-Manipulation Subsystem Modification. The channel coding subsystems, namely, the LDPC and repetition encoders and decoders, are at the core of the HARQ system. *LabVIEW FPGA Compiler* also eases the implementation of *bit-manipulation* subsystems like these. For example, the 9x repetition encoder description in *LabVIEW FPGA* is shown in Figure 15. Comparing this to the algorithmic description shown in Figure 16, it is evident that modification without much time and effort is facilitated by *LabVIEW FPGA Compiler*. It is important to emphasize here that *LabVIEW FPGA* provides a high-level abstraction to VHDL. However, it is not the same as the *algorithmic description* that we refer to, throughout this brief. This is because *LabVIEW FPGA* is a lower-level description language relative to the algorithmic description that is input to *LabVIEW FPGA Compiler*.

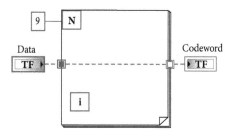

FIGURE 16: Schematic depiction of the description of a 9x repetition encoder using HLS using just a *for-loop* without any logic specific to the code.

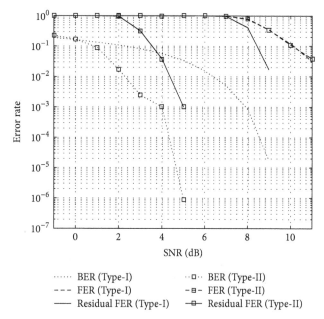

FIGURE 17: FER performance of Type-I and Type-II schemes. Note that the FER of Type-I and Type-II overlap as expected.

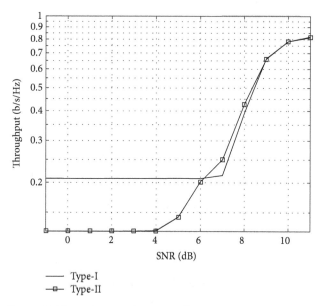

FIGURE 18: Throughput performance of Type-I and Type-II schemes.

TABLE 9: Performance and resource utilization, after mapping onto the FPGA, for the HARQ system (that supports both Type-I and Type-II mode of operation) on the *NI USRP-2953R* containing the *Xilinx Kintex-7 (410t)* FPGA.

	Utilization
Clock rate (MHz)	80
Time to generate VHDL (min)	5
Total slice (%)	54
LUT (%)	32
FF (%)	19
DSP (%)	12
BRAM (%)	30

5.3.2. Results.

The HARQ system has been implemented on the *Xilinx Kintex-7* series of FPGAs and the algorithmic description was input using *LabVIEW CSDS*. We chose these sets of tools as the FPGA is available in the *NI USRP 2943R* series used for real-world prototyping of our research. At the time of writing this paper, the system performance has been evaluated for the *IEEE 802.16 (2012)* [36] set of QC-LDPC codes. We would like to emphasize here that owing to the ease of modification, we can, in short development cycles, replace the channel codes with other code structures being researched such as the one described in [42]. The error-rate performance for 1k frames of codeword size of $n = 2304$ is shown in Figure 17. The residual Frame Error-Rate (FER) accounts for the errors that the HARQ protocol failed to correct, whereas the FER accounts for errors that happen without the use of the HARQ protocol. The data throughput of the system, defined as R/RTN, and the throughput averaged over the frames per SNR point are plotted in Figure 18. As expected, the performance of the system is improved with HARQ at the cost of a decrease in the throughput. The FPGA resource utilization for the same is given in Table 9.

Scalable Simulation Speedup. Each time any change in the system is made, there is a need to evaluate the performance of the system. This is especially true for testing code structures under research. Error-rate performance in excess of 10^8 bits is required to observe phenomena such as the error-floor of a code [24]. This makes time-efficient simulations not only a luxury but a necessity. In our implementation, while developing a real-world prototype we also get the benefit of a 4x speedup in simulation time using a decoder without pipelining. We measured the execution time for 10k frames over 40 SNR values. We used the *IEEE 802.16 (2012)* specified (2304, 1152) QC-LDPC code, with a 1/9 and a 1/40 repetition code for the header and the feedback, respectively. The decoder was set to perform 4 decoding iterations.

On a host machine, a *Dell Precision T3600* 3.6 GHz *Quad Core Xeon (i7)* with a 16 GB RAM, it took about 4.28 min, whereas on our FPGA testbed it took about 1.02 min resulting in a 4x speedup with a one time *time-to-compile* of approximately 45 min. While the time-to-compile seems significant,

TABLE 10: Comparative survey of the state-of-the-art. Note that, while there are multiple implementation case studies in [19, 21], we only list here those cases which are the closest in terms of the QC-LDPC code used in our case study, namely the *IEEE 802.11n (WiFi)* (1944, 972) QC-LDPC code with $z = 81$. *Development time (wherever reported) quantifies the programming effort required. This measure of the programming effort has been defined in [20] and is adopted here to facilitate an unambiguous comparison. In our work, the development effort is of the order of a few days of programming effort, once the algorithm to be implemented is finalized; including the total compile time which is of the order of tens of minutes.

Work →	Andrade et al. [19]	Pratas et al. [20]	Andrade et al. [21]	Scheiber et al. [22]	This work
HLS Technology	*Altera OpenCL*	*Maxeler MaxCompiler*	*Altera OpenCL*	*Xilinx Vivado HLS*	*National Instruments LabVIEW FPGA Compiler*
Standard	*IEEE WiMAX*	*ETSI DVB-S2*	*IEEE WiFi*	*IEEE WiFi*	*IEEE WiFi*
LDPC Parameters (n, k, z)	$(1152, 576, 48)$	$(64800, 32400, —)$	$(1944, 972, 81)$	$(648, 324, 27)$	$(1944, 972, 81)$
BP Decoding Schedule	flooding	flooding	flooding	layered	serial and layered
Throughput (Mb/s)	103.9	540	21	13.4	608
Decoding Iterations	10	10	10	3	4
Developement Time*	n.a.	~weeks	n.a.	n.a.	~days
FPGA Device	*Altera Stratix 5 D5*	*Xilinx Virtex-5 LX330T*	*Altera Stratix 5 D5*	*Xilinx Spartan-6 LX150T*	*Xilinx Kintex-7 K410T*
Fixed-point Precision (total bits)	8	n.a.	n.a.	n.a.	10
Clock Rate (MHz)	222.6	150	157	122	200
LUT (%)	42.9	n.a.	41	3	8.2
FF (%)	42.3	n.a.	36	2	5.3
BRAM (%)	75.3	n.a.	67	20.9	6.4
DSP (%)	3.8	n.a.	0	0	5.2

n.a.: not available (i.e. not reported in the cited work).

once compiled, for several trials with larger datasets (orders of magnitude larger than experimental value specified above), this time becomes insignificant.

6. A Comparative Survey of State of the Art

A survey of the state of the art for channel code architectures and their implementation using HLS technology reveals that insightful work on the topic has been done. In this section, we list some of the notable contemporary works. While there are a myriad of LDPC architecture designs implemented on the FPGA platform, here we restrict ourselves to a subset of those works that utilize HLS technology. In this section, we list some of the notable contemporary works that fall into this category.

The performance of an implementation depends on a host of factors such as the vendor specific device(s) with its associated HLS technology and the type of channel code in consideration. Thus, the intent of the authors is not to claim an all-encompassing performance comparison demonstrating gains or losses with respect to each other, but to provide the reader with a qualitative survey of the state of the art. Table 10 lists works [19–22] based on the settings from each that are chosen according to the proximity of their relevance to our work.

7. Conclusion

We use an HLS compiler that without expert-level hardware domain knowledge enables us to reliably prototype our research in a short amount of time. With techniques

such as timing estimation, pipelining, loop unrolling, and memory inference from arrays, *LabVIEW FPGA Compiler* compiles untimed dataflow algorithms written with loops, arrays, and feedback into VHDL descriptions that achieve a high clock rate and high-throughput. The employed HLS technology significantly reduced the time to explore the system parameter space and optimized it in terms of the error-rate performance and the resource utilization. We propose techniques to achieve a high-throughput FPGA architecture for a QC-LDPC code. The strategies are validated by implementing a standard compliant QC-LDPC decoder on an FPGA. The decoder architecture is scaled up to achieve another highly-parallel realization that has a throughput of 2.48 Gb/s. The HLS compilation process is used to rapidly prototype a HARQ experimentation system using LDPC codes that not only comprises bit-manipulation subsystems but also protocol-sensitive subsystems. This facilitated the error-rate performance measurement of the system over large, realistic data sets at a 4x greater speed than the conventional CPU-based experimentation. Finally, the use of HLS and reconfigurable hardware platforms holds the promise of realizing the architecture suited for the evolving research requirements of 5G wireless technology.

Appendix

A. MAC-Level HARQ Operation

Here, we briefly discuss the operation of the protocol-sensitive subsystems (Section 5.3.1) in the HARQ system for the interested reader. Without loss of generality, for N RVs

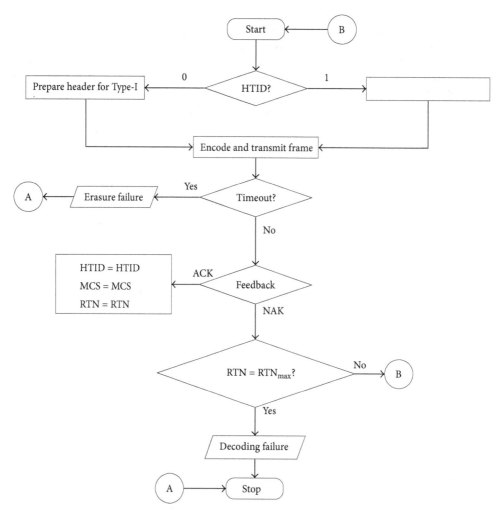

FIGURE 19: Flowchart showing the *master* mode of operation for the HARQ control algorithm. HTID: HARQ type identifier, MCS: Modulation and Coding Scheme, RTN: ReTransmission Number, and CRC: Cyclic Redundancy Check.

and the maximum number of retransmissions set to $\text{RTN}_{\max}$, the MAC-level operation of the HARQ protocol is shown in Figure 19 for the master mode and Figure 20 for slave mode. For Type-I scheme of HARQ, the RV generator does not puncture any bits and sends the whole *mother* codeword every transmit instance, whereas, in the Type-II scheme, it generates RVs as detailed in [40].

At the receiver, for the Type-I scheme of HARQ, the *i*th transmit instance performs $\mathbf{B}_i = \mathbf{B}_{i-1} + \mathbf{RV}_i$, where $\mathbf{B}$ denotes the buffer contents and $|\mathbf{B}| = n$ with $\mathbf{B}_0 = \mathbf{0}$. For the Type-II scheme, the RV combiner performs $\mathbf{B}[\sigma(j)] = \mathbf{RV}_i(j)$, where $0 \le i \le (N-1), 0 \le j \le (|\mathbf{RV}| - 1)$, and $\sigma(j)$ is the position of the *j*th code bit in the mother codeword determined by the puncturing method.

B. Parallelizing Block Columns

In Section 4, it was concluded that increasing the number of layers to more than two layers in the pipeline provides diminishing returns in efficiency of the pipelining scheme.

Here, we present a technique for a multifold increase in throughput by processing multiple blocks in a particular layer. We would like to note that this technique has not been implemented in any of the case studies provided in this article. To gain further throughput improvement, in this approach, we take advantage of the following fact. There is no message exchange across the blocks of a particular layer. In other words, message exchange (and hence dependency) happens only in the vertical direction in $\boldsymbol{\beta}_{\mathbf{I}}'$, where, $\forall u \in \{1, 2, \dots, I\}$ and $\forall w, w' \in \{1, 2, \dots, J\}$,

$$\boldsymbol{\beta}_{\mathbf{I}}'(u, w) \neq \boldsymbol{\beta}_{\mathbf{I}}'(u, w'). \tag{B.1}$$

The matrix $\boldsymbol{\beta}_{\mathbf{I}}'$ is defined in Section 4.4. In the pipelined version, the NPU array processes each block (within a layer) sequentially as shown in Figure 21. However, if we split the blocks into two sets and process each set independent of the other (requiring 2 NPU arrays), we can double the throughput. Owing to this fact, we call this version as the 4x version. Similarly, by employing 4 NPU arrays, we have the 8x version

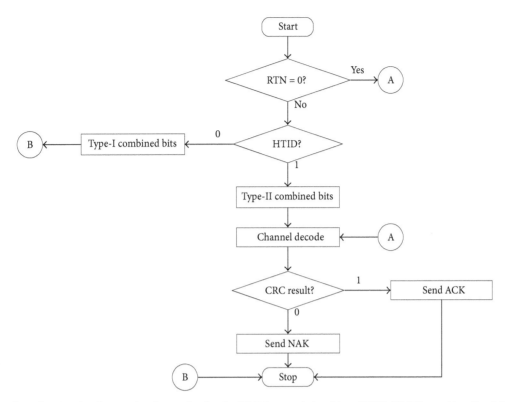

FIGURE 20: Flowchart showing the *slave* mode of operation for the HARQ control algorithm. HTID: HARQ type identifier, MCS: Modulation and Coding Scheme, RTN: ReTransmission Number, and CRC: Cyclic Redundancy Check.

GNPU array	$\beta'_I(1,1)$	$\beta'_I(1,2)$	$\cdots$	$\beta'_I(1,n_\beta)$	$\beta'_I(2,1)$	$\beta'_I(2,2)$	$\cdots$	$\beta'_I(2,n_\beta)$	$\beta'_I(3,1)$	$\beta'_I(3,2)$	$\cdots$	$\beta'_I(3,n_\beta)$	$\cdots$
LNPU array		Block			$\beta'_I(1,1)$	$\beta'_I(1,2)$	$\cdots$	$\beta'_I(1,n_\beta)$	$\beta'_I(2,1)$	$\beta'_I(2,2)$	$\cdots$	$\beta'_I(2,n_\beta)$	$\cdots$

Layer → (a)

GNPU array-1	$\beta'_I(1,1)$	$\beta'_I(1,2)$	$\cdots$	$\beta'_I(1,n_\beta/2)$	$\beta'_I(2,1)$	$\beta'_I(2,2)$	$\cdots$	$\beta'_I(2,n_\beta/2)$	$\beta'_I(3,1)$	$\beta'_I(3,2)$	$\cdots$	$\beta'_I(3,n_\beta/2)$	$\cdots$
GNPU array-2	$\beta'_I(1,n_\beta/2+1)$	$\beta'_I(1,n_\beta/2+2)$	$\cdots$	$\beta'_I(1,n_\beta)$	$\beta'_I(2,n_\beta/2+1)$	$\beta'_I(2,n_\beta/2+2)$	$\cdots$	$\beta'_I(2,n_\beta)$	$\beta'_I(3,n_\beta/2+1)$	$\beta'_I(3,n_\beta/2+2)$	$\cdots$	$\beta'_I(3,n_\beta)$	$\cdots$
LNPU array-1	—	—	$\cdots$	—	$\beta'_I(1,1)$	$\beta'_I(1,2)$	$\cdots$	$\beta'_I(1,n_\beta/2)$	$\beta'_I(2,1)$	$\beta'_I(2,2)$	$\cdots$	$\beta'_I(2,n_\beta/2)$	$\cdots$
LNPU array-2	—	—	$\cdots$	—	$\beta'_I(1,n_\beta/2+1)$	$\beta'_I(1,n_\beta/2+2)$	$\cdots$	$\beta'_I(1,n_\beta)$	$\beta'_I(2,n_\beta/2+1)$	$\beta'_I(2,n_\beta/2+2)$	$\cdots$	$\beta'_I(2,n_\beta)$	$\cdots$

(b)

Time

FIGURE 21: Pipeline timing diagram from the block processing perspective for (a) the 2x version and (b) the 4x version of the massively-parallel decoder architecture. Note that the ordering of $\beta'_I(u,w)$ blocks, $\forall u \in \{1,2,\ldots,I\}$ and $\forall w \in \{1,2,\ldots,J\}$ shown here, is not unique, owing to the independence of the blocks as shown earlier. Here, n_β represents the number of columns of β'_I.

and finally, if we employ 8 NPU arrays, we have the 16x version, thus increasing throughput gradually at each stage.

Acknowledgments

The authors would like to thank the Department of Electrical and Computer Engineering, Rutgers University, NJ, USA, and the National Instruments Corporation, Austin, TX, USA, for their continual support for this research work.

References

[1] B. Raaf, W. Zirwas, K.-J. Friederichs et al., "Vision for Beyond 4G broadband radio systems," in *Proceedings of the IEEE 22nd International Symposium on Personal, Indoor and Mobile Radio Communications, (PIMRC '11)*, pp. 2369–2373, IEEE, Toronto, Canada, September 2011.

[2] C. Berrou, A. Glavieux, and P. Thitimajshima, "Near Shannon limit error-correcting coding and encoding: turbo-codes," in

Proceedings of the IEEE International Conference on Communications, pp. 1064–1070, Geneve, Switzerland, May 1993.

[3] R. G. Gallager, "Low-Density Parity-Check Codes," *IRE Transactions on Information Theory*, vol. 8, no. 1, pp. 21–28, 1962.

[4] "3GPP RAN WG1," in *3rd Generation Partnership Project (3GPP)*, 2016, http://www.3gpp.org/specifications-groups/ranplenary/ran1-radio-layer-1/home.

[5] H. Kee, S. Mhaske, D. Uliana et al., "Rapid and high-level constraint-driven prototyping using lab VIEW FPGA," in *Proceedings of 2014 IEEE Global Conference on Signal and Information Processing, GlobalSIP 2014*, pp. 45–49, USA, December 2014.

[6] H. Kee, T. Ly, N. Petersen, J. Washington, H. Yi, and D. Blasig, "Compile time exec ut ion," *U.S. Patent 9 081 583*, 2015.

[7] T. Riche, N. Petersen, H. Kee et al., "Convergence analysis of program variables," *U.S. Patent 9 189 215*, 2015.

[8] H. Kee, H. Yi, T. Ly et al., "Correlation analysis of program structures," U.S. Patent 9 489 181, 2016.

[9] T. Ly, S. Mhaske, H. Kee, A. Arnesen, D. Uliana, and N. Petersen, "Self-addressing memory," U.S. Patent 9 569 119, 2017.

[10] W. Ryan and S. Lin, *Channel Codes: Classical and Modern*, Cambridge University Press, Cambridge, 2009.

[11] Y. Sun and J. R. Cavallaro, "VLSI architecture for layered decoding of QC-LDPC codes with high circulant weight," *IEEE Transactions on Very Large Scale Integration (VLSI) Systems*, vol. 21, no. 10, pp. 1960–1964, 2013.

[12] K. Zhang, X. Huang, and Z. Wang, "High-throughput layered decoder implementation for quasi-cyclic LDPC codes," *IEEE Journal on Selected Areas in Communications*, vol. 27, no. 6, pp. 985–994, 2009.

[13] N. Onizawa, T. Hanyu, and V. C. Gaudet, "Design of high-throughput fully parallel LDPC decoders based on wire partitioning," *IEEE Transactions on Very Large Scale Integration (VLSI) Systems*, vol. 18, no. 3, pp. 482–489, 2010.

[14] T. Mohsenin, D. N. Truong, and B. M. Baas, "A low-complexity message-passing algorithm for reduced routing congestion in LDPC decoders," *IEEE Transactions on Circuits and Systems. I. Regular Papers*, vol. 57, no. 5, pp. 1048–1061, 2010.

[15] A. Balatsoukas-Stimming and A. Dollas, "FPGA-based design and implementation of a multi-GBPS LDPC decoder," in *Proceedings of 22nd International Conference on Field Programmable Logic and Applications, FPL 2012*, pp. 262–269, nor, August 2012.

[16] V. A. Chandrasetty and S. M. Aziz, "FPGA implementation of high performance ldpc decoder using modified 2-bit Min-Sum algorithm," in *Proceedings of 2nd International Conference on Computer Research and Development, ICCRD 2010*, pp. 881–885, mys, May 2010.

[17] R. Zarubica, S. G. Wilson, and E. Hall, "Multi-Gbps FPGA-based Low Density Parity Check (LDPC) decoder design," in *Proceedings of 50th Annual IEEE Global Telecommunications Conference, GLOBECOM 2007*, pp. 548–552, usa, November 2007.

[18] P. Schläfer, C. Weis, N. Wehn, and M. Alles, "Design space of flexible multigigabit LDPC decoders," *VLSI Design*, vol. 2012, Article ID 942893, 2012.

[19] J. Andrade, G. Falcao, and V. Silva, "Flexible design of wide-pipeline-based WiMAX QC-LDPC decoder architectures on FPGAs using high-level synthesis," *Electronics Letters*, vol. 50, no. 11, pp. 839–840, 2014.

[20] F. Pratas, J. Andrade, G. Falcao, V. Silva, and L. Sousa, "Open the Gates: Using High-level Synthesis towards programmable LDPC decoders on FPGAs," in *Proceedings of 2013 1st IEEE Global Conference on Signal and Information Processing, GlobalSIP 2013*, pp. 1274–1277, usa, December 2013.

[21] J. Andrade, F. Pratas, G. Falcao, V. Silva, and L. Sousa, "Combining flexibility with low power: Dataflow and wide-pipeline LDPC decoding engines in the Gbit/s era," in *Proceedings of 25th IEEE International Conference on Application-Specific Systems, Architectures and Processors, ASAP 2014*, pp. 264–269, che, June 2014.

[22] E. Scheiber, G. H. Bruck, and P. Jung, "mplementation of an LDPC decoder for IEEE 802.11n using Vivado TM high-level synthesis," in *Proceedings of int. Conf. Electron., Signal Process. and Commun. Syst.*, pp. 45–48, 2013.

[23] H. Kee, D. Uliana, A. Arnesen et al., "A 2.06Gb/s LDPC decoder (exhibit floor demonstration)," in *Proceedings of IEEE Global Commun. Conf.*, 2014, https://www.youtube.com/watch?v=o58keq-eP1A.

[24] D. Costello and S. Lin, *Error Control Coding*, Pearson, 2004.

[25] R. M. Tanner, "A recursive approach to low complexity codes," *Institute of Electrical and Electronics Engineers. Transactions on Information Theory*, vol. 27, no. 5, pp. 533–547, 1981.

[26] L. Chen, J. Xu, I. Djurdjevic, and S. Lin, "Near-Shannon-limit quasi-cyclic low-density parity-check codes," *IEEE Transactions on Communications*, vol. 52, no. 7, pp. 1038–1042, 2004.

[27] "EEE Std. for information technology–telecommunications and information exchange between LAN and MAN–Part 11: Wireless LAN medium access control (MAC) and physical layer (PHY) specifications," in *IEEE P802.11-REVmb/D12*, pp. 1–2910, 2011.

[28] F. R. Kschischang, B. J. Frey, and H.-A. Loeliger, "Factor graphs and the sum-product algorithm," *Institute of Electrical and Electronics Engineers. Transactions on Information Theory*, vol. 47, no. 2, pp. 498–519, 2001.

[29] E. Sharon, S. Litsyn, and J. Goldberger, "Efficient serial message-passing schedules for LDPC decoding," *Institute of Electrical and Electronics Engineers. Transactions on Information Theory*, vol. 53, no. 11, pp. 4076–4091, 2007.

[30] M. M. Mansour and N. R. Shanbhag, "High-throughput LDPC decoders," *IEEE Transactions on Very Large Scale Integration (VLSI) Systems*, vol. 11, no. 6, pp. 976–996, 2003.

[31] J. Chen and M. Fossorier, "Near optimum universal belief propagation based decoding of LDPC codes and extension to turbo decoding," in *IEEE Int. Symp. Inf. Theory*, p. 189, June 2001.

[32] National Instruments Corp., *LabVIEW Communications System Design Suite Overview*, 2014, http://www.ni.com/white-paper/52502/en/.

[33] J. L. Hennessy and D. A. Patterson, *Computer Architecture: A Quantitative Approach*, Morgan Kaufmann, 1995.

[34] Q. Liu, T. Todman, and W. Luk, "Combining optimizations in automated low power design," in *Proceedings of Design, Automation and Test in Europe Conference and Exhibition*, pp. 1791–1796, March 2010.

[35] K. K. Gunnam, G. S. Choi, M. B. Yeary, and M. Atiquzzaman, "VLSI architectures for layered decoding for irregular LDPC codes of WiMax," in *Proceedings of 2007 IEEE International Conference on Communications, ICC'07*, pp. 4542–4547, gbr, June 2007.

[36] "IEEE standard for wireless MAN-advanced air interface for broadband wireless access systems," IEEE Std 802.16.1-2012, 2012.

[37] S. Mhaske, H. Kee, T. Ly, A. Aziz, and P. Spasojevic, "High-throughput FPGA-based QC-LDPC decoder architecture," in *Proceedings of 82nd IEEE Vehicular Technology Conference, VTC Fall 2015*, usa, September 2015.

[38] S. Mhaske, D. Uliana, H. Kee, T. Ly, A. Aziz, and P. Spasojevic, "A 2.48Gb/s FPGA-based QC-LDPC decoder: An algorithmic compiler implementation," in *Proceedings of 36th IEEE Sarnoff Symposium, Sarnoff 2015*, pp. 88–93, usa, September 2015.

[39] D. Chase, "Code combining—a maximum-likelihood decoding approach for combining and arbitrary number of noisy packets," *IEEE Transactions on Communications*, vol. 33, no. 5, pp. 385–393, 1985.

[40] S. Mhaske, H. Kee, T. Ly, and P. Spasojevic, "FPGA-accelerated simulation of a hybrid-ARQ system using high level synthesis," in *Proceedings of 2016 IEEE 37th Sarnoff Symposium*, pp. 19–21, Newark, NJ, USA, September 2016.

[41] N. I. Rafla and B. L. Davis, "A study of finite state machine coding styles for implementation in FPGAs," in *Proceedings of 2006 49th Midwest Symposium on Circuits and Systems, MWSCAS'06*, pp. 337–341, pri, August 2007.

[42] B. Young, S. Mhaske, and P. Spasojevic, "Rate compatible IRA codes using row splitting for 5G wireless," in *Proceedings of 2015 49th Annual Conference on Information Sciences and Systems, CISS 2015*, usa, March 2015.

14

An Efficient FPGA Implementation of Optimized Anisotropic Diffusion Filtering of Images

Chandrajit Pal,[1] **Avik Kotal,**[2] **Asit Samanta,**[1] **Amlan Chakrabarti,**[1] **and Ranjan Ghosh**[3]

[1]*A. K. Choudhury School of Information Technology, University of Calcutta, JD-2, Sector III, Salt Lake City, Kolkata 700098, India*
[2]*Department of Applied Optics and Photonics, University of Calcutta, JD-2, Sector III, Salt Lake City, Kolkata 700098, India*
[3]*Institute of Radio Physics and Electronics, University of Calcutta, JD-2, Sector III, Salt Lake City, Kolkata 700098, India*

Correspondence should be addressed to Chandrajit Pal; palchandrajit@gmail.com

Academic Editor: John Kalomiros

Digital image processing is an exciting area of research with a variety of applications including medical, surveillance security systems, defence, and space applications. Noise removal as a preprocessing step helps to improve the performance of the signal processing algorithms, thereby enhancing image quality. Anisotropic diffusion filtering proposed by Perona and Malik can be used as an edge-preserving smoother, removing high-frequency components of images without blurring their edges. In this paper, we present the FPGA implementation of an edge-preserving anisotropic diffusion filter for digital images. The designed architecture completely replaced the convolution operation and implemented the same using simple arithmetic subtraction of the neighboring intensities within a kernel, preceded by multiple operations in parallel within the kernel. To improve the image reconstruction quality, the diffusion coefficient parameter, responsible for controlling the filtering process, has been properly analyzed. Its signal behavior has been studied by subsequently scaling and differentiating the signal. The hardware implementation of the proposed design shows better performance in terms of reconstruction quality and accelerated performance with respect to its software implementation. It also reduces computation, power consumption, and resource utilization with respect to other related works.

1. Introduction

Image denoising is often employed as a preprocessing step in various applications like medical imaging, microscopy, and remote sensing. It helps to reduce speckles in the image and preserves edge information leading to higher image quality for further information processing [1]. Normal smoothing operations using low-pass filtering do not take into account intensity variations within an image and hence blurring occurs. Anisotropic diffusion filter performs edge-preserving smoothing and is a popular technique for image denoising [2]. Anisotropic diffusion filtering follows an iterative process and it requires a fairly large amount of computations to compute each successive denoised image version after every iteration. This process is continued until a sufficient degree of smoothing is obtained. However, a proper selection of parameters as well as complexity reduction of the algorithm can make it simple. Various edge-preserving denoising filters do exist targeting various applications according to the cost,

power, and performance requirements. However, as a case study, we have undertaken to optimize the anisotropic diffusion algorithm and design an efficient hardware equivalent to the diffusion filter that can be applied to embedded imaging systems.

Traditional digital signal processors are microprocessors designed to perform a special purpose. They are well suited to algorithmic-intensive tasks but are limited in performance by clock rate and the sequential nature of their internal design, limiting their maximum number of operations per unit time. A solution to this increasing complexity of DSP (Digital Signal Processing) implementations (e.g., digital filter design for multimedia applications) came with the introduction of FPGA technology. This serves as a means to combine and concentrate discrete memory and logic, enabling higher integration, higher performance, and increased flexibility with their massively parallel structures. FPGA contains a uniform array of configurable logic blocks (CLBs) [3–5], memory, and DSP slices, along with other elements [6]. Most machine vision algorithms are dominated by low and intermediate level image processing operations, many of which are inherently parallel. This makes them amenable to parallel hardware implementation on an FPGA [7], which have the potential to significantly accelerate the image processing component of a machine vision system.

2. Related Works

A lot of research can be found on the requirements and challenges of designing digital image processing algorithms using reconfigurable hardware [3, 8]. In [1], the authors have designed an optimized architecture capable of processing real-time ultrasound images for speckle reduction using anisotropic diffusion. The architecture has been optimized in both software and hardware. A prototype of the speckle reducing anisotropic diffusion (SRAD) algorithm on a Virtex-4 FPGA has been designed and tested. It achieves real-time processing of 128×128 video sequences at 30 fps as well as 320×240 pixels with a video rate speed of 30 fps [8, 9]. Atabany and Degenaar [10] described the architecture of splitting the data stream into multiple processing pipelines. It reduced the power consumption in contrast to the traditional spatial (pipeline) parallel processing technique. But their system partitioning architecture clearly reveals nonoptimized architecture as the $N \times N$ kernel has been repeated over each partition (complexity of which is $O(N^2)$). Moreover, their power value is completely estimated. The power measurements of very recent hardware designed filters, namely, the bilateral and the trilateral filter [11–13], have also been undertaken. In [14], the authors have introduced a novel FPGA-based implementation of 3D anisotropic diffusion filtering capable of processing intraoperative 3D images in real time making them suitable for applications like image-guided interventions. However, it did not reveal the acceleration rate achieved in hardware with respect to the software counterpart (anisotropic diffusion) and energy efficiency information as well as any filtered output image analysis. Authors in [15] have utilized the ability of Very Long Instruction Word (VLIW) processor to perform multiple operations in parallel using a low cost Texas Instruments (TI) digital signal processor (DSP) of series TMS320C64x+. However, they have used the traditional approach of 3×3 filter masks for the convolution operation used to calculate the filter gradients within the window. It increased the computation of arithmetic operations. There is also no information regarding the power consumption and energy efficiency.

We have also compared our design with the GPU implementations of anisotropic diffusion filters for 3D biomedical datasets [16]. In [16], the authors have implemented biomedical image datasets in NVIDIA's CUDA programming language to take advantage of the high computational throughput of GPU accelerators. Their results show an execution time of 0.206 sec for a 128^3 dataset for 9 iterations, that is, for a total number of $(128^3 * 9)$ pixels where 9 is the number of iterations to receive a denoised image. However, once we consider 3D image information, the number of pixels increases thrice. In this scenario, we need only 0.1 seconds of execution time

in FPGA platform as an approximation ratio with a much reduced MSE (Mean Square Error) of 53.67 instead of their average of 174. The acceleration rate becomes 91x with respect to CPU implementation platform unlike the case in GPU with 13x. Secondly, their timing (execution) data does not include the constant cost of data transfer (cost of transferring data between main memory on the host system and the GPU's memory which is around 0.1 seconds). It measures only the runtime of the actual CUDA kernel which is an inherent drawback of GPU. This is due to the architecture which separates the memory space of the GPU from that of its controlling processor. Actually, GPU implementation takes more time to execute the same [17] due to lot of memory overhead and thread synchronization. Besides GPU implementation or customized implementations on DSP kits of Texas Instruments have got their own separate purpose of implementation.

3. Our Approach

The main contributions of our work are highlighted as follows:

(i) Firstly, the independent sections of the algorithm that can be executed in parallel have been identified followed by a detailed analysis of algorithm optimization. Thereafter, a complete pipeline hardware design of the parallel sections of the algorithm has been accomplished (gradient computations, diffusion coefficients, and CORDIC divisions).

(ii) Our proposed hardware design architecture completely substituted standard convolution operation [18], required for the evaluation of the intensity gradients within the mask. We used simple arithmetic subtraction to calculate the intensity gradients of the neighboring pixels within a window kernel, by computing only one arithmetic (pixel intensity subtraction) operation. The proposed operation saved 9 multiplications and 8 addition operations per convolution, respectively (in a 3×3 window).

(iii) The number of iterations, which is required during the filtering process, has been made completely adaptive.

(iv) Besides increasing the accuracy and reducing the power reduction, a huge amount of computational time has been reduced and the system has achieved constant computational complexity, that is, $O(1)$.

(v) We performed some performance analysis on the diffusion coefficient responsible for controlling the filtering process, by subsequently differentiating and scaling, which resulted in enhanced denoising and better quality of reconstruction.

(vi) Due to its low power consumption and resource utilization with respect to other implementations, the proposed system can be considered to be used in low power, battery operated portable medical devices.

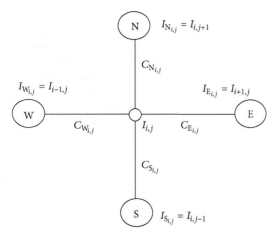

FIGURE 1: The structure of the discrete computational scheme for simulating the diffusion equation. The brightness values $I_{i,j}$ are associated with the nodes of a lattice and the conduction coefficients C with the arcs. One node of the lattice and its four north, east, west, and south neighbors are shown [2].

The detailed description of the algorithm optimization and the hardware parallelism as well as the achieved acceleration are described in Section 5. As discussed above, in order to implement each equation, one convolution operation needs to be computed with a specified mask as per the directional gradient. Further optimization has been achieved by parallel execution of multiple operations, namely, the intensity gradient (∇I) and the diffusion coefficients (C_n) within the filter kernel architecture, being discussed in hardware design sections. To the best of our knowledge, this is one of the first efficient implementations of the anisotropic diffusion filtering, with respect to throughput, energy efficiency, and image quality realized in hardware.

The paper is organized as follows. Section 4 describes the algorithm background, Section 5 briefly explains the materials and methods of the approach in multiple subsections, Section 6 discusses the results, and Section 7 ends up with the conclusions and future projections.

4. Algorithm (Background Work)

The well known anisotropic diffusion equation is given in [2]

$$I_t = \text{div}\left(C\left(x, y, t\right) \nabla I\right) = C\left(x, y, t\right) \Delta I + \nabla C \cdot \nabla I, \quad (1)$$

where div is the divergence operator and ∇ and Δ, respectively, denote the gradient and Laplacian operator with respect to the space variables. t denotes the time (scale) where the locations of the region boundaries appropriate for that scale are known with coordinate (x, y). The anisotropic diffusion equation can be expressed as a simple numerical scheme explained as follows.

Equation (1) above can be discretized on a square lattice with vertices representing the brightness, and arcs representing the conduction coefficients, as shown in Figure 1.

An 8-nearest-neighbor discretization of the Laplacian operator can be used:

$$E_N = \nabla_N I_{i,j} \equiv I_{i-1,j} - I_{i,j},$$

$$E_S = \nabla_S I_{i,j} \equiv I_{i+1,j} - I_{i,j} \quad (2)$$

$$\vdots$$

leading to

$$I_{i,j}^{t+1} = I_{i,j}^t + \lambda \left[C_N \cdot \nabla_N I + C_S \cdot \nabla_S I + C_E \cdot \nabla_E I + C_W \right.$$

$$\cdot \nabla_W I + C_{NE} \cdot \nabla_{NE} I + C_{NW} \cdot \nabla_{NW} I + C_{SE} \cdot \nabla_{SE} I \quad (3)$$

$$\left. + C_{SW} \cdot \nabla_{SW} I\right],$$

where $0 \leq \lambda \leq 1/4$ for the numerical scheme to be stable, N, S, E, W are the mnemonic subscripts for north, south, east, and west, the superscripts and subscripts on the square brackets are applied to all the terms they enclose, the symbol ∇, the gradient operator, indicates nearest-neighbor differences, which defines the edge estimation method, say E, and t is the number of iterations.

Perona and Malik [2] tried with two different g definitions, which controls blurring intensity according to $\|E\|$; g has to be a monotonically decreasing function:

$$g\left(\|E\|\right) = e^{-\left(\left(\frac{\|E\|}{\kappa}\right)^2\right)},$$

$$g\left(\|E\|\right) = \frac{1}{1 + \left(\|E\|/\kappa\right)^2}. \quad (4)$$

We define new "C" to identify the conduction coefficients. The conduction coefficients are updated at every iteration as a function of the brightness gradient shown in equationarray (2). The coefficients control the amount of smoothing done at each pixel position (x, y) represented as

$$C\left(x, y, t\right) = g\left(\left\|\nabla I\left(x, y, t\right)\right\|\right). \quad (5)$$

Considering all the directions, we have

$$C_{N_{i,j}}^t = g\left(\left|\nabla_N I_{i,j}^t\right|\right),$$

$$C_{S_{i,j}}^t = g\left(\left|\nabla_S I_{i,j}^t\right|\right) \quad (6)$$

$$\vdots$$

If $C(x, y, t)$ is large, then x, y is not a part of an edge and vice versa. Thus, substituting the value of the coefficient (C_n) by $g()$ as shown in (6), this is performed for all the gradient directions which is finally substituted to get (3).

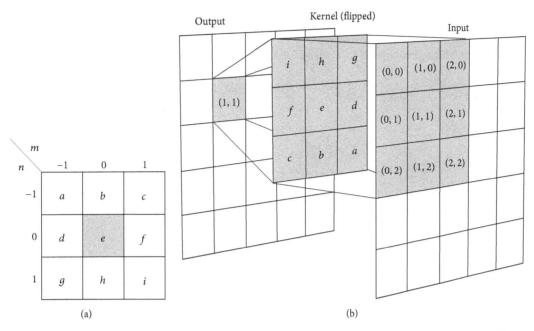

FIGURE 2: Convolution architecture concept. (a) 3×3 filter kernel. (b) Convolution operation (see equations (8) and (10)).

5. Design Method and Hardware Details

5.1. Replacing the Convolution Architecture (Proposed by Us).
Consider

$$y[1,1] = \sum_{j=-1}^{1} \sum_{i=-1}^{1} x[i,j] \cdot h[1-i, 1-j]$$

$$= x[0,0] \, h[1,1] + x[1,0] \, h[0,1]$$

$$+ x[2,0] \, h[-1,1]$$

$$= x[0,1] \, h[1,0] + x[1,1] \, h[0,0] \qquad (7)$$

$$+ x[2,1] \, h[-1,0]$$

$$= x[0,2] \, h[1,-1] + x[1,2] \, h[0,-1]$$

$$+ x[2,2] \, h[-1,-1].$$

Equation (7) describes a simple 2-dimensional convolution. Referring to Figure 2, we use x as the input image and h as the filter coefficient kernel to perform the convolution as shown in (7). Now, as a case study, substituting the value of the filter coefficient kernel (north gradient filter coefficient) is shown as follows:

$$h_{N} = \begin{pmatrix} 0 & 1 & 0 \\ 0 & -1 & 0 \\ 0 & 0 & 0 \end{pmatrix}. \qquad (8)$$

In (7), we get

$$y[1,1] = 0 + \cdots + x[1,0] - x[1,1] + \cdots + 0$$

$$= x[1,0] - x[1,1]. \qquad (9)$$

Similarly, for south gradient filter coefficient

$$h_{S} = \begin{pmatrix} 0 & 0 & 0 \\ 0 & -1 & 0 \\ 0 & 1 & 0 \end{pmatrix}, \qquad (10)$$

we get the south directional gradient as

$$y[1,1] = 0 + \cdots + x[1,2] - x[1,1] + \cdots + 0$$

$$= x[1,2] - x[1,1]. \qquad (11)$$

This operation is continued for all other directions. This shows that the convolution operation can be simplified down to a single arithmetic subtraction, thereby drastically reducing the number of operations, the complexity, and the hardware resources. It also enhances the speed, as discussed in the latter sections of the paper.

The gradient estimation of the algorithm for various directions is shown in equationarray (2), which was originally realized in software [19] by means of convolution of 3×3 gradient kernel sliding over the image. It consisted of 9 multiplications and 8 additions for a single convolution operation (so total of 17 operations). Therefore, our hardware realization of the convolution kernel operation (computing gradient (2)) has been substituted by a single arithmetic subtraction operation, reducing a huge amount of computation. The detailed hardware implementation is described in Section 5.5.

5.2. Adaptive Iteration (Proposed by Us). The iteration step of the filter shown in (3) needs to be manually set in the classical version of the algorithm, which was its main drawback. However, that has been made adaptive by the proposed Algorithm 1. The number of iterations completely depend upon nature of the image under consideration.

> **Input:** Denoised images $I_{i,j}$ at every iteration step of (3).
> **Comments:** Referring (3).
> (1) The differences between denoised output images at every iteration step is found out.
> $$Id^t = I_{i,j}^{t+1} - I_{i,j}^t$$
> (2) The difference between the maximum and minimum of the difference matrix found out in Step (1) is computed at every iteration step.
> $$Id_{\text{diff}}^t = \max(Id)^t - \min(Id)^t$$
> (3) Steps (1) and (2) are continued until the condition shown below is met.
> $$\|Id_{\text{diff}}^{t+1} - Id_{\text{diff}}^t\| = 0$$
> (4) Once the condition in Step (3) is met the execution is stopped which in turn stops the number of iteration thereby making it adaptive.
> (5) Display the number of iteration thus encountered and exit.

ALGORITHM 1: Adaptive iteration algorithm.

5.3. In-Depth Analysis of the Diffusion Coefficient (Proposed by Us). To control of the properties of the diffusion coefficient in (5) is required to analyze the signal behavior. Considering a 1-dimensional diffusion coefficient of the form shown in (12) as $1/(1 + x^2)$, which is a function of the gradient, we get

$$C(\nabla I_x) = \frac{1}{(1 + \nabla I_x^2)}, \tag{12}$$

where ∇I_x is the gradient computation shown in equation-array (2). Observing the coefficients timing variation by computing the differentiation of the coefficient C, we get

$$\nabla I_t = \frac{dC(\nabla I_x)}{dx} = C'(\nabla I_x) \cdot \nabla I_x' = -\frac{2x}{(x^2 + 1)^2}, \tag{13}$$

where $C(\nabla I_x) > 0$ and the differentiation order may be complimented since we are interested in its timing variance:

$$\frac{d(\nabla I_t)}{dt} = \frac{d(dC(\nabla I_x)/dx)}{dt} = C'' \cdot \nabla I_x'^2 + C' \cdot \nabla I_x''. \tag{14}$$

Therefore, substituting the value of $C(\nabla I_x)$, we get

$$\begin{aligned}
\frac{d(\nabla I_t)}{dt} &= \frac{d\left[-2\nabla I_x/\left(\nabla I_x^2 + 1\right)^2\right]}{dx} \\
&= -\frac{2\left(\left(\nabla I_x^2 + 1\right)^2 - 4\nabla I_x^2\left(\nabla I_x^2 + 1\right)\right)}{\left(\nabla I_x^2 + 1\right)^4}.
\end{aligned} \tag{15}$$

Upon performing some algebra and rewriting, we get

$$\frac{d(\nabla I_t)}{dt} = \frac{8\nabla I_x^2}{\left(\nabla I_x^2 + 1\right)^3} - \frac{2}{\left(\nabla I_x^2 + 1\right)^2} = \frac{2\left(3\nabla I_x^2 - 1\right)}{\left(\nabla I_x^2 + 1\right)^3}. \tag{16}$$

Now, as a test case, the magnitude of the second-order derivative of the coefficient is scaled by 3 (tested on images) which changes the signal attribute as shown in Figure 3(b):

$$\frac{d(\nabla I_t)}{dt} = \frac{6\left(3\nabla I_x^2 - 1\right)}{\left(\nabla I_x^2 + 1\right)^3}. \tag{17}$$

Upon solving (17), the roots appear as $\pm 1/\sqrt{3}$. However, keeping the roots coordinate the same, the magnitude increases upon scaling as is clear from graphs (see Figure 3(b)).

So we can conclude here that the smoothing effect can be performed in a controlled manner by properly scaling the derivative of the coefficient. As a result, images with high-frequency spectrum are handled in a different way unlike their counterpart.

Since the coefficient controls the smoothing effect while denoising, it also effects the number of iterations incurred to achieve the magnitude threshold κ in (4) for smoothing. This signal behavior of the diffusion coefficient should be very carefully handled. Proper selection of its magnitude depends upon the image selected for denoising.

5.4. Algorithm of Hardware Design Flow. The first step requires a detailed algorithmic understanding and its corresponding software implementation. Secondly, the design should be optimized after some numerical analysis (e.g., using algebraic transforms) to reduce its complexity. This is followed by the hardware design (using efficient storage schemes and adjusting fixed-point computation specifications) and its efficient and robust implementation. Finally, the overall evaluation in terms of speed, resource utilization, and image fidelity decides whether additional adjustments in the design decisions are needed (ref. Figure 4). The algorithm background has been described in the previous Section 4.

The workflow graph shown in Figure 5 shows the basic steps of our design implementation in hardware.

5.5. Proposed Hardware Design Implementation. The noisy image is taken as an input to the FPGA through the *Gateway_In* (see Figure 5) which defines the FPGA boundary and converts the pixel values from floating to fixed-point types for the hardware to execute. The anisotropic diffusion filtering is carried out after this. The processed pixels are then moved out through the *Gateway_Out* again converting the System Generator fixed-point or floating-point data type.

Figure 5 describes the abstract view of the implementation process. The core filter design has been elaborated

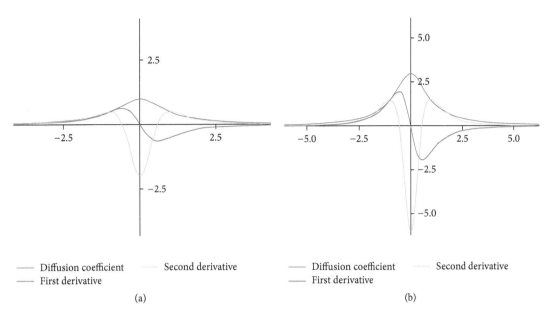

FIGURE 3: Diffusion coefficient C_n signal analysis of (12).

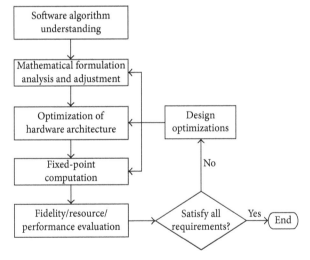

FIGURE 4: Algorithm to hardware design flow graph.

in descriptive components in a workflow modular structure shown in Figure 6. The hardware design of the corresponding algorithm is described in Figures 7–14.

Explanation of Hardware Modules as per the Workflow Diagram. Figure 7 shows the magnified view of the blue boundary block implementing equation (3) of Figure 5 (i.e., the anisotropic diffusion filtering block). Figure 7 shows the hardware design which gets fired t times due to t number of iterations from the script when executed.

Equation (3) has been described in words in detail in Figure 6 with iteration required to meet the necessary condition for the classical anisotropic diffusion equation. Equation (3) shows that $I_{i,j}^t$ gets updated at every iteration and has been realized with the hardware design in Figure 8. The

green outlined box in Figure 7 has been detailed in Figure 8. The line buffer reference block buffers a sequential stream of pixels to construct 3 lines of output. Each line is delayed by 150 samples, where 150 is the length of the line. Line 1 is delayed by $(2 * 150 = 300)$ samples, each of the following lines are delayed by 150 fewer samples, and line 3 is a copy of the input. It is to be noted that the image under consideration used here is of resolution 150×150, and in order to properly align and buffer the streaming pixels, the line buffer should be of the same size as the image. As shown in Figure 9, $X1$ to $X9$ imply a chunk of 9 pixels and their corresponding positions with respect to the middle pixel $X5$ as north (N), south (S), east (E), west (W), north-east (NE), north-west (NW), and so forth, as shown with a one-to-one mapping in the lower second square box.

This hardware realization of the gradient computation is achieved by a single arithmetic subtraction as described in Section 5.1.

Now, referring to this window, the difference in pixel intensities from the center position of the window to its neighbors gives its gradient as explained in equationarray (2). This difference in pixel intensities is calculated in the middle of the hardware section as shown in Figure 8. Here, $X1$ denotes the central pixel of the processing window and the corresponding differences with pixel intensities in position $X1, X2, X3, \ldots, X9$ denote the directional gradient ($X1 - X5 = grad\_northwest$, $X2 - X5 = grad\_west, \ldots, X9 - X5 = grad\_southeast$). The pixels are passed through the line buffers (discussed in Section 5.6) needed for proper alignment of the pixels before computation. This underlying architecture is basically a memory buffer needed to store two image lines (see Section 5.6) implemented in the FPGA as a RAM block. The deep brown outlined block in Figure 8 (from where the three *out* lines are coming out) contains the detailed diagram and working principle of the buffering scheme in Figure 12.

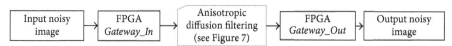

FIGURE 5: Work flow of design modules.

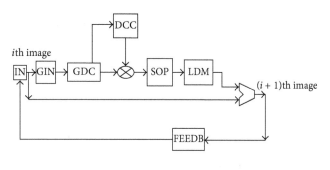

IN: input noisy image

GIN: input image is passed into the boundary of the FPGA through the *Gateway_In*

GDC: computing the image gradient in all eight directions within a filter window

DCC: computing the diffusion coefficient using the image gradients

SOP: summing up all the product of the image gradient as well as the diffusion coefficient

LDM: the summed up component is then multiplied with a constant quantity lambda for the numerical scheme to be stable

FEEDB: the input image gets updated at every iteration, which is shown by this feedback path

FIGURE 6: Work flow of design module of anisotropic diffusion filter of Figure 5 in detail.

The pixels $X1$ to $X9$ are passed out of the buffer line blocks through various delays into the next level of circuitry as shown in Figure 8. Referring to Figure 8, the Out 1 of the line buffer block which outputs three pixels $X7$ to $X1$ as per Figure 9 of which $X7$ moves out first, then $X8$ and $X9$ after encountering the delay blocks. Similarly, pixel data flow occurs for Out 2 and Out 3 blocks, respectively, with the pixel positions as shown from $X1$ to $X9$. Pixel positions at this instant of time shown in Figure 8 have been shown after encountering the buffer delays. In this model, pixel $X5$ denotes the center pixel and subtracting it from the remaining pixels denotes the gradient in their corresponding positions as shown in the following:

$$
\begin{aligned}
X1 - X5 &= \nabla_{NW}I, \\
X2 - X5 &= \nabla_{W}I, \\
X3 - X5 &= \nabla_{SW}I, \\
X4 - X5 &= \nabla_{N}I, \\
X6 - X5 &= \nabla_{S}I, \\
X7 - X5 &= \nabla_{NE}I, \\
X8 - X5 &= \nabla_{E}I, \\
X9 - X5 &= \nabla_{SE}I.
\end{aligned}
\tag{18}
$$

Now, let us discuss the bottom-up design approach to make things more transparent. Referring to (3), the coefficient C_n is defined in equationarray (6) which has been realized in hardware as shown in Figure 11 where $\|E\|$ is the intensity gradient calculating variable and κ is the constant value 15. So $1/\kappa = 1/15 = 0.0667$ which gets multiplied with the input gradient $\|E\|$ squared up and then added with a unitary value and the resultant becomes the divisor with 1 the dividend. Referring to the hardware design in Figure 11, the CORDIC divisor has been used to compute the division operation in (4) and the rest is quite clear. Now, Figure 10 is the hardware design of the equations C_nE_n and $1/2C_nE_n$ as per the individual components of (3). For the gradient north, south, east, and west, it is needed to multiply only $1/2$ with C_nE_n and 1 for others. We have seen the coefficient computation of equationarray (6) where the input is the gradient $E_n = \nabla I_n$. This is the same input in the hardware module in Figure 10 needed to compute coefficient C_n. The output of Figure 10 is nothing but the coefficient multiplied with the gradient E_n as shown.

The delays are injected at the intervals to properly balance (synchronize) the net propagation delays. Finally, all the output individual components of the design shown in Figure 8 are summed up and the lambda (λ) is finally multiplied with the added results. This implementation of the line buffer is described in the next subsection.

Each component in (3), that is, $C \cdot \nabla I$, requires an initial 41-unit delay for each processed pixel to produce (CORDIC: 31-unit delay, multiplier: 3-unit delay, and register: 1-unit delay). The delay balancing is done as per the circuitry. However, this delay is encountered at first and from the next clock pulse each pixel gets executed per clock pulse since the CORDIC architecture is completely pipelined.

5.6. Efficient Storage/Buffering Schemes. Figure 12 describes the efficiency in the storage/buffering scheme. Figures 12 and 13 describe a window generator to buffer reused image intensities diminishing data redundancies. This implementation of the line buffer uses a single port RAM block with the read before write option as shown in Figure 13. Two buffer lines are used to generate eight neighborhood pixels. The length of the buffer line depends on the number of pixels in a row of an image. A FIFO structure is used to implement a 3×3 window kernel used for filtering to maximize the pipeline implementation. Leaving the first 9 clock cycles, each pixel is processed per clock cycle starting from the 10th clock cycle. The processing hardware elements never remain idle due to the buffering scheme implemented with FIFO (Figure 14). Basically, this FIFO architecture is used to implement the buffer lines.

With reference to Figure 14, it is necessary that the output of the window architecture should be vectors for pixels in the window, together with an enable which is used to inform an algorithm using the window generation unit as to when the data is ready to process. To achieve maximum performance in a relatively small space, FIFO architectural units specific to the target FPGA were used.

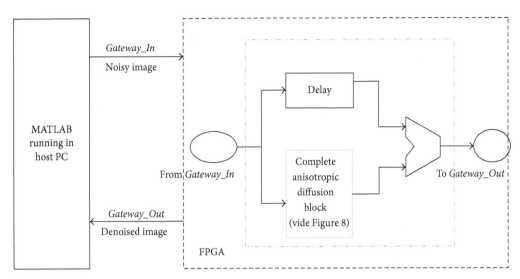

FIGURE 7: This hardware design shows a single instance of the iterative diffusion step shown in (3). The overall architecture with the pixels passing from the host PC to the FPGA platform and the processed pixels being reconstructed back to the host PC.

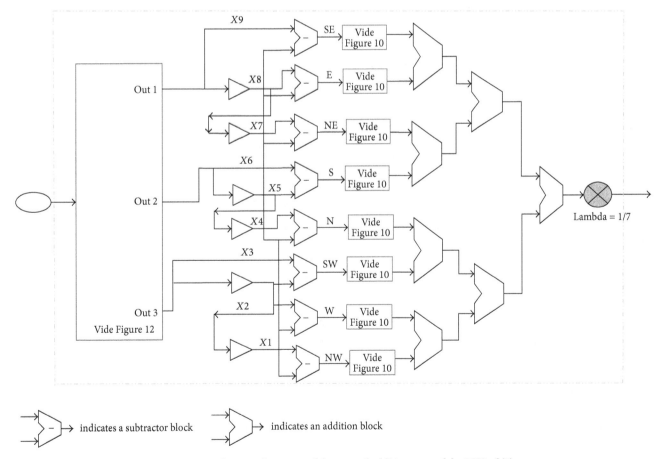

FIGURE 8: Hardware architecture of the second additive term of the RHS of (3).

6. Results and Discussion

In this paper, we presented an efficient architecture of the FPGA prototyped hardware design of an optimized anisotropic diffusion filtering on image. The algorithm has been successfully implemented using FPGA hardware using the System Generator platform with Intel(R) Core(TM) 2 Duo CPU T6600 @ 3.2 GHz platform and Xilinx Virtex-5 LX110T OpenSPARC Evaluation Platform (100 MHz) as well as Avnet Spartan-6 FPGA IVK.

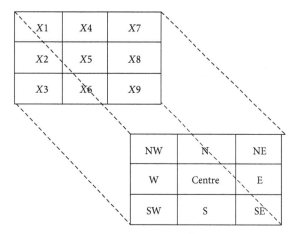

FIGURE 9: The figure is showing a section of an image and the neighborhood pixel directions with respect to the middle pixel.

TABLE 1: Runtime comparison between acceleration rates of our proposed hardware implementation of anisotropic diffusion filter for different image resolutions.

Image resolution	Software execution time (seconds)	Hardware execution time (seconds)	Accelerate rate
150×150	0.101	0.0011	**(0.101/0.0011) = 91**
512×512	0.402	0.0131	**(0.402/0.0131) = 30**

Here, the hardware filter design is made using the Xilinx DSP blockset. The algorithm [2] has been analyzed and optimally implemented in hardware with a complete parallel architecture. The proposed system leads to improved acceleration and performance of the design. The throughput is increased by 12 to 33% in terms of frame rate, with respect to the existing state-of-the-art works like [20–22]. Figures 15, 16, and 17 show the denoising performances. Figure 15 shows a denoised image of various human skeletal regions which was affected by noise. Figure 16 shows the quality comparison between the hardware and its corresponding software implementations. Figure 17 shows the various denoising filter performances. Fine texture regions have been magnified to show the achieved differences and improvement.

Figures 18 and 19 denote the accuracy measures.

With regard to data transfer requirement, there is a huge demand for fast data exchange between the image sensor and the computing platform. For example, transferring a 1024×1024 grayscale video sequence in real time requires a minimum data transfer rate of 1024×1024 pixels/frame * 1 byte/pixel * 30 fps = 30 Mbps. In order to achieve this data rate, a high performance I/O interface, such as a PCI or USB, is necessary. We have used USB 2.0 (Hi-Speed USB mode) supporting 60 Mbps data rate.

For a 512×512 image resolution, time taken to execute in software is 0.402 seconds and 0.101 seconds for 150×150 size grayscale image approximately (cf. Table 1).

Simulation activity files (SAIF) from simulation is used for accurate power analysis of a complete placed and routed design.

As already explained, the buffer line length needs to be equal to that of the image resolution. Now, as the resolution increases, the buffering time increases too. Now, it is obvious that increasing image resolution, the number of pixels to be processed in both hardware and software increases. This difference is proportionate. But what makes the difference in acceleration rate as a result of change in resolution (see Table 1) is created by the buffering scheme of the hardware. In software, the image can be read at one go unlike in hardware

where the pixels need to be serialized while reading (see Figures 12 and 14).

Case 1. The image resolution used for this experiment is 150×150, so a total of 22500 pixels. Therefore, a sum total of $(22500 * 5) = 112500$ pixels have been processed for five iterations of the algorithm. Our proposed hardware architecture is such that it can process per pixel per clock pulse (duration 10 ns). The clock frequency of the FPGA platform on which the experiment has been performed is 100 MHz (period = 10 ns). The *Gateway_In* of the FPGA boundary has an unit sample period. Therefore, the total time taken to process is 22500 pixels * 5 iterations * 10 ns = **0.0011** seconds in hardware (also has been cross-checked complying with (19)).

Whereas only in software environment the total time taken to execute in the host PC configuration mentioned above is **0.101** seconds, thus a total acceleration of (**0.101/0.0011 = 91x**) in execution speed has been achieved in FPGA-in-the-loop [23] experimental setting.

Case 2. Therefore, for image resolution 512×512, the total hardware time required to process is 262144 pixels * 5 iterations * 10 ns = 0.0131 seconds (also has been cross-checked complying with (19)). Figure 20 shows that per pixel gets executed per clock cycle starting from the FPGA boundary *Gateway_In* to *Gateway_Out*.

The experiment has been implemented 10 times and the corresponding mean squared error (MSE) obtained has been averaged by 10 to get the averaged MSE_{av}, which is used to calculate the PSNR. Since the noise is random, therefore averaging is performed while computing the PSNR.

As seen from the processed images, our result resembles the exact output very closely. The difference is also clear from the difference of the PSNR and SSIM values (Table 2).

A closer look has been plotted with a one-dimensional plot shown in Figure 21, which clearly exposes the smoothing effect at every iterative step.

FPGA-in-the-loop (FIL) verification [23] has been carried out. It includes the flow of data from the outside world to move into the FPGA through its input boundary (a.k.a *Gateway_In*), get processed with the hardware prototype in the FPGA, and be returned back to the end user across the *Gateway_Out* of the FPGA boundary [24, 25]. This approach also ensures that the algorithm will behave as expected in the real world.

TABLE 2: Quality measures (performance metrics): SSIM (structural similarity) and PSNR (peak signal-to-noise ratio) for the experiments. For each column, the best value has been highlighted for three different noise standard deviations. Our proposed technique OAD (optimized anisotropic diffusion) shows better result except for the SSIM parameter for standard deviation, 20. Comparison has been made with different types of benchmark edge preserving denoising filters.

Method	Std. dev. = 12		Std. dev. = 15		Std. dev. = 20	
	SSIM	PSNR (dB)	SSIM	PSNR (dB)	SSIM	PSNR (dB)
(a) ADF [2]	0.9128	29	0.8729	27.82	0.8551	24.93
(b) NLM [27]	0.9346	28.2	0.9067	27.29	0.8732	25.64
(c) BF [12]	0.9277	27	0.8983	28.54	**0.8809**	24.28
(d) TF [13]	0.8139	25.22	0.7289	22.87	0.6990	21.98
(e) OAD (Our proposed optimized anisotropic diffusion filter)	**0.9424**	**30.01**	**0.9245**	**28.87**	0.8621	**25.86**

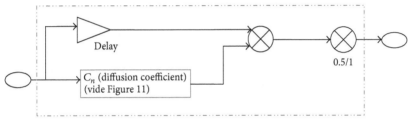

FIGURE 10: This hardware module multiplies the diffusion coefficient C_n with the pixel gradient ∇I to produce $C_n \nabla I$.

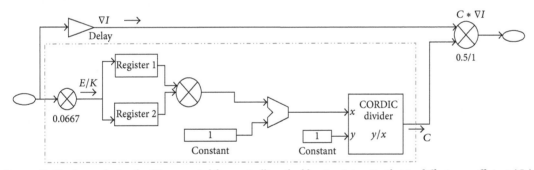

FIGURE 11: Hardware design for (5) generated for controlling the blurring intensity, that is, diffusion coefficient (C_n).

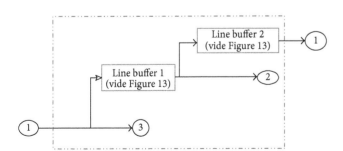

FIGURE 12: Hardware module showing the line buffering scheme of the pixels as described in Section 5.6 and hardware design (Section 4).

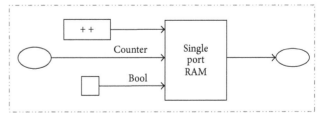

FIGURE 13: Hardware design within the line buffer shown in Figure 12.

Figure 22 shows the frames per second achieved for images of various resolutions. The power measurements in our proposed method have been analyzed after the implementation phase (placement and routing) and are found to be more accurate and less than their stronger counterpart,

namely, the hardware implementation of the bilateral and trilateral filter as shown in Table 3.

Table 4 denotes the resource utilization for both the hardware platforms for our implementation and a very strong benchmark implementation (its counterpart) of bilateral filter. It shows that a lot of acceleration has been achieved for anisotropic (cf. Table 5) with respect to its counterpart

w11	w12	w13
w21	w22	w23
w31	w32	w33

Output 3 × 3 window

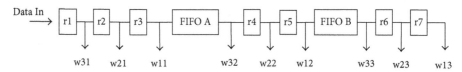

FIGURE 14: Data flow architecture of the window kernel implemented using the FIFO architecture.

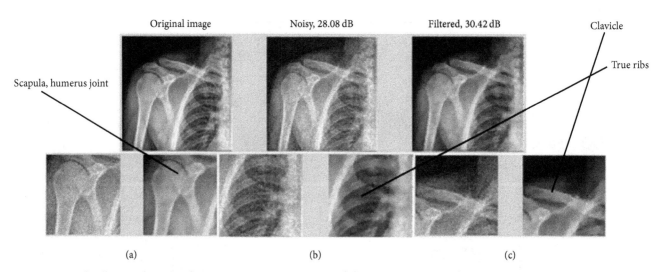

FIGURE 15: Results showing the original image, its noisy counterpart, and the denoised image and its various magnified portions of various sections of the denoised image of human skeleton. Image size = 512 × 512; the filter settings are as follows: Sigma (σ) for random noise = 12, number of iterations = 4, λ in (3) = 1/7, and Kappa (κ) in (4) = 15. (a), (b), and (c) show the zoomed insets of the scapula-humerus joint, true rib region, and the clavicle bone, respectively.

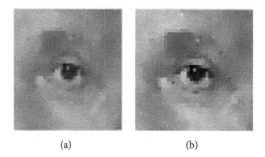

FIGURE 16: Image quality comparison between (a) FPGA implementation for the natural Einstein image (zoomed eye inset) and (b) MATLAB implementation. Filter parameters: Sigma (σ) for random noise = 12, number of iterations = 4, λ in (3) = 1/7, and Kappa (κ) in (4) = 15.

bilateral at the cost of a marginal increase in percentage of resource utilization (cf. Table 5).

The complexity analysis has been compared with some of the benchmark works and is shown in Table 6.

6.1. Considerations for Real-Time Implementations. There remain some considerations while planning to implement complex image processing algorithms in real time. One such issue is to process a particular frame of a video sequence within 33 ms in order to process with a speed of 30 (frames per second) fps. In order to make correct design decisions, a well known standard formula is given by

$$t_{\text{frame}} = \frac{C}{f} = \frac{\left(M \cdot N/t_p + \xi\right)}{n_{\text{core}}} \cdot f \leq 33 \, \text{ms}, \quad (19)$$

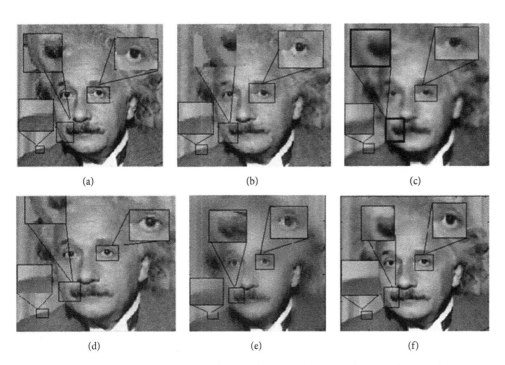

(a)   (b)   (c)

(d)   (e)   (f)

FIGURE 17: Comparison of various edge-preserving filters implemented using hardware on the natural grayscale image Einstein of size 150 × 150 measured for similar number of iterations. (a) Original image. (b) Direct implementation of the anisotropic diffusion filter (software implementation). (c) Output of the bilateral filter realized using FPGA. (d) Output of nonlocal means filter. (e) Trilateral filter output. (f) Output of our implementation of optimized anisotropic diffusion filtering using a novel hardware design. Note that the fine boundary transitions in the moustache area (see zoomed insets) are clearly visible in our implementation in (f) unlike others which is clear from the visual experience. Similarly, the zoomed portions of the left eye show the clear distinctions of the lower and upper lid (also holds the contrast information); moreover, the magnified area of the neck portion also shows a sharp transition. All the comparisons should be done keeping the original image in (a) in mind as the reference image. The PSNR difference is as shown in Table 2.

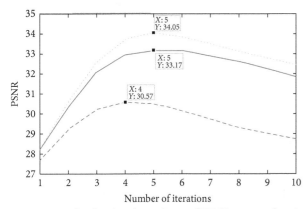

Number of iterations

FIGURE 18: Results showing the variance of PSNR measured against the number of iterations measured for images of various resolutions. It has been found that the number of iterations ranges between 4 and 5 to attain the most denoised output close to the original. The filter settings are as follows: Sigma (σ) for random noise = 12, number of iterations = 4, λ in (3) = 1/7, and Kappa (κ) in (4) = 15. ($\cdots$): image resolution 150 × 150, (—): image resolution 256 × 256, and (- - -): image resolution 512 × 512. Various images with the similar resolution have been tested and the averages have been plotted with identical curves with their respective resolutions.

TABLE 3: Power utilization for Virtex-5 OpenSPARC architecture measured for an image of resolution 150 × 150.

Filter type	Quiescent power (watt)	Dynamic power (watt)	Total power (watt)
OAD (our proposed)	**1.190**	**0.200**	(1.100 + 0.070) = **1.170**
TF [13]	2.305	0.422	(2.305 + 0.422) = 2.727
BF [12]	1.196	0.504	(1.196 + 0.504) = 1.700
Reference [10]	NA	NA	1.240

pixels, f is the maximum clock frequency at which the design can run, n_{core} is the number of processing units, t_p is the pixel-level throughput with one processing unit ($0 < t_p < 1$), N is the number of iterations in an iterative algorithm, and ξ is the overhead (latency) in clock cycles for one frame [1].

So in order to process one frame, the total number of clock cycles required is given by ($M \cdot N/t_p + \xi$) for a single processing unit. For $n_{\text{core}} > 1$, one can employ multiple processing units.

Let us evaluate a case study applying (19) for our experiment.

where t_{frame} is the processing time for one frame, C is the total number of clock cycles required to process one frame of M

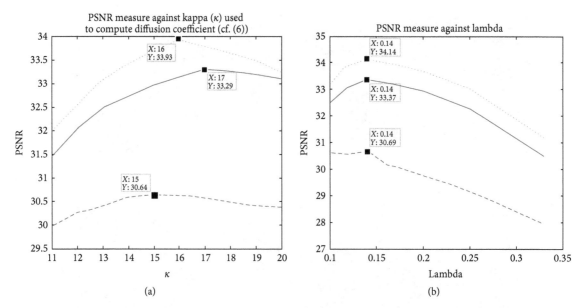

FIGURE 19: Results show two graphical plots: (a) measures the change of PSNR values against the parameter kappa (κ) (cf. in (4)) used to compute the diffusion coefficient (C_n), which reflects an optimum value in the range of 15 to 17 needed to obtain the denoised accuracy as shown with the pointers in the graphs. (b) shows a single value for $\lambda = 1/7$ yields the maximum denoised output for different images of varying resolutions; the rest of the filter settings remain the same.

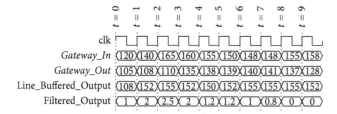

FIGURE 20: Simulation results showing the time interval taken to process the image pixels. Each clock pulse duration is 10 ns. Each pixel requires one clock pulse to process from the FPGA boundary *Gateway_In* to *Gateway_Out* together with the intermediary signal lines as probed, following the same rate (ref. Figure 7).

For 512×512 resolution image, $M = 262144$, $N = 5$, $t_p = 1$, that is, per pixel processed per clock pulse, $\xi = 1050$, that is, the latency in clock cycle, $f = 100\,\text{MHz}$, and $n_{\text{core}} = 1$. Therefore, $t_{\text{frame}} = 0.013$ seconds = 13 ms ≤ 33 ms (i.e., much less than the minimum timer threshold required to process per frame in real-time video rate). With regard to data transfer requirement, there is a huge demand for fast data exchange between the image sensor and the computing platform. For example, transferring a 1024×1024 grayscale video sequence in real time requires a minimum data transfer rate of 1024×1024 pixels/frame $* 1$ byte/pixel $* 30$ fps = 30 Mbps. In order to achieve this data rate, a high performance I/O interface, such as a PCI or USB, is necessary. Our USB 2.0 (Hi-Speed USB mode) supports 60 Mbps data rate, which is just double the minimum requirement of 30 Mbps which catered our purpose with ease.

The highlights of our approach are the following:

(i) *Accuracy*. We have performed our experiments on approximately 65–70 images (both natural and medical) and they are producing successful results. We discovered that every time they yielded the max PSNR for the following selected parameter values shown in Figures 18 and 19.

(ii) *Power*. We can claim our design to be energy efficient as the power consumption for the design has reduced in comparison to other benchmark works for an example image of a given resolution as shown (cf. Table 3 by reducing the number of computations [26], NB also tested for images of various resolutions) with respect to other state-of-the-art works cited previously [11, 12].

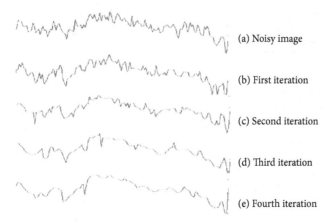

FIGURE 21: Family of 1D signals showing the plot of only one particular row of an image, the variation of which is shown at different iterations, starting from noisy to final denoised output.

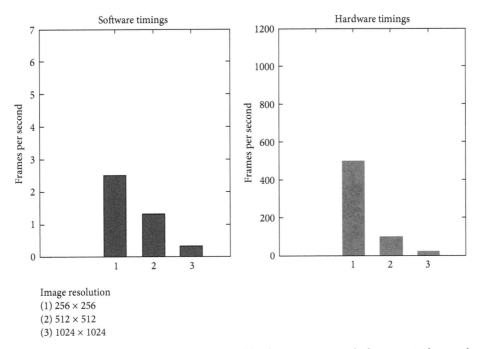

Image resolution
(1) 256 × 256
(2) 512 × 512
(3) 1024 × 1024

FIGURE 22: The figure shows the frame processing rate of software and hardware processing platform. x-axis denotes the image resolutions and y-axis the frames per second, respectively, for image of different resolutions as shown from 1 to 3 in x-axis.

TABLE 4: Comparison showing resource utilization of the various optimized hardware architectures for image resolution 150 × 150 implemented in Virtex-5 LX110T OpenSPARC Evaluation Platform [28] and Spartan 6 IVK [29] realizing bilateral [12] and anisotropic diffusion filtering.

	Image size *(150 × 150)*		
Percentage utilization	Virtex-5 LX110T OpenSPARC FPGA (utilized/total number) *(anisotropic diffusion)*	Fully parallel and separable single dimensional architecture *(bilateral filter)* for the same OpenSPARC device	Avnet Spartan 6 industrial video processing kit *(anisotropic diffusion)*
Occupied slices	5225/17280 (30%)	6342 and 3144 (37% and 18%)	3810/23038 (16%)
Slice LUTs	14452/69120 (20%)	11689 and 8535 (17% and 12%)	11552/92152 (12%)
Block-RAM/FIFO/RAMB8BWERs	1/148 (1%)	22 and 22 (15% and 15%)	2/536 (1%)
Flip flops	17309/69120 (25%)	16167 and 5440 (23% and 8%)	15214/69120 (22%)
Bonded IOBs	46/640 (7%)	1 and 1 (1% and 1%)	46/396 (11%)
Mults/DSP48Es/DSP48A1s	55/64 (85%)	0 and 0 (0% and 0%)	81/180 (45%)
BUFGs/BUFCTRLs	1/32 (3%)	4 and 4 (13% and 13%)	1 (3%)

(iii) *Diffusion Coefficient Analysis.* We performed some performance analysis on the diffusion coefficient responsible for controlling the filtering process, subsequently by differentiation and scaling. The changes in the signal behavior help to perform a proper selection of the scaling parameter needed for filtering different image types. PSNR and SSIM performance measures reflect the reconstructed denoising quality affected by random noise.

(iv) *Complexity.* Previous implementations [10, 15] used normal convolution operation to calculate the intensity gradients whose computational complexity is of

TABLE 5: Runtime comparison in software and hardware for bilateral filtering (BF) and anisotropic diffusion (AD) filtering (note that A = 150 × 150, B = 256 × 256, C = 512 × 512, and D = 1024 × 1024). The processing platform was done on an Intel(R) Core(TM) 2 Duo CPU T6600 3.2 GHz system.

Filtering techniques	AD filtering				BF			
Image resolution	A	B	C	D	A	B	C	D
Execution time (software in seconds)	0.101	0.153	0.402	1.1	0.5	1.1	2.5	11.5
Acceleration rate in software for anisotropic over bilateral (approx.)	3x	3x	3x	3x	—	—	—	—
Acceleration rate when executed in hardware with respect to software for BF	—	—	—	—	70x	6x	7x	3x
Acceleration rate when executed in hardware with respect to software for AD	91x	46x	30x	21x	—	—	—	—

TABLE 6: Complexity analysis report. The set S of all possible image locations. The set R of all possible pixel values. σ is the kernel standard deviation. $M \times N$ denotes the image resolution, x is patch size, and y is the search window size.

Algorithm	Complexity
Constant time polynomial range approach [30]	$O(1)$
Trilateral filter [13]	More than the [12, 27, 30–35]
NLM [27]	$x^2 \cdot y^2 \cdot N \cdot M$
Brut force approach [31]	$O(|S|^2)$
Layered approach [32]	$O(|S| + (|S|/\sigma_s^2)(|R|/\sigma_r))$
Bilateral grid [33] approach	$O(|S| + (|S|/\sigma_s^2)(|R|/\sigma_r))$
Separable filter kernel approach [34]	$O(|S| \sigma_s)$
Local histogram approach [35]	$O(|S| \log \sigma_s)$
Constant time trigonometric range approach [12]	$O(1)$
Classical anisotropic diffusion [2]	Nonlinear
Optimized anisotropic diffusion (OAD) (our approach)	$O(1)$

$O(N^2)$. Even if the normal convolution is substituted by single dimensional architecture [12], the computational complexity would reduce to $O(N)$. However, we have realized the same with a single arithmetic subtraction operation, making it convenient by arranging the pixels in the favorable order, thereby reducing the complexity to $O(1)$. That is, $O(N^2) \rightarrow O(N) \rightarrow O(1)$, that is, the least complexity achievable.

(v) *Speed.* Besides having $O(1)$ complexity, our hardware architecture of the algorithm has been formulated in parallel. This allows us to further accelerate its speed, since all the directional gradient computations have been done in parallel, thereby saving the CORDIC (processor) divider delay time by $(41 * 7 * 10) = 2870$ ns. Each CORDIC block has 31-unit delay, together with multipliers and registers and thereby

saving 7 directions (due to parallel executing) where 10 ns is each clock pulse.

(vi) *Adaptive Iteration.* We have designed Algorithm 1, which shows the steps of intelligent adaptation of the number of iterations.

(vii) The filter design has been implemented in one grayscale channel; however, it can be replicated for all other color channels.

(viii) *Reconstruction Quality.* Last but not least, the denoised image quality has been measured against benchmark quality performance metrics.

7. Conclusions

In this paper, we presented an efficient hardware implementation of edge-preserving anisotropic diffusion filter. Considerable gain with respect to accuracy, power, complexity, speed, and reconstruction quality has been obtained as discussed in Section 6. Our design has been compared to the hardware implementation of state-of-the-art works with respect to acceleration, energy consumption, PSNR, SSIM, and so forth. From the point of view of the hardware realization of edge-preserving filters, both bilateral and anisotropic diffusion yield satisfying results, but still the research community prefers bilateral filter as it has less parameters to tune and is noniterative in nature. However, recent implementations of the same are iterative for achieving higher denoised image quality. So it can be concluded that if a proper selection of parameters can be done (has been made adaptive without manual intervention in our case) in case of anisotropic diffusion filtering, then real-time constraints can be overcome without much overhead. We have not performed the hardware implementation of the nonlocal means algorithm as it contains exponential operations at every step. Hardware implementation of the exponential operation introduces a lot of approximation errors.

While GPU implementations of the same do exist, however, we have undertaken this work as a case study to measure the hardware performance of the same.

Additional work on testing with more images, design optimization, and real-time demonstration of the system and a suitable physical design (floorplanning to masking) is to be carried out in future. It is to be noted that we have designed one extended trilateral filter algorithm (edge-preserving/denoising) which is also producing promising results (not been published yet).

Till now, there have been more advanced versions of anisotropic diffusion algorithms even with more optimized/modified versions. But they are all optimized and targeted to specific applications. However, this design forms the base architecture for all the other designs. Any kind of modification of the algorithm and its corresponding hardware design can be done keeping the similar base architecture.

Competing Interests

The authors declare that there are no competing interests regarding the publication of this paper.

Acknowledgments

This work has been supported by the Department of Science and Technology, Government of India, under Grant no. DST/INSPIRE FELLOWSHIP/2012/320 as well as the grant from TEQIP phase 2 (COE) of the University of Calcutta providing fund for this research. The authors also wish to thank Mr. Pabitra Das and Dr. Kunal Narayan Choudhury for their valuable suggestions.

References

[1] W. Wu, S. T. Acton, and J. Lach, "Real-time processing of ultrasound images with speckle reducing anisotropic diffusion," in *Proceedings of the 40th Asilomar Conference on Signals, Systems, and Computers (ACSSC '06)*, pp. 1458–1464, Pacific Grove, Calif, USA, November 2006.

[2] P. Perona and J. Malik, "Scale-space and edge detection using anisotropic diffusion," *IEEE Transactions on Pattern Analysis and Machine Intelligence*, vol. 12, no. 7, pp. 629–639, 1990.

[3] D. Bailey, "Implementing machine vision systems using FPGAs," in *Machine Vision Handbook*, B. G. Batchelor, Ed., pp. 1103–1136, Springer, London, UK, 2012.

[4] R. Zatrepalek, *Using FPGAs to Solve Tough DSP Design Challenges*, 2007, http://www.eetimes.com/document.asp?piddl_msgpage=2&doc_id=1279776&page_number=1.

[5] J. A. Kalomiros and J. Lygouras, "Design and evaluation of a hardware/software FPGA-based system for fast image processing," *Microprocessors and Microsystems*, vol. 32, no. 2, pp. 95–106, 2008.

[6] A. E. Nelson, "Implementation of image processing algorithms on FPGA hardware," May 2000, http://www.isis.vanderbilt.edu/sites/default/files/Nelson_T_0_0_2000_Implementa.pdf.

[7] B. G. Batchelor, *Machine Vision Handbook*, Springer, London, UK, 2012.

[8] K. T. Gribbon, D. G. Bailey, and C. T. Johnston, "Design patterns for image processing algorithm development on FPGAs," in *Proceedings of the IEEE Region 10 Conference (TENCON '05)*, pp. 1–6, Melbourne, Australia, November 2005.

[9] S.-K. Han, M.-H. Jeong, S. Woo, and B.-J. You, "Architecture and implementation of real-time stereo vision with bilateral background subtraction," in *Advanced Intelligent Computing Theories and Applications. With Aspects of Theoretical and Methodological Issues*, D.-S. Huang, L. Heutte, and M. Loog, Eds., vol. 4681 of *Lecture Notes in Computer Science*, pp. 906–912, Springer, Berlin, Germany, 2007.

[10] W. Atabany and P. Degenaar, "Parallelism to reduce power consumption on FPGA spatiotemporal image processing," in *Proceedings of the IEEE International Symposium on Circuits and Systems (ISCAS '08)*, pp. 1476–1479, Seattle, Wash, USA, May 2008.

[11] K. N. Chaudhury, D. Sage, and M. Unser, "Fast O(1) bilateral filtering using trigonometric range kernels," *IEEE Transactions on Image Processing*, vol. 20, no. 12, pp. 3376–3382, 2011.

[12] C. Pal, K. N. Chaudhury, A. Samanta, A. Chakrabarti, and R. Ghosh, "Hardware software co-design of a fast bilateral filter in FPGA," in *Proceedings of the 10th Annual Conference of the IEEE India Council (INDICON '13)*, pp. 1–6, Mumbai, India, December 2013.

[13] P. Choudhury and J. Tumblin, "The trilateral filter for high contrast images and meshes," in *Proceedings of the 14th Eurographics Symposium on Rendering*, pp. 186–196, 2003.

[14] O. Dandekar, C. Castro-Pareja, and R. Shekhar, "FPGA-based real-time 3D image preprocessing for image-guided medical interventions," *Journal of Real-Time Image Processing*, vol. 1, no. 4, pp. 285–301, 2007.

[15] D. Bera and S. Banerjee, "Pipelined DSP implementation of nonlinear anisotropic diffusion for speckle reduction of USG images," in *Proceedings of the 2nd International Conference on Computer Engineering and Technology (ICCET '10)*, pp. V249–V253, Chengdu, China, April 2010.

[16] M. Howison, "Comparing GPU implementations of bilateral and anisotropic diffusion filters for 3D biomedical datasets," Tech. Rep., 2010.

[17] S. Che, J. Li, J. W. Sheaffer, K. Skadron, and J. Lach, "Accelerating compute-intensive applications with GPUs and FPGAs," in *Proceedings of the Symposium on Application Specific Processors (SASP '08)*, pp. 101–107, Anaheim, Calif, USA, June 2008.

[18] R. C. Gonzalez and E. Richard, *Woods, Digital Image Processing*, Pearson, 3rd edition, 2008.

[19] D. Lopes, *Anisotropic Diffusion (Perona & Malik)*, 2007, http://www.mathworks.in/matlabcentral/fileexchange/14995-anisotropic-diffusion-perona-malik.

[20] I. Bravo, P. Jiménez, M. Mazo, J. L. Lázaro, and E. Martín, "Architecture based on FPGA's for real-time image processing," in *Reconfigurable Computing: Architectures and Applications: Second International Workshop, ARC 2006, Delft, The Netherlands, March 1–3, 2006, Revised Selected Papers*, vol. 3985 of *Lecture Notes in Computer Science*, pp. 152–157, Springer, Berlin, Germany, 2006.

[21] K. P. Sarawadekar, H. B. Indana, D. Bera, and S. Banerjee, "VLSI-DSP based real time solution of DSC-SRI for an ultrasound system," *Microprocessors and Microsystems*, vol. 36, no. 1, pp. 1–12, 2012.

[22] S. McBader and P. Lee, "An FPGA implementation of a flexible, parallel image processing architecture suitable for embedded vision systems," in *Proceedings of the International Parallel and Distributed Processing Symposium (IPDPS '03)*, pp. 1–5, Nice, France, April 2003.

[23] http://www.mathworks.com/products/hdl-verifier.

[24] System Generator for DSP Getting Started Guide. Release 10.1, March 2008.

[25] A. T. Moreo, P. N. Lorente, F. S. Valles, J. S. Muro, and C. F. Andrés, "Experiences on developing computer vision hardware algorithms using Xilinx system generator," *Microprocessors and Microsystems*, vol. 29, no. 8-9, pp. 411–419, 2005.

[26] Xilinx Power Tools Tutorial, *Spartan-6 and Virtex-6 FPGAs [Optional] UG733 (v13.1)*, 2011.

[27] A. Buades, B. Coll, and J. M. Morel, "Denoising image sequences does not require motion estimation," in *Proceedings of the IEEE Conference on Advanced Video and Signal Based Surveillance (AVSS '05)*, pp. 70–74, Como, Italy, September 2005.

[28] Virtex-5 OpenSPARC Evaluation Platform (ML509), http://www.digilentinc.com/Products/Detail.cfm?Prod=XUPV5.

[29] Xilinx Spartan-6 FPGA Industrial Video Processing Kit, http://www.em.avnet.com/en-us/design/drc/Pages/Xilinx-Spartan-6-FPGA-Industrial-Video-Processing-Kit.aspx.

[30] F. Porikli, "Constant time O(1) bilateral filtering," in *Proceedings of the IEEE Conference on Computer Vision and Pattern Recognition (CVPR '08)*, pp. 1–8, IEEE, Anchorage, Alaska, June 2008.

[31] M. Elad, "On the origin of the bilateral filter and ways to improve it," *IEEE Transactions on Image Processing*, vol. 11, no. 10, pp. 1141–1151, 2002.

[32] F. Durand and J. Dorsey, "Fast bilateral filtering for the display of high-dynamic-range images," *ACM Siggraph*, vol. 21, no. 3, pp. 257–266, 2002.

[33] J. Chen, S. Paris, and F. Durand, "Real-time edge-aware image processing with the bilateral grid," in *Special Interest Group on Computer Graphics and Interactive Techniques Conference (SIGGRAPH '07)*, ACM, New York, NY, USA, 2007.

[34] T. Q. Pham and L. J. van Vliet, "Separable bilateral filtering for fast video preprocessing," in *IEEE International Conference on Multimedia and Expo (ICME '05)*, pp. 454–457, July 2005.

[35] B. Weiss, "Fast median and bilateral filtering," *ACM Siggraph*, vol. 25, no. 3, pp. 519–526, 2006.

Permissions

List of Contributors

Aous H. Kurdi, Janos L. Grantner and Ikhlas M. Abdel-Qader
Electrical and Computer Engineering Department,Western Michigan University, Kalamazoo, MI 49009, USA

Lekhobola Tsoeunyane and Simon Winberg
Department of Electrical Engineering, University of Cape Town, Software Defined Radio Group, Rondebosch, Cape Town 7701, South Africa

Michael Inggs
Department of Electrical Engineering, University of Cape Town, Radar Remote Sensing Group, Rondebosch,Cape Town 7701, South Africa

Amit Kulkarni and Dirk Stroobandt
ELIS Department, Computer Systems Lab, Ghent University, Sint-Pietersnieuwstraat 41, 9000 Ghent, Belgium

David Wilson and Greg Stitt
Department of Electrical and Computer Engineering, University of Florida, Gainesville, FL 32611, USA

Aniruddha Shastri
National Instruments Corp., 11500 N Mopac Expwy, Austin, TX 78759, USA

Y. H. Lee, M. Khalil-Hani and M. N.Marsono
VeCAD Research Laboratory, Faculty of Electrical Engineering, Universiti Teknologi Malaysia (UTM), 81310 Skudai,Johor Bahru, Malaysia

Khalid Javeed
Electrical Engineering Department, COMSATS Institute of Information Technology, Abbottabad, Pakistan
School of Electronic Engineering, Dublin City University, Dublin, Ireland

Xiaojun Wang
School of Electronic Engineering, Dublin City University, Dublin, Ireland
School of Comuputer & Software, Nanjing University of Information Science and Technology, Nanjing, Jiangsu, China

Hasitha Muthumala Waidyasooriya, Tsukasa Endo and Masanori Hariyama
Graduate School of Information Sciences, Tohoku University, Aoba 6-3-09, Aramaki-Aza-Aoba, Sendai, Miyagi 980-8579, Japan

Yasuo Ohtera
Graduate School of Information Sciences, Tohoku University, Aoba 6-3-05, Aramaki-Aza-Aoba, Sendai, Miyagi 980-8579, Japan

Ali Asghar, Muhammad Mazher Iqbal, Waqar Ahmed, Mujahid Ali and Husain Parvez
Karachi Institute of Economics and Technology, Karachi, Pakistan

Muhammad Rashid
Umm Al-Qura University, Makkah, Saudi Arabia

Satheesh Bojja Venkatakrishnan, Elias A. Alwan and John L. Volakis
Department of Electrical and Computer Engineering, Florida International University, Miami, FL 33174, USA

Jia Wei Tang, Nasir Shaikh-Husin, Usman Ullah Sheikh, andM. N.Marsono
Faculty of Electrical Engineering, Universiti Teknologi Malaysia (UTM), 81310 Skudai, Johor Bahru, Malaysia

Shuli Gao, Dhamin Al-Khalili and Noureddine Chabini
Department of Electrical and Computer Engineering, Royal Military College of Canada, Kingston, ON, Canada

J. M. Pierre Langlois
Department of Computer Engineering, ´Ecole Polytechnique de Montr´eal, Montr´eal, QC, Canada

Gilberto Ochoa-Ruiz,
CONACYT-Universidad Autonoma de Guadalajara, Guadalajara, JAL, Mexico

Romain Bevan, Florent de Lamotte and Jean-Philippe Diguet
Lab-STICC-CNRS/ComposiTIC, Lorient, France

Cheng-Cong Bao
Coriolis Composites, Lorient, France

Swapnil Mhaske and Predrag Spasojevic
Wireless Information Networking Laboratory, Rutgers University, New Brunswick, NJ 08902, USA

Hojin Kee, Tai Ly and Ahsan Aziz
National Instruments Corporation, Austin, TX 78759, USA

Chandrajit Pal, Asit Samanta and Amlan Chakrabarti
A. K. Choudhury School of Information Technology, University of Calcutta, JD-2, Sector III, Salt Lake City, Kolkata 700098, India

Avik Kotal
Department of Applied Optics and Photonics, University of Calcutta, JD-2, Sector III, Salt Lake City, Kolkata 700098, India

Ranjan Ghosh
Institute of Radio Physics and Electronics, University of Calcutta, JD-2, Sector III, Salt Lake City, Kolkata 700098, India

Index

Printed in the USA
CPSIA information can be obtained
at www.ICGtesting.com
JSHW052023301024
72690JS00004B/143